FRIENDS OF GOD AND PROPHETS

FRIENDS OF
GOD AND
PROPHETS

**A Feminist Theological Reading
of the Communion of Saints**

ELIZABETH A. JOHNSON

CONTINUUM • NEW YORK

1998

The Continuum Publishing Company
370 Lexington Avenue, New York, NY 10017

Printed in the United States of America

Library of Congress Cataloging-in-Publication Data

Johnson, Elizabeth A., 1941-
    Friends of God and prophets : a feminist theological reading of the communion of saints / Elizabeth A. Johnson.
        p. cm.
    Includes bibliographical references and index.
    ISBN 0-8264-1078-2
    1. Communion of saints. 2. Feminist theology. I. Title.
BT972.J57   1998
262'.73'082–dc21   97-46452
                                                                CIP

In memory of my father
Walter T. Johnson
1915–1959

Contents

Part III
THEOLOGY OF THE FRIENDS OF GOD
AND PROPHETS

Acknowledgments

A book like this, in the making for several years, cannot reach a favorable conclusion without the help of many people, and my debts are legion. First of all I am grateful to Fordham University for granting me a Faculty Fellowship Award, which allowed a year's priceless time for concentrated research and writing. In particular I want to thank Mary Callaway, Chair of the Department of Theology, Joseph McShane SJ, Dean of Fordham College at Rose Hill, Robert Himmelberg, Dean of the Graduate School of Arts and Sciences, and Robert Carrubba, Vice-President for Academic Affairs, for their consistent and imaginative support of my efforts to combine scholarship with teaching, support shown in gifts of both time and research grants. My graduate assistant, Antoinette Gutzler MM, served this project well beyond the call of duty, researching, checking, and delivering to me great quantities of material; I am most grateful for her cheerful and enthusiastic help, without which this book would be much the poorer. In addition, Robert Hinkle, Betty Garrity, and Charlotte Labbé of the Fordham University Library staff provided constant and highly professional assistance.

During my sabbatical the invitation to deliver the Rauschenbusch Lectures at Colgate-Rochester Divinity School provided me with the opportunity to test ideas as they were developing. The hospitality of faculty and students provided a wonderful atmosphere for intellectual exchange, and the insights offered there have left their imprint on this book. My colleagues Mary Catherine Hilkert and Susan Simonaitis read central chapters and provided irreplaceably valuable criticism. And time would fail me to tell of the inspired and inspiring support of my editor, Frank Oveis, whose intelligence, patience, and good humor makes producing a book such a wonderful collaboration. Finally, my family and friends, and my religious community, the Sisters of St. Joseph of Brentwood, New York, have backed and encouraged me through the whole writing process. To all, my heartfelt thanks.

Introduction

I began this research as a project in Mariology with the idea that the communion of saints would provide an untapped resource for developing a contemporary theology of Mary of Nazareth. One of the strongest criticisms of feminist theology against traditional Mariology, captured in the striking title of Marina Warner's book, *Alone of All Her Sex: The Myth and Cult of the Virgin Mary*,[1] censures the way it separates the mother of Jesus out from all other women and places her on a pedestal, theologically as well as in the concrete. From there, standing head and shoulders above all other women, her figure looms as the feminine ideal against which patriarchy judges her sisters to their endless detriment. Feminist theologians such as Rosemary Radford Ruether and Elisabeth Moltmann-Wendel have already shown ways in which Mary can be reconnected back to the company of women.[2] I thought to carry on in this direction by exploring a theological interpretation of Mary of Nazareth enfolded in the communion of saints, which seems on the face of it to be an intrinsically inclusive and egalitarian doctrinal symbol.

Working the communion of saints into a hermeneutical key for a feminist theological interpretation of Mary grew into dozens of pages and then multiple chapters as the dearth of recent critical reflection on this symbol as well as its power and value in its own right became more apparent. The result is the present volume on the doctrinal symbol of the communion of saints alone, and a projected companion volume in which Mary will be interpreted in its light. Although there is an overarching unity between the two, each volume can stand on its own. Thus the vagaries — and the surprise — of research.

Given common misperceptions about this subject, a cautionary word about what the communion of saints is *not* is in order. This doctrinal symbol does not in the first instance refer to paradigmatic figures, those outstanding individuals traditionally called "saints," but rather names the whole community of people graced by the Spirit of God. Neither does it point exclusively to those who have died; rather, the community of living persons is its primary referent. Furthermore,

while obviously interested in human beings, the symbol does not al-
lude to them exclusively but embraces the whole natural world in
a "communion of the holy." Put positively, the symbol signifies the
relationship flowing among an intergenerational company of persons
profoundly touched by the sacred, sharing in the cosmic community of
life which is also sacred. Ultimately it points to the Creator Spirit who
vivifies creation, weaves interconnections, and makes holy the world.

For many centuries the communion of saints has been structured
according to the social system of patronage, taken from earth and
writ large into heaven. The imagination of this construal sees God like
a monarch ruling in splendor, with hosts of courtiers ranked in descending order of importance. Being far from the throne, people need
intercessors who will plead their cause and obtain spiritual and material favors that would otherwise not be forthcoming. This is put rather
baldly but it is not inaccurate. Not only did the Reformation criticize
this patronage structure for the way it disrupts the gospel, overshad-
owing Christ in whom God's gracious mercy has been poured out
on the earth so that there is no need of other go-betweens; but contemporary feminist analysis also shows the pattern to be profoundly
patriarchal, shaped according to a graded pyramid of power with an
elite corps near the top and a male ruling figure at the point.

What this patronage model obscures is the belief that the whole
community of redeemed sinners participates in the holiness of God,
a liberating dignity that can be claimed equally by each and every one.
Seeking a different pattern of relationship, I found a rich metaphor
in the Book of Wisdom, where the work of Sophia is described in
this way:

> Although she is but one, she can do all things,
> and while remaining in herself, she renews all things;
> in every generation she passes into holy souls
> and makes them friends of God, and prophets.[3]

This text, when applied to the communion of saints, succeeds in structuring those who respond to grace into a circle of companions by
the power of Spirit-Sophia. It became the guiding intuition of my
exploration.

Support for this inclusive, companionship paradigm of the communion of saints comes from two sources, corresponding to the second
and third sections of this book. One resource is a strand of the living Christian tradition discovered in Scripture, the early age of the

martyrs, creed, liturgy, and conciliar teaching that understands the graced relationships between members of the community to be equal and mutual. The other is the contemporary work of women bringing these same relationships to the fore, whether by actually relating to each other in struggles for justice, the ideal here being solidarity in difference, or in feminist religious scholarship, discovering in history a whole lost company of forgotten women with whom to bond and advocating the value of mutual, reciprocal, egalitarian relations as most coherent with the dynamism of God's own life. Using both these sources as clues for interpreting the communion of saints as a company of the friends of God and prophets brings the symbol alive with unsuspected liberating power.

Part I frames the question of the meaning of the communion of saints within two contexts of faith experience: contemporary secular culture that largely ignores the communion of saints, and Christian feminism that provides method and resources for a nonpatriarchal approach. Guided by the metaphor of friends of God and prophets, Part II sets out to dialogue with the living Christian tradition. The purpose here is not to give a full account of the development of this doctrinal symbol and its devotional practice but to cull insights that can serve to interpret its liberating meaning for today. There are discoveries to be made that warn of dead ends and point to genuine ways forward. As part of a two-millennia-long tradition we do not have to start searching for meaning in a vacuum but may find wisdom in the past that can germinate into future fruitfulness. Provisioned with these historical gleanings, Part III sets about the work of a feminist theological interpretation of the communion of saints. Starting with women's practices of memory and the critical power of hope, it moves to analysis of the levels of meaning in the communion of saints itself, ending with examples of spiritual practice that make the symbol come alive in the life of different church communities, to practical and critical effect. The whole point is to retrieve this symbol in such a way that it itself functions in a befriending and prophetic way, nourishing women in the struggle for life and equal human dignity and nurturing the church through memory and hope into being a true community of the friends of God and prophets.

At the beginning of an earlier book, *She Who Is: The Mystery of God in Feminist Theological Discourse,*[4] I used the image of braiding a footbridge to describe the task of connecting Christian tradition with the contemporary religious experience of women in their struggle for the fullness of their genuine human dignity in theory and practice. I had in mind those constructions of thick vines or rope flung over narrow gorges as seen in *National Geographic* or travel journals. After reading the book, one of my Jesuit colleagues commented, "You don't need a footbridge; you need the Verrazano!"[5] He may be right. But in seeking an understanding of this somewhat diffident doctrinal symbol, I think that what has been created here is again a simple footbridge. May those who hang on and cross in either direction discover the ongoing beauty of Spirit-Sophia in the face of all God-seekers who are friends of God and prophets.

Part I

Framing the Question

Chapter 1

A Sleeping Symbol

Basic Meanings

A circle of women who gather for prayer remembers the names of Mary Magdalene, Joanna, and other women witnesses of Christ's resurrection, lamenting the suppression of these voices in the church but gaining strength to lift up their own voices now, regardless. Before crossing onto a military installation to protest the arming of submarines with nuclear bombs, a group committed to peace pauses for prayer, calling upon Franz Jägenstatter to be present with them. In a cathedral of a southern U.S. city, All Saints Day rituals pay reverence to "anonymous," the millions of people whose lives have shaped this world for the better, the numerical majority of whom, it is noted with a paradoxical mixture of regret and praise, are women. A roll call of Salvadoran martyrs — read to the response of *Presente!* — strengthens the commitment of a parish toward local activities for justice. An Asian woman theologian welcomes a world assembly of Christian churches by calling upon the spirits of those unjustly dead, including among others Uriah, killed for David's lust, the women burned as witches during the Inquisition, the Jewish victims of Nazi genocide, the earth, air, and water being poisoned by human greed, and last of all, the Liberator, our brother Jesus, tortured and killed on the cross, all enfolded in the vivifying power of the Holy Spirit.[1] In every instance, although not explicitly noticed or named, the traditional doctrine of the communion of saints is being brought to new, liberating expression.

The communion of saints is a Christian symbol that speaks of profound relationship. In traditional usage it points to an ongoing connection between the living and the dead, implying that the dead have found new life thanks to the merciful power of God. It also posits a bond of companionship among living persons themselves who, though widely separated geographically, form one church community. Since the range of those who seek God is as broad as the human race it-

self, it furthermore affirms a link between all who have been brushed
with the fire of divine love and witness to this in their lives. Insofar
as the original Latin term *communio sanctorum* is ambiguous, referring in one instance to a communion of holy people but in another
instance to a communion of holy things, it also signifies eucharistic
sharing and, by extension, sharing in the sacred community of life that
is creation itself. From every angle the symbol of the communion of
saints crosses boundaries, bespeaking a communal participation in the
gracious holiness of God brought about by the play of Spirit-Sophia
from generation to generation and across the wide world. The public appearances of this symbol in creed and liturgy shed light on its
basic meanings.

Apostles' Creed

Following belief in God who creates the world and Jesus Christ who
redeems it, the third major section of the creed testifies to the vivifying and renewing work of the Holy Spirit. There the communion of
saints nestles quietly, between "the holy catholic church" and "the forgiveness of sins," forming along with "the resurrection of the body"
and "life everlasting" a sign of the compassionate presence and action of divine mystery in the world of life and death. The fact of its
inclusion in the creed signifies that the communion of saints is not
immediately evident but a matter for faith, as are all salvific realities. Its location precisely in the creed also indicates the importance
of this deep relationship, an abiding gift of the Spirit, freely given.
For the symbol, somewhat abstract in itself, comes to birth in a river
of holy lives through the centuries, a great crowd to which those
confessing the creed today also belong, to which generations yet unborn are destined, and to which the natural world forms both matrix
and partner.

Liturgy

The practical import of this symbol comes to the fore in the annual celebration of All Saints Day, that feast of splendid nobodies. While every
eucharistic prayer remembers the great community of the dead "who
have left this world in your friendship"[2] and makes explicit mention
of Mary, the apostles, martyrs, and all the saints, this feast spells out
in a special way the challenge and hope of their memory. In the first
reading of the day's liturgy, an awesome vision is evoked: a huge heavenly crowd "which no one could count from every nation and race and

people and tongue."[3] Robed in white, they stand before the throne of the Lamb, singing and feasting, sheltered, comforted, given to drink of the water of life. These are people who suffered, who knew sin and forgiveness and something of the laughter and tears of love, who gave a cup of cold water, who sought the face of God. Now they have died, passing beyond the veil to the place where "God will wipe away every tear from their eyes."[4] Joined with them in a community of "God's children," persons living today hear a word of hope in the face of the great darkness of death. Although what happens after death is unknown and "what we shall be has not yet come to light,"[5] nevertheless we too will share in divine, unimaginable glory. This comforting promise is then accompanied by a word of vigorous challenge. The gospel proclaims that the road to joining this blessed company is the way of Jesus the Christ, crucified and risen, and entails being poor in spirit, merciful, pure of heart, peacemaking, and hungry and thirsty for righteousness.[6] Accessed through memory and hope, the communion of saints can be believed only by being practiced in faithful deeds of discipleship.

These basic meanings embedded in creed and liturgy seem to me to bear exploring in view of the worldwide movement of women for equal participation in church and society. A symbol so pneumatological, so relational, so intrinsically inclusive and egalitarian, so respectful of persons who are defeated and praising of those who succeed against all odds, so hope-filled and so pragmatic, has the potential to empower all those who struggle for human dignity in the name of God. At the outset, however, an interesting research obstacle presents itself. The symbol of the communion of saints is largely passed over both in theological work and in everyday experience.

A Dearth and Wealth of Research

The communion of saints is one of the least developed symbols in the history of theological explanation. There are sermons and meditations aplenty, but no systematic treatises from the early Christian centuries, no extended medieval discussions in the form of the *quaestio*, no organization into a neo-scholastic tract, and very few sustained attempts to explore this belief in any methodical fashion whether in Protestant, Orthodox, or Catholic theology.[7] Despite the conflict over devotional practices at the time of the Reformation, neither Protestant

nor Catholic opponents situated their theological battles in the context
of the communion of saints, focusing instead on the power of discrete
saints as intercessors. The Council of Trent, which met intermittently
for eighteen years, treated the issue only on its last two rushed days(!),
contenting itself with defending the disputed practice of invoking the
saints as "good and useful" and articulating in a few sentences a concise program of practical reform.[8] When the Second Vatican Council
included a chapter on the communion of saints in its Dogmatic Constitution on the Church, *Lumen Gentium,* it was the first time that
pope or council had ever offered a sustained teaching on the subject,
and this itself was more a sketch than a full-blown treatment.[9] Since
that time, ecumenical dialogue has revisited the sixteenth century with
more irenic results, and occasional theological essays and books have
consulted the saints as a source for theology or explored facets of their
meaning.[10] But twenty-five years after Vatican II, a three-volume work
assessing how theology on an international scale developed the council's themes records no significant work on the subject.[11] And the field
of systematic theology still enjoys no consensus about the location
or systematic meaning of the communion of saints. Instead, pieces of
the subject are found scattered throughout discussions of other major
themes such as the holiness of the church, the Spirit's sanctifying work,
the life of grace, the mediatorship of Christ, life after death in heaven
or hell, and the proper level of veneration of saints compared to the
adoration due to God.[12]

The dearth of a well-developed, integrated approach in theology
is cast into sharp relief by comparison with burgeoning new lines
of scholarly research in related disciplines. Social history studies the
saints with an eye to the communal context of the lives of religious
individuals, charting the power politics, cultural mentalities, and social mores with which they interacted, and uncovering the impact of
their lives on political and social forces. Equally worthy of analysis are construals of saints' memories and orchestration of their cults
which, depending on circumstances, could be used equally well by civil
or ecclesiastical rulers to enhance their position or by those ruled to
resist structures of governance that they found oppressive.[13] Social
histories of women in particular, highlight the frequency of gender
transgression in the life of holy women, and open a window onto
sexual politics in different eras.[14] In another field, comparative studies
produce fascinating insight into the role of the saint in cross-cultural
perspective, finding "family resemblances" between Christianity's mar-

tyrs, monks, ascetics, teachers, wonder workers, and other types of holy persons and the function of the Buddhist *arahant* (Theravada) and *bodhisattva* (Mahayana), the Islamic *wali* (Sufi), the Confucian sage, the Hindu *rsis,* and the Jewish *saddiq* and *hasid.*[15] These types are not reducible to each other, for each religious tradition has unique patterns of interpretation. Yet study of the similarities and differences enhances understanding of the religions and the complex field of comparative theology. Philosophy weighs in with studies that analyze the existence of holy persons as empirical evidence for the Christian community's talk of the presence of the Spirit in history, or that develop new approaches to ethics grounded on the example of holy people. Focusing on the saintly life as a model for moral living has long been a staple of preaching. In light of the postmodern critique of totalizing accounts of reality, however, reading the narrative text of holy lives yields a method of ethical thinking with compassion that may counter the horrors of genocide and other evils.[16] Psychological studies of saints and aesthetic studies of devotion to saints shed unique light on the phenomenon.[17] There is also growing scholarly interest in popular religion, long neglected because of rationalistic bias. By no means restricted to unsophisticated lay people, popular cultic expressions are signs of a worldview and set of relationships shared by bishops, clergy, and lay people alike which strengthen confidence and help communities to create meaningful lives in stressful circumstances. Robert Orsi's beautiful study *Thank You, St. Jude,* for example, movingly explores how in the United States second-generation women moving out of immigrant enclaves found help in the new and sometimes hopeless circumstances of their uncharted lives by turning to this particular saint.[18]

This flowering of scholarship about the phenomenon of saints illumines a subject all too often bogged down in less than critical discussion and provides rich material for theological reflection. In its own integrity, however, it does not supply theology with answers to its own proper question which, precisely defined, inquires about the meaning of the communion of saints *coram Deo,* before the face of God, and about how this belief can function in the community of disciples today. It is here in seeking to construe an interpretation that we face a paucity of theological material. In a most interesting twist of history, this theoretical silence of traditional theology is now matched by an absence of traditional, existentially felt devotion to saints in advanced industrialized cultures, a situation that also shapes our quest.

Global Differences in Experience

In an essay on Vatican II's teaching on the saints, Karl Rahner made the shrewd observation that while the council set forth an exemplary doctrine, it simply did not engage the important existential issue of how this could be meaningful to people of "today" (by which he meant persons in his own culture). But such people find little or nothing in their own religious experience to correspond to the objective reality of the saints as described by the council. It is, to use his dated but interesting analogy, similar to a situation in which a mother is describing the good qualities of her daughter to a young man who might be a prospective marriage partner. He does not dispute the accuracy of the description, but no love is aroused in him due to a lack of connection with his own desire. Thus while the council described the reality of the saints with unobjectionable accuracy, it did not appeal to the subjective experience of people conditioned by the atmosphere of contemporary life so as to elicit a response. As a result, "the present situation is such that at least in the Cisalpine countries of Europe veneration of the saints has suffered an extraordinary decline even among Catholics, so that the ability to practice such veneration seems to have undergone some kind of process of atrophy and decay."[19] In the United States, the Notre Dame Study of parish life reveals the same pattern, with fewer than half of the respondents reporting that they prayed to Mary or the saints, with that number decreasing ever further among those younger in age so that the future may well bring even further diminishment.[20] Reflecting on the contrast with his own upbringing when the saints were part of the warp and woof of life at Mass, on feasts, when things got lost — "they were always there" — James Wallace, while urging a form of preaching that would restore this rich heritage, joins many commentators with his rueful remark that "it is true to say that the saints no longer play much of a role in contemporary popular piety."[21]

This situation does not define the whole world scene, however. The affective experience of peoples in different cultures, colored by basic emotional moods and intellectual assumptions, has given rise to a globally multifaceted situation with regard to the communion of saints. It is important to be clear about this because this book does not pretend to give a universally relevant explanation but speaks out of and back to a situation that is at once idiosyncratic and new.

In Latin America intense veneration of saints and of that special saint, Mary, continues to flourish in two distinctly different ways. According to traditional piety, on the one hand, each locale has its own patron saint, often celebrated with a special festival day, and its own Marian image, title, and shrine which link the community to the great Mother of God. Often sharing characteristics of ancient indigenous deities, these popular saints are helpers of the people in their daily struggle for life. By providing them with understanding and power to deal effectively with harsh situations, these saints open an avenue of relationship to God who can then be thought to be actively present in their midst. Despite traditional teaching that minimizes the value of life on earth in view of heaven, and despite scholarly attempts to label their behavior as ignorant or worse, millions of people have set about creating meaningful lives for themselves and their families in the company of their saints. As sociologists June Macklin and Luise Margolies observe, "They care little about whether they are 'coercing' or 'petitioning' the powerful dead, whether they are practicing 'magic' or 'religion,' whether their deeds are sacramental or extra-sacramental, if the required results are forthcoming."[22] The point is that devotion to the saints works to build personal and communal meaning where life is desperately hard. It is an expression of an existential faith, developed in a culture "brushed only ever so lightly by the wings of the Enlightenment."[23]

In base communities, on the other hand, the people reclaim saints as partners in the struggle against an oppression that is analyzed in explicitly social and political terms. Critical of the present roster of canonized and liturgically celebrated saints, the majority of whom are white Europeans of upper- and middle-class standing and thus unrepresentative of the poor on the underside of history, the search is made for new models of holiness among those in the ancient and recent past who have struggled for justice. Leonardo Boff, for example, rereads the significance of Francis Assisi through the filter of liberation theology, finding in his story powerful witness to God's love for the poor and the need to speak truth to power on their behalf.[24] Taking poignant note of the new generation of martyrs being created on this continent, theologians furthermore argue the need for political saints today as revelatory of the grace of God in the midst of social conflict.[25] In this perspective, the eyes of the poor have rediscovered Mary's solidarity with them in a startlingly apt way insofar as she was a village woman, a poor woman of the people, a member of a people oppressed by an occupying force, a refugee woman fleeing with her newborn child from the wrath of a murderous ruler, a bereaved mother of a victim of unjust execution. Through it all she was a herald of liberation, singing the song of justice of the coming reign of God, her "Magnificat."[26] This solidarity carries political significance, for it is to *this* kind of woman that God has done great things. Her veneration aids and abets the realization of the dignity of all those treated as nonpersons.

In Africa the unseen but powerful presence of ancestors undergirds the sense of selfhood and is foundational for the whole social fabric including ethical values. Drawing on this genius of the African peoples for sensing a vital relationship between the living and the "living dead," various local communities and theologians are attempting to incorporate this ancient cult into veneration of the saints and Mary. Several Christian corrections are introduced to ancestor worship: only God is all-powerful, so ancestors can do no harm; and the foundation for relationship is the grace of Christ rather than family blood ties. With these provisos, the living presence of ancestral spirits is recognized as part of the working of divine providence and the mystical bond connecting the living and the living dead is celebrated, especially at Eucharist.[27]

Amid the religious pluralism and poverty of Asia, Christians, a minority of tiny proportions (3 percent), creatively appropriate the saints through symbols that resonate with the holy men and women of the great Eastern religious traditions and that vast continent's diverse traditions of veneration of ancestors. Among them, too, liberation-oriented communities reclaim Mary from her disappearance in Protestantism and her domestication in Catholicism, seeing her as a graced woman of poverty and suffering who walks with them in their struggle for justice and particularly for the dignity of women.[28]

In eastern Europe and the Mediterranean countries a thriving veneration of the saints and Mary is visible, at times related to national aspirations, but more often the expression of a national character that is warmhearted and affectionate.[29] The resurgence of Orthodoxy in Russia likewise brings to the fore a highly conscious mystical union with the saints and the great Theotokos in accord with the doctrine of deification. An example from the sixth-century Dorotheus of Gaza illustrates the dynamism of this union:

> Imagine a circle marked out on the ground. Suppose that this circle is the world and that the center of the circle is God. Leading

from the edge to the center are a number of lines, representing ways of life. In their desire to draw near to God, the saints advance along these lines to the middle of the circle, so that the further they go, the nearer they approach to one another as well as to God. The closer they come to God, the closer they come to one another.... Such is the nature of love: the nearer we draw to God in love, the more we are united together by love for our neighbor.[30]

Saints are those who have drawn so close to the center of the circle that Uncreated Light streams through them into the world. And the closer people draw to them, the closer they get to the divine, an understanding that nourishes a resurgence of interest in the saints.

By contrast, what is striking in this global panorama is the noticeable diminishment of private devotion among dominant sectors of the population in the democratic, capitalist nations of western Europe, North America, Australia, and wherever Western secular culture has gained a foothold. In this setting, as sociologists Weinstein and Bell observe, "It is undeniable that there has been an overall great decline in the role of cult and of saints as intermediaries between the faithful and their God."[31] This diminishment has become a matter for some puzzlement and distress. In his elegant study of the meaning of saints, Lawrence Cunningham speaks of this generation's deep estrangement from the subject, due in part to the way saints have been trivialized or romanticized: "When we describe persons of perspicacious sanctity today, we hasten to report that they are not 'plaster of paris' saints. The qualifier betrays how deeply we have been alienated from the tradition of saints."[32] How is it, he goes on to wonder, we have come to ignore the saints just when renewed interest in spirituality and the role of story in theology is on the rise? From a sociological point of view, John Coleman also judges this "passing of the saint" to be regrettable. In a strong jeremiad he declares, "Alasdair McIntyre claims in his provocative book *After Virtue* that we have lost the essential vocabulary of virtue, and by titling this essay 'After Sainthood' I am proposing that we have experienced a similar loss in regard to saints. Taken together, these two losses indicate a considerable cultural disarray, which will not be easy to repair."[33] One aspect of the loss to society is the dearth of visually imaginable models at a time when the use of video media is sweeping text alone to the side. Historian John Howe notes that while Catholics have always depended on pictorial models as vehicles for specific teachings, today in this post-book era even some biblical fundamentalists may depend for the knowledge of Scripture on charismatic media figures. "Yet just when one would expect a tremendous need for holy models, traditional devotions to the saints often appear to be declining. Why?"[34]

Interpreting the Silence

Many analysts note that this state of affairs results in part from the success of the Second Vatican Council's reforms, which laid renewed emphasis on biblical, eucharistic, and christocentric piety.[35] The annual calendar of the Roman Catholic Church was redesigned with the express purpose of replacing the priority formerly given to saints with relationship to Christ through the reading of Scripture and the prayers of the liturgical seasons; statues of saints were removed from churches or shifted to inconspicuous places; the eucharistic liturgy was made more accessible through use of the vernacular, revised rites, and emphasis on people's participation both as ministers and as congregation; translations of the Bible and encouragement of its use set loose new appreciation of the great themes of salvation history, central among them God's gracious will to save. With new realization that access to God's mercy is assured through Jesus Christ, and with the nourishment of word and sacrament easily at hand, there was no longer such a strongly felt need for mediators like the saints and Mary to whom one could thankfully turn, confident that they would intercede with a God who was quite distant and judgmental. Consequently, it was no exaggeration when an article on the resulting decline of attention characterized this as a time "when the saints went marching out."[36]

Since this result did not occur everywhere after the council, however, there are obviously cultural forces at play as well. In North America the timing of these reforms intensified their impact, coinciding as they did with the end of the period of European immigration begun in the nineteenth century. The election of John F. Kennedy announced a newly confident Catholicism among the descendants of those immigrants, less rooted in ethnic folk piety and, as they moved into the economic and social mainstream of North American life, more inclined toward a secular, searching spirit.[37] The explanation of the silence about the saints does not stop there, however. In subsequent decades, a concrete set of changes in the social, economic, and intellectual order has rapidly reconfigured this mainstream itself. This new state of affairs and its attendant consciousness is increasingly referred to as "postmodern," a chameleon-like term. But however diverse the definitions, it is essential to come to grips with the basic claim carried in the term "postmodern" itself, namely, as Edward Farley puts it, that starting in the last quarter of the twentieth century "European and North American industrialized peoples now participate in a historical shift so massive and deep-running that the human being that comes with it is as different from its Victorian ancestors as the Hellenes of classical Greece were from their predecessor civilizations."[38]

According to Farley's analysis, this shift involves the movement of people from rural villages and small towns to large, anonymous, urban centers; a concomitant change from a culture of thrift to a mass consumer culture; the economy's shift from industrial output to product delivery systems and communication technologies; and existential changes from a rhythm of talk and silence to a daily world pervaded by video and audio media and rapidly changing popular culture. In this upheaval, many extended or strong nuclear families are broken up while a startling variety of domestic arrangements emerge. The spotlight of public interest turns to business, entertainment, and government while the traditional bearers of normative values such as education, art, and religious traditions are pushed to the shadowy margins. Disconnected from meaningful community, many people also experience a broken connection between themselves and the divine, however transcendent or immanent. In academic, literary, and artistic circles the master narrative that shaped modern Western culture comes under fire. No longer do the clear and distinct ideas of universal reason, the gains of unending progress, the supremacy of white, male culture supported by violence, and human domination over nature drive interpretation, but attention focuses on what is disruptive, ironic, contingent, different, ambiguous. Overall, a new cultural epoch is dawning with power to displace customary ways of thinking, acting, and relating. The ambiguity of the phenomenon can be seen in the fact that one can celebrate the breakup of old dominations at the same time that one can also lament the dissolution of fixed meanings that traditionally supported identity and gave one a place to stand.

The modern and postmodern spirit offers a poor fit for traditional appreciation of the saints. Not only does this age deflate heroes, but the hagiography and iconography of many established saints render them remote and even singularly unattractive to contemporary concerns. Tales of their holy lives and images of their devout selves make them seem too perfect, too miraculous, too otherworldly, too eccentric to have anything useful to say. The process of canonization, moreover, which removes the power of naming saints from the local church to a central bureaucracy, further distances the saints from persons in the current intellectual ambience, who in any event are more likely to be inspired by unofficial saints such as peacemakers or those with creative charisms who have brought faith to bear on the human dilemma.

The traditional cosmology and timetable of the afterlife, presumed by customary practices of venerating saints, also withers under critical scrutiny. The old story included the particular judgment at death, followed by time in purgatory, and then the fulfillment of blessedness in heaven or the damnation of hell. It also allowed for modes of contact between heaven and earth which made it possible for the dead in general, or the saints in particular, to be in touch with the living, to take their needs to heart, even to play a direct part in their lives. The naive realism that has made such a picture possible has disappeared before the critical spirit of this age. As David Power observes, it "presumes a certainty about the other world that leaves even many believers uncomfortable."[39] In addition, the belief in indulgences and the treasury of merits that accompanied the traditional scenario plays little role in Catholic spirituality and practice anymore. Indeed, as Susan Rabe has summarized, people "no longer think in these terms of measurement and accounting, and modern spiritual needs are very different."[40] These discrete criticisms indicate that the devotional forms and interpretive categories of a previous era do not match the spirituality of a new time, a not unusual situation that has occurred before in the course of a living tradition.

At the deepest level, I wager that the characteristic experience of God in this epoch undergirds what has happened to piety regarding the saints. Shaped by the climate of thought and the situation in the modern/postmodern world, religious experience encounters the radically incomprehensible mystery of God precisely as mystery: unfathomable, uncontrollable, and unimaginable. Thought and experience find this holy mystery first and foremost not as a particular being among other beings but as the gracious Spirit embracing the world with compassionate love while dwelling in light so inaccessible it remains darkness to human perception. Speaking of this existential quality of contemporary faith, Rahner notes that it is precisely the people today who really and genuinely believe in God who, even while they know that the gracious divine mystery is infinitely close, feel this strangeness and distance:

> Naturally this is something which has always been known and recognized. But modern persons experience it with a new and radical keenness because the world has become so inescapably vast and at the same time so profane, and also because, not surprisingly, God does not appear as one factor "along with" others which are given in the everyday experience of this world. God is, to a large extent, experienced as the silent mystery, infinite in ineffability and inconceivability. And the more persons advance in the religious life the more *these* aspects of God come consistently to the fore, instead of diminishing.[41]

The characteristic experience of faith today is pervaded by a certain darkness, emptiness, silence, risk, the cross, akin to the dynamic of apophatic mysticism, even while the drawing near of the sacred is recognized in fragments of healing, beauty, liberation, and love in the human and natural world, understood anew as luminous sacraments of divine presence.[42]

In this milieu, theology itself is more tentative about what can be known about the present condition of persons who have died, those traditionally called "all saints." We are aware of the limits of language and the nature of symbols, and our experience of God, in Michael Perham's telling phrases, may compel us to repeat with Mother Julian that all will be well, but we feel unable to specify further or to paint vivid pictures as the Bible does.[43] In truth, people in this culture tend to sense as a rule that those who have died have truly disappeared from this world. They are no longer accessible to the living in any direct fashion, as was possible to imagine in a previous age. Imaginatively, the clear and easy trafficking between heaven and earth enjoyed by early Christian and medieval ancestors in the faith has broken down. While graves may be tidily kept and commemorative ceremonies carried out at military cemeteries, the sense of the dead's presence has radically diminished; there is no celebration of the Day of the Dead, with offerings of flowers, food, and candles at the family graves as in Mexico. Instead, while some persons' spiritual inclinations allow them to experience the presence of their beloved dead, most people feel that the departed exist way beyond their everyday sphere of existence. God is incomprehensible holy mystery. And "into this silent, unfathomable, and ineffable mystery the dead disappear. They depart. They no longer make themselves felt. They cease any further to belong to the world of our experience."[44] If this is the typical experience with even friends and family members who have died, it is not surprising that saints of old seem remote and inaccessible. As Rahner queries, "But if people think of their own nearest and dearest as disappearing at death into that darkness which surrounds the meager light of our existence with its silent infinitude, how can they then find it in themselves to take up an attitude of veneration towards other dead persons merely on the grounds that they were holier?"[45]

In this culture, secular and fragmented but also dreaming of new forms of relationship, where people experience God's presence in absence as absolute mystery while knowing death to be the real end of life as they know it, little spiritual energy is generated by the traditional question of the saints. Existentially, Christians in this culture cannot seem to connect with them; intellectually, such a connection seems irrelevant to the burning religious questions of the day. As a result, private devotion directed toward the saints has disappeared as a spiritual practice for many people; feast days are ignored, wanly celebrated, or become street festivals attractive for their food and games of chance; and public preaching and theological reflection on the subject, at least as traditionally carried out, is of marginal interest.

It is important to note that this description does not apply to all peoples living in modern societies. Officially, the liturgical calendar of the church continues the public veneration of the saints while teaching and exhortation maintain some emphasis on the subject. In addition, many older persons with a lifelong habit of venerating the saints continue to do so to their spirits' benefit. In particular in the United States, where more than one-third of the members of the Catholic Church are Hispanic, the saints and Mary play a strong role in popular piety coherent with this people's historical roots. A growing body of Latina/Latino theological literature, representing some of the most exciting and significant theology being done in this country today, analyzes popular religion as a genuine locus for theology that reflects the *sensus fidelium* of a suffering people with a significant history and sense of community. Orlando Espín, for example, argues convincingly that the people's intuition of faith and the practices which express it, such as home altars, fiestas, graphic images, and the custom of the *manda,* are legitimate bearers of authentic gospel tradition.[46] These symbols point to basic truths such as God's compassionate solidarity with the oppressed and vanquished, and do so in a way reflective of late medieval

Iberian Catholicism meshed with Amerindian and African symbols, the mix itself being a lasting sign of this people's origins in slavery, rape, plunder, and violence. The result has a definite flair — it is oral, visual, dramatic — at the same time that it indubitably connects the faith with the daily lives of suffering people. And this devotion operates independently of the ecclesiastical institution insofar as it works in the intimacy of the home and the public space of the neighborhood, and is led by the laity. For Hispanic communities under pressure to assimilate, saintly rites and symbols actually function as a protection and protest against the dominant U.S. culture, fueling their spiritual and cultural identity and their struggles for basic justice.

The silence is thus not universal, even within the borders of advanced industrialized nations. Furthermore, Hispanic religious sensibility has much to teach secular culture about cultivating a sense of the self in which relationship to the other is intrinsic and fostering "habits of the heart" that cherish community and tradition. Nevertheless, the dwindling of interest in the communion of saints does mark the religious consciousness of large numbers of people of the dominant culture in developed nations, including and especially the young. Due to powerful cultural forces, the traditional symbol has faded as a vital conduit of religious energy. If not dead, at least it sleeps. Our quest for understanding is situated firmly in this setting and keeps its parameters in view when construing meaning. I seek to avoid the pitfall Rahner noted about Vatican II's teaching, which simply crafted a set of ideas without reference to lived experience. But neither can I make appeal to the experience of an ancestor tradition or a dramatic popular culture of the saints, for such does not characterize the people of the church in Western secular culture. This situation provides a nonnegotiable context for the present theological exploration. While this may seem restrictive, finding a way forward may prove to be widely beneficial; as Elizabeth Dreyer has observed, "an accurate grasp of our own situation frees us to be a contributing member of the global community."[47]

Communities of Memory and Hope

In their illuminating work on the American character, *Habits of the Heart,* Robert Bellah and his associates make a persuasive case that for society to flourish it needs multiple communities that form persons whose identity is bound up in relationships. Their argument under-scores how the primary American emphasis on self-reliance, a keystone of the national myth and a unique source of strength, also tends to cre-ate a personal distance from tradition, obligation, commitment, and social responsibility, leading in the extreme to an empty, radically sep-arated self. The antidote they envision is a constituted self, created when the private life of an individual is interwoven with a larger public whole. Such a self is formed when a person grows up within a commu-nity and a tradition capable of nurturing individual autonomy that is intrinsically related to society. Without such relational selfhood, even the private life of an individual cannot sustain itself but collapses in self-reference; society also pays the price in the form of disinterest or damage to the public good.

Bellah and his colleagues offer an illuminating description of a genuine community as a group composed of diverse people who par-ticipate together in sharing certain goods and in celebrating the distinct callings of all. Such a community is not quickly formed. Instead, it gains its character in the course of a certain history,

> and for this reason we can speak of a real community as a "com-munity of memory," one that does not forget its past. In order not to forget that past, a community is involved in telling its story, its constitutive narrative, and in so doing it offers exam-ples of the men and women who have embodied and exemplified the meaning of the community. These stories of collective history and exemplary individuals are an important part of the tradition that is so central to a community of memory.[48]

Some of the stories in such a community contain ideas about char-acter and the attributes of a good person; some carry reminders of corporate achievements as also of shared sufferings endured in the past; some, too, painfully remember sufferings the community has in-flicted on others, with the call to remedy ancient evils. These memories carry a vital élan that inspires and energizes action for the good. Thus, by their inner dynamism, "the communities of memory that tie us to the past also turn us toward the future as communities of hope. They carry a context of meaning that can allow us to connect our aspira-tions for ourselves and those closest to us with the aspirations of a larger whole and see our own efforts as being, in part, contributions to a common good."[49]

Examples of such genuine communities can include ethnic and racial communities, each with its own story and exemplary personages; religious communities that recall their stories in the weekly and annual cycles of the ritual year, in their Scripture readings, and in the saints and martyrs who embody their identity; the national community with its democratic ideals and representative leaders; and some neighborhoods, towns, and families. As this list suggests, there is one more element in a nurturing community:

> People growing up in communities of memory not only hear the stories that tell how the community came to be, what its hopes and fears are, and how its ideals are exemplified in outstanding men and women; they also participate in the practices — ritual, aesthetic, ethical — that define the community as a way of life. We call these "practices of commitment" for they define the patterns of loyalty and obligation that keep the community alive.[50]

Where memory, hope, and practices of commitment disappear, the "empty self" proliferates and society degenerates into defensive amalgamations of the like-minded in gated communities. Where they thrive, socially responsible individualism grows and holds society together, even in periods of rapid change. The need for communities of memory and hope at the turn of the millennium could hardly be stated more clearly and compellingly.

The memory and hope of the Christian community of faith are grounded on the foundational narrative of the life, death, and resurrection of Jesus the Christ. Interwoven with this story are the stories of countless other women and men who have responded in vastly different ways to the Spirit's call to discipleship. In a particular way, the stories of the world's forgotten and unnamed resonate with the promise of the Crucified. Losing a sense of connection with these lives weakens the ability of the church to pass on gospel values and to empower the growth of constituted selves who live with "habits of the heart" in free and caring relationships. Retrieving the symbol of the communion of saints would therefore contribute to a mature spirituality. Bellah's analysis underscores the importance of ending the silence of the saints. But this is no simple matter, for the traditional construal of the communion of saints fails to connect with contemporary experience on deep cultural, psychological, and spiritual levels.

The resistance of this circumstance to easy solution is further under-scored when the symbolic character of the communion of saints comes into view. In Paul Tillich's well-known analysis, a genuine symbol can neither be created nor replaced at will by a conventional deci-sion, for it arises from a dimension of nutritive darkness not under immediate rational control, becoming a symbol when accepted by a community at that same level. As a consequence, a symbol is dynamic; it is born, grows, and may die in relation to a group.[51] The latter has been happening with the communion of saints in advanced industrial-ized nations. Simply repeating understandings arrived at by past eras or other cultures has no discernible effect on either fervor or enlight-enment, for there is no deep point of connection in the wider matrix of spiritual experience. Can the symbol of the communion of saints be awakened in this context? From what deep level of experience can it arise and with what dream of the future can it be connected? How shall it be construed? In the face of the tendency of North Ameri-can culture to foster a rugged individualism neglectful of the common good, can this doctrine be revived to foster "habits of the heart" that cherish community? Can it draw people into deeper friendship with the heart of divine mystery and turn them toward the praxis of justice and compassion for the world, both human beings and the earth? The exploration in this book is framed in part by these questions. With a wager that a positive answer can be found, we set out guided by an evocative text from the Book of Wisdom: "from generation to gener-ation, she passes into holy souls and makes them friends of God, and prophets,"[52] an unceasing work of love and challenge whereby Holy Wisdom marks the world as her own.

– Chapter 2 –

Christian Feminism

An Intriguing Possibility

In addition to the context of faith in a secular culture, the exploration in this book is also framed by questions arising specifically from women's contemporary experiences of being subjects of their own lives before God. Now, women have always walked in active, creative partnership with the divine Spirit. But in our day a worldwide movement of women that presses their right to live with the freedom and dignity befitting a human person has emerged in the political, social, and economic orders with, given the unity of life, strong ramifications in the religious sphere as well. Change occurs in women's consciousness when they become aware of the contrast between their own human worth and the subordinate status they are assigned by patriarchal systems in public and private realms. Then all theory and praxis, all institutions and laws, all traditions and structures come under scrutiny for the overt or subtle ways they either promote or block the realization of the full humanity of women. Novelist Keri Hulme captures the dynamism of this movement when she writes, "They were nothing more than people, by themselves. Even paired, any pairing, they would have been nothing more than people by themselves. But all together, they have become the heart and muscles and mind of something perilous and new, something strange and growing and great. Together, all together, they are the instruments of change."[1]

Theology is no exception to this challenge. In this discipline, the equal dignity of both women and men created in the image of God, redeemed by Christ, and graced by the Spirit is now basic doctrine, with the result that, as the Second Vatican Council teaches, "every type of discrimination" on the basis of sex "is to be overcome and eradicated as contrary to God's intent."[2] But such discrimination is precisely part of the heritage of the church both in theory and practice, continuing to the present moment. This book's exploration is situated within the struggle of women to wrest a life-giving blessing from religious tradition on their concrete, historical, embodied selves and their girl children, in the process seeking to transform the church into a community of mutuality among equal persons. Can the symbol of the communion of saints be so construed that it becomes an ally in the movement for women's equal participation in church and society? Can it be interpreted so as to foster "habits of the heart" that cherish a community of the discipleship of equals? Can it function to promote the dignity of women, poor and disparaged women in particular? The goal of this book is to show how this is possible within the spiritual climate of secular culture.

Immediately, a most interesting phenomenon draws our attention, namely, the current resurgence of women's practices of memory. In an explosion of critical scholarship, women are engaged in new efforts to recover the lost memory of women of ages past as food for their hungering spirits and as an eloquent factor in forming communities of resistance to patriarchy in all of its forms. A veritable renaissance of historical research is in progress, coupled with new forms of keeping memory. When this research meets feminist theological reflection that highly prizes mutual relationship and egalitarian community, an intriguing possibility begins to emerge. Might women's practices of memory rediscover the communion of saints as a source of strength in the struggle toward a world where justice reigns? And in return, might this symbol itself help to interpret spiritually the depth of what is occurring in women's experience of remembrance? If this be the case, then the exchange between women's experience and religious symbol can chart a path along which the whole *ekklesia* in secular culture can reclaim this symbol as an element in its transformation into a liberating community of memory and hope.

Whereas this whole book is an exploration of this intriguing possibility, the present chapter completes our framing of the question by describing elements of feminist theology that contribute to our reading of the communion of saints. First, a feminist critique of the tradition of the saints pinpoints areas where male dominance has weakened the liberating power of the communion of saints. Then, elements contributing to a positive, constructive interpretation are noted in women's historical research and the diverse, worldwide practice of feminist theologies. Finally, an analysis of the guiding metaphor "friends of God and prophets" unveils the reality toward which this study points and from which liberating power flows: Holy Wisdom who makes the world sacred and connects people to each other as a great sea of support.

Critique of the System of Sainthood

Theology from the perspective of diverse women's flourishing, or feminist theology, interprets Christian tradition so as to uncover what oppresses the full humanity of women in all dimensions of their being and to release what enhances this, a goal that is inseparable from the truth of the compassionate God to which the tradition testifies.[3] In feminist perspective, the standard construal of the communion of saints in canonizations, liturgical feast days, exemplary lives, and practices of devotion has been a decidedly mixed blessing for women. While upholding a blessed destiny for human life and the world itself, and while offering the possibility of relationship with helpful ancestors in the faith, the tradition about saints is pervaded with the values and virtues of the overarching system of patriarchy in which it took shape. As a result, women's history of holiness has been largely erased from the collective memory of the church. Furthermore, even when they are remembered, exemplary women's lives are interpreted as models of virtue that support the male-dominated status quo and cast women into submission. Overarching the erasure and the male-oriented narration is the system of relationships whereby saints are limned as heavenly patrons to whom earthly petitioners address requests, a transferral of patriarchal power patterns into heaven that molds both women and men into spiritual dependency. Silence, distortion, subordination: a potpourri that makes the communion of saints at first glance even more irrelevant to women than does secular culture's estrangement from the dead.

• A simple head count shows that the number of biblical saints, martyrs, confessors, ascetics, and holy people of later ages honored in the church are overwhelmingly men. Even before canonization as a juridical process went into effect in the twelfth century, men outnumbered women saints by a seven to one margin; since then, the imbalance has been sedimented into an official list of holy people who are mainly male, European, upper class, and clerics. In the first eight decades of the twentieth century, for example, the proportion of canonized saints numbered 75 percent men to 25 percent women.[4] Least represented among the canonized saints are married women, reflecting the dualistic assessment that to be female is a handicap, but to be a sexually active woman renders one almost incapable of embodying the sacred. The current liturgical calendar encodes this erasure into daily worship; roughly three-fourths of the annual feast days honor men and one-fourth honor women, if Mary be counted once. This silence is abetted by the fact that biblical stories of women's initiative and fidelity are largely omitted from the lectionary; it is exacerbated by the lectionary's inclusion of readings that advise women's submissiveness to men.[5] If in view of the traditional group of "saints" we ask what is missing, we must answer with Adrienne Rich, "the particularity and commonality of this vast turbulence of female becoming, which is continually being erased or generalized."[6]

• Not only is the history of women's holiness suppressed in this way, but when narratives of sainted women are told, they are distorted by the patriarchal point of view that controls interpretation. Acts of radical discipleship are transmuted into obedience to the male hierarchical leadership; women's sufferings in the struggle for their own religious identity are veiled as a proper asceticism; stereotypical feminine virtues are promoted in place of women's history of raw courage in the Spirit. The outcome is a meager feast for women's souls. Instead of the empowerment that comes from knowing one is part of a struggling, creative, vital history of women with God, stories of the saints function as a means of ecclesiastical control. They sustain the status quo of male authority, foster spiritual elitism, and inculcate virtue that is unattractive and even oppressive to any woman whose goal is mature adult personhood. Recalling an experience now typical of women, Elisabeth Schüssler Fiorenza poignantly expresses the discomforting feeling of being "out of synch" with the ideal held up in the saints. When she and her classmates made a high school retreat, although they had been brought up on a rich diet of stories of the saints, including women who had enacted very strong roles, they were shocked into new recognition by their priest's preaching that so contrasted with the desires of their burgeoning women-selves:

> Our images of ourselves, our problems as young women, and our goals for life were totally different from the images of the female saints that were preached to us. The lives of the saints presented more of a hindrance than a help in finding our own self-identity. These stories stressed suffering, sexual purity, submission, outmoded piety, and total obedience. They were anti-intellectual and

anti-erotic; they told about many nuns and widows and some queens, but rarely did they speak about ordinary women. While we desired our own independence and love, the glorification of the saints demanded humble feminine submission and fostered sexual neuroses.[7]

As this experience is repeated in the reflection of numerous women, the lives of the saints become what Anne Patrick strongly calls "narratives of fading power,"[8] ignored or rejected by women with even a flicker of consciousness of their own desire and historical power.

• A third critique moves beyond the concrete lives of women to examine the dominant-subordinate patterns of relationship that the system of sainthood prescribes. Ideally, remembrance of forebears in the faith enhances self-identity, releasing a power to go forward in their spirit and with their unfinished agendas. Structurally, however, by singling out an elite core, the traditional, male-defined system of sainthood does not return a sense of their own holiness to women but rather deprives them of it: "I'm no saint." Furthermore, rather than understanding the relationship between the living and the dead as one of mutual companionship, a circle of "friends of God, and prophets," traditional prayers and devotions promote a pattern of unequal relationships whereby earthly neediness on the one hand forever calls out to heavenly power on the other, thus reinscribing the patriarchal pyramid of power into eternity. It is not that people should not be of help to one another, including praying for each other. But the system of sainthood is so designed that relationships pivot on inequality while solidarity is undermined.

In sum, feminist theological analysis from the perspective of women's flourishing measures the official tradition of the saints and finds it wanting. Its vision, structure, and practices promote and sustain a system of religious patriarchy. Women's history of holiness has been neither remembered nor truthfully told; nor does relationship with the saints in heaven generally redound to the empowerment of the saints on earth in their struggle for human and religious dignity. In fact, the patriarchal structure of powerful heavenly patrons and needy petitioners, coupled with the erasure of the memory of women's discipleship and approval of the male-defined virtue of even those women who have made it onto official lists, conspire to block women's realization of their own sacredness, bringing about a corresponding decline in religious energy.

A Renaissance of Research

Both the oppressive character of the system of sainthood and its current irrelevance might indicate that it should be consigned to oblivion. But something new has appeared on the horizon. The blossoming of feminist historical scholarship, received in women's gatherings for prayer and ministry, and the burgeoning of feminist theologies, reprising relationship and mutuality as characteristic even of God's own being, provide a venue for creative advance.

Historical research into the lives, the sufferings and defeats, the achievements and victories of women who walked with God proceeds on the assumption that women's lives have been little recorded or remembered in official versions of important events not because women were not there and actively contributing but because they are not deemed important. A consummate example of this mind-set can be seen in Matthew's account of the feeding of the multitude. The gospel story concludes: "And those who ate were about five thousand men, besides women and children."[9] "Besides women and children," or as some translations would have it, "not counting women and children," or "to say nothing of women and children" — surely this is not because their appetites are so small as to be unworthy of mention, but because their persons are unimportant. Their presence does not count. But in truth they were there, and they were hungry and ate, so that the traditional nomenclature "the feeding of the five thousand" needs to be revised upward. This pattern holds true through the centuries: denied power and voice, women in the churches yet have a story of creative fidelity and participation to tell.

Contemporary feminist research into biblical and historical materials vigorously develops methods to tease out the stories of women rendered invisible and silent by patriarchal texts, bringing to light long-neglected women and their overlooked impact. The mind-set here, in contrast to androcentric erasure, is one of critical and conscious remembering, bringing forth the subversive meanings in texts and the silences within texts using a multitude of strategies. Scholars now explicitly note the presence of women in a story, interpreting this as the tip of an iceberg rather than an exhaustively accurate account; they reconceive the framework of interpretation so that women's active contributions stand out; they read women into generic language such as prophet and apostle, remark their lack of a name, and call them by name where possible; they indict the violence inflicted on them, interpret criticisms and strictures against them as revelatory of how women were in fact resisting the limited domain assigned them. With these and other strategies that look not *at* women in texts but at the world *through their eyes,* scholars are erasing the erasure of the memory of women's lives in the Spirit. Women in the history of Israel, women in the ministry of Jesus, women at the center of the cross and resurrection event, women in the apostolic church, women as prophets, apostles, and leaders of house churches, women martyrs, women ascetics, nonconformist women, wives and mothers, nuns and single lay women, women mystics, women reformers, women theologians, women burning with charity for the poor and distressed, women burned at the stake, slave women, poor women, working women, women creating art and beauty, women working crafts, women feeding, women healing, women in solidarity with each other, women seeking equal partnership with men, women preaching, women interpreting the Bible, women leading others in the ways of the spirit, peacemaking women, women loving their children, women loving their husbands, women escaping their husbands, women fighting male restrictions on their lives and ministry, women resisting injustice, "ordinary" women of fidelity and valor — all have been there, living their lives before God. To discover these foresisters with their sufferings and defeats, their accomplishments and victories, and to recover their lives from the judgment that labels them insignificant is to break through a long and debilitating amnesia.[10]

New, liberating readings of the significance of particular women customarily seen as fitting quietly into a man's world abound. There are the Hebrew midwives Shifrah and Puah, who in fidelity to their conscience defy the murderous decree of the Pharaoh to kill the male babies; and the girl child Miriam, quick-witted protector of her little brother Moses, who herself grows up to be a leader of the Exodus community and the head of their liturgical thanksgiving in dance and song.[11] There is the concubine from Bethlehem, gang-raped and dismembered, whom Phyllis Trible interprets as a Christ figure: "her body was broken and given to many";[12] and the daughter of Jephthah, sacrificed by her father's foolish vow to a patriarchal God but mourned every year by the daughters of Israel in a ritual that Renita Weems interprets as person-forming in its impact: "weeping helped to clarify their vision...she was not the first woman to have been treated unjustly, nor unfortunately would she be the last."[13] There are the women disciples of Jesus' ministry with their irreplaceable relationship to him in death and risen life; Mary Magdalene in particular emerges as the apostle to the apostles, a leader in ministry who meets with resistance from the male disciples and is later metamorphosed into a repentant prostitute; Martha of Bethany, spokesperson of the apostolic confession of Jesus' messianic identity in the Johannine community, thus assuming a role similar to that of Peter in the synoptic tradition; hosts of others in the Scriptures.[14] Women's leadership in the early Christian centuries and in the synagogue of the diaspora is played off against male criticism of their participation, revealing how the public defeat of women's ministry was determinative for the formation of rabbinic Judaism and orthodox Christianity.[15] Mystics such as Hildegard of Bingen and Julian of Norwich are prized for their theological acumen as much as their spiritual wisdom.[16] Carolyn Walker Bynum and Clarissa Atkinson sensitively interpret other medieval women mystics so as to rescue them from weirdness into the identity of self-defining God-seekers within a highly particularized situation; Anne Llewellyn Barstow details the religious sadism and female suffering of the early modern witch hunts; Jo Ann McNamara explores the strength found in the initiatives of women in religious orders; Brenda Meehan recovers the memories of contemplative Russian women as pointers to vital spiritual energy today; Delores Williams brings black American slave women's experience of surrogacy to the fore as historical fact and theological metaphor.[17]

New readings of traditional, official saints covered over with the sickly pale of patriarchal interpretation yield surprisingly strong pictures. Doctor of the church and activist mystic Catherine of Siena wrote in the spirit of the prophets to the cardinals behind the church schism, "You are not sweet-smelling flowers but corruptions which cause the whole world to stink"; doctor of the church and reformer Teresa of Avila confided in agony over the restrictions of women's activity within the church, "When you were in the world, Lord, you did not despise women but did always help them and show them great compassion. You did find more faith and no less love in them than in men.... When I see what the times are like, I feel it is not right to repel spirits which are virtuous and brave, even though they be the spirits of women"; young Carmelite Thérèse of Lisieux internalized the stricture that she ought to be satisfied with being Jesus' spouse, yet could not bridle her own desire, writing "I feel within me the vocation of the PRIEST" (emphasis in the original).[18] Putting to rest the idea that women were forever silent on matters religious, busy librarian Andrew

Kadel, hounded by requests for sources, compiles a bibliography of writings by Christian women from the first to the fifteenth centuries; Patricia Wilson-Kastner and her colleagues translate the lost tradition of women writers in the early church; Marla Selvidge uncovers the notorious voices of feminist biblical interpretation from 1500 to 1920; and Rosemary Radford Ruether and Rosemary Skinner Keller collect the distinct voices of four centuries of American women's religious writing.[19] Nor does this list even scratch the surface of the work being done during this veritable renaissance of feminist theological retrieval of women's history of life with God.

In face of the erasure of women's participation in Christian history, so that relatively few female figures stand out and those that do have been reshaped according to patriarchal norms, discovery of women's lives requires a critical revision of the overarching story into which they are received. If men are the only or the chief players, then women are inevitably auxiliary to their deeds. But if women's contributions and struggles are equally valuable, then the story must be told a different way. The point is not just to include women in existing narrative structures in order to make the dominant paradigm look inclusive (the "add women and stir" strategy); rather, the goal is to reshape that narrative paradigm so that female perspectives are as central as male ones in a community of mutuality (the "change the recipe" strategy). Allowing the storyline to trace the community of women and men through feminist rather than patriarchal imagination, such a critical hermeneutic liberates the text and its hearers together.

Such narrative remembrance fosters a sense of connectedness among women with the great crowd of women who have lived before now. This solidarity arouses pride in a legitimate past, enhances self-respect, awakens resistance to oppression, and provides exemplars who encourage greatness of spirit. In these ways it intuitively arouses energy for the struggle for the well-being of the world today. By bonding in memory with suffering, victimized, creative, and victorious foresisters and foremothers in the tradition, women draw strength and are nourished in their own human, spiritual powers. They are not alone, but part of a whole river of historic efforts. In a culture where promotion of the latest excitement has lifted forgetfulness to a fine art, the option to connect with ancestors, as Adrienne Rich has wisely pointed out, has the character of an act of moral responsibility. Resisting the temptation to drift along with every veering wind and tide, women take their bearings toward a worthwhile life from a living tradition, one moreover that is ripe with promise: "seeds stored for generations can still germinate."[20]

From a theological perspective, what I see taking shape in these practices of memory, received and made effective in women's lives through personal reflection and communal rituals, is a contemporary form of the doctrine of the communion of saints. What Scripture refers to as "so great a cloud of witnesses"[21] that inspires our running, and what the church of the martyrs praises as a living community of companions who give us "lessons of encouragement"[22] and make our way a little less rough, is functioning once again with liberating power. It now becomes clear why bringing this retrieval of women's history of life in the Spirit into explicit correlation with the symbol of the communion of saints can be mutually advantageous. The research and its reception gives new life to the meaning of the symbol in contemporary spiritual life; in turn, the religious symbol gives the historical discoveries a spiritual place to dwell. The exploration that follows in this book pursues this connection. Can generations of women's lives as friends of God and prophets be reclaimed as theological doctrine? Can saints be friends rather than foes of women's search for their full measure of human equality and their Christian identity as *imago Dei, imago Christi,* temple of the Spirit? Can women connect with each other in and through our differences? How can resources arising from women's intelligent wisdom illuminate the meaning of the communion of saints, and resources encoded in this symbol be tapped to promote the flourishing of women and thereby all the relationships and communities of which they are a part? Finally, in what way might this conjunction offer a clue for revitalizing the communion of saints as a practical doctrine for the whole church?

Feminist Theologies

This exploration is situated in the enterprise of women doing theology that is today a worldwide phenomenon. Feminism, in Sandra Schneiders's definition, is a comprehensive worldview that "engages in a critique of patriarchy as an essentially dysfunctional system, embraces an alternative vision for humanity and the earth, and actively seeks to bring this vision to realization."[23] Christian feminism does this within and toward the tradition and community of the church, while feminist theology is that aspect of the endeavor that seeks to interpret the intelligibility and accountability of the faith through the lens of women's flourishing. As the endeavor has matured, its qualities as a fundamental, ethical, and pluralist quest for understanding become ever more apparent. These three aspects bear on a feminist reading of the communion of saints in a particular way.

Fundamental

It is a truism to say that feminist theology is concerned not only with "women's issues" but with the whole range of Christian tradition, its beliefs, moral values, rituals, images, and structures. Analyzing this tradition brings to the fore an ambiguous result. Not only has it been the bearer of the gracious and liberating good news of salvation and of life-affirming ways to follow Christ, but it also bears deeply embedded attitudes of the male's privileged place before God coupled with practices of exclusion that have severely limited and harmed women in their spiritual search. In 1964 the biblical scholar Margaret Brackenbury Crook described her discovery in this way:

> A masculine monopoly in religion begins when Miriam raises her indignant question: "Does the Lord speak only through Moses?" Since then, in all three of the great religious groups stemming from the land and books of Israel — Judaism, Christianity, and Islam — men have formulated doctrine and established systems of worship offering only meager opportunity for expression of the religious genius of womankind.... If a woman born and bred in any of these faiths takes a comprehensive look at the form of theology best known to her, she discovers that it is masculine in administration, in the phrasing of its doctrines, liturgies, and hymns. It is man-formulated, man-argued, man-directed.[24]

Lured by the Spirit, women now turn away from the disparagement of their embodied selves imbibed from the patriarchal tradition and turn toward a full embrace of their own blessed worth, cherishing themselves anew as religious subjects, created by God, redeemed by Christ, graced by the Spirit, called to responsibility in this world, and destined for life in glory. This becomes a baseline from which critical and creative thinking and action proceed. Amid incalculable personal, political, and spiritual suffering resulting from women's subordination in theory and practice, Christian feminism labors to bring the community, its symbols and practices, into a closer coherence with the reign of God's justice. In face of the patriarchal dominance of creed, ethics, ritual, law, and symbol, it seeks to reinterpret the symbols and ethics of faith at the deepest level so as to subvert misogyny and release a public and permanent blessing on being female. Therefore the venture is concerned not simply with "women's questions" but with the whole meaning and praxis of Christian faith as it bears on salvific wholeness of relationships, human beings with each other and with the earth, which in turn are inseparable from the truth of the all-holy, compassionate God. No superficial endeavor, feminist theology works to heal patriarchy's broken heart, in Rita Nakashima Brock's beautiful metaphor,[25] or to liberate women and men together into a community of the discipleship of equals, in Elisabeth Schüssler Fiorenza's powerful symbol,[26] or to communicate the Spirit's offer of transforming grace to the church in this age, as Anne Carr prophetically states.[27]

Ethical

In a remarkable insight, Pope John XXIII in 1963 discerned the participation of women in common, public life to be one of the "signs of the times" to which the church should attend. His words still ring: "Since women are becoming ever more conscious of their human dignity, they will not tolerate being treated as inanimate objects or mere instruments, but claim, both in domestic and in public life, the rights and duties that befit a human person."[28] It is that refusal to tolerate, enacted in individual and collective resistance, and that claim, pressed in arenas from the intimate to the global, that signal an epochal ethical event in the history of the human spirit. For despite some important recent advances, serious obstacles impede women's enjoyment of their full human dignity in the concrete.

The world conference on women sponsored by the United Nations in Beijing in 1995 took the measure of the difficulty when it noted that despite the fact that women and girl children in all their diversity are genuine human beings with the inherent dignity and inalienable rights belonging with that identity,

> women's concerns are still given second priority almost everywhere. Women face discrimination and marginalization in subtle as well as in flagrant ways. They do not share equally in the fruits of production: women constitute 70 percent of the world's poor.... Women and men still live in an unequal world. Gender disparities and unacceptable inequalities persist in all countries. In 1995 there is no country in the world where men and

women enjoy complete equality.... Deeply entrenched attitudes and practices perpetuate inequality and discrimination against women, in public and private life, on a daily basis, in all parts of the world.[29]

The Beijing Conference's "Platform for Action" points out major stumbling blocks that need attention. These include women's systemic absence from economic and political decision-making; the resulting desperate poverty and violation of human rights suffered by them and their children; the lack of equal access to education, literacy, and training, as well as to health care appropriate to the female life-cycle; the violence directed against women in the home, in public places, and in war, including the use of rape as an instrument of control; dehumanizing women into sex objects by the media in a consumer culture; and environmental degradation which directly affects the well-being particularly of poor women. "Look at the world through women's eyes." With this theme, the conference saw clearly that women's issues are global and universal, basically human issues, and that women's access to power and their equal participation in all spheres of society are fundamental for the achievement of social justice, world peace, and sustainable development of the economy in harmony with the environment.

As Beijing made clear, gender equality and the advancement and empowerment of women confront not only sexism but also racism, classism, ageism, heterosexism, colonialism, and supremacy over the earth, the whole interstructured edifice of oppressions that allow some to lord it over others. This ethical concern is intrinsic to feminist theology's quest for understanding religious beliefs, morals, and rituals, for if they do not liberate, how true can they be? Or, put in other words, if the God revealed in creation and in Scripture is the life-giving, compassionate, gracious, and self-giving Holy Mystery who cares for all, then Christian teachings must serve that care in every instance.

Pluralist

As Beijing showed, women are willing to link together in moral struggle to move the cause of women's human dignity forward and are in general agreement about the direction in which "forward" lies. Even with this baseline, there is no one feminism. Women of different countries and cultures, different races and classes, different philosophies and social theories, and different historical and religious backgrounds approach issues with different sufferings, different wisdoms, and multiple angles of vision. This gives the enterprise a profoundly pluralist cast.

With the exception of Antarctica, every continent is now home to published work interpreting faith and morals from the perspective of women. A recent dictionary, under the heading of feminist theology, carries entries for the following geographic locations: Africa, Asia, Europe, Latin America, North America, Pacific Islands, South Asia.[30] The inclusion of "dozens of black, yellow, brown, and red women" whose work represents diverse cultural complexities and varies "in questions, emphases, theoretical stance, method, and ecclesial relation" projects into Christian theological reflection, Shawn Copeland rightly suggests, a radically new element, namely, "the voices and experiences of women who have been ignored, abused, exploited, and oppressed."[31] The cross-fertilization of insight provides unexpected, fruitful directions for thought as well as challenging problems which themselves become the source of new insight.

A key issue arises from the fact that women in every instance consult their own interpreted experience as a hermeneutical tool, thus gaining a foothold from which to wrestle with patriarchal tradition.[32] This very practice introduces the question of difference among women, for no one group of women's experience is universal or provides exclusive access to the truth. The question of whose experience counts has been pressed particularly by women in minority groups who direct it against the hegemony of the discourse of the majority. As feminist theological work has matured in the United States, this challenge has been mounted by womanist (African-American), *mujerista* (Hispanic), and Asian-American thinkers against the dominance of European-American women's experience, values, and perspectives assumed by many such women to be common to all. But this experience of the white majority lacks the suffering visited upon minority women because of their race or economic or immigration status; it misses the cultural strength of belonging to "my people" and an extended network of family; it operates from a position of privilege assumed by the majority race in this country. It becomes clear that white women, by ignoring the difference made by race, class, and other particulars of women's lives, actually exercise dominance over women of color, even if and precisely as they intend to speak for all. They do to women of minority groups what male dominant thinking has long done to women in general, namely, include everyone in the universal subject, thereby obscuring their actual historical sufferings, wisdom, and joy, their concrete reality. It is a great cover for oppression. The importance of difference, by contrast, lies in the way it allows each woman her own integrity and life story.

As the discussion has progressed, feminist ethicists have warned against a kind of emphasis on difference that would cut the nerve of common struggle in resistance to women's marginalization. Lisa Cahill argues that "it cannot be emphasized too strongly that, despite the immediate practical importance of recovering the differences (whether racial, ethnic, economic, or religious) of women who have too quickly been assimilated to a white, middle-class paradigm of women's experience, the eradication of all unity worldwide among women or, for that matter, among men and women, would have monstrous moral consequences."[33] The ethical imperative "Resist domination!" will be disabled, especially in cross-cultural situations, if all generalization is disallowed because of diversity. Rather, women's movements gather momentum to the degree that women come together and realize that other women share similar difficulties and aspirations. Commonality is essential to the fight against cruelty at the concrete level.

In view of this debate, the optimal intellectual option consists in a conversion of mind and heart in which one admits the limits of one's own experience and stands open to the world of the other with interest and respect, willing to hear and be taught by different women's stories, at the same time building respectful and vigorous solidarity in action. Accordingly, sensitivity to difference and efforts toward nonhierarchical, positive valuations of difference have become a major motif in theorizing, all the while a common solidarity in the face of women's historic marginalization is sought.[34] The rich, radiant array of voices in feminist-womanist-*mujerista*-Asian-American women's theologies, in Third World women's theologies, and in theology done by women on all continents has come to be not only expected but sought after for the insight that it brings, even when tensions play among conflicting interpretations. This diversity makes "feminist theology" itself problematic as a univocal term, although it continues to function to some degree internationally as a broad umbrella term for women's unified efforts.

In this symphony, my own voice is but one, that of a European-American, middle-class, educated, Catholic woman in conversation with many others. While clearly rooted in the context of the church in a secular culture and hoping to speak a word back to it, the reading of the communion of saints that we seek draws from the insights of women in different circumstances and benefits from their critique and discoveries. Playing out the thesis that this symbol carries a liberating impulse that can disrupt present injustice, the goal of this reading is to interpret the symbol in such a way that it will serve the practical and spiritual well-being of all women, releasing redemptive possibilities of life. It aims at the liberation of women as valued human persons in their own right and, not incidentally, the emancipation of men, freed from gender-determined expectations of dominance. The goal is ultimately a renewed Christian community in service to the world according to the vibrant, life-giving Spirit of Christ, and a transformed society of mutuality and compassionate respect, both among human beings and between human beings and the earth.

Toward that end, we complete the framing of the question by limning the core metaphor, replete with equality in the power of the Spirit, that will guide our interpretation.

Friends of God and Prophets

In the biblical Book of Wisdom the unseen, incomprehensible mystery of God is spoken of by means of an elusive, appealing image, a female figure of power and might called Wisdom (*Hokmah* in Hebrew, *Sophia* in Greek). Creating and vivifying the natural world, she knows the ways of equinoxes, wild animals, and herbs. Also at play among human beings, she shapes a history of salvation, leading the oppressed to freedom, establishing justice, and teaching whoever will listen her ways which lead to life: "whoever finds me finds life."[35] Her gracious effects extend to the human heart, where she draws persons toward her divine mystery, shaping them in the process into a wisdom community:

> Although she is but one, she can do all things,
> and while remaining in herself, she renews all things;
> in every generation she passes into holy souls
> and makes them friends of God, and prophets.[36]

Age after age! Kindling friendship with God and prophecy in God's name! From the beginning of the human race's emergence into consciousness and responsibility, the breath of the power of Spirit-Sophia has been pervading the human heart and conscience, awakening the fire of affection for divine mystery and the flame of compassion wherever injustice eviscerates what that love requires in the world. Down through the centuries as Holy Wisdom graces person after person in land after land, situation after situation, they form together a grand company of the friends of God and prophets; a wisdom community of holy people praising God, loving each other, and struggling for justice and peace in this world; a company that stretches backward and forward in time and encircles the globe in space.

Friends of God: freely connected in a reciprocal relationship characterized by deep affection, joy, trust, delight, support in adversity, and sharing life; knowing and letting oneself be known in an intimacy that flows into common activities; as in Abraham, "friend of God."[37] Just as clear, still water reflects the face, so one heart reflects another in friendship; perfume and incense make the heart glad, but the sweetness of a friend is ever greater.[38] In the relationship of friendship with Sophia-God, one's love and energy flow toward the world, its persons, its other living creatures, its social structures, all so befriended by divine compassion.[39]

Prophets: moved to comfort those who suffer, for this pain is not Sophia-God's last word and there is hope; raising visions of "on that day." Anointed with the Spirit "to bring good news to the oppressed, to bind up the brokenhearted, to proclaim liberty to the captives, and release to the prisoners; to proclaim a year of favor from the Lord."[40] Called to criticize in God's name because, passionately bonded in friendship, one's heart loves what God loves and one's imagination sees how it should flourish; when this collides with the social arrangements people make at one another's expense or the expense of the earth, prophets are moved to speak truth to power about injustice, thus creating possibilities of resistance and resurrection.[41]

The twofold aspect of the communion of saints suggested by the idiom "friends of God, and prophets" can be analyzed with profit in light of the biblical wisdom tradition, the gospel tradition, and the notion of the religious classic.

The symbol and story of Wisdom herself suggest that friendship and prophecy are inherent to God's own relationship with the world. There is a joyfulness in the way she plays in the natural world; there is great cheer in the way she finds those who are seeking and teaches them her ways; there is profound gladness in the way she prepares food and sets a copious table, inviting those far and wide to come and eat. The festivity and abundance are signs of the irreplaceable blessing which is her primordial gift — life. At the same time, the beloved world is being destroyed by injustice, ignorance, greed. "I walk," she declares, "in the way of righteousness, along the paths of justice,"[42] and just governance is characteristic of her inspiration. Therefore there is measured fury in the way she strides forth, lifting her voice in the streets, the marketplace, and on the city walls, insisting on attention, declaring punishment for those who will not hear but well-being for those who change. These actions likewise signal the approach of her inestimable blessing of life, but now offered amid the gagging struggle for breath. Overall, her figure limns in a primordial way what friend and prophet mean: delighting in the good and denouncing the evil. Those whom she makes friends of God and prophets are shaped according to this cadence, being a people who bear both the feast of joy and the challenging word into the world.

Just how this works out in the practical order receives a fascinating nuance in the biblical wisdom tradition itself. In the centuries following the Enlightenment scholars tended to sideline the wisdom writings in favor of the historical and prophetic books of the Bible. At the center of Jewish religious experience, it was alleged, was encounter with the Holy One through God's mighty acts in history. Therefore "Yahwism" was considered to be an essential characteristic of Jewish faith, and the narrative interpretation of salvation history to be the primary form of biblical witness.

The wisdom literature does not easily fit into the type of faith exhibited in the historical and prophetic literature so described; it has a different way of discerning God's manifestations. It focuses not so much on once-for-all sacred deeds in history, although it does remember and cherish these, as on the continuing world of natural, everyday, mundane life, being interested in interpersonal and societal relationships, in nature and its workings, in the meaning of human life and the anguishing problem of suffering. Furthermore, wisdom is not exclusive to Israel but has an affinity with the insights of the sages of Egypt and other advanced cultures of the ancient Near East, and in fact is often borrowed from them. Unlike traditions of law and cult which were interpreted and administered by official guardians such as Pharisees and priests, wisdom escapes the control of any one group. It does not find its center in the temple but is given to anyone who searches out the order of creation in order to live in harmony with it. Its religious focus is not on personal sin and its overcoming or other intrareligious matters, but on walking the way of righteousness in human responsibility for culture, with the goal of a rightly ordered life amid the good things of this world.

In recent decades biblical scholars have criticized the way their forebears relegated wisdom writings to secondary status, arguing that the wisdom tradition reflects a genuine, primary element of biblical faith itself. The narrow track of encounter with God in salvation history is not the only way, indeed for some not even the primary way, that religious experience occurs. People connect with the holy mystery that surrounds their lives as they actually *live* in the world, in the non-heroic moments, in the efforts to be decent and just, in puzzling over setbacks and suffering, in appreciating and trying to protect nature, in trying to work out relationships harmoniously, in the gift and task of every day — in this, every bit as much as in the peak religious experiences of personal or communal life. Since the whole world is God's creation, life cannot be neatly divided into sacred and profane times or places. Life in its dailiness mediates connections with the mystery of Holy Wisdom, hidden and present. Such is the vision of the wisdom tradition. It widens the playing field for discourse about the communion of saints insofar as it allows the praxis of the friends of God and prophets to take place in home and other private spaces, in workplace and other public spaces, as vigorously as in the sanctuary. This tradition makes room for women today, largely excluded from official religious circles, to claim their own friendship with God and call to prophecy experienced in the beauty and struggle of every day and to know that this is religiously important — every bit as significant as what occurs in more explicitly sacred times and places. In this manner, new ways of appreciating holiness are being born, less associated with patriarchal control and more in tune with women's collective wisdom, so often discounted as a source of insight.

In a move of surpassing creativity, the early Christian community used the wisdom tradition as one interpretative element in their reflection on Jesus of Nazareth and his ministry, death, and new life in the Spirit. New Testament scholarship reveals the various ways different local churches identified him as Wisdom's child and prophet, promise of new life for all the brokenhearted. The gospels depict him speaking her words and doing her deeds; the gospel of John even confesses him to be Wisdom incarnate in history.[43] Seeking and finding, feeding and nourishing, teaching and enlightening, criticizing and comforting, shining as light in the darkness, Jesus' life embodies her ways in the world: "I am the way, and the truth, and the life."[44]

The realities of friendship and prophecy course through the gospel narrations. Jesus is a friend of Sophia-God par excellence, delighting in being with people and spelling out in imaginative parables, compassionate healings, startling exorcisms, and festive meals the graciousness of God drawing near to confound the powers of evil. In a way that merits criticism from religious authorities, he extends divine friendship to outcast and poor persons through table companionship, being himself "a glutton and a drunkard, a friend of tax collectors and sinners. Yet wisdom is vindicated by her deeds."[45] In his circle, new relationships patterned according to the mutual services of friendship rather than domination-subordination flower among the women and men who cast their lot with his movement. Indeed, the change begins with Jesus himself: "I do not call you servants any longer,... but I have called you friends."[46] Anointed with the Spirit, this prophet from Nazareth of Galilee lifts up his voice passionately to challenge the hardness of heart that bruises and destroys the wholeness of life, and he suffers the consequences. Anointed with the same Spirit, his disciples, Jew and Greek, slave and free, male and female, are sent to announce prophetically the good news of life's victory to the ends of the earth. Interpreting the friendship and prophecy of the gospel tradition in the context of the wisdom tradition shows that the passion of God is clearly directed toward lifting oppressions and bringing life to the world. The table is set for those who will come; the bread and wine are ready to nourish the struggle. What is needed is for his disciples to listen to the loud cries of Jesus-Sophia resounding in the cries of the poor, violated, and desperate, and to ally their efforts with God's creative and redeeming work of establishing a wise order of relationship in the world.

The "friends of God, and prophets" idiom is further elucidated by the idea, trenchantly developed by David Tracy, that there are two classical forms of expression throughout religious traditions, namely, manifestation and proclamation.[47] The first exists where human experience releases a sense of positive participation with the forces of life; then the emphasis falls on the symbolic, festive, mystical, aesthetic character of relationship with the divine. God is manifest in joy; friendship abounds. The second abides where human experience generates a radical sense of negative contrast to the forces of life; then emphasis arises on a challengingly verbal, historical, political, ethical emphasis. God is hidden in suffering; prophecy is called forth. One reflects the graceful connection between God and the world expressed in the incarnation. The other gives voice to the agonizing discontinuity felt in the suffering of the cross and its overcoming in resurrection. Though at opposite ends of the spectrum and embodying truly different types of spirituality, the two classic expressions are intimately related: manifestation and proclamation; disclosing sacred presence and exposing illusory pretensions to totality; connecting to the holy and shattering idols; the analogical and dialectical imagination; grace and judgment, friend of God and prophet — neither alone is adequate to the totality of life in encounter with God or with the world. Though one or other tends to predominate, both ideal types interact in historical religious communities and mature personalities, yielding a completeness of expression seen in nurturing and critically liberating love.

◆ ◆ ◆

These first two chapters have introduced this exploration into the communion of saints, situating it within the sensibility that marks religious believers in a secular culture and within Christian feminism, and sketching the metaphor of Wisdom's "friends of God, and prophets" that will guide our work. In the following section we search out light from the living tradition. As we track the origins of the communion of saints and watch it develop from a company of friends to a patronage system, and thence to institutionalized practice and movements of reform, we gain valuable glimmers of insight as to how this symbol can be retrieved in an empowering way within the discipleship of equals today.

Part II

Dialogue with a Living Tradition

– Chapter 3 –

A Holy Nation,
a People Belonging to God

The Search for Biblical Meaning

One of the outstanding characteristics of Jesus' ministry was his table companionship with a great variety of people. Rich and poor, sinners and righteous, tax collectors and the taxed, religious leaders and ordinary folk, those healed, those forgiven, Pharisees and disciples, women and men, all shared common food and drink in the spirit of Jesus' preaching of the coming reign of God. These suppers formed community out of unlikely associates, and the discovery of common bonds in the light of God's merciful approach released a wave of joy. To be included when you had been excluded! To find a path when you were lost! To have nourishment when you were poor! To be healthy when you had been sick! To be challenged to deeper life when you were self-satisfied! To discover a right relation to God when you had been alienated, by your own actions or the religious system! To be part of the company of friends and prophets around the table of this eschatological prophet was to discover a new energy of life by inclusion in this new community, which was itself a foretaste of the plenitude to come in the reign of God.

Critical reaction to these meals was vigorous and blunt. In Luke's description: "For John the Baptist has come eating no bread and drinking no wine, and you say, 'He has a demon'; the Son of Man has come eating and drinking, and you say, 'Look, a glutton and a drunkard, a friend of tax collectors and sinners!' "[1] Despite the criticism, Jesus' presence and words communicated the gracious presence and challenging call of Sophia-God and galvanized response. As Luke's text continues, "Nevertheless, wisdom is vindicated by all her children."[2] In Edward Schillebeeckx's beautiful phrases, Jesus as companion at table liberated people and made them glad; "being sad in Jesus' presence is an existential impossibility: his disciples do not fast"; "Jesus' eating and drinking in fellowship with his own and with outcasts, tax-gatherers and sinners brings freedom and salvation"; and, "Jesus as host: a copious gift from God."[3] What Christians have come to call the Last Supper was only the last of many, albeit a special one now tied into the events of his unjust and miserable death.

Under the guiding image of the shared meal, the experience of being a new community took on central significance for the women and men of the early church. Through their sharing in the bread and cup of salvation they understood that the power of the Spirit was forming them into a company of the friends of the crucified and risen Jesus the Christ, with responsibility to bear good news into the world. At the heart of their connectedness to each other was a new experience of the graciousness of God which led them to a sense of identity as a holy people. They called each other saints.

While the precise term "communion of saints" is nowhere to be found in the Christian Scriptures, the reality of a vital community of holy people sharing in holy things is expressed in a multitude of ways, a founding moment being the gathering of people at Jesus' festive meals. A rich vein of interpretation opens up when we realize how deeply this notion is rooted in the Jewish tradition, where a covenant relationship with the God who led them out of bondage constitutes the Jewish people as God's holy people. This identity, in turn, is not simply an ethical matter, being holy as being morally perfect, but is a participation in the very life of God's own being. Our search for the biblical roots of the communion of saints, therefore, begins with the holiness of God, tracks this into the identity of the Jewish people, and thence into Christian self-understanding.

Jewish Roots: The One Holy God

In a general sense, the Hebrew word "holy" (*kadosh*) means dedicated or set apart. It carries the connotation of something separate, pure and clear, unmixed with evil, like a wellspring of clean running water, something rock hard in the strength of its integrity, something burning bright in contrast to the darkness. These overtones of meaning coalesce when the term is used in reference to God, "the Holy One of Israel."[4] It points to God's being utterly transcendent, completely apart from what is finite or sinful. Yet divine holiness does not refer primarily to moral perfection or ritual purity. Instead, it bespeaks the mystery and power of a gracious God, the numinous quality of the divine who dwells in unapproachable light, God as the *mysterium tremendum et fascinans* by whom the human heart is terribly awed and irresistibly attracted.[5] While remaining always hidden, this divine mystery is manifested in theophanies that serve only to deepen the mystery: a promise of a great multitude of offspring to a runaway slave woman in the desert, a burning bush that is not consumed, a band of slaves breaking free, words burning on a prophet's tongue, a gentle breeze. The word "holy" bespeaks the experience of God's being unlike anything or anyone else, in face of which people are moved to fall silent, sing, dance, raise their arms or fall on their knees in adoration. "The holiness of God," writes Claus Westermann, "is the being God of God."[6] It is God's own godliness, the very divine essence, alive with inconceivable energy that people cannot manipulate but that sparks their own existence.

The meaning of the idea cannot be left here, however. In biblical usage, the holiness of God is never used simply and undialectically to indicate God's otherness and separateness, for the Holy One is precisely the Holy One of Israel. Set within the narrative framework of exodus and covenant, holiness is at the same time a profoundly relational term that refers to God's involvement with the world in creative and redeeming care. A case in point: when the Israelites had crossed the Sea of Reeds, the prophet Miriam took up her tambourine and led the other women in a song and dance of praise. Telling the story of their breathless escape, one version of the song exclaims:

> Who is like to you, O Lord, among the gods,
> Who is like to you, majestic in holiness,
> awesome in splendor, doing wonders?[7]

What is so typical of the biblical view of holiness is that here God's immeasurable grandeur shows itself in the rescue of this ragtag but determined group of slaves. Over and over again the psalms and the prophets bring this connection between divine transcendence and immanence to clear expression, linking holiness and justice, holiness and love of the truth, holiness and glory throughout the earth. This link is so consistently made that we can say that compassionate and challenging engagement is the very form in which divine transcendent holiness makes itself known. As Abraham Heschel has powerfully demonstrated, "What Abraham and the prophets encountered was not a numen, but the fullness of God's care."[8]

This is a point that needs to be emphasized. Exploring more deeply the biblical connection between God's holiness and its appearance in justice, truth, or glory makes clear the deep understanding that the untouchable, wholly other God is always encountered in saving relation to the world. We work here with glory, starting with the well-known text of Isaiah's vocational vision. Called to be a prophet, he sees himself ushered before the lofty throne of God, with incense smoking to the corners of the room and angels everywhere in attendance. He hears the praise resound:

> Holy, holy, holy is the Lord of hosts;
> the whole earth is full of his glory.[9]

The triple repetition of "holy" expresses the superlative degree; but rather than leave the enthroned One simply sitting as the awe-inspiring subject of worship, the text radiates this holiness as glory upon the world. The God of Israel is no mere high God, however high, but indwells the earth. Holiness and glory — the second gives precision to the meaning of the first. A closer scrutiny of the meaning of glory can bring us to the very heart of the biblical notion of holiness, which is never described apart from divine graciousness and compassion.

In ordinary speech "glory" is a word that signifies splendor, magnificence, brilliance, luster, rich ornamentation, power, and worth. It connotes something beautiful and desirable. The Hebrew word for glory, *kabod,* is derived from the verb meaning "to weigh heavily," and so weaves these connotations round with a sense of heaviness or deep importance. Glory then signifies something akin to a weighty radiance.[10] When used in reference to the holy mystery of God, the *kabod YHWH* is a light-filled metaphor meaning the weighty radiance of divine presence in the world, the heavy, plump, fat brightness of God's immanence drawing near and passing by to enlighten, warm, and set things right. The more the infinite transcendence of God is stressed in Israel's experience, the more *kabod YHWH* becomes a technical term in the biblical books for divine presence within the world and its happenings. Though God dwells beyond the heavens and can be compared with nothing created, God's glory pervades and leaps out from things, God's weighty radiance surrounds us. Getting a glimpse of it puts one in relation to the self-disclosure of God's being, the publicly engaged, unhidden character of the incomprehensible Holy One.

Even as it functions as a code for the presence of God, however, divine glory is never directly perceived. Rather, it is revealed in and through the world and its events. Chief among these revelatory bearers is the natural world with its power and beauty: "The heavens are telling the glory of God," exults the psalmist.[11] Typically, divine glory is depicted by a cloud or the land's fruitfulness or fire or a thunderstorm with its crashing noise, flashing lights, and rushing waters. Indeed all of the natural world is *capax Dei,* capable of revealing the unseen, hidden Creator. As Isaiah's mystical vision of the One who is "holy, holy, holy" perceives, the natural earth is full of God's glory. In the biblical vision, glory is thus a category of divine immanence perceived through the world's participation in divine beauty. The world shares in the weighty radiance of God: the starry heavens sing of it, other natural creatures reveal it in flashes of speed, methods of feeding, and all their intricate, mysterious workings. Human beings, too, reflect divine splendor, and when they realize this in moments of insight they "give glory" to God. This response entails upwelling sentiments of praise and thanks, as well as efforts to correspond to divine glory through their own loving deeds of righteousness.

But divine glory, God's weighty radiance, is not confined to the beauty and magnificence of the world. Sin, sorrow, and injustice mar the world's well-being. Wars erupt, the innocent suffer, the poor starve, a history of blood and tears tracks through the centuries. Therefore, the *kabod YHWH,* never directly perceived, is also manifest in and through historical events of peacemaking and liberation. The Exodus narratives make great play with this symbol, using it to manifest the God who frees the Israelites from slavery and accompanies them in the glory of cloud and fire through the desert into their own covenanted history. The Book of Wisdom puts it this way: "A holy people and blameless race Wisdom delivered from a nation of oppressors.... She guided them along a marvelous way and became a shelter to them by day, and a starry flame through the night."[12] The radiance of cloud and fire bespeaks the active, compassionate presence of the transcendently holy God.

In this connection, and to an extraordinary degree, the glory of God is a biblical theme of religious hope. Uttering words of comfort to people suffering the distress of Babylonian exile, second Isaiah proclaims that "the glory of the Lord will be revealed,"[13] namely, when they are delivered. Then they will see a resplendent manifestation of divine power in a historical moment of liberation and homecoming, sign of that even greater future day when evil will be overcome and the whole world will be filled with the glory of God. In biblical terms, yearning for salvation, for victory in the struggle with evil, for deliverance of the poor from want and of the war-torn from violence is consistently expressed in the hope that God's glory will dwell in the land or will fill the earth or will shine throughout heaven and earth.[14]

Biblically, then, the glory of God does not point to God as a bigger and better Solomon sitting on a throne in isolated splendor. Rather, it signifies divine beauty flashing out in the world and in particular bent over brokenness and anguish, moving to heal, redeem, and liberate. It is a synonym for the holy God's elusive presence and action in the midst of historical trouble. As such, it is a category of relationship and help.

It is interesting to see how resonant the idea of glory is with the related concepts of spirit (*ruah*), wisdom (*hokmah/sophia*), and divine presence (*shekinah*), those great grammatically feminine metaphors of God's indwelling power and concern. Chief among the biblical images for the Spirit are fire and the shining cloud. Wisdom writings are replete with glowing and blazing images. It is said that "She is a pure radiance of the glory of the Almighty"; "She is the brightness that streams from everlasting light"; and "She is more splendid than the sun, and outshines every constellation of the stars; compared with the light of day she is found to excel, for day gives place to night, but against wisdom evil does not prevail."[15] In the writings of early rabbinic Judaism, glory and the *shekinah* are used as virtual equivalents, the *shekinah* being God's compassionate spirit who accompanies the people through the tragedies of history, weeping with them and occasioning hope. Here the typical expression of the *kabod shekinah YHWH*, the glory of God's indwelling spirit, signifies no mere feminine dimension of God but the radiance of God as She-Who-Dwells-Within, divine Spirit in compassionate engagement with the conflictual world as source of vitality in the struggle.

The correlations, the mutual amplifications, at times even the identity, between the glory of God and the divine metaphors of *ruah*, *sophia*, and *shekinah* indicate that we are dealing with the active presence of great and healing beauty that can fittingly be imaged in female metaphors. The glory of God adorns the world with justice the way women beautify themselves. In the film *Steel Magnolias*, which deals with the life struggles of a group of women in the American South, there is a memorable scene in a beauty salon where, in the midst of a group of friends getting their hair curled in preparation for a wedding, an older woman observes, "What distinguishes us from the animals is our ability to accessorize." You have to hear these words uttered in an inimitable southern drawl to appreciate their impact! The ability to accessorize well describes what the glory of God has wrought in the world, filled with the marvels of nature as well as fragmentary shapes of freedom and justice happening amid destruction and despair. She has adorned the world with beauty and her own gracious radiance shines out, even in and despite the darkness.[16]

To complete the depiction of glory, we leap ahead to Christian usage. The New Testament taps deeply into the Jewish meaning of glory, now translated by the Greek word *doxa*. It proclaims that the weighty radiance of divine presence is in the world in a new way through the very human flesh of Jesus the Christ, whose ministry makes strikingly manifest how divine glory operates in the world. It does so by enacting Wisdom's deeds: the blind see, the lame walk, the dead are raised up, the poor have the gospel preached to them.[17] It is especially in the light of Easter, as the crucified one is raised to glory by the power of the Spirit, that divine *doxa* pervades the world. Glory now rests on the whole community of believers, women as well as men, who are thereby being transformed amid weakness and sin into the image of Christ. Paul writes: "And all of us, with unveiled faces, seeing the glory of the Lord as though reflected in a mirror, are being transformed into the same image from one degree of glory to another."[18] The natural world, too, is involved in this drama of salvation, groaning in the present age but with the hope that it "will obtain the freedom of the glory of the children of God."[19] The Jewish orientation toward promise is likewise strong throughout these writings: "Christ in you, the hope of glory."[20] Once again, glory is a category of participation in the holy God's redeeming beauty that draws near to share the brokenness of the world in order to heal and set free.

To sum up: In the abstract, the notion of divine holiness stands for infinite otherness and separation — the Godness of God; but in the concrete, glory as well as other metaphors function as a hermeneutic of holiness that affirms the elusive Holy One is powerfully near in and through the wondrous processes of nature, the history of struggle for freedom and life, and communities where justice and peace prevail. When connected with the biblical narrative, the incomprehensible holy mystery of God indwells the natural and human world as source, sustaining power, and goal of the universe, enlivening and loving it into liberating communion. The synergy between divine holiness and glory, or between holiness and the many other phrases with which it is connected in the Jewish sacred writings, is instructive, for these phrases give a distinct nuance to the concept of holiness that keeps it from being merely a term of distance and separation. At once ontological and ethical, holiness is essentially God's unfathomable splendor drawing near and passing by to create and to beautify, to heal, redeem, and liberate the beloved world.

Jewish Identity: Be Holy for I Am Holy

In the Hebrew Scriptures holiness is proper to God alone. But the biblical God in loving kindness and fidelity gathers a people to share in that holiness. The most characteristic religious mark of the Jewish people lies in the awareness that, liberated from bondage and chosen for covenant, they are called to share in the very holiness of God. As written in Exodus, "You have seen what I did to the Egyptians, and how I bore you on eagles' wings and brought you to myself. Now therefore, if you obey my voice and keep my covenant, you shall be my treasured possession out of all the peoples. Indeed, the whole earth is mine, but you shall be for me a priestly kingdom and a holy nation."[21] Applied to the people, *kadosh* takes on the connotation of "belonging to God." Loved and cherished as God's special possession on the earth, this is a people shaped by a profound relationship with the Holy One that acts like a deep spring of creative power at their very core. This relationship is not won because of their great achievements or merits but is offered them as a free gift: "It was not because you were more numerous than any other people that the Lord set his heart on you and chose you — for you were the fewest of all peoples. It was because the Lord loved you."[22] It is a gift of inestimable largesse, rife with ethical implications but not limited to them. All of the transcendent otherness and the passion for the repair of the world conveyed by the holiness of God come to a focus in the divine mandate that now shapes a new identity: "For I am the Lord who brought you up from the land of Egypt, to be your God; you shall be holy, for I am holy."[23]

This holiness does not consist first and foremost in ethical or pious practices, nor does it imply innocence of experience or perfection of moral achievement. Rather, it is a consecration of their very being. The people are imbued with a sacred quality that flows into responsibility to bear witness and serve the good of the world, in accord with the world-loving dynamics of the holiness of God in which they participate. When the people are called holy, and when certain times, places, things, and acts are regarded as ritually holy, and when a holy life is considered to be one lived according to Torah, the same quality marks them all, namely, a certain sharing in divine energy that dedicates their very being as sacred in distinction to what is evil and unclean: "For you are a people holy to the Lord your God."[24]

The concrete ways in which this profound and intimate relationship were construed in the course of history present difficulties for contemporary interpretation, for "belonging to God" can tend toward a separateness that occasions intolerance and violence toward those outside the community. It can also create divisions of superiority and inferiority among those inside. In her insightful wrestling with the biblical idea of the holy people, Judith Plaskow brings to critical light how within a patriarchal context holiness-as-separation came to be interpreted in oppositional and hierarchical terms, rather than the distinctiveness of Jewish identity, belief, and practice being interpreted in relational terms that connect. Furthermore, the separation motif, used to demarcate the Jewish people from surrounding nations, also turned inward to create a graded system of holiness within the community itself. "Paralleling external differentiation were a host of internal separations that set apart distinct and unequal objects, states, and modes of being," she analyzes. "On a religious level, to be a holy people was both to be different from one's neighbors and to distinguish between, and differently honor, pure and impure, Sabbath and week, kosher and nonkosher, Cohen, Levi, and Israel (grades of priests and ordinary Jews), and male and female."[25] Emphasis on clean and unclean, especially in a ritual sense, tended to stratify society according to the measure of one's adherence to observable modes of being or codes of conduct. Groups who did not measure up then became separated out and classified as deficient compared to the more elite whose lives cohered with the holiness code.

Socially, the subordination of women was the first and most persistent result of this hierarchical interpretation of what was more or less holy. The covenant was made with Abraham, circumcision is its sign, and the voice at Sinai addresses male hearers. Within a male-defined system of law and ritual, while women are granted theoretical equality as images of God, the natural workings of women's bodies especially in menstruation and childbirth are classified among things that are unclean. Thus, while many women find their way to God by following the path of Torah, the construal of holiness in a patriarchal perspective functions to exclude them publicly from the realm of the sacred, or at least to marginalize their access to the Holy One. From a feminist perspective, argues Plaskow, Jewish emphasis on the holy community is "deeply ambiguous and ironic.... Affirming community, Judaism affirms a male community in which the place of women is an open and puzzling question,"[26] women either being overlooked altogether or perceived in a peripheral way.

Concerned to deconstruct the construal of women as Judaism's "Other" as well as other separations that divide the community, Plaskow's own reinterpretation of what it means to be "chosen" utilizes a part-whole model rather than a hierarchical one. There is a greater unity to which different groups belong; the distinctiveness of each part is legitimate in itself and necessary to the whole; boundaries between parts need not be guarded by rigid separations but can be points of contact where differences enrich; denying the value of the part not one's own entails spiritual injury, for God is known in and through the experience of the empowered whole community. "It is not in the chosenness that cuts off," she concludes, "but in the distinctiveness that opens itself to difference that we find the God of Israel and of each and every people."[27] Her work demonstrates that the history of exclusivist interpretations connected with the idea of being God's holy people does not exhaust the possibilities.

I would suggest further that the biblical idea of divine holiness itself, when joined to its typical expression in glory, also carries the potential for inclusive interpretation. Set within the biblical narrative, the holiness of God shows itself in a deeply relational manner, reaching out to the poor and enslaved in a special way and seeking the good of the whole world. The call to be holy as God is holy implies a share in this world-embracing love. Whereas both Jewish and Christian male leaders have traditionally aggrandized their position to the detriment of the whole community and created powerful categories of "in" and "out," "near" and "far" from the divine, such separations are not an essential requirement of being a holy people. If the holiness of the people is indeed a result of the initiative of God, "the Holy One in your midst,"[28] in the midst of every person as well as of the whole community, such hierarchical divisions can be judged to be a grave distortion. Aware of the ambiguity of the notion of the holy people of God, its attractive and inclusive possibilities but also its potential for misuse, we turn to early Christian reception of the idea, still seeking the biblical roots of the communion of saints.

Christian Identity: All the Saints Greet You

Although not a people in the same sense that the Jewish people are, Christians drew upon the biblical theme of the holy people who participate in God's holiness to articulate their own sense of identity. This comes to expression in the term *koinonia,* variously translated as community, sharing, fellowship, participation, or communion, a word that easily slides from one connected meaning to another. It points to a eucharistic sharing that results in bondedness with each other: "The cup of blessing which we bless, is it not a *koinonia* in the blood of Christ? The bread which we break, is it not a *koinonia* in the body of Christ? Because there is one bread, we who are many are one body, for we all partake of the one bread."[29] The word also refers to a solidarity with the Spirit of God: "The grace of the Lord Jesus Christ and the love of God and the *koinonia* of the Holy Spirit be with you all."[30] In this text grace, love, and fellowship all play variations on the theme of God's threefold gracious self-gift which transforms persons who are sinners into a redeemed community. In more picturesque terms, the second-century bishop Irenaeus displayed the same sense of living unity in the Spirit:

> Just as dry wheat cannot be shaped into a cohesive lump of dough or a loaf held together without moisture, so in the same way we many could not become one...without the water that comes from heaven. As dry earth bears no fruit unless it receives moisture, so we also were originally dry wood and could never have borne the fruit of life without the rain freely given from above.... [We] have received it through the Spirit.[31]

However spread out they are in different local communities, and despite internal tensions and external harassment, early Christians are conscious of being really one communion, one *koinonia* through the waters of baptism and the shared bread and cup of salvation. As with the Jewish sense of being a holy people, their community's center of gravity is not located in itself but in relation to a divine gift and claim. They interrelate as a community of the friends of God and prophets in the risen Christ by the power of the Spirit.

The net effect of being part of this community is that all members are considered participants in the holy life of God. This comes about not because of a state of life they choose or set of virtues they practice, not because of their innocence or perfection, but because of the gift of the Spirit who is given to all.[32] The Spirit of life who raised Jesus from the dead is poured out on them and they are clothed with Christ, being transformed into the very image of Christ. As always, this is a gift freely given. Its effect is to create a community in grace.

In the New Testament, the term "the saints" comes into play to express this sense of being a holy community. This term, too, is multivalent, referring on different occasions in the New Testament to the angels, to pious Jews who have already died, or to Christians who die under persecution.[33] Its most extensive meaning, occurring some sixty times, is as a denomination for the Christian community as a whole. In addition to the general notion of Israel as the holy people of God, some scholars believe that the specific background for this usage is found in late Jewish apocalyptic literature where "the saints" describe the elect who will share in the blessings of the messianic age. In the Book of Daniel, after bitter conflict with the enemies of God, the "saints of the Most High" gain possession of the kingdom forever.[34] These holy ones are the faithful, righteous remnant of Israel who would inherit the eschatological kingdom when the Messiah comes. In the belief that Jesus of Nazareth is the Messiah, the anointed one, the Christ, Christians adapted the idea of this faithful eschatological band as an element in their own self-identity.

Paul's letters are a chief locus for this usage. "The saints" becomes the common designation of those to whom he writes, frequently appearing in the opening and closing salutations: "To all God's beloved in Rome, who are called to be saints";[35] "To all the saints in Christ Jesus who are in Philippi";[36] "To the church of God that is in Corinth, to those who are sanctified in Christ Jesus, called to be saints";[37] "Greet one another with a holy kiss. All the saints greet you."[38] Its extensive use in reference to the community of living Christians reflects the heat and vigor of their sense of the presence and action of God in their midst through the life, death, and resurrection of Jesus Christ, which leads to a sharing of physical and spiritual goods among themselves and an impulse to proclaim this messianic coming as good news. The whole church is a communion of saints. Saints are all the living people who form the eschatological community, chosen and beloved, called, gifted, and sent by God. While sinners, they are nevertheless redeemed in Christ and their lives aim to reflect this in their passionate faith in God and their loving responsibility toward the world.

Several implications flow from the consistent New Testament appellation of Christians as "the saints." Pertinent to our investigation, the title is essentially corporate in significance, directly designating not individual believers but the members of the church collectively. As befits the roots of the concept in Israel as the holy people of God, "the saints of the New Testament are not an aggregate of individuals who are characterized by a special quality of holiness; they are a holy community."[39] An individual may be regarded as a saint or holy one, but only in virtue of belonging to the community. Furthermore, the designation implies that the community is theocentric, for its existence is grounded on the call of God, the living memory of Jesus Christ, and the consecrating gift of the Holy Spirit. It intimates that the community has a strong sense of ethical integrity, for while its sanctity is a gift given without regard for deservingness, the gift brings a responsibility to live worthy of this calling in love and justice. In its context in late Jewish apocalyptic, the term also indicates that the community is eschatological, oriented in hope toward God's final victory over evil, already experienced in the resurrection of the crucified and other shapes of freedom in history. The all-encompassing scope of the term implies that the community is an inclusive one, open to persons of any race or nationality or class or sex whom God chooses and calls. And, since in the community persons enter into a new relationship with the divine, the term "the saints" conveys an equality of persons in value and religious status without discrimination. Galatians puts this radical idea clearly: "As many of you as were baptized into Christ have clothed yourselves with Christ. There is no longer Jew or Greek, slave or free, male and female; for all of you are one in Christ Jesus."[40]

As happened with the idea of Israel as the holy people of God, the inclusive equality of "all the saints in Christ Jesus" has been submerged in the concrete by patterns of exclusivity typical of the history of patriarchy. Biblical interpretation of the passage from Galatians cited above is one place where the androcentric mind-set is clearly evident. Baptism indeed establishes each person as equal before God, the argument goes, but this is a purely spiritual matter. No conclusions should be drawn from this religious equality to the political and social arrangements of church or society.[41] Instead, current arrangements of the distribution of power in a dominant-subordinate pattern can be justified from other sources. By holding tight to a dualism of religious and political realms, such exegesis manages to affirm a certain equality before God while confining it to social irrelevance. While in the nineteenth century this purely spiritual interpretation was often mounted against the emancipation of slaves, it is currently used against the liberation of women into full equality in the public order.

In an astute essay, Elisabeth Schüssler Fiorenza offers a contrasting interpretation that disputes the ploy of relegating equality before God to the purely spiritual realm. In the period of this text's composition, the early church was struggling between two visions of itself: the house church's democratic structures and vision of well-being for all on the one hand, and customary social-political-familial-religious stratifications on the other. Set in this context, "no more Jew or Greek, no more slave or free, no more male and female" carries the experience and imagination of historical "losers." For them, the social experience of baptism and the gathering around the table for the breaking of the bread meant entering into a sociopolitical community different from what they had encountered all their lives, an "assembly of equals in the power of the spirit."[42] Their voice, heard in this text, proclaims that not only does the privilege of following Torah grant one no special standing over the non-Israelite; not only does the exploitative relationship between master and slave not define association in the Christian community; but the socially constructed gender roles of dominance and submission characteristic of the patriarchal household are also transcended in this new life in the Spirit. "The text repeats with different social categories that no structures of domination and socioreligious elite male privileges exist within the Christian community. By denying the religious and social prerogatives of Jewish males as well as masters and husbands, it accords wives, Jewish women, gentile and slave women and men the new status, equality, and freedom of ecclesial citizenship."[43]

Biblical scholars have come to the consensus that this Galatians text contains pre-Pauline material connected with baptism, probably a baptismal blessing or hymn. Used on such an important ritual occasion, the text would not function as a purely spiritual statement about the individual Christian. Rather, it would be a statement of the church's own identity as a social body called into existence through the sacred waters. Concludes Schüssler Fiorenza, "Galatians 3:28 is therefore best understood as a communal-ecclesial self-definition."[44] As such, it says: this is who we are, a community of social equals, before God and before each other. Like the work of Plaskow, this hermeneutical labor demonstrates that the history of exclusivist interpretations connected with the idea of being God's holy people does not exhaust its possibilities. The subversive memory of baptismal and other texts lies waiting, part of a submerged heritage that in our day is being retrieved to powerful effect by women who struggle to overcome patriarchal relations in church and society.

Connecting this feminist exegesis with its social, egalitarian interest to the grounding notion of the community as "saints in Christ Jesus," we highlight the inclusive practice and equal valuing of persons implied by the New Testament term "saints." In the Christian Scriptures there is never any assignment of degrees of holiness to different saints. Since all are baptized the same way into the death and resurrection of Jesus, and all have received the gifts of the Spirit, then all have equal standing before God and in the community. This does not level out differences: "there are varieties of gifts but the same Spirit; . . . to each is given the manifestation of the Spirit for the common good."[45] But these distinctions are not the occasion for the saints to divide themselves in the usual oppressive ways of humankind. Thanks to God's ways implementing a new order, the old categories that are typically used to subordinate some and elevate others become profoundly inoperative.

It should be remembered that there was as yet no highly structured sacramental system, ordained priesthood, or monastic life such as would develop in the course of later centuries. Indeed, the only priest mentioned for the community is the lay preacher Jesus who, metaphorically speaking, performed the service of merciful and faithful high priest by his sacrificial death.[46] Everyone else is priestly, consecrated to the service of God, by virtue of participating in Christ's work. The Christian phenomenon of holiness is essentially lay, belonging to the people (Greek laos): "you are a chosen race, a royal priesthood, a holy nation, a people belonging to God."[47] This identity inheres in the community and every person belonging to it without distinction.

Seen in this way, the biblical grounding of the communion of saints gives to this doctrinal symbol a prophetic luminosity. Called by God, baptized in Christ, and empowered by the gifts of the Spirit, the whole community enjoys a radical equality of relationship with the Holy One and, as sacred, each and every person has equal standing. The symbol sheds light on the darkness where this fails to be embodied socially, politically, or religiously and challenges the church to a new life of transformed relationships among all the friends of God and prophets.

Cloud of Witnesses

Throughout the Jewish Scriptures certain deceased individuals are singled out as embodying the values of the community in a unique way. Remembered for centuries after their death because of the role they played in the nation's history or religious development, especially at times of crisis, these persons are described in terms such as holy or righteous, just, blameless, blessed, friend of God, finding favor with God, or filled with the Spirit. In postexilic Judaism, as ideas of future resurrection and immortality grew strong in some quarters, a distinctive remembrance and veneration of these celebrated deceased ancestors emerged in a public way. Honor was given to the founding mothers and fathers of Israel, to kings from the dynasty of David, and to murdered prophets such as Zechariah. Burial sites of such people were known by fact or tradition, Rachel near Bethlehem or Abraham and Sarah in Hebron, and their graves were visited and held in respect. Special honor was paid to the memory of those who had suffered or died because of their Jewish faith in times of persecution. Outstanding among these were the aged scribe Eleazar and a Jewish woman with her seven sons, tortured and killed under Antiochus IV (Epiphanes) because of their refusal to betray Torah. The books of Maccabees detail their suffering, even citing the epitaph appropriate for their tomb: "Here lie buried an aged priest, a woman full of years, and her seven sons, because of the violence of a tyrant bent on destroying the way of life of the Hebrews. They vindicated their nation, looking to God and enduring torture even to death."[48] The example of such commitment encouraged others to be strong in their own faith even when not put to such a test. This honoring of the saints of old in popular religion led in the last two pre-Christian centuries to building "tombs of the prophets" and decorating "monuments of the righteous," a practice depicted even in Matthew's gospel.[49]

In light of the death and resurrection of Jesus Christ, early Christians vigorously developed this vein of belief. In their experience, the power of the Spirit shaping them into a community of the friends of God in Christ was so strong that death could not break the relationship. This intuition was eloquently elucidated by Paul, who asks rhetorically: "Who will separate us from the love of Christ? Will hardship or distress or persecution or famine or nakedness or peril or sword?" And he answers: "No, in all these things we are more than conquerors through him who loved us. For I am convinced that neither death nor life, nor angels nor rulers, nor things present nor things to come, nor powers, nor height nor depth nor anything else in all creation, will be able to separate us from the love of God in Christ Jesus our Lord."[50] If even death cannot separate persons from God's gracious and compassionate love, no one who dies, then, is lost. The same Spirit who raised Jesus from the dead will likewise bring them into the new life of glory. To cite the agricultural metaphor used in 1 Corinthians, the risen Christ can be seen as the first of the fruits to ripen and be plucked, but all the beloved dead will make up the rest of the harvest.[51] They are embraced by the love of God who holds the whole world in being. In fact, the Holy One "who gives life to the dead and brings into being the things that do not exist"[52] becomes one of the distinctive designations of the Christian God.

Teasing out the logic of the early Christians' intuition of faith, we see that they forged a certain syllogism. If living persons shared in the life of God, and if the dead were likewise still clasped by the living God, then both the living and the dead were united to each other, forged into one community by the same vivifying Spirit. Paul put this insight quite succinctly when he wrote, "whether we live or whether we die, we are the Lord's. For to this end Christ died and rose again, that he might be Lord of both the living and the dead."[53] This was not a belief that pertained primarily to the individual but is a corporate idea, linked with the sense of the church as a holy people. Thus grew the idea that the community of sinful yet redeemed people of God extends not only across spatial boundaries to include those living in different lands at the present moment, but also extends across time boundaries to include those living in different historical periods, as the wide earth rolls. This belief, later expressed as the communion of saints, is not held because of logical deduction but as an act of hope in the fidelity of God. But intellectually it is an expression of that trust within a Christian framework of ideas.

There are no individual persons named "saints" in the New Testament, the term being reserved for the whole community. But just as passages in the Hebrew Scriptures speak at times of individual holy persons and recall their faith, so too in the Christian Scriptures certain individuals are singled out in a noteworthy way. They are described as upright in the sight of God, living blamelessly, highly favored, a just one, full of faith and the Holy Spirit, full of grace and power — in a word, holy. None of these persons is explicitly proposed for imitation or direct address in prayer. It is enough to remember their exemplary character, which is the fruit of the Spirit's presence in the historical circumstances of their lives. The configuration of their lives adds luster to the community and gives glory to God; their memory releases energy for discipleship.

As in late Judaism, special reverence is paid to the memory of those who have died for their faith. In a context of persecution, the Book of Revelation makes use of apocalyptic devices to present a host of faithful ones who "have come forth from the great tribulation, having washed their robes and made them white in the blood of the Lamb."[54] A beatitude is uttered over them: "Blessed are the dead who die in the Lord,"[55] and they are seen now to have rest from their struggles, for their deeds follow them. By myriad rhetorical devices the author implies a corporate relationship between those already put to death who have achieved their eternal destiny and those on earth who are still undergoing testing.

A late first-century Christian letter addressed to the "Hebrews" contains a powerful example of venerating the memory of ancestors in the faith. Writing in a persuasive style that gives the work the character of a sermon, the author invokes a solidarity between Jewish people of faith in times gone by and Christian readers now. In the following excerpt, notice how the first example of faith is not a particular person but "we," implying that the community is the primary bearer of the faith exemplified in the individuals who follow. Notice too how the roll call of the deceased friends of God flows into exhortation to the community currently alive on earth to find courage and heart for the journey:

> Now faith is the assurance of things hoped for, the conviction of things not seen. Indeed, by faith our ancestors received approval. By faith we understand that the worlds were prepared by the word of God....
>
> By faith Abel offered to God a more acceptable sacrifice than Cain's. Through this he received approval as righteous, God's own self giving approval to his gifts; he died, but through his faith he still speaks.... By faith Noah, warned by God about events as yet unseen, respected the warning and built an ark to save his household....
>
> By faith Abraham obeyed when he was called to set out for a place that he was to receive as an inheritance; and he set out,

not knowing where he was going.... By faith Sarah herself received power to conceive, even though she was too old, because she considered God faithful who had promised. Therefore from one person, and this one as good as dead, descendants were born, "as many as the stars of heaven and as the innumerable grains of sand by the seashore."

By faith Moses was hidden by his parents for three months after his birth, because they saw that the child was beautiful, and they were not afraid of the king's edict. By faith Moses, when he was grown up, refused to be called a son of Pharaoh's daughter, choosing rather to share ill treatment with the people of God than to enjoy the fleeting pleasures of sin....

By faith the people passed through the Red Sea as if it were dry land, but when the Egyptians attempted to do so they were drowned. By faith the walls of Jericho fell after they had been encircled for seven days. By faith Rahab the prostitute did not perish with those who were disobedient, because she had received the spies in peace.

And what more should I say? For time would fail me to tell of Gideon, Barak, Samson, Jephthah, of David and Samuel and the prophets — who through faith conquered kingdoms, administered justice, obtained promises, shut the mouths of lions, quenched raging fire, escaped the edge of the sword, won strength out of weakness, became mighty in war, put foreign armies to flight. Women received their dead by resurrection. Others were tortured, refusing to accept release, in order to obtain a greater resurrection. Others suffered mocking and flogging, and even chains and imprisonment. They were stoned to death, they were sawn in two, they were killed by the sword; they went about in skins of sheep and goats, destitute, persecuted, tormented — of whom the world was not worthy. They wandered in deserts and mountains, and in caves and holes in the ground....

Therefore, since we are surrounded by so great a cloud of witnesses, let us also lay aside every weight and the sin that clings so closely, and let us run with perseverance the race that is set before us, looking to Jesus the pioneer and perfecter of our faith, who for the joy that was set before him endured the cross, disregarding its shame, and has taken his seat at the right hand of the throne of God.[56]

The dynamism of this passage moves from the narrative of faithful individuals (nineteen in all) to whole groups of persons in the past and thence into enthusiastic exhortation for the contemporary community of disciples. The movement of the text expresses a strong sense of communion or solidarity, which comes to a pitch in the metaphor of the cloud of witnesses surrounding the living community on earth. Here the faithful dead are proposed not as the objects of a cult, nor even as exemplars to be imitated in any one particular, but as a compact throng of faithful people whose journey Christians are now called upon to share and continue. Remembrance of their lives already lived, by the intrinsic power of memory itself, galvanizes the courage of those presently running the course. It is a matter of being inspired by the whole lot of them in their wonderful witness to the living God. It is interesting that this Christian litany of the cloud of witnesses honors figures who were important in the history of Israel but does not include Christian persons who would be equally good candidates, Stephen, for example, the first Christian martyr, or Mary Magdalen, first apostolic witness of the resurrection. Reflecting reverence for the history of God's holy people before the Christian community came into existence, the passage sees its own audience as recipients of that tradition now configured in Jesus, pioneer of faith, whose advent does not discredit but rather enhances the history of holiness of his own people.

Feminist biblical interpretation critiques the patriarchal tenor of this passage with its emphasis on descent through the male, omission of key women such as Deborah the judge and Miriam, a leader of the Exodus, and inclusion of men such as Jephthah, who acted abominably toward his daughter. As with all such biblical texts, the mind and heart struggle to wrest a liberating meaning reflective of God's gracious intent carried in, through, and despite the distortion of women's reality. What can be gathered here does have potential for a rich use in an inclusive community of the friends of God and prophets. The linguistic practice of remembering celebrated ancestors in the faith by naming them and telling their story, coupled with the act of counting even unnamed, unknown women and men whose lives give witness in less public but no less dramatic ways, and combining this in the vision of them gathered all together as that wondrously named "cloud of witnesses" inspires moral and religious energy that buoys up the *ekklesia* today in its own ongoing, stumbling journey toward the reign of God.

Gleanings

Though "the communion of saints" as such is not a biblical expression, the reality of this community is present throughout the Scriptures. From the early Christian people's sense of themselves as a holy people sharing equally in the holy things of God through Christ Jesus, and from their dozens of uses of the term "saints," we learn that the whole community of the living is considered to be saints. Participants with each other in the waters of baptism and the bread and cup of salvation, they share in the very life of God through the grace of the Spirit. Though still struggling amid the sinfulness of the world and of their own hearts as part of that world, they are in fact a consecrated people. Such an identity is not dependent on gender, race, class, age, sexual orientation, or any other specific characteristics that mark persons' concrete lives. It is rather a gift given to each and every one and all together by the loving-kindness of God. This realization releases a powerful experience of new relationships in which the dominant-subordinate structure of social, political, familial, and religious organization is challenged and in some instances overcome. Equality of the saints before God has social implications.

We learn, furthermore, that this sense of identity would be inconceivable without the Jewish covenant tradition. Here the original notion of being a holy people through participating in the holiness of God is born and developed. Probing this tradition brings forth the insight that holiness is primarily a mark of the whole community rather than the individual, who shares in the quality of holiness not primarily by pious or ethical practices or by means of having a certain role or office but by virtue of membership in the people. Furthermore, the gift is given by the free, gracious, merciful initiative of Israel's God, who loved them when they were oppressed and bore them up on eagles' wings to freedom. Consequently, life in the holy covenant community is inscribed with a deep relationship to the Holy One expressed in gratitude and lament, praise and repentance, and a deep relationship to each other in deeds of love and justice. Although ambiguity inheres in the notion of separateness, living the holy life means essentially living relationally and compassionately in coherence with God.

At the root of both Jewish and Christian notions of being a holy people lie assumptions about the holiness of God in which the community participates. Searching out the meaning of this unfathomable reality brings to light the insight that far from indicating merely a transcendent, awesome deity over against the world, holiness, because it is precisely the holiness of Israel's God, connotes infinite mystery engaged with the world in infinite care. Thrice holy, divine mystery fills the world with glory. Pointing to God's distinct otherness in the narrative framework of the Exodus, holiness is thus a category of beauty, of rescue, and of hope. The resounding call to be a holy people as God is holy carries an entire program for compassionate, liberating engagement with the world.

Finally, investigating Jewish and early Christian inclusion of persons who have died into the holy community, we see that in the context of faith this is no mere wish but a radical extension of hope in God. Death's destructive power cannot sever the bonds holding persons in communion, for these bonds are the grace, love, and community of God's own being. In dying, one falls into the hands of the living God and is quickened by loving-kindness which is forever faithful. For Christians this hope is grounded in the resurrection of the Crucified, a pledge already given of coming life for all people and the whole world itself. In the case of both traditions, the living and the dead are held in a community of life and memory centered in God.

These salient points form one usable resource for a contemporary theology of the communion of saints and offer clues for further development. To state the obvious, the practices of venerating the saints characteristic of later church tradition are nowhere observed in Scripture. Taking soundings from the next few centuries will make clear how a cult of the saints emerged in Christian tradition. It will also present us with two clear models of relationship between the living and the dead in Christ, one patterned according to the biblical model of community and one according to the late Roman system of patronage.

Chapter 4

Patterns in the Age of the Martyrs

Martyrs: Stories and Devotion

The distinctive practice known in later centuries as the cult of the saints, not to be confused with a sociological cult, had its origins in the veneration of the martyrs. During its first three centuries until it became an established religion under Constantine, Christianity around the Roman empire was put to the test, not continuously but in discrete outbreaks of violence in different times and places. Constituting a small, politically and artistically insignificant minority within the pagan classical world, the members of this religious movement served when necessary as convenient scapegoats for ills or tragedies that afflicted society. The main source of contention was their refusal to offer gestures of civic piety to the gods of Rome. Even a pinch of incense went counter to their belief in the one God whose mercy was made known in Jesus Christ. Therefore, Christian communities were liable to be looked upon with suspicion as dangerous to the common good. Leaders feared that a semi-secret group that refused its patriotic duty could turn into a subversive, revolutionary movement, while the urban masses feared that this group's "atheistic" refusal to honor the gods could earn divine displeasure in the form of famine, plague, or war. At root, given the intertwining of political and religious power in the Roman order, their refusal implicitly undermined the foundations of empire. Under pressure to conform, some persons resisted, even to the point of death under torture, giving a remarkable witness to their faith in Jesus Christ in a culture hostile to that belief. Called martyrs, from the Greek word *martyres* meaning witnesses, these persons were especially cherished by others in the community. As persecution intensified and as the number of witnesses increased, they began to form a distinct group within the memory of the Christian people.[1]

In his study of different character types in the Christian heritage, Lawrence Cunningham notes how deeply rooted in human consciousness is the desire to recognize those who die for an issue that is dear to the heart of a community. Voluntary death, chosen not out of masochism but as a by-product of commitment to a cause, is a touchstone that depicts in the most concrete and moving way possible what is ultimately worthwhile. The death of the individual "gives specific reference to an otherwise objective and somewhat abstract idea,"[2] creating an attraction to the cause that can be generated in no other way. Especially in situations of oppression, the symbolic power of a sacrificial death unleashes powerful forces that galvanize resistance and energize commitment. In the first three centuries, the conscious decision to reject the demands of Roman authority by confessing Jesus Christ in spite of probable death had this kind of existential impact.

For the martyrs themselves, the decision was usually not a sudden one but a maturing step on their faith journey toward Christ. In an intriguing study, Maureen Tilley demonstrates how persons prepared for their trials by a regimen of ascetic training guaranteed to strengthen them against the debilitating effects of pain. Seeing "the body as a field of combat on which the torturers and their victims duel,"[3] she argues that extreme pain normally has the effect of psychic disintegration, the breakdown of the world of the victim. The martyrs confounded the dynamic of this process by the discipline of severe fasting and prayer, buttressed by a view of the world centered on the cross of Christ. Cyprian of Carthage taught a group of confessors, for example, that each instrument of torture could be a means of uniting themselves to the passion of Christ, thus "training them in the skill of reconfiguring their own bodies."[4] Wooden clubs evoke the wood of the cross that brought salvation to the world; chains are ornaments; scant clothing recalls that they are clothed with Christ; shaved heads remind them that Christ is their head. Prepared in this way by bold bodily asceticism and mental habits, martyrs were not surprised or distressed when gross pain arrived but saw it as a continuation of their discipline. Instead of breakdown they experienced fulfillment; instead of dissociating under torture they found a new level of integration; instead of being deconstructed their world was reinforced because it had already been deeply reconfigured to the cross, both physically and psychologically. Calling into question the standard interpretation of the history of sanctity, Tilley argues that "this evidence refutes the claim that asceticism was a substitute for martyrdom which Christians adopted once their religion was legalized. On the contrary, asceticism logically and practically preceded martyrdom. In fact, it made martyrdom possible."[5] The final act of witness was not an anomaly but was understood, anticipated, and practiced for within the framework of the ascetic following of Jesus Christ.

Local churches where the killing had occurred frequently took pains to write up accounts of the martyrs' struggles and victories to send to other local groups for their edification and encouragement. In doing so, they drew on motifs and conceptions in parallel Jewish and pagan literature, for the phenomenon of persecution was not without precedent. Intertestamental and later rabbinical Jewish literature is replete with narratives of those who had witnessed unto death;[6] a similar literature of resistance recounts the trials and death of educated Greeks in Alexandria who opposed repressive and rapacious Roman rule.[7] Analogous in literary form and motifs, Christian martyr literature nonetheless sounded its own distinct religious themes.[8] Most central is the idea that martyrs are the ideal disciples because they follow Jesus Christ even to his death on the cross. Jesus himself is the first martyr, as Revelation expresses it, "the faithful witness [martyr], the firstborn of the dead."[9] As they participate in his suffering they become icons of Christ; in turn, Christ suffers in them to strengthen and comfort. The result of their mutual struggle is the entrance of the martyr into new, risen life in glory in accord with Christ's own pasch. Besides being a christological phenomenon, the martyrs were also interpreted in pneumatological terms. In case you think the Spirit worked only in days of old, wrote the redactor of Perpetua's prison diary and narrator of her martyrdom, recent events show a new outpouring of the Spirit's power as promised in the prophecy of Joel. As time goes on these events will soon be part of the past; since they are vital to posterity, "we deem it necessary to disseminate this written account for the glory of God, lest anyone with a weak or despairing faith might think that supernatural grace prevailed only among the ancients."[10] Charismatic creations, martyrs testify to God in boldness and freedom of speech, the Spirit speaking in them before their persecutors as Jesus had promised. Their courage in suffering shows the presence of the Spirit's anointing. Another interpretive theme was struggle with the powers of darkness; martyrs contend with Satan embodied in the form of wild beasts or other torments, receiving their victory thanks to God's mighty power alone. Faithful to God and the integrity of their conscience, they themselves become a living word testifying to the truth of the faith and the hope that it inspires.

These theological motifs find clear expression in the narrative of the slave woman Blandina, martyred along with forty-seven other persons in Lyons around 177 C.E. Notice in this account how the ideal of Galatians 3:28 comes to light as the prisoner who is slave and female becomes "filled with such power" that she takes the lead in encouraging others and is recognized to be "in her person" an image of Christ fighting victoriously with Satan to win the crown of life.

All of us were in terror; and Blandina's earthly mistress, who was herself among the martyrs in the conflict, was in agony lest because of her bodily weakness she would not be able to make a bold confession of faith. Yet Blandina was filled with such power that even those who were taking turns to torture her in every way from dawn to dusk were weary and exhausted. They themselves admitted that they were beaten, that there was nothing further they could do to her, and they were surprised that she was still breathing, for her entire body was broken and torn. They testified that even one kind of torture was enough to release her soul, let alone the many they applied with such intensity. Instead, this blessed woman like a noble athlete got renewed strength with her confession of faith. Her admission "I am a Christian; we do nothing to be ashamed of" brought her refreshment, rest, and insensibility to her present pain. . . .

Maturus, then Sanctus, Blandina, and Attalus were led into the amphitheatre to be exposed to the beasts and to give a public spectacle of the pagans' inhumanity, for a day of gladiatorial games was expressly arranged for our sake. Once again in the amphitheatre Maturus and Sanctus went through the whole gamut of suffering. . . . Though their spirits endured much throughout the long contest, they were in the end sacrificed after being made all the day long a spectacle to the world to replace the varied entertainment of the gladiatorial combat.

Blandina was hung on a post and exposed as bait for the wild animals that were let loose on her. She seemed to hang there in the form of a cross, and by her fervent prayer she aroused intense enthusiasm in those who were undergoing their ordeal, for in their torment with their physical eyes they saw in the person of their sister him who was crucified for them, that he might convince all who believe in him that all who suffer for Christ's glory will have eternal fellowship in the living God.

But none of the animals had touched her, and so she was taken down from the post and brought back to the gaol to be preserved for another ordeal: and thus for her victory in further contests she would make irreversible the condemnation of the crooked serpent, and tiny, weak, and insignificant as she was she would give inspiration to her brothers and sisters, for she had put on Christ, that mighty and invincible athlete, and had overcome the Adversary in many contests, and through her conflict had won the crown of immortality.…

Finally, on the last day of the gladiatorial games, they brought back Blandina again, this time with a boy of fifteen named Ponticus. Every day they had been brought in to watch the torture of the others, while attempts were made to force them to swear by the pagan idols. And because they persevered the crowd grew angry with them, so that they had little pity for the child's age and no respect for the woman. Instead, they subjected them to every atrocity and led them through every torture in turn, constantly trying to force them to swear, but to no avail.

Ponticus, after being encouraged by his sister in Christ so that even the pagans realized that she was urging him on and strengthening him, and after nobly enduring every torment, gave up his spirit. The blessed Blandina was last of all. Like a noble mother encouraging her children, she sent them before her in triumph to the King, and then, after duplicating in her body all her children's sufferings, she hastened to join them, rejoicing and glorying in her death as though she had been invited to a bridal banquet instead of being a victim of the beasts. After the scourges, the animals, and the hot griddle, she was at last tossed into a net and exposed to a bull. After being tossed a good deal by the animal, she no longer perceived what was happening because of the hope and possession of all she believed in and because of her intimacy with Christ. Thus she too was offered in sacrifice, while the pagans themselves admitted that no woman had ever suffered so much in their experience.[11]

As this Letter from Lyons indicates, Roman authorities drew no line between the sexes when designating persons for death. At Lyons twenty-four men were martyred and twenty-three women; the Scillitan martyrs counted seven men and five women; at Abatina the number of those arrested was thirty-one men and seventeen women. It is interesting to observe in these accounts how the idea of women's weakness and frailty, an assumption also reflected in Jewish and pagan sources, is overridden by the gift of the Spirit. Blandina, a slave woman who encourages her companions, comes to embody in her own person the crucified Christ, thus becoming the noble, powerful "mother" of all the other martyrs.

In another incident in Carthage, the gift of the Spirit enables the young nursing mother Perpetua to emerge as the spokesperson and moral leader of her fellow prisoners. Almost half the narrative of their road to martyrdom is written by Perpetua herself. Probing the reasons why, Stuart Hall argues that awareness of the importance of her own experience at trial and in prison prompts this initiative: "she recognizes herself as a competent confessor and records her own sayings, visions, and spiritual experiences because they are of value to the church."[12] This is the Christian perception of the women martyrs in general, who triumph in the face of horrendous death thanks to the gift of the Spirit. The equal status of women in the church is not thereby recognized, for during this period patriarchal ecclesial structures are in their ascendancy. Even in lists of the martyrs women's names are usually last, indicating a subordinate rank. But in the actual event and memory of the event, women's witness is so strong that a breakthrough in consciousness occurs despite cultural denial. As Peter Brown observes, "in the legacy of courage, at least, men and women were remembered as equal within the Christian Church."[13]

The imagination of later centuries stylized the martyrdom of early Christians into marvelous occurrences. But the haze of hagiography and stereotypical art cannot rub out the flesh-and-blood reality of suffering for God's truth that is at the heart of the latent power of the martyr. Condemned, tortured, bloodied, executed, women and men were perceived in a religious sense by other Christians as having entered in a graphic, physical way into the dying of the crucified Jesus. Configured to his likeness in death, they were thereby also configured by God's mercy to the glory of his rising. In their terrible death and certain entrance into heaven, they became images of Christ through the power of the Spirit and icons of the community's hope. Their splendid and striking witness became a source of encouragement for believers and of attraction to the Christian way for pagans.

The community's appraisal of the martyrs had implications for devotion. Archaeological and textual evidence shows that from the second century in the East and the third century in the West, Christians loved these martyrs and, even after the passing of the generation that knew them, cherished their memory. Ways were found to express this respect and esteem and to release the power of their witness to transform other lives.[14] When possible, their bodily remains, considered to belong to the realm of the sacred, were carefully gathered up and buried. The Christians of Smyrna, to cite a well-known example, revered their bishop Polycarp, who had been burned to death after torture in the fifth or sixth decade of the second century. In the first Christian document to have martyrdom as its exclusive subject, and the earliest evidence for the veneration that then arose, they wrote to neighbor churches:

> Thus at last, collecting the remains that were dearer to us than precious stones and finer than gold, we buried them in a fitting spot. Gathering there so far as we can, in joy and gladness, we will be allowed by the Lord to celebrate the anniversary day of his martyrdom, both as a memorial for those who have already fought the contest and for the training and preparation of those who will do so one day.[15]

Small shrines were built on or near the martyrs' graves, which became places of prayer and pilgrimage. On the yearly anniversary of their death, considered their birthday into heaven, nightlong vigil would be kept at their graves ending with the Eucharist celebrated at dawn. Following pagan funeral custom, the liturgy was often followed by a meal among the participants at graveside. If more than one martyr belonged to a city or region, each of their anniversaries would be celebrated on the appropriate day, thus beginning the practice of a liturgical calendar of the saints. As stories of the martyrs spread, other regions would commemorate the more appealing ones despite the absence of their tombs, thus expanding their own local calendar. With the coming of the Constantinian peace and the building of churches, the desire to have a martyr's body buried under the altar or, failing that, a segment of the body, led to local communities' moving and exchanging relics. Now the feast day celebration included reading the acts of their martyrdom in church assemblies and sermons on the lessons their witness taught.

Within this historical setting, the custom of directly calling upon a martyr for prayers arose, originally as the expression of the private piety of individuals. No one in an official position said this was to be done; it simply seemed to some to be a coherent and good thing to do. Graffiti scratched on the walls near martyrs' graves both in Roman and other cemeteries give evidence of the invocation of these outstanding members of the confessing church: "Vincent, you are in Christ, pray for Phoebe"; "Januaria...pray for us"; "...intercede and pray for your brothers and sisters"; "Paul, Peter, pray for Eratus"; faithful Sentianus "in your prayers pray for us, for we know that you are in Christ."[16] Calling upon the martyrs for their prayers was a specific way of evoking the solidarity that existed between pilgrims on earth and those who had been sealed with the victory of Christ. These latter were asked to participate in Christ's continuing intercession and remember before God their sisters and brothers who had not yet run the whole course. During the times of persecution, a sense of bondedness across the spheres between heaven and earth and across the years between the martyrs and those who asked for their prayers supported those who might be called next to give the supreme witness of their lives.

It is hard to underestimate what the memory of the martyrs meant for the hope and self-understanding of other Christians. Thousands were heartened by the witness of these women and men to the vitality of Christian faith in times of violence; even when the threat had passed, their dreadful deaths underscored the worth of belief in Christ and opened a glimpse of the future to which all were heading. Remembering them served to nourish the sense of community belonging. It is interesting to note that Mary the mother of Jesus did not receive any public veneration during these centuries, since she was not a martyr.

Once the age of Roman persecution had passed and martyrdom was no longer an imminent possibility, other holy women and men whose lives had given witness in the church were also honored. The Christian cloud of witnesses grew to include confessors who had been tortured for the faith but not killed; ascetics, especially those who lived a life of celibacy; wise teachers and prudent church leaders; and those who cared for the poor, the sick, and the ignorant. But the general habit of publicly venerating persons who witnessed in a unique way to the community's common hope had taken root in the age of the martyrs.[17]

An important line of inquiry opens up if we ask precisely how persons in the community envisioned their relationship to the martyrs and other holy persons who had died, and how they conceived of all of them, living and dead together, standing in relation to God. My study of the literature suggests that two distinctly different patterns can be glimpsed, one an egalitarian model that names others companions and friends, the other a patriarchal one that casts certain privileged dead into positions of patronage. In the first, the holy dead are an inspiration as a cloud of witnesses in the one Spirit surrounding the living with lessons of encouragement; in the second, they are heavenly intercessors before the distant throne of God obtaining good things for needy petitioners. Attention in the first instance is focused on remembrance with a view to nourishing faith; in the second, interest in thaumaturgic, miracle-working power is paramount. The boundaries are not absolute, there being room for intercession in the companionship model and for keeping memory in the patronage model, but the overall shape of relationship is different enough to warrant naming them two distinct models. A closer analysis reveals how the circle of companions idea, now long buried under the pyramid of patronage idea, can prove to be a resource for a contemporary reading of the communion of saints.

Paradigm 1: Companionship of Friends

Early in the age of the martyrs, the Christian community envisioned its relationship with its honored dead in terms of mutual companionship in Christ. In a sense this was easy for them to do, because remembering the martyrs put the community in solidarity not with distant figures who had died in previous centuries and distant cultures but with contemporaries who had been known and loved in this life and who had died for the faith within living memory. Connected in a common, recent history, the living look upon the dead as the cloud of witnesses who encourage the community in the struggle to be faithful disciples. Essentially, however, the prerequisite for this pattern is not proximity in time but a lively sense of the presence of the Spirit in the people as a whole, shaping them into a holy community. Since God's mercy flows into every crevasse of the broken world, offering forgiveness to every sinful heart, all are called and blessed. Assured by the biblical sensibility that "there is therefore now no more condemnation for those who are in Christ Jesus,"[18] the community struggles to live faithfully, joyfully, in the midst of suffering. When through a combination of personal giftedness and historical circumstance some persons stand out in witness to this hope even to death, their lives are received with profound gratitude because of how their witness to God nourishes the faith of the rest. The living and the dead form a circle of friendship centered on the graciousness of the living God.

The church at Smyrna reveals this pattern when, in the same letter mentioned above, they respond to a phony criticism about the meaning of their veneration of their beloved bishop. Prevented at first by the authorities from gathering up his bones on the pretext that they would then switch allegiance from Jesus to Polycarp, they replied:

> Little did they know that we could never abandon Christ, who suffered for the redemption of those who are saved in the whole world, the innocent one dying on behalf of sinners. Nor could we worship anyone else. For him we worship as the Son of God. But the martyrs we love as disciples and imitators of the Lord, and rightly so because of their matchless affection for their own king and teacher. May we too become their comrades and fellow disciples.[19]

The living were partners, companions, codisciples with those who had given their lives, one witnessing to the other, both carried along by the saving grace poured out in Christ. This same lively sense of friendship appears even a century after persecution had ceased in one of Augustine's sermons on the feast of Perpetua and Felicity:

> The martyrs of Christ for the sake of the name and justice of Christ won a twofold victory: they feared neither death nor suffering pain. The one who lived in them conquered in them; so that they who lived not for themselves but for him did not die even in death itself.... Let it not seem a small thing to us that we are members of the same body as these.... We marvel at them, they have compassion on us. We rejoice for them, they pray for us.... Yet do we all serve the one Lord, follow the same teacher, accompany the same leader. We are all joined to the one head, journey to the same Jerusalem, follow after the one love, embrace the same unity.[20]

There is a mutual give and take that recognizes differences, all built on the foundation of the shared call to discipleship. At its best, veneration of the martyrs was pervaded by this lively sense of community between the living and the dead, between those struggling to live faithfully on earth and those known and beloved persons who were now alive in God beyond the reach of trouble. They are companions in hope.

The companionship model structures relations along the lines of mutuality. To use a spatial metaphor, here the saints are not situated *between* God and living disciples, but are *with* their sisters and brothers through the one Spirit poured out in the crucified and risen Jesus Christ. It is not distance from God, nor fear of "his" judgment, nor impression of "his" cold disinterest, nor need for grace given only in small portions, nor a sense of one's own utter unimportance in the hierarchy of power, nor any other such motivation found in the patronage model that impels the community to turn to the saints. Rather, gratitude and delight in this cloud of witnesses with whom they share a common humanity, a common struggle, and a common faith commend their memory to contemporary interest. The living now bear the heat of the day; it is their turn to contribute to the care of the world. But communion in hope with those who already walked this path releases great energies for their own fidelity. In the light of redeeming grace, the relationship among those living on earth and those with God in glory is fundamentally mutual and collegial. They comprise a community of the friends of God and prophets, a true *koinonia*.

Preaching on the feasts of the martyrs over a long span of years, Augustine provides a vocabulary for this partnership. In this as in so much else, his legacy is ambiguous, showing use of first the companionship model and then the patronage model. Late in his life he showed great interest in miracles and other accoutrements of the patronage relationship, especially after relics of the first martyr, St. Stephen, were transferred from Palestine to North Africa.[21] But throughout his earlier years as bishop, many of his sermons on the festival days of the martyrs reveal a strong grasp of the value of the companionship model and give it eloquent expression: "When we pay honor to the martyrs, we are honoring the friends of Christ."[22]

As required by this pattern, a strong grasp of the compassionate and gracious presence of the Spirit making the church a holy people undergirds relationship with the living dead. Augustine proclaims this truth with a plenitude of images. Holy Wisdom is already at work among you, searching for her lost coins; God is building you up into a house in which the Spirit is pleased to dwell; your lives can be a song of praise better than any hymn; your lives can be danced to the rhythm of the love of God better than dancers keep time with their bodies and their feet; you are the branches of Christ the vine; God is cultivating you like an orchard of trees, causing growth, producing buds, putting strength in the branches, clothing you with leaves and loading you with fruit. These images come to fullest expression in references to the community that celebrates Eucharist as itself the body of Christ. Speaking on Easter Day to the newly baptized about the bread and wine soon to become the body and blood of Christ, Augustine puts it with startling simplicity: "If you receive them well, you are yourselves what you receive."[23] Being made christic in eucharistic communion, the people comprise together a genuine partnership in grace seeking the face of the living God. On more than one occasion, the preacher appeals to this reality with a vigor that is quite affecting: "Let us be companions in believing. What am I saying? Let us be companions in seeking."[24] Without this theology of the call of the whole people to life in the Spirit, the companionship model has no foundation.

In this context of becoming a holy people, remembering those who have died and especially those who have given tremendous witness by their martyrdom becomes a communal act of identity: "You are the people of God, you are the Catholic people, you are members of Christ. You are not separated from the unity. You are in communion with the members of the apostles, in communion with the memorial shrines of the holy martyrs who are scattered throughout the world."[25] The martyrs in particular stand out because they were human just like ourselves and struggled through very severe testing with the help of the same God who is still faithful. They did so because they were lovers who clung to the divine promise of life despite the threats of their persecutors. Now the church cherishes their legacy by means of festivals: "Blessed be the saints in whose memory we are celebrating the day they suffered on; ... they have left us lessons of encouragement."[26]

This phrase, "lessons of encouragement," carries the heart of Augustine's companionship theology of the saints. For whereas he exhorts the community to commend themselves to the prayer of the saints, what is absolutely central is emulation, or following their footsteps. As companions in faith they gave their very lives; in response, the community matures in its own life of love in accord with the contours of their witness. It is simply false flattery and idle superficiality to send up songs of praise and then to go on ignoring what their example teaches. "So as we reflect on all this, let us be on our toes to imitate the martyrs, if we want the feast day we celebrate to be of any use to us";[27] and again, "That's absolutely the only value of this festivity, there isn't any other at all."[28] Sometimes a saint teaches us a particular path to follow: "Come then brothers and sisters, let us follow him; you see if we follow Stephen, we shall be crowned with the victor's laurels. It is above all in the matter of loving our enemies that he is to be followed and imitated."[29] More often the martyrs act like members of that great cloud of witnesses who inspire us by the general tenor and trust of their lives. Perpetua and Felicity, for example, outstanding for their surpassing courage and now dwelling in "perpetual felicity," were the closest of companions who held on tight to each other in the struggle; by their example they now encourage our own love. To pay attention to what the martyr sets before us, to believe this, to embody this in our own lives, is the truest way to celebrate and venerate their memory. They are like jewels that flash in the sun or like jars of aromatic ointment whose fragrance fills the house. Since they did what they did by the outpouring of the gift of God, in their company we find light and warmth and direction in our struggles to be faithful: "The fountain is still flowing, it hasn't dried up."[30]

One might raise the objection that since the time of persecution has ceased, there is no longer any point in drawing strength from the memory of the martyrs. But this is to be terribly shortsighted. The affairs of everyday life continually cast us into situations in which we are tested and persecuted in the struggle for the truth. For example, an aristocrat who holds your life in his grasp compels you to give false evidence; if you do not deny Christ with a lie, you will pay a very high price; if you are truthful, you will suffer. Or again, many people endure martyrdom on their sickbeds, struggling to remain faithful amid the many temptations that illness brings. As many situations as there are in human life, that is how many opportunities there are for showing courage and love of God.[31]

Unfortunately, in his efforts to draw out the inspiring connections between the martyrs and the current community, Augustine is impaled on the spike of androcentric thinking. Assuming that to be female means to be weak, he found it amazing that women were able to give such strong witness. Commenting on the two young African women who had been martyred while they yet had their infants at the breast, he preached: "Both the merits and the names of Perpetua and Felicity, God's holy servants, shine out brightly and preeminently among their fellow martyrs. A more splendid crown, I mean, is owed to those of the weaker sex, because a manly spirit has clearly done much more in women when their feminine frailty has not been undone under such enormous pressure."[32] In an interesting sequence of reasoning, he comes at one point to see baptism as freeing women from the constraints of patriarchal marriage and conducting them into a zone of equality in Christ:

> But how were women able to imitate this cunning of the snake in order to win the prize medal, the crown of martyrdom? Christ, you see, is called the head of man, while the man is the head of the woman. And these women didn't die for their husbands, did they, seeing that in order to suffer they spurned the appeals even of their husbands trying to call them back from the brink. Well, of course, they too through the same faith are members of the Church, and thus Christ, who is head of the whole Church, is head of all his members.... When women also suffered for Christ, they fought for their head with the cunning of the snake.[33]

This insight, however, did not motivate Augustine to move from spiritual equality to the need for social or political equality; as with patriarchal reflection in general, his thought remains less than perfectly coherent.[34] In dealing with these texts that reveal male assumption of the inferiority of the female, feminist analysis has to name the subordinationist premises while critically searching at the same time for the bread of meaning the text may yet offer. In a way more ambiguous than most, Augustine stands under judgment for his androcentric anthropology while his notions of the holy community and mutual relationship with the martyrs has much to offer.

What exchange occurs between the saints in heaven and on earth in this companionship model? In these sermons Augustine describes a free-flowing reciprocity with different actions on both sides. The best gift the saints give the church is their own lives, whose witness acts like strong beacons of light. When their festivals are celebrated, their lives yield up these "lessons of encouragement" that inspire and teach us on our own journey. Moreover, in union with Christ they pray for those on earth who are now struggling to be faithful lovers of God. The local community, meanwhile, honors them by keeping festival in their memory; it is remembrance that affects the nature of the communion. Once we listen to their story, our response wells up in various ways. We sing in gratitude to God for them, or praise God for the beauty of their lives, or rejoice in their victory, or draw hope from their witness in our despair, or commend ourselves to their prayers, or simply love them. Most important of all, we are inspired to follow in the footsteps of their example.

They are human like us, they know what it means to suffer and be tempted, and now they are victorious by the grace of God. "Therefore, dearly beloved, exult and rejoice on the days of the holy martyrs; pray that you may be able to follow in their footsteps."[35] An underlying sense of companionship centered in God pervades this pattern of relationship. The living and the dead together are a holy people at different stages of the journey; each one gives and receives what is appropriate, while the whole group of friends of God and prophets is centered on the incomprehensible mystery of divine love poured out in Jesus Christ for the sake of the world: "venerate the martyrs, praise, love, proclaim, honor them. But worship the God of the martyrs";[36] and even more clearly, "honor the martyrs and with the martyrs worship God."[37]

In the companionship model, the effect of the presence of the martyrs and other saints in the consciousness of the living community is profound and far-reaching. Like the biblical cloud of witnesses, this group of ancestors surrounds the living church with witness to God, with lessons of encouragement, and with inspiration to hope. Augustine was aware of how fragile the church's beginnings had been historically, and of how indebted the present generation is to those who went before. The earliest generations of Christians deserve special appreciation, he thought, for they pioneered a whole new way of life: "When numbers were few, courage had to be great. By passing along the narrow road they widened it. . . . They went ahead of us."[38] Those earlier people had no idea that one day there would be a community in Carthage, a church of the future praising God: "They weren't yet able to see it, yet they were already constructing it out of themselves."[39] To realize as a people that we are the heirs of the tradition shaped by such persons makes us grateful and rejuvenates our desire to contribute to this heritage for the next generation. Their adventure of faith opened a way for us, and now we go ahead of others in an ongoing river of companions seeking God. And when our own journey grows hard, we can draw strength from the memory of our forebears' sufferings and victories: "How can the way be rough when it has been smoothed by the feet of so many walking along it?"[40] The communion of saints in the companionship model forges intergenerational bonds across time that sustain faith in strange new times and places. Surrounded by the cloud of witnesses, we cherish in very different circumstances what they cared enough to live and die for.

Paradigm 2: Patrons-Petitioners

Starting in the late third century and coming to dominance by the late fifth, a different understanding of the relationship between the living and the dead in Christ arose. In raw terms, the saints in heaven went from being primarily witnesses in a partnership of hope to being primarily intercessors in a structure of power and neediness. For this model, which has no precedent in Scripture, to develop and take root, a diminished sense of being a holy people and an increase in the distance felt to exist between sinful, needy people and the majesty of God were necessary. Into this gap the Christian imagination cast the saints in the role of sponsors who could plead one's cause before the throne of God and even dispense favors in their own right. Henceforth the major way of connecting with the honored dead is not effective remembrance but pleas for their intercession before God for protection from both physical and spiritual dangers. Now their attractiveness to Christian consciousness results in the first instance not from their lessons of encouragement but from their ability to mediate the presence and power of the transcendent God, and thus to help.[41]

Many forces coalesced to cause and cement this shift. The whole church changed in these centuries. Sociologically, the establishment of the church under Constantine resulted in church leadership and a growing class of clerics becoming inculturated into the prevailing forms of Roman authority and imperial rule. Spiritually, a vigorous growth in the value of ascetic practice created clear distinctions between those who engaged in such practice and those who did not. Theologically, the Arian controversy, fiercely fought and barely won, led to strong emphasis on the divinity of Christ, with a consequent obscuring of his human nature by which he is related to human beings as their brother. The net effect of these and other major changes was that the official presence of the Spirit moved out from the community as a whole to rest in more specifically holy hands and places, or, to put it another way, "the sacred" migrated from the nave to the sanctuary. The Christ who reigned from that sanctuary was now identified with the omnipotent ruling power of God and, while he had mercifully died to save sinners, was now authorized to exercise righteous judgment against them. The eschatological prophet from Nazareth was now commonly depicted seated in glory surrounded by a heavenly court. I realize I am painting this picture with very broad brush strokes, and exceptions to the general picture exist. But the configuration of the church is not the same in every age, and these developments pointed the church in a direction of living out the gospel that was discernibly different from the age of the martyrs.

Use of the nomenclature "saints" to include the living community as the whole holy people of God was now far in the past. The saints were those among the dead who were safely in the glory of heaven. What better than to turn to these persons whom God has graciously allowed to be courtiers at the throne of grace, the mother of the King increasingly seen as having the best access of all. Though subject to God themselves, these mediators have their own spheres of influence, in descending order according to their place in the hierarchy of importance, and may prove to be benefactors in return for prayers and devotions such as pilgrimage to their tombs or reverence to their relics. The notion of the saints and the Virgin Mary as intercessors was increasingly proclaimed in the official theology of the church and variously adapted or understood by the faithful. "Here saints might be seen," writes Stephen Wilson, "as advocates pleading causes before a stern divine judge, as mediators, as go-betweens, as intriguers or wire-pullers at the court of Heaven — all metaphors were used. It is significant also that the saints themselves were arranged in a hierarchy, in both the liturgy and official iconography, the Virgin Mary as the arch-intercessor through whom petitions of other saints were directed."[42] The chief analogue for the relationship between the living community and the saints in heaven now became the institution of patronage which was an intrinsic part of the social order of the Roman empire. A closer examination of this system reveals important nuances which affected the communion of saints for centuries to come.

In general, the patronage system arises when concentrations of wealth and political power in the hands of the few, coupled with neediness of the many and lack of democratic processes, conspire to create permanent social stratifications. History presents a varied panorama, but basic to all patronage systems is inequality — marked social and economic inequality accompanied by pronounced differences in privileges and honor. According to Carl Landé, whose definition reflects a wide consensus, "a patron-client relationship is a vertical dyadic alliance, i.e., an alliance between two persons of unequal status, power, or resources each of whom finds it useful to have as an ally someone superior or inferior to himself. The superior member of such an alliance is called a patron. The inferior is called his client."[43] The purpose of this relationship is an exchange of benefits. Typically, the favors which patrons do for their clients are material in kind, such as economic assistance or physical protection in times of danger, while clients repay the favors with more intangible benefits such as loyalty, support, and the giving of honor. It is common for patron-client systems "to be pyramided upon each other so that several patrons, each with their own sets of clients, are in turn the clients of a higher patron who is in turn the client of a patron even higher than himself."[44] As a result, the system ultimately extends upward to a single shared patron who sits at the peak of the pyramid. A low-status participant in this system, furthermore, personally approaches a high-status member only on rare occasions; normally he depends on a series of linkages with intermediate brokers, usually his own patron with whom he has face-to-face contact.

In the ancient world, patronage pervaded both urban and rural life, but its character is limned most starkly in the world of the peasant.[45] Most peasants lived by subsistence farming, growing crops they used to feed the family, to barter for implements they could not make themselves, and to pay rent for the land, upon which owners or tax collectors often leveled gouging demands. In terms of the sheer requirements for survival, their existence was precarious, marked by economic stress, malnutrition, and unremitting struggle. It was virtually impossible to save. One bad year, and free peasants could be tipped over into serfdom or debt slavery, a dreaded but frequent occurrence. Politically they were powerless with neither organization nor voice to protect their rights. Hemmed in on every side, peasants saw their only chance at security lay in establishing some form of client relationship with a person of power, usually the neighboring large landowner. If all went well, the patron would lend a hand in time of extreme need. The risk was, however, that the patron might act to exploit the relationship and the peasants' situation would deteriorate even to the point of destitution.

Systems of patronage perdure as long as clients accept their subordinate status, receiving benefits that are necessary for life itself due to the paternalistic kindness of the patron while the patron amasses power through the allegiance of many such needy clients. Tensions appear once clients query and resist their status — seeking land reform, for example. The coercive nature of the relationship then becomes apparent as patrons use threats, the withholding of benefits, and even violence to repress erosion of the system and to reinforce loyalty, usually resulting, at most, in resentful, fearful, and begrudging obedience.

In either case, current anthropological studies stress the disparity of power in the system, with dominance on the one hand playing off dependency on the other. John Dominic Crossan points out that even studies that emphasize the positive gain to social order that results from a peacefully working patronage system acknowledge the underlying injustice, as persons take up positions of subordination in order to gain access to essential resources. Deepening the analysis, Crossan's own map of patronal society links patronage strongly to antiquity's institution of slavery, the two forming complementary arrangements.[46] In sum, patronage is a system of exchange founded on asymmetrical relations between persons of unequal status — the antithesis of friendship between equals.

The Roman empire was no stranger to the structure of patronage, which formed a linchpin of its social, economic, and political organization. A "mass of little pyramids of influence" cascaded upward to form the warp and woof of public life, with not only individuals and families but even towns and whole regions dependently seeking benefit by subservient alliance with personages more powerfully placed than themselves, the closer to the emperor the better.[47] Given the church's inculturation into this system, it is perhaps not surprising that the patronage pattern also began to govern transactions with the realm of heaven. According to the study of G. E. M. de Ste. Croix, "By the later fourth century the term *patrocinium* (patronage) has begun to be applied to the activity of the apostles and martyrs on behalf of the faithful: in the writings of St. Ambrose, and later Prudentius, St. Augustine, St. Paulinus of Nola and others, the martyrs are the most powerful of *patroni*.... Just as the terrestrial patron is asked to use his influence with the emperor, so the celestial patron, the saint, is asked to use his influence with the Almighty."[48] Such a religious arrangement would not be foreign to those who had grown up in a world pervaded with the patronage system.

In his illuminating study of the rise of the cult of the saints in the West, historian Peter Brown virtually equates the cult of the saints with the structure of patronage. "The need for intimacy with a protector with whom one could identify as a fellow human being, relations with whom could be conceived of in terms open to the nuances of known human relations between patron and client, is the hallmark of late-fourth-century Christian piety."[49] His analysis sympathetically details both the spiritual and social dynamics of how this transfer was accomplished. Spiritually, the change was not trivial, merely replicating in heaven the hard facts of patronage that people took for granted in the late Roman world, but was a response to deeply felt existential needs. At the heart of the move was a certain spiritual anxiety resulting from the rapidly spreading ascetic movement's emphasis on sin and judgment. The world was a battleground between the dark desires of one's heart, deserving of God's judgment, and the mercy of God that promised forgiveness. Writes Brown, "It is this hope of amnesty that pushed the saint to the foreground as *patronus*."[50] For joined with an invisible companion according to the pattern of a late Roman patron-client relationship, one could negotiate the difficult demands of holiness that led to the distant reward of heaven and find, especially at death, warm confidence in a human presence that could lead one over the terrifying chasm.

If the pressure of anxiety moved the heart, then competition between an elite group of wealthy laity and a newly powerful group of bishops, often from the same class, drove the social dynamics of saints' patronage. In this age of increasing ecclesial wealth and power, whoever had control of a martyr's grave could designate who had the privilege of being buried nearby; whoever orchestrated the celebration of the martyr's day could choose who would be admitted to the feasting; whoever thus opened access to the sacred functioned as a patron to the community as a whole. A rising tide of lay patronage, interested in expressing influence in the sacred realm of the church in this way, was met by the determination of the bishops that they alone would exercise the influence of patrons of the Christian community. This conflict between rival systems of patronage was ultimately decided in favor of the bishops who took initiatives in bringing to a local community the remains of martyrs in the form of relics, building lavish shrines and churches to house saints' tombs or relics, and celebrating their festivals with splendid eucharistic liturgies and with inclusively communal, rather than restricted family, feasting. As the balance of social power shifted to the advantage of the bishop, visible patron of an invisible one, shrines became the mechanism for the growth of ecclesiastical power structures. In Brown's assessment, this change was accompanied by "intense personal links which those who acted as *impresarios* of the cult established with their invisible friends and protectors. But the outcome was plain — the martyr took on a distinctive late Roman face. He was the *patronus*, the invisible, heavenly concomitant of the patronage exercised palpably on earth by the bishop."[51] The saint became the good patron whose intercessions were successful, whose power was exercised benevolently, and in whose name the church's wealth was at the disposal of the whole community. The bishop stood for him or her. Loyalty was due them both.

Episcopal orchestration of the cult of the martyrs and other saints according to the pattern of late Roman patron-client relationships reconfigured the understanding of the church's relationship with the cloud of witnesses in significant ways. The notion of being friends and comrades in the egalitarian experience of grace receded in favor of living persons being needy petitioners vis-à-vis powerful heavenly intercessors. It is important to remember that the bishops did not invent the cult of the martyrs, which has its roots in late Jewish and early Christian reverence for those who had lived holy lives even unto death. But they did give this veneration a new aristocratic shape in their own social circumstances, one that enhanced the altar of the bishop and the intercessory power of the saint in direct proportion. Henceforth patron saints became vitally important for their thaumaturgic powers; by the sixth century miracles had become the primary norm for legitimating the veneration of holy persons even if they had not shed the blood of martyrdom.

Brown makes a good case that we should look at this development with greater empathy than is usually shown, for by introducing a gentle, holy, human face into the system of patronage, late antique Christians were taking care to ensure that "in their world, there should be places where men could stand in the searching and merciful presence of a fellow human being."[52] While this may be true as a historical interpretation, the problems this development poses for theology today are too numerous not to allow appreciation to be followed by critique. Not only does the heavenly patronage system reinforce the imperial model of God's relation to the world, so contrary to feminist and liberation theologies' vision of reality.[53] And not only does it diminish awareness of the gracious and compassionate love of God freely poured out in Jesus Christ, thereby setting forth a potential for abusive obscuring of the gospel brought to a high pitch in subsequent centuries.[54] And not only does the heavenly patronage system serve to support dominant-dependency relationships even on earth, being thus a spiritual form in which patriarchal structures obscure the community of the discipleship of equals. But with regard to the communion of saints the patronage relationship itself also ensures the loss of the "lessons of encouragement" that flow from the narrative remembrance of their witness. Gone now was the mutuality and reciprocity of earlier Christian experience in which the living and the dead were filled with the Spirit and joined in a community of codiscipleship. In its place was the patron-client relationship whereby saints became powerful intercessors for needy petitioners before the distant throne of God, and thus were elite "friends of God" in a higher sense than the rest of the community.

In a way that obscures the difference between these two paradigms, Brown consistently equates friendship and patronage: "I would suggest that only language shot through with the *grandeur et misère* of friendship and patronage could do justice to so potentially hazardous an enterprise."[55] I would suggest, to the contrary, that the two relationships are vastly distinct, one signifying mutuality and reciprocity in a fundamentally egalitarian sense, and the other signifying the unequal play of power and need in a patriarchal system. True, persons within dominant-subordinate relationships may call each other "friends." But unless they intend to subvert the system that structures their association, the word has only the thinnest connection with genuine friendship. A clear example, meant with no disrespect but offered because it makes the point: even Mafia dons call people "my friend"; but they imply an exchange of favors for loyalty that carries a subliminal menace, the antithesis of genuine mutuality. If patriarchy be the shaping force of a relationship, and in an authentic patronage system it is, then a Spirit-filled community of friends of God and prophets is not a possibility.

The patron-client paradigm gained ascendency through the period of late antiquity, becoming the predominant feature of medieval devotion to the saints and a main target of Reformation criticism. It still waxes strong where social and spiritual forces conspire to rob the community of its identity as a worthy and holy people, but wanes with the weakening of those forces. In a study of the interrelation between earthly and heavenly patrons in Malta, for example, Jeremy Boissevain observes that both earthly and heavenly types of patronage "seem to have thrived in periods when power was concentrated in the hands of a few, when economic and political uncertainty prevailed, when widespread poverty induced dependency."[56] His next observation is pertinent; due to changing circumstances, "In Malta, as elsewhere in Europe, the saints are marching out."[57] I would suggest, rather, that the patronage system is marching out. People may be losing their client status, but they do not need to be bereft of their cloud of witnesses.

Gleanings

The age of the martyrs and its outgrowth in a developing cult of the saints presents us with two major paradigms of what would come to be called the communion of saints. One, more continuous with the biblical notion of the holy people of God, affirms a relationship of companions and comrades in the one Spirit-filled community. The other, influenced by the civil system of patronage, structures relationship according to patron-client dynamics. While at first the two interacted with each other in an ever-changing cultural context, eventually, the patronage model took a commanding lead and carried the torch of the communion of saints into the medieval period and beyond. It is this model that is so incompatible with feminist values and with the religious spirit of persons in modern/postmodern culture.

Speaking of her research into the creation of patriarchy, Gerda Lerner has famously observed that to see something coming into historical existence is also to be able to see it passing away.[58] This is so because historical knowledge enables one to realize that what exists today is not necessarily there by nature or immutable decree, but began and developed in particular circumstances and for reasons of benefit to at least a few people. The freedom exists then to take a hand in reshaping the trajectory of the institution or idea according to new, changing conditions. The rise of patronage left earlier themes undeveloped in the theology of the saints. The more ancient companionship model, however, can still be discerned in certain texts and bears the promise of being a fruitful resource for a feminist reading of the communion of saints.

– *Chapter 5* –

Institutional Settling

During the next millennium, both the companionship and patronage models of the communion of saints coexisted and, through a series of official decisions, became variously embedded in institutional elements of creed, liturgy, and law. The phrase *sanctorum communionem* was added to the Apostles' Creed by the beginning of the fifth century; a feast to celebrate all the saints entered the annual calendar in the ninth; and by the high Middle Ages the process of canonization was instituted in the Roman Catholic Church. Together with popular practices of veneration, these official developments shaped the tradition that endures to this day. Each element carries critical and constructive significance that can contribute to a present rereading of the communion of saints.

An Elusive Creedal Phrase

The actual origin of the phrase *communio sanctorum* seems to be lost in the mists of history. While possibly used by Jerome or religious writers in the East, it first shows its head in a creed when it is interpolated as a late addition into the already existing Apostles' Creed recited in the West, soon to be followed by use in other creeds in Gaul and elsewhere. In the creed it is placed after belief in the Holy Spirit as one of the fruits of the Spirit's vivifying presence: "I believe in the Holy Spirit, the holy catholic church, the communion of saints, the forgiveness of sins, the resurrection of the body and life everlasting. Amen." Here the Latin language opens up a fascinating ambiguity, for the *sanctorum* in the creed's original language can be read in two different ways.[1] The traditional interpretation takes the word to be the genitive form of *sancti,* the grammatically masculine noun meaning holy persons. In this case, the phrase can be translated "the communion of saints" and affirms belief in a living community among all holy persons, living and dead. Since the nineteenth century, however, another line of interpretation has opened up that takes the earliest sense of the word to be the genitive plural of the grammatically neuter noun *santa,* or holy things. The phrase should then be understood to refer to participation in sacred things, most specifically the Eucharist.

J. N. D. Kelly offers persuasive pointers that the term originally flowed to the West from the East, where it had the objective, sacramental rather than the subjective, personal meaning, and contemporary scholarship tends more and more to agree. While the expression *communio sanctorum* was relatively rare and its meaning was fluctuating in the West, he writes, the Greek equivalent, *koinonia ton hagion,* and related phrases "were firmly established in the East and bore the clear-cut sense of participation in the holy things, i.e., the eucharistic elements. This makes it highly probable that the idea and the language expressing it originated in the East."[2] In the West, however, the phrase came to bear the personal sense. This can be seen in a commentary on the Apostles' Creed by one Nicetas, bishop of Remesiana (c. 400 C.E.), whose work is the first evidence we have that *sanctorum communionem* was actually being recited as part of a creedal formula. Explaining to his people the meaning of the articles of faith they were confessing, he wrote of this phrase:

> What is the church but the congregation of all saints? From the beginning of the world patriarchs, prophets, martyrs, and all other righteous people who have lived, or who are now alive, or who shall live in time to come, comprise the church, since they have been sanctified by one faith and manner of life, and sealed by one Spirit, and so made one body, of which Christ is declared to be the head, as the Scripture says.... So you believe that in this church you will attain to the communion of saints.[3]

Clearly here the *communio sanctorum* stands for a relationship among the holy people of all ages, including the whole company of heaven, which is anticipated and partially realized in the community of the church on earth. In addition to this text's recognition of illustrious persons who have died, Jewish and Christian alike, it also includes the future in a fascinating way, for generations as yet unborn also belong to this community. Similarly, the whole company is not settled in the present but moving toward the eschatological fullness yet to come — "you will attain." The whole community through time shares in a communion of hope.

While this personal meaning predominates in the tradition of the West, the sacramental meaning has also occurred with some frequency, as an often quoted Norman-French version of this creedal phrase as *la communion des seintes choses* attests. Medieval theologians such as Abelard, Bonaventure, and Aquinas play with both meanings, connecting them in a unified vision as the holy sacrament of the altar which forms its recipients into a holy people. In his short essay on the Apostles' Creed, Aquinas writes in this vein: "Because all the faithful form one body, the benefits belonging to one are communicated to the others. There is thus a sharing of benefits (*communio bonorum*) in the church, and this is what we mean by *communio sanctorum.*"[4] Aquinas explains that the goods shared comprise everything worthwhile done on earth by the members of the community, for different gifts and charisms given to one person, when well used, strengthen and encourage others. In particular the goods shared include the sacraments which gift the church with the power flowing from Christ's passion. Corporate solidarity and sharing in holy things, the personal and realist meanings, mutually reinforce each other.

Scholars today point out that there is no absolute need to choose between the personal, predominantly Western, and the sacramental, predominantly Eastern, meanings of the *communio sanctorum*. The elusive quality of the phrase's original meaning is a happy circumstance, allowing it to bring forth a complex, multilayered reality, namely, the kinship of God's friends and prophets in a Spirit-filled company grounded in Christ and constituted by a sharing in the holy things, these being each other's lives and witness plus the sacraments, particularly the eucharistic bread and cup of salvation. As Berard Marthaler suggests, the ambiguity of the phrase *communio sanctorum* allows us to see that holy people and holy things are inextricably linked in the one Spirit of God.[5] The fact that the phrase is included in the creed brings this activity of the Spirit, renewing and blessing the world and the human community, into explicit consciousness.

Interpretation of this creedal statement today is enhanced by new experiences in a truly global world. Encounter and dialogue among the world's religious traditions results in ecumenical and comparative theology that discovers Spirit-Sophia at work in the broad expanse of humankind. Thus the boundaries of the community of the saints are far from rigid and certainly include persons of persuasions other than Christian and even of no religious belief who live according to the light of their conscience. In discussing this issue, Mary Ann Fatula makes the important point that this perspective must guide not only new formulations but even interpretation of the tradition:

> It must be noted also that the ecumenical perspective opened up by Vatican II is of great import in interpreting past texts relevant to the communion of saints. Vatican Council II affirmed that the Holy Spirit is at work wherever people labor to make life more human, and that the Spirit's gifts "can be found outside the visible boundaries of the Catholic Church." These insights provide an entirely new context for understanding that, in the Holy Spirit, the communion of saints extends beyond the bounds of the Church to all persons of truth and love.[6]

An equally interesting possibility opens up with the notion that *communio sanctorum* refers to participation in sacred things. Ecological theology, born of a marriage of the wonder of scientific discovery and the tragedy of environmental degradation, is reflecting anew on the ancient theme that the natural world is a sacred creation with its own intrinsic, rather than just instrumental, value.[7] The universe itself is the primordial sacrament through which life and all potential for the holy is communicated. At its best, theology of the sacraments has always drawn on the connection between the natural world and the signs of bread, wine, water, and oil which, when taken into the narrative of Jesus' life, death, and resurrection, become avenues of God's healing grace. Now, in the time of earth's agony, the *communio sanctorum* can be interpreted to include the primordially sacred gifts of air, water, land, all life systems, and the myriad species that share the planet with human beings. The community of persons partakes of these holy things as the very first gift, life itself. This sharing imparts to the *communio sanctorum* a prophetic character that stands against the degradation of the earth. On balance, the elusive, double-entendre character of *communio sanctorum* holds the promise of new readings. Through the power of the Spirit there is deep intermingling of holy persons and holy things in God's good creation.

A Great Festival

The origins of the feast of All Saints are also lost in the mists of time, but what can be traced of its history illuminates its meaning. During the early centuries of persecution, the anniversary day of martyrs' deaths was already remembered with prayer and a shared meal. When the violence ceased, appreciation grew of the witness given by these courageous persons, both singly and collectively. By the end of the fourth century, the Syriac church in the East celebrated a feast day in honor of the company of *all* the holy martyrs, the first such memorial on record. Placing this observation on Easter Friday meant that the martyrs' death and victory were closely linked to the dying and rising of Jesus Christ.

At around the same time, other Eastern cities observed a festival of the martyrs on the Sunday following Pentecost, the day marked on Western calendars in more recent centuries as the feast of the Holy Trinity. A movable feast held in May or June, Pentecost was originally an agricultural festival marking the harvest of the first barley crop, already ripened in the warm Mediterranean climate. In Jewish tradition it also commemorates the giving of the Law to Moses on Sinai. Yet another layer of meaning is added by the Christian story which tells of the outpouring of the Spirit in wind and fire giving birth to the church. Placing a festival of all the martyrs on the Sunday after this irruption of the Spirit depicts a new kind of harvest, the fruit of God's work amid the sufferings of history. This feast, later expanded to include all the holy people, All Saints, is still celebrated on the octave day of Pentecost in the Orthodox church.

In the Latin West there were a series of variable dates for the feast: Easter Friday in some places; the Sunday after Pentecost in others; May 13, a commemoration of "all the martyrs of the earth" in the rededicated Pantheon in Rome; and by the eighth century, November 1 in transalpine Europe. This latter date corresponds to a celebration of the "old religion," the Druid festival of the dead called *Samhain*, and may well represent an effort to reinterpret a popular Celtic feast within a Christian framework. In the northern climate, the gathering of the harvest coupled with the waning of the sun and the approach of dark winter signaled the beginning of the new year on November 1. The Celts believed that the souls of those who had died during the year traveled to the other world at this time. Animals were sacrificed, fruits and vegetables offered, and bonfires lit to help the pilgrim dead find their way on the journey. A darker side to the occasion arose with the belief that this was also the time when the Lord of death sent evil spirits abroad to harass humans; the fires, sacrifices, tricks, treats, and disguises were needed as protection from their onslaught. Introducing the feast of All Saints, the church invited people to celebrate the season differently, by recognizing the God of life and resurrection who gathers in not only the courageous martyrs and outstanding ascetics but all the blessed dead, including family members and friends and loved ones. Instead of the terror of chains, moaning ghosts, and evil spirits tormenting humans, the day celebrated the victory of Christ over evil and death, epitomized in all the beloved dead who have gone through darkness into light forever.

By the ninth century, the November 1 date was observed throughout the Western church as the feast of All Saints. It is the festival par excellence of the communion of saints, giving comfort and consolation to those who are grieving the loss of beloved persons and awakening in all community members hope and joy in their solidarity with the friends of God and prophets of all ages. Soon, however, due to the growth of the idea of purgatory, people were no longer certain that all those who had died were covered by this commemoration. On the cusp of the second millennium, an abbot of the monastery of Cluny added the day of All Souls on November 2, when those still being purified were remembered in prayer. This has resulted in the festival of All Saints losing some of its ringing clarity. It is boxed in on one side by the hijinks of Halloween, the remnant of *Samhain* that has proved highly resistant to Christian reinterpretation, and by the somber scene of souls in painful transit on the other. This conjunction has left the great festival of the communion of saints "framed by the almost equally bizarre phenomena of Halloween and the singing of the *Dies Irae* over a black-draped empty coffin."[8] Unlike developments in Eastern Christianity, where the Pentecost setting assures a deep, narrative connection with the Spirit who raised Christ from the dead and is at work in the world even now, in the West the vagaries of history have landed the day of All Saints in a somewhat less favorable position. But its theological meaning is still there to be burnished and appreciated. The festival of all the redeemed including, in the light of the sacramental meaning of *communio sanctorum*, the redeemed earth and its creatures, sheds its light on the community today that keeps memorial in hope.

Entering the List: Canonization

During the first millennium of Christianity, the question of who among the dead would be lifted up for public veneration was decided by the local church. The people themselves through a certain collective intuition in the Spirit recognized who among the post-martyr generations had given witness of a holy life and would salute their luminous example by naming them aloud at the Eucharist on the anniversary of their death, most often with the collaboration of their bishop. In this process of "spontaneous canonization of the saints,"[9] veneration of specific saints was deeply rooted in the living remembrance and piety of the people. If the appeal of the holy person was universal enough, other local churches would follow suit.

By the tenth century it became common for bishops, once the people had recognized a holy person, to enhance the solemn dignity of a local saint by requesting that the pope recognize the saint or even proclaim the saint's worthiness. This happened with more frequency until, in keeping with the growth of papal power, the twelfth and thirteenth centuries saw the right to canonize reserved to the papacy alone. In his study of the whole process, Kenneth Woodward details the key decrees:

> Like other dimensions of church activity, the making of saints was gradually placed under the jurisdiction of the Holy See and its lawyers. In 1170, Alexander III decreed that no one, regardless of his or her reputation for holiness or wonder-working, could be venerated locally without papal authorization. However, his decree by no means spelled an immediate end to episcopal canonizations, nor did it quench the popular thirst for new cults. In 1234, Pope Gregory IX published his *Decretals,* or collection of pontifical laws, in which he asserted the absolute jurisdiction of the Roman pontiff over all causes of saints and made it binding on the universal church. Since saints were objects of devotion for the entire church, he reasoned, only the pope with his universal jurisdiction possessed the authority to canonize. From this point on, the canonization process became increasingly fastidious.[10]

Public recognition of worthiness, including a place in the calendar of saints, was now to be granted from a single authoritative source, thus shifting what had been an acclamation close to the spiritual life of the people to an increasingly centralized bureaucratic process.

Recent sociological studies have deepened our understanding of the results.[11] Since the right to name the community's exemplars reinforces the authority of the one who canonizes, this was one more element in the centralization of power in the hands of the papacy, aggrandizing that office even at the expense of local episcopal authority. Inevitably the process became political. By means of this honor, the pope was able to reward his allies in battles against heretical groups or recalcitrant monarchs, maintain popular support by naming favored saints, and punish those whose orthodoxy was questionable. Given the length of time and money the process increasingly demanded, it began to favor members of religious orders and royal houses who had resources sufficient for the required research and lobbying. As Pierre Delooz describes, "moral reputation and financial credit, competence in canon law and perseverance well beyond a single human life-span became essential elements here. Religious, whose orders could play the necessary role of pressure groups, thus came to have a considerable advantage over lay candidates for canonization."[12] These results were felt slowly at first for in the high Middle Ages the Roman procedures were not well worked out and public acceptance of them was far from universal. Slowly but surely a set of centralized procedures was crafted and progressively fine-tuned to regulate the process of being canonized, or entering the list (canon) of saints approved for public veneration. The procedures have continued to evolve to our own day, being recently reformed in 1983 and now administered by the Vatican office known as the Congregation for the Causes of the Saints.

Contemporary scholarly discussion of what canonization has wrought tends to highlight the unfortunate effects of the move from local recognition to certification through a bureaucratic process, although some gains may be recorded. In a positive sense it allows for careful scrutiny to ensure authenticity in persons whom the whole church venerates, preventing fabrication or credulous enthusiasm from winning the day. The history of saint-making does show a vein of fancifulness, love of the fabulous, even of anarchy, seen for example in the early medieval period when "saints sprang up from the fertile imaginations of hagiographers like so many spring mushrooms."[13] Concern for the integrity of the gospel and for good pastoral care would see to it that such tendencies toward the stupendous are kept in check. Another positive outcome results when the witness of a person's life on one continent is lifted up for appreciation by the church in different countries and cultures. Provincialism is overcome as the consciousness of the world church expands to appreciate the graced work of the Spirit beyond one's own immediate world. People can draw benefit from the rich diversity of lives singled out as exemplars, and find their racism and ethnic prejudices being subtly subverted.[14]

While canonization developed in response to historical forces, its exercise at this point in time also has negative impact on popular and theological awareness of the communion of saints. Saints have become an ever more elite group, proclaimed for their heroic virtue and their power to produce spectacular miracle. The unfortunate result has been that the meaning of the term "saint" itself has shrunk in Christian usage to refer mostly to those who have been named as a result of this official juridical scrutiny. Not only does this overshadow the theological meaning of the terms "saints" which embraces all persons of love and truth, but existentially the official ideal of perfection rewarded by this process becomes rarefied to the point where people reject their own identity as holy and blessed: "I'm no saint."

Transferring what ideally is a grace-filled discernment by a local community to a centralized bureaucracy, furthermore, has resulted in a certain uniformity among the canonized saints reflective of the face of that bureaucracy itself. Product of a clericalized culture, both the roster of canonized saints and the liturgical calendar of saints drawn from it reflect a worldview that is overwhelmingly favorable toward men who are priests or bishops and toward persons of aristocratic and upper-class origins. These "canons" are likewise biased against lay people in general and women in particular, and prejudiced against the full and legitimate use of human sexuality by both women and men. Even before canonization became a regular procedure, social status and power in the hierarchical order of church and society largely determined who would be candidates for public sainthood. Researching lists of some several thousand names of the holy dead from 500 to 1200 C.E., Jane Tibbetts Schulenburg found that "despite claims of spiritual egalitarianism by the Church, it was much more difficult for women to be recognized as saints than it was for men. For this period of some seven hundred years, the average percentage of women recognized as saints was less than 15 percent of the total."[15] Covering mostly centuries when canonization was in effect, Pierre Delooz's statistical analysis demonstrates that between the tenth and nineteenth centuries, 87 percent of those whom Rome recognized as saints were men while only 13 percent were women; in the first eight decades of the twentieth century, the proportion was 75 percent men and 25 percent women, a small gain but far from equality. Similarly, those recognized as saints from the tenth to the nineteenth centuries were

82 percent clergy and 18 percent laity, as compared with the twentieth century's 79 percent clerical and 21 percent lay saints, hardly a change at all.[16] The vast majority of those on the list are Europeans, although that balance is slowly shifting as John Paul II has canonized groups of lay martyrs from developing nations.[17] Glaringly missing from the canonized lists are married people honored for the goodness and exemplarity of their lives precisely as actively married. The official ideal of holiness thus marginalizes lives in which sexual activity is integrated rather than excluded, sending a message that most people live in a less-than-holy way. "What is it about the passionate life of the body," asks Kenneth Woodward, "which the church finds unbecoming in a saint? Why in particular are there no examples of happily married saints?"[18] It is obvious from this roster that the history of women's holiness is given extremely short shrift. Furthermore, female exemplars approved by a patriarchal bureaucracy, almost by definition, need at least on the surface to be accepting of a self-definition of femininity that is far from adequate to the drive for women's wholeness in contemporary society. Given dedication and prophetic zeal, passion for justice and hope in the face of despair, could a feminist ever be canonized? Sexual stereotyping limits the appeal of even those women who are on the list.

Another flag is raised by the fact that saints must pass muster before a narrow definition of doctrinal orthodoxy, thereby largely excluding pioneering thinkers, intellectuals, artists, or anyone with a critical or challenging spirit. The process thus becomes an instrument of control to ensure a certain doctrinal and spiritual conformity, having the power to tame even charismatic lives into symbols of institutional loyalty. From yet another angle, the need to have an objective standard by which to judge holiness in the canonization procedure has skewed miraculous happenings all out of proportion to their true importance in the life of a holy community. The luminous quality of a life well-lived and of witness given in the midst of struggle have their own powerful validity apart from any "wonders" worked during life or after death, which may actually be distractions from the authentic activity of the Spirit. Finally, today as in the high Middle Ages, the process itself requires large investments of time and money, thus giving the edge to groups such as religious orders or organized lay societies and disqualifying the poor and other struggling segments of the church from even beginning pursuit of official recognition of those whose holy lives have touched them, presuming they would even want to.

After much study and with a desire to promote the saints, Lawrence Cunningham proposes that the formal canonization process, perhaps necessary in certain historical circumstances, has become so irrelevant and obstructionist that it should be abandoned or, at the least, radically modified. Far from promoting piety it induces in some quarters a strong alienation as a result of the process losing touch with the people:

> Any fair and impartial student of the saints would agree, it seems to me, that the very process of canonization tends to produce saints for our veneration who are outside the interests of the average intelligent modern Catholic. It could be argued, in fact, that the almost total decline in the interest in the subject of saints, apart from a certain residual sentimentality or loyalty to the old forms, can be traced to a quiet rebellion of the modern mind against the roster of saints that has been bequeathed to us as a result of the bureaucratization of the saints.[19]

The purpose of taking this sounding in the debate about canonization has been to put this process in a certain perspective that would remove it as a stumbling block to a feminist theological understanding and practicing of the communion of saints today. In truth, canonization's purpose is to determine who among the deceased have given such evidence of holy lives that they may receive public veneration in the church. There must still be some mechanism for this, as the difficulties experienced by Protestant churches trying to restore a calendar of saints make clear.[20] But current bureaucratic processes operate under patriarchal assumptions that neither focus on nor respect the living memory and living hope of local communities. To retrieve the vitality of the communion of saints it is necessary for local churches to reclaim the power of naming. The communion of holy people sharing in holy things is not limited to the list of those canonized but includes all the friends of God and prophets who try to live according to truth and love. Occasionally some people give such striking witness in the midst of the struggles of their own time and place that their story becomes a source of empowerment and warm encouragement for others in the community. In actual fact, as David Power has observed, the earlier process of local canonization is in some respects being recovered as "people in their faith are calling up the memory of those who exemplify hope for them and are often in acts including their naming in public acts of worship. This is in essence the process of putting persons on the calendar,"[21] although it still lacks the mechanism of formal ecclesiastical approval. Long before the juridical process was invented, local communities, through the power of the Spirit, could recognize these persons who made the face of God present in uniquely different circumstances and gave brave witness in their life of discipleship. That power has not deserted the church.

Gleanings

By the thirteenth century in the West a public pattern is set in creed, liturgy, and law recognizable even to this day. The symbol of the communion of saints is affirmed in a phrase in the Apostles' Creed, celebrated in a November festival, and controlled by the practical norms of canonization. There are gains as well as losses to this symbol's becoming thus official: benefits in recognizing the community of the friends of God and prophets in a communal statement of belief and an annual festival day, and defeats in the bureaucratizing of sanctity which creates official models remote and distant from people's hopes. The fact that most average Christians struggling to live their lives as best they can do not consider themselves "saints" may be an expression of humility and awareness of their sinfulness. It is just as likely to be the result of the reduction of the idea of holiness to the rarefied realm of a clericalized or monastic ideal.

From a feminist theological perspective, the symbol of the communion of saints understood through its historical development becomes ripe for retrieval within the companionship model. The creedal affirmation of the *communio sanctorum* and the festival of All Saints are already gender inclusive. In fact, the nonhierarchical nature of the mutual sharing of persons and goods attested to by this *communio*, interpreted traditionally to signify the very essence of the church, stands as a prophetic sign against the divine right of patriarchal institutions. In keeping with consciousness of the sacredness of being female, feminist theological reflection can reclaim this symbol, reading women, poor women, women of color, marginalized women, raped and brutalized women, caring and ministering women, strong and vibrant and artistic women, sexually active women, setting-out-not-knowing-where-they-are-going women, women who are all of the above, all holy women of the world, into the creed, into the feast, onto the list as equal partners in the holy community sharing in sacred things.

Chapter 6

Movements for Reform

Mending the Practice, Reviving the Sense

In late medieval times, devotion to the saints blossomed in the Christian West with a profusion that is impossible to codify. On the one hand, the public liturgy honored the saints with a certain sobriety. On feast days the church offered thanks to God for the grace given to them, held up their lives as sterling examples to be imitated, and joined with this heavenly company to sing the praises of God. On the other hand, despite the growing centralized process of canonization, popular piety honored uncounted thousands of local saints, some of them of dubious merit, some even legendary. Emphasis on the miraculous powers of the saints overshadowed other aspects of veneration, and zeal for collecting relics, use of auguries and incantations, and superheated hagiography contributed to the divorce of piety from ethics. There were reasons for this odd explosion, so different from the pattern of the gospel.[1] Daily life was hard and dangerous, with suffering and sudden death through plague, war, and civil unrest ever-present possibilities; how could an ordinary person survive? Given the juridical cast of church teaching and practice about human sinfulness and the need for satisfaction, spiritual life was also a struggle. Jesus Christ was the merciful Savior, but he was also the just Judge who would weigh each person's good or wrongful deeds against each other and assign a rightful destiny in heaven or, more likely, hell; how could a sinner survive? An underlying anxiety pervaded the cultural climate. Nor did the Latin liturgy or scholastic theology, ever more remote from ordinary people's experience, offset the fear with the good news of God's mercy poured out in Christ Jesus.

In response, there was a felt need for the saints to act as powerful mediators who would intercede for material and spiritual blessings for vulnerable, unworthy sinners. Human themselves, the saints could bring compassion to the struggles people were going through; not needing to pay attention to governing the whole universe, they could care more about individual devotees; now redeemed themselves, they could plead sinners' cases before Christ's searing judgment. Thanks to her maternal relationship with Christ and her eloquent powers on behalf of others, so clearly demonstrated at Cana where she persuaded Jesus to perform his first miracle, the Mother of God was thought to be the best intercessor of all. This resulted in a religious situation where the confidence and trust that the heart should have in God's abundant goodness was transferred to saints. In spite of the efforts of some bishops and theologians to curb abuses, many pastors benefitted financially and socially from these practices and so condoned them, leaving the veneration of the saints open to the criticism that it was a distortion of the gospel. As Martin Luther was later to recollect:

> Consider what we used to do in our blindness under the papacy. If anyone had a toothache, he fasted to the honor of St. Apollonia; if he feared fire, he sought St. Lawrence as his patron; if he feared the plague, he made a vow to St. Sebastian or Roch. There were countless other abominations, and every person selected his own saint and worshiped and invoked him in time of need.... All these fix their heart and trust elsewhere than in the true God. They neither expect nor seek anything from him."[2]

In terms of the two historic patterns of relationship we traced earlier, by the sixteenth century the patronage model was operating with a vengeance and to excess.

Two movements for reform, the Protestant Reformation in the sixteenth century and the Second Vatican Council in the twentieth, sought to mend the practice and revive the original sense of the communion of saints. It is fascinating to see how these efforts at reform thought to accomplish their goal largely by restoring the companionship model in theology and practice. Our purpose here is not to rehearse the history and complexities of Reformation debates or conciliar deliberations surrounding this subject, which comprise a vast and complex literature.[3] Rather, we are sifting the material for insight that will contribute to a contemporary retrieval of the symbol.

Protestant Reform: "Living Members of Christ and Friends of God"

The theological leaders of the Reformation did not turn against the communion of saints or even the saints in themselves. But they did stringently criticize what we have identified as the patronage model of veneration which related to saints as intercessors before the distant high throne of a judgmental God. Having rediscovered the good news of God's mercy, freely given while we were yet sinners and without any merit on our part, they pressed the glad insight that there is no need for subordinate mediators because the flood of divine kindness reaches us through the cross of the one mediator, Jesus Christ. "There is therefore now no condemnation for those who are in Christ Jesus" (Rom 8:1). Reflecting on this liberating religious experience, rooted in the gospel, Luther recommends that the only appropriate response is to cling with all our heart to God alone, the one, eternal, loving good. It is as if God were now saying, "What you formerly sought from the saints, or what you hoped to receive from mammon or anything else, turn to me for all this; look upon me as the one who wishes to help you and to lavish all good upon you richly."[4]

Criticism focused in particular on the practice of invoking the saints, or calling upon them for their prayers and favors. This became the nub of the controversy surrounding the saints. Not only is there no scriptural warrant for this practice, the reformers argued, and thus it is not assured by the word of God, but by setting up a whole series of intercessors between ourselves and Christ it dangerously detracts from the heart of the gospel's revelation that Christ alone is the bringer of God's mercy. It distorts faith, turning the "kindly Mediator" into a "dreaded Judge" who needs to be placated by the intercession of the saints, and causing people to have greater confidence in the saints than in Christ. The hinge of debate turns on whether and to what extent the God made known in Jesus is to be trusted. So sure was Luther of the attractive power of the mercy of God, and so disgusted at the quid pro quo of the abuse of invocation, that he predicted rather accurately, "When physical and spiritual benefit and help are no longer expected, the saints will cease to be molested in their graves and in heaven, for no one will long remember, esteem, or honor them out of love when there is no expectation of return."[5]

While forbidding invocation of the saints, however, the reformers had a theological vision in which there was room to honor the saints in heaven. Rediscovering the biblical notion of God's holy people and the early Christian usage of "saints" to name the whole community, they interpreted the creed's "communion of saints" to mean the church itself. A sinful yet redeemed community, a little flock led by the shepherd Christ, a gathering of saints, an assembly of prophetic, priestly, and kingly believers, the church itself is the place of encounter with the mercy of God. Those in this living community who have died in the peace of Christ join the great cloud of witnesses in heaven. Perhaps they pray for us (opinion was divided, as Scripture gives no sure word). But what is most important is the witness of their lives. We honor them because they are living stories of God's grace and mercy, because they instruct us by the example of their bold faith, and because their destiny with God strengthens our hope. Thus the Reformation rediscovered in a new historical setting the contours of the early companionship pattern of believing and practicing the communion of saints. Several key examples from Lutheran and Reformed writings illuminate how this happened in the concrete.

The *Augsburg Confession,* written in 1530 by Philip Melanchthon for the historic public hearing vis-à-vis the Roman party at the Diet of Augsburg, is one of the founding confessional statements of the Lutheran Church. Explaining the church's position on the saints, the document declares, "It is also taught among us that the saints should be kept in remembrance so that our faith may be strengthened when we see what grace they received and how they were sustained by faith. Moreover, their good works are to be an example for us, each of us in his own calling.... However, it cannot be proved from the Scriptures that we are to invoke saints or seek help from them,"[6] for Scripture attests that there is only one mediator, Jesus Christ. One year later, responding to Catholic criticism of this position, the *Apology of the Augsburg Confession* asserts that the Lutheran Confession approves of giving honor to the saints, and goes on to explain that this honor should be shown in three ways. The first way is by thanking: we thank God for showing such divine mercy to sinners and for "giving teachers and other gifts to the church." The second way is by allowing our faith to be strengthened by theirs; seeing Peter forgiven after his denial we are encouraged to trust that grace does indeed abound more than sin. The third way is by imitating the saints' example and virtues, according to our own calling in this world. Together, these practices of reverence enrich the life of faith lived in the light of God's mercy. But, the *Apology* continues in criticism of the Catholic position, "our opponents do not require these real honors; they only argue about invocation which, even if it were not dangerous, is certainly unnecessary."[7] In the light of this teaching, the Lutheran Church continued liturgical observation of the traditional All Saints Day and memorial days of apostolic saints such as Mary Magdalene and John the Baptist, along with Lutheran martyrs and other select holy people, including in time Martin Luther himself. In these commemorations emphasis focused strongly on the courage to follow after Christ in the footsteps of these redeemed sinners. Research by Robert Kolb has shown that by the end of the sixteenth century there was little polemic in Lutheran writings on the veneration of saints, indicating that preaching and piety had shifted successfully into a new mode.[8] The whole church is a community of saints; paradigmatic figures stand out as foremost examples of the grace of God; invocation disappears but mutual regard endures as together we praise God's mercy in the following of Christ.[9]

More severe in their judgment were John Calvin and the ensuing Reformed tradition which rejected the sanctoral cycle altogether along with images, martyrologies, pilgrimages, and other devotional practices. Focused on the worship of God alone through Jesus Christ the sole mediator, this branch of the Reformation found the veneration of saints an appalling distortion. In his *Institutes of the Christian Religion,* Calvin unerringly found the neuralgic point to be the practice of invoking the saints and abjured it in no uncertain terms. It is "the height of stupidity, not to say madness" to be so intent on gaining access to God through the saints that we lose that very access offered to us in Christ; it is "a drunken dream of our brain" to imagine that the saints in heaven are more kindly disposed to help us than is Christ, who has an affection for us "than which nothing can be gentler or more tender." Those who delight in the intercession of the saints do so because "they are burdened by anxiety, as if Christ were insufficient or too severe." But by this attitude they "make void the cross" and "cast out the kindness of God."[10] Indeed, one wonders why such people even want to call themselves Christian: "in contending that we need the advocacy of the saints, they have no stronger argument than to object that we are unworthy to approach God intimately. This we admit to be very true indeed, but we conclude from it that those who account Christ's intercession worthless unless George and Hippolytus and such specters come forward leave nothing for Christ to do."[11]

Even here, however, there is no ultimate rejection of the communion of saints; indeed, how could there be? Commenting on this phrase in the creed, Calvin notes that the communion of saints "well expresses what the church is."[12] It refers to the society of those redeemed by Christ and filled with a rich diversity of graces accordingly as the gifts of the Spirit are variously distributed. There is a wealth of comfort in this phrase, for our hope is strengthened by the gifts given to others that are shared among us. The phrase, furthermore, refers "not only to the visible church but also to all God's elect, in whose number are also included the dead."[13] Regarding these persons who have died in the flesh but are alive in Christ, the second Helvetic Confession, although rejecting invocation, nevertheless affirms:

At the same time, we do not despise the saints or think basely of them. For we acknowledge them to be living members of Christ and friends of God who have gloriously overcome the flesh and the world. Hence we love them as brothers [sic], and also honor them; yet not with any kind of worship but by an honorable opinion of them and just praise of them. We also imitate them. For with ardent longings and supplications we earnestly desire to be imitators of their faith and virtues, to share eternal salvation with them, to dwell eternally with them in the presence of God, and to rejoice with them in Christ.[14]

Remembering the cloud of witnesses, and doing so in comradeship and hope, spurs on the living community in its attempts to live the gospel. Here is yet another articulation of the companionship model.

Although the sixteenth-century Reformers had drawn the line in the sand over the practice of invoking the saints, the Council of Trent, called to address the crisis, gave this subject no theological analysis or systematic defense. As it drew to a hasty close it simply reaffirmed that the practice was "good and useful" (bonum atque utile) and laid down guidelines for reform of the more egregious abuses connected with veneration of the saints in general.[15] As the polemic of the Reformation dispute wore on and turned bloody, positions on both sides hardened. Honoring the saints became a badge of Catholic identity, while Protestant worship and spirituality diminished interest in the saints to the vanishing point: on the one hand, a certain fixation; on the other, a case of amnesia.

The Anglican communion remained closest to traditional perspectives regarding the saints even while it, too, abjured the practice of invocation. This church also continued to observe the feast days of biblical saints and some martyrs, culminating in the annual festival of All Saints. Two centuries after the Anglican tradition took shape, John and Charles Wesley transformed the spiritual atmosphere of the Church of England with the warmth and light of the Methodist revival. With its new passion for fellowship in the Spirit, Methodism rediscovered the power inherent in the communion of saints both in local societies and as a *koinonia* across time. In his explanation of the ecclesiological phrases of the creed, John Wesley notes the global and transcendent dimensions of this communion, writing that in the Spirit the members of the church have fellowship with the trinitarian God and also "with all the living members of Christ on earth, as well as all who are departed in his faith and fear."[16] That this belief was honored in vigorous celebration of All Saints Day is expressed in a series of entries into John Wesley's journal on November 1 of successive years. In 1756 he wrote, "November 1, Monday, was a day of triumphant joy, as All Saints Day generally is — how superstitious are they who scruple giving God solemn thanks for the lives and death of His saints!"[17] His meditation for 1767 reveals where his own heart lies: "Being all Saints Day, a festival I dearly love...."[18] That same entry shows how rooted his intuitions are in the Anglican tradition: "I could not but observe the admirable propriety with which the Collect, Epistle, and Gospel for the day are suited to each other."[19] The Collect, taken from the 1662 Book of Common Prayer and still in use today, runs thus: "O almighty God, who has knit together thine elect in one communion and fellowship in the mystical body of thy Son Christ our Lord, grant us grace so to follow thy blessed saints in all virtuous and godly living that we may come to those ineffable joys which thou hast prepared for those who unfeignedly love thee; through the same Jesus Christ our Lord...."[20] When coupled with the epistle, which then as now depicts a great throng from every nation gathered around the throne of the Lamb (Rev 7), and the gospel, which promises beatitude upon those who yearn for the reign of God (Mt 5), this Collect prayer gives living voice to the ancient sensibility of comradeship in the great company of all the saints.

In an insightful essay Geoffrey Wainwright suggests that while Methodism refrains from using many artistic images, its hymns can be considered "a kind of musical iconography,"[21] similar to pictorial icons used by the Orthodox to enact the presence of the saints in liturgy so that the joy of heaven may be known upon earth. Referring to one such hymn, John Wesley's journal entry for November 1, 1766, gives evidence that such may be the case: "On this day in particular, I commonly find the truth of these words:

> The Church triumphant in His love,
> Their mighty joys we know;
> They praise the Lamb in hymns above,
> And we in hymns below."[22]

This and other Methodist hymns written by Charles Wesley, one of the greatest hymn writers in the English language, reveal the basic doxological character of the Wesleyan practice of the communion of saints. United in one community that transcends time and death, those alive in the Spirit share a bond of fellowship that issues in praise and confidence in God. Charles Wesley's great funeral hymn captures this sense of transcendent comradeship between the living and the dead with stunning power; despite its use of military and servant imagery, common to its day, it expresses a closeness to each other in God that is intrinsic to the communion of saints:

> Come, let us join our friends above / That have obtained the prize,
> And on the eagle wings of love / To joys celestial rise:
> Let all the saints terrestrial sing / With those to glory gone;
> For all the servants of our King / In earth and heaven, are one.
>
> One family we dwell in him, / One church, above, beneath,
> Though now divided by the stream, / The narrow stream of death;
> One army of the living God, / To his command we bow,
> Part of his host have crossed the flood / And part are crossing now.
>
> Ten thousand to their endless home / This solemn moment fly;
> And we are to the margin come, / And we expect to die;
> Ev'n now by faith we join our hands / With those who went before,
> And greet the blood-besprinkled bands / On the eternal shore.
>
> Our spirits too shall quickly join, / Like theirs with glory crowned,
> And shout to see our captain's sign, / To hear his trumpet sound.
> O that we now might grasp our guide! / O that the word were given!

Come, Lord of Hosts, the waves divide, / And land us all in heaven.[23]

This vision of joining with our friends, one family dwelling in God, one church "above, beneath" divided only by death, one company crossing to heaven with the living now on the edge of the stream, joining hands across the divide, a vision shot through with hope, inspires in those who sing this hymn a joyful confidence in being part of such a community that carries God's promise of victory in Christ. Despite this promising beginning in Methodism, however, time and circumstance dimmed the practice of the communion of saints in local congregations, as with the Protestant tradition in general.

Catholic Reform: "Companionship with the Saints"

The Reformation critique was certainly in the mind of the Second Vatican Council when it presented the first systematic teaching about the saints ever given at the papal or conciliar level. It is not that the council directly answers the reformers' criticisms against invoking the saints; indeed, Trent's teaching that the practice is "good and useful" is simply assumed and restated, still unexplained. But Vatican II makes three moves to reform thinking and practice about the saints: it connects teaching on the saints to the broader theology of the church, itself refreshed by biblical and early Christian sources; it develops this teaching in a trinitarian framework centered on the mercy of God in Christ; and, rather surprisingly in view of traditional practice, it recommends a new version of the companionship relationship while criticizing the excesses that gather around practices of patronage.

What is essential for the conciliar view of the communion of saints is the shift in its understanding of the whole church as a communion. Since the council, fierce debates have continued over the nature of its teaching on the church, and ecclesiology as a theological discipline is still searching for a common critical method and integrating goal.[24] But it cannot be denied — the debate itself demonstrates this — that at the council a new image and idea of the church came into play. In post-Reformation Catholic ecclesiology, *communio* had referred to the church as a visible society, united by the profession of faith, the sacraments, and juridical allegiance to the authority of bishops and pope; emphasis lay on what separated members of this communion

from other Christians and from other religious traditions and unbe-
lievers; the world was treated as a separate and largely antagonistic
entity that needed to be converted to the visible communion of the institutional church. There was little sense of a redemptive *communio*
already at work as an inner-historical reality across all these borders.
In contrast to this theology, the council worked with a concept of *communio* at once more spiritual and more historical. While respecting
legitimate social authority, it understands the *communio* of the church
to be constituted first of all by a common participation in the trinitarian mystery of God, which grounds it as a holy people of God sharing
a communion of life, love, and truth; these bonds of union in the saving grace of the Spirit are not exclusionary but open and dialogical,
linking the church in real ways to other Christian communities, and
extending also to other religious believers and even atheists, in whose
conscience and heart the Spirit works in ways known only to God; the
historical world itself is the zone of God's creative and redemptive activity toward *communio,* not only needing the church's ministry but
also having something to teach. In these respects the council not only
expanded the framework within which the church as a community was
to be understood; it also recentered the purpose of its existence from
self-referential maintenance to being a sacrament (sign and means)
of a *communio* that God desires to be realized in the whole historical world. Analyzing this profound conciliar shift, Joseph Komanchak
astutely highlights its outcome for policy and spirituality:

> The jealous exclusion of others from its own *communio* once
> provided Catholics with a clear identity, but this was an iden-
> tity that, as articulated in theory and realized in practice, itself
> often contributed to the divisions and alienations of humanity
> and postponed the realization of redemptive *communio* in his-
> tory. The challenge today is to recognize that the very *communio*
> constitutive of the Church and defining its identity requires the
> recognition of a larger *communio* both as reality already at work
> in the world and as eschatological goal, which, confessed in
> faith and yearned for in hope, serves even now as a measure of
> its love.[25]

Vatican II's teaching on the saints carries this latter option in ecclesiology forward, delineating the communion of saints at once in ways
historical and eschatological.

Structure

This teaching appears in chapter 7 of *Lumen Gentium,* the Dogmatic Constitution on the Church, and its very placement there is an important key for interpretation.[26]

Despite debates over the number and content of *Lumen Gentium*'s chapters, most famously the fierce floor fight and close vote over including the chapter on Mary, a clear intrinsic structure marks the final form of this document. The progression of chapters reveals a train of thought that illumines meaning.

• Chapter 1 roots the mystery of the church in the grace of God poured out in Jesus Christ. Indeed, the *lumen gentium,* or light of all nations, is Christ, whose radiance brightens the face of the community called together in his name and Spirit; they in turn, by proclaiming the gospel to every creature, shed this light to all the world. This chapter makes clear that the foundational relationship that constitutes the essence of the church is a saving relation to God through Christ in the power of the Spirit.

• Chapter 2, entitled "The People of God," effected what Yves Congar called a revolution that was no less than "Copernican" in placing consideration of the whole community of disciples before mention of a hierarchical structure.[27] Using the biblical metaphor of the pilgrim people of God, the text describes the church as a community stemming from Israel and now stretching across all times and places whom God has made into a royal priesthood, a holy nation, a company of prophets. The seed of a whole theology of the fundamental equality of all members united in one calling and one hope is placed in the soil of the redeeming grace of Christ and the indwelling of the Spirit, which makes holy the whole messianic people. From descriptions of the charisms of the Spirit distributed freely among the faithful to statements about their rights and duties in virtue of their rebirth through baptism — "all the faithful can baptize"[28] — the chapter rediscovers the powerful biblical notion of the whole community as God's holy people. Their shared heritage is the dignity and freedom of the children of God; the heart of their life is love; their goal together, to bring the reign of God into all creation through all the vagaries of history.

• Subsequent chapters carry out these themes in view of the various functions of different ministries in the church: episcopacy and clergy (chapter 3), laity (chapter 4), and those in religious orders (chapter 6). The existence of various ministries and paths of life does not erase the fundamental reality that "all have received an equal privilege of faith through the justice of God," and that "all share a true equality with regard to the dignity and to the activity common to all the faithful for building up the Body of Christ."[29]

• The shift occurring throughout *Lumen Gentium* from the institutional, juridical, and hierarchical image of the church typical of theology since the Middle Ages bursts fully into the open with chapter 5, "The Call of the Whole Church to Holiness," which returns to the second chapter's theology of the pilgrim people of God and amplifies the identity of this people as a holy community. The wonder of this move, which erases a centuries-old assignment of holiness according to ecclesial rank, is caught by an early commentator: "we catch sight here of an astonishing process. The Church is in the throes of a portentous transformation. She is changing her whole countenance and bearing"[30] to include the sacredness of the life of the baptized. The text roots the universality of the life of grace in the inclusive nature of God's love, in the pattern of Jesus' preaching which excluded no one from the call to discipleship, and in the boundless gift of the Spirit who transforms persons from within. The power of baptism justifies all persons in the church and makes them together sharers in the divine nature. "In this way they are really made holy."[31] This holiness is not in the first instance a moral perfection but a participation in the glory (*doxa*) and love (*agape*) of God, given freely without previous merit or accomplishment on anyone's part. God is holy, and the people share in this through the grace of Christ in the Spirit.

It is not necessary for people to be ordained or enter a religious order to pursue the path of holiness. The call is there, an intrinsic part of the identity of Christians, and whatever the circumstances of persons' lives, they can "grow in holiness day by day *through these very situations*."[32] The result will be an abundant harvest of good as, energized by the same love with which God so loves the world, people commit themselves to promoting a more human way of life in earthly society, especially for the poor and suffering. Gifts given by the Spirit may differ. But about the participation in God's life that blesses every heart there is no doubt — it is the same essential holiness: "in the various types and duties of life, *one and the same holiness* is cultivated by all who are moved by the Spirit of God."[33]

• Having theologized about the holy people of God and the various paths of life that characterize the church, *Lumen Gentium* could have come to a conclusion. But the reality of the church is not exhausted here, in the community of those who are alive at any given moment. Some of the faithful have already arrived in the promised future. To them the pilgrim church is still united, for the bonds which join believers to Christ in the Spirit are so strong that not even death can break them. One does not leave the church by dying. Therefore, the Constitution on the Church turns attention in chapter 7 to the faithful dead, those "friends and fellow heirs of Jesus Christ"[34] with whom the living form one community. This it does in tandem with reflection on the eschatological nature of the pilgrim church, to which these definitively redeemed persons give concrete expression. The final chapter 8 then teaches about Mary, mother of Jesus and a preeminent member of the church, who takes her place amid this company of saints.

The placement of the chapters on the saints and Mary yields a hermeneutical clue for fruitful interpretation of the communion of saints. For the intrinsic structure of *Lumen Gentium* enfolds all the saints in heaven into the community of God's holy people, living and dead, energized by the fire of the Spirit and equally called to discipleship. Now with God in glory, they once struggled to be faithful to this call amid the sufferings of history, dramatic or everyday. The church remembers their bright patterns of holiness. They are a sign of our joy.

Content

Chapter 7 opens its teaching on the saints with a corporate and cosmic vision. Corporately, human beings walk a path that ends in death; cosmically, the world as a whole is also groaning and in travail through the course of time. Inspired by the resurrection of Jesus, the Christian community lives a pilgrimage of hope, looking forward to "a new heaven and a new earth where justice dwells."[35] This eschatological dynamism moves people to love the entire world and to yearn and work for its fulfillment on that day when Christ will come and death will be destroyed. Meanwhile, some disciples are living on earth, some have died and are being purified, and some have entered into the glory of God. Between them all there is a genuine community, based on the truth that "in various ways and degrees we all partake in the same love for God and neighbor, and all sing the same hymn of glory to our God. For all who belong to Christ, having his Spirit, form one church and cleave together in him."[36]

This is not a new belief. Historically, continues the text, the church from its beginning centuries has understood that the apostles and martyrs as well as Mary and other holy people who have died are alive in

God and thus still allied with those living on earth. While not claiming detailed knowledge about the condition of the saints, the church believes that, joined with Christ, they contribute to the upbuilding of the church on earth through their holiness and their prayer offered in and with Christ. It therefore venerates their memory in special ways. The benefits that accrue to the living by remembering the saints are many. Our quest is inspired by theirs; our path is made more sure by their example; and the communion of the whole church is strengthened. The right response of living disciples is to love these "friends of Jesus Christ," to thank God for them, to follow their example, and (quoting Trent) to have recourse to their prayers. When we praise God in their company during the eucharistic liturgy, each of these actions terminates through Christ in God, who is wonderful in the saints.[37]

The council then offers a particularly intense theocentric interpretation of the saints. "In the lives of those who shared in our humanity and yet were transformed into especially successful images of Christ, God vividly manifests" to human beings the divine "presence." Even more, in these grace-filled lives, God clearly and compellingly shows to human beings the divine "face," which no one has ever seen or can see. Furthermore, God "speaks to us in them," and gives us a sign of the coming reign of God, "to which we are powerfully drawn, surrounded as we are by so many witnesses and having such an argument for the truth of the gospel."[38] This strong affirmation of the sacramental function of the saints is rooted in the *imago Dei* doctrine. If the glory of God is the human being fully alive, then in the saints God's glory shines through in most attractive, even poignant ways. Saints are a sign of God's presence, a symbol of the Holy One, a living parable. Through their lives God sends a message to the world, communicating something which helps unfold the meaning of faith. Through their love, living evidence of God is revealed to all people.

Concerned that veneration of the saints has not always hewn to a rightly ordered pattern, the constitution calls for hard work to correct abuses which have crept in and to restore the veneration of the saints to ample praise of God in Christ. Significantly, it exhorts: "Let the faithful be taught, therefore, that the authentic cult of the saints consists not so much in the multiplying of external acts, but rather in the intensity of our active love."[39] Provided it is understood in the light of faith, communion with those in heaven serves but to enrich our worship and service of God through Christ in the Spirit. The council's Constitution on the Sacred Liturgy translates these exhortations into concrete directives. Saints' feasts proclaim the victory of Jesus Christ's paschal mystery in them and set an example before us. Consequently, feasts of Christ take precedence over those of the saints; the number of universal feasts of the saints is to be pruned; private devotions should be harmonized with the liturgy which far surpasses any of them.[40]

To sum up, *Lumen Gentium*'s chapter 7 weaves biblical and traditional ideas into a new and appealing idiom in light of its teaching on the church as the people of God called to be holy. Its theology of the saints is centered in God, based on the vital, Spirit-filled community of all disciples who are following Christ, and pointed toward the hope of future *shalom*. Remembering the saints brings the blessings of encouragement and good example and issues in the praise of God, ancient themes already emphasized by the Reformers. Even where the text affirms the intercession of the saints, it ultimately envisions the saints in glory praying with and for those on earth in a great chorus of praise of God. Eschewed altogether is any explicit mention of the term or idea of patronage, except in references to Trent, and it would appear that the excesses the council warns against have clustered around practices associated with the patron-client model. In its place, the text appeals to the existential experience of companionship, partnership, friendship, and collaboration known by people in their life and worship in the church. In a summary sentence the text explains, "just as Christian communion among wayfarers brings us closer to Christ, so our companionship with the saints joins us to Christ, from whom as from their fountain and head issue every grace and the life of God's people itself."[41] In terms of the two models we have been tracking this is a clear favoring of the companionship model, seeing communion with one another in mutual love as the "deepest vocation" of the church and a way that believers have a foretaste of the joy to come.[42]

Gleanings

These two historic efforts at reform offer key insights for a contemporary reading of the communion of saints. After a millennium of honoring holy people whose lives configured them to Jesus Christ, exuberant variations on devotional acts throughout the Middle Ages coupled with increased worry over salvation and attendant practices of indulgences, Masses, and prayers for the dead had dimmed the original meaning of the communion of saints. It seems clear that the abuses criticized by the Reformers were the result of the patronage model run wild. Furthermore, in historical context, their interpretation that the practice of invoking the saints placed these intercessors between needy believers and the mercy of God in Christ must be judged to be fundamentally correct. In a positive vein, the Reformation's endorsement of the holiness of all the baptized and the community of mutual regard between the living and the dead brought to the fore a rediscovery of the ancient companionship model in accord with biblical sensibility and the age of the early martyrs. Unfortunately, in the subsequent hostilities, this rediscovery was lost again for all practical purposes. A historic opportunity to develop the communion of saints in a collegial way both doctrinally and in practice was missed. We get only a glimpse of what could be. Nevertheless, it is still a glimpse — a small coin of insight.

Meanwhile, although the reforms of Trent succeeded in reigning in the more egregious abuses, Catholic theology did not investigate the fundamental premises upon which devotion to the saints was based. In the heat of battle it defended the patronage model as if it were the only possible way to honor the saints, and ever new practices aligned with this pattern arose in the following centuries. In its own way, however, this theology did succeed in maintaining a sense of the connection between the living and the dead in Christ, even if the relationship was structured according to hierarchical patronage. It also insisted on the reality of the saints' intercessory prayer for the church and the consequent validity of calling upon them in prayer, ideas which can find new meaning when transposed to a companionship model.

The teaching of Vatican II restores the companionship model to the forefront of theology, and does so with a zest that results from a deep shift in its theology of the church. Specifically, the profound connection that *Lumen Gentium* forges between the people of God, called to be holy, and those faithful friends of God already in glory articulates the biblical and early martyrs' pattern in a new idiom. Far from being isolated patrons, saints in heaven are enfolded into the whole people of God as companions in Christ who are the beginning of the great harvest. Their example as fellow pilgrims has left us a bright pattern of holiness; having reached the end of the journey, they now signal to us what lies ahead. Remembering them strengthens hope as the community forges ahead in the struggle of history; joining with their praise of God enriches our own worship. This ecclesial sense of the communion of saints is ushered into an even greater plenitude of meaning through the council's vision of all peoples and the whole world itself being re-deemed and renewed by the gracious mercy of God, for *communio* defines not only the basic calling and destiny of the church but also of all peoples and the whole world as God created and calls it to be. The communion of saints therefore functions as a symbol of redemptive communion in the sacred that is as broad and deep as history itself.

Basic rudiments needed for a contemporary theology of the communion of saints find a place in this conciliar teaching, although they are not systematized: the universality of the communion among people, the possibility of holiness in ordinary and secular situations, paradigmatic figures as companions, relationship through memory and hope, and the inclusion of the cosmic world. Furthermore, the theocentric view of the saints as fellow travelers in whom we are shown God's presence, face, and voice has powerful implications for inclusive theologies from the perspective of those marginalized by race, class, and gender. In this ecumenical age, a vast field of experimentation lies ahead as Anglican and some Protestant churches now seek appropriate ways to restore the lost practice of an annual sanctoral cycle,[43] while Catholic conciliar teaching turns veneration of the saints in a more evangelical direction.[44] At the same time, by tracing how the Reformation and Vatican II each glimpsed the original Christian intuition of a community of the friends of God and prophets, living and dead, united in the Spirit of Christ, we have minted new insight for our task.

Chapter 7

Serenely Free

Our trek through the historical permutations of the communion of saints makes clear that this is one belief never long separated from devotional practice. Given that theological theory is so intertwined with religious practice in this instance, we will conclude our dialogue with history by considering two traditionally contentious questions: whether practices of venerating the saints in general are actually required, and what the particular practice of invoking the saints might intelligibly mean. If it can be established that a zone of legitimate freedom exists in these areas, then room for creative rethinking and new practice opens up in tranquillity.

Good and Useful — but Not Necessary

Is it required that Christian people, and in particular Catholics, venerate the saints and Mary? This is not a question about belief. Since the communion of saints is confessed in the creed, it forms part of the doctrine of God's saving concern to which those who profess the creed entrust their lives. But is the overt practice of honoring the saints mandatory, either in the theological sense of being necessary for salvation or in the more juridical sense of being an obligation which Catholics assume with membership in the church?

A heritage of consensus on this question has wisdom to contribute that may be surprising in view of traditional practice. The answer hinges on a technical distinction that theology has long made between the public, liturgical prayer of the church as a community of faith and the private prayer of local groups or individual persons. Officially the church venerates the saints in its public liturgy, the paramount instance being the celebration of the Eucharist. In every eucharistic prayer of the Catholic Church, in the context of thanks to God for the life, death, and resurrection of Jesus Christ made present around the shared table, the church calls to mind the memory of all who have died in God's friendship including, in some combination, Mary, the apostles, the martyrs, and all the saints. In their company the assembled community praises God's glory and sets its hopes on sharing with them in this glory forever. In addition to this daily eucharistic remembrance, a calendar of annual feast days brings particular saints to mind in the course of the year. There are also some few occasions such as the great Easter Vigil and the sacraments of baptism and ordination when the Litany of the Saints is prayed in the context of prayer addressed to God through Jesus Christ in the Spirit. Insofar as they participate in this daily, weekly, annual, or occasional public prayer, individual persons participate in honoring the memory of the saints. Nowhere are they bound to more than this public liturgical remembrance, which is considered the highest form of veneration because it is a component of the direct worship of God. If there is any obligation attached to honoring the saints, it resides in the requirement that an individual not repudiate this public veneration of the church's liturgy.

As for private veneration of the saints by groups or individuals, this is encouraged but nowhere mandated as a requirement of conscience. Official church teaching and law do not hold that the individual believer must of necessity honor the saints or Mary in one's own personal prayer or in nonliturgical communal practices of piety. Whereas the advantages of honoring the saints are pointed out in some official exhortations, preaching, and spiritual books, the matter is left to personal discretion. For this is a matter of spirituality, and the Spirit leads people in diverse ways, as the multifaceted history of Christian spirituality makes clear.

A brief review finds that a number of sources traditionally consulted by Catholic theology support this conclusion both explicitly and by the argument from silence.

Scripture

There is no text in the Bible that could be even remotely construed as mandating the practice of invoking the saints.

Early Christian Tradition

Neither do the creeds, liturgies, conciliar teachings, or theological writings of the first Christian centuries make this a requirement.

Teaching of Councils

The twenty-fifth and last session of the Council of Trent dealt with
this issue in the decree "On the Invocation, Veneration, and Relics of
Saints, and on Sacred Images." Previous to this decree in its teaching on the Mass, the council had clarified the point that sacrifice is
not offered to the saints but to God alone who crowns their efforts.[1]
Now attention is turned to the customs of piety that had been matters of dispute with the Reformers, especially the practice of invoking
the saints or calling upon them for prayers and favors. The key passage states that bishops and other pastoral leaders should diligently
teach the faithful that (1) the saints who are with Christ pray to God
for us; that (2) it is good and beneficial to call upon their prayers in
order to obtain benefits from God through Jesus Christ who alone is
our savior and redeemer; and that (3) those who think otherwise are
thinking impiously. Here the practice of invoking the saints is being
defended, but it is not being laid on consciences as a requirement. "It
is good and useful [bonum atque utile] suppliantly to invoke them"[2] —
such language affixes a value and implicitly encourages such practice,
but does not make a necessity of it. This is the virtually unanimous
opinion of Trent's interpreters. Kretschmer and Laurentin's ecumenical
commentary is typical, commenting that while Trent did indeed defend
the legitimacy of practices which the Reformation rejected, it did not
make them obligatory.[3]

The Second Vatican Council delineates a much broader theology of
the saints and Mary, enfolding them into its vision of the church as
the holy people of God. As persons who have shared our humanity in
the struggle of history, they reveal God's face and voice, give splendid
examples of the following of Christ, and signal to the pilgrim church
that it is worthwhile to hope. In response, according to Lumen Gentium, it is "supremely fitting"[4] for the living to love these friends of
Christ, to thank God for them, to imitate their discipleship, and to ask
them to pray to God for us. This is the key phrase for our inquiry,
and it clearly employs a rhetoric of persuasion. Honoring the saints
would be very much an appropriate behavior. But fittingness does
not imply obligation. This interpretation is buttressed by the council's document on the liturgy, concerned with connecting the central
act of praise in the Eucharist to the vast outpouring and diversity of
personal and communal prayer practices. "Popular devotions of the
Christian people are warmly commended," it declares, "provided they

accord with the norms and laws of the church."[5] Nevertheless, the teaching goes on, these devotions should be so drawn up that they harmonize with the liturgical seasons, cohere with liturgical prayer, and lead people to the shared table, for this is at the center of Christian life. Again, not only is there no obligation but an explicit ordering of values in which devotional practice does not have an essential place, although it is commended. In keeping with its pastoral concern, furthermore, the council calls for a correction of abuses, excesses, or defects that have cropped up in the veneration of the saints, emphasizing the value of active love in imitation of the saints' example. This principle is also reiterated with regard to the veneration of Mary. Exhorting people to avoid the opposite excesses of false exaggeration and narrow-mindedness, the council urges all to remember that in honoring Mary "true devotion consists neither in fruitless and passing emotion, nor in a certain vain credulity. Rather, it proceeds from true faith by which we are led to know the excellence of the Mother of God, and are moved to a filial love toward our mother and to the imitation of her virtues."[6] The obvious intent of these texts is to teach, guide, and persuade the community about the value of remembering the saints and Mary and the proper way to honor them. Publicly the church is committed to do this, and it invites individual members to join in. With regard to necessity, however, the council cannot be construed as teaching that honoring the saints or Mary is required as a practice of personal piety.

Canon Law

Echoes of Trent can be heard again in the 1917 version of the *Code of Canon Law* which dealt with "The Cult of the Saints, of Sacred Images, and of Relics" in fourteen separate canons. The first simply notes that practices of devotion such as invoking the saints or venerating their images and relics are "good and useful";[7] the other thirteen set parameters to the use of images and other expressions of public honor. The 1993 revision of the *Code* reduces the number of canons dealing with veneration of the saints to five. The first one relates to the question of obligation. To foster the sanctification of the people, the church commends (*commendat*) the Blessed Virgin Mary to the special and filial veneration of all the faithful; the church also promotes (*promovet*) the authentic veneration of the other saints who help the faithful by their example and their prayers.[8] The language of this and subsequent canons highlights the church's public position on veneration and is clearly designed to encourage responsible private practice on the part of individuals. Nowhere in the law, however, is an obligation laid on consciences in this regard. Recommendation is not requirement.

Pre-Vatican II Manuals of Theology

Veneration of the saints and Mary was seldom matter for more than passing theological discussion in these books, used in the education of seminarians and thus influential in the daily life of the church. The authors of theology manuals and encyclopedia articles ordinarily taught simply that it is "good and useful" to venerate the saints and Mary. Most of their attention was taken up with explaining the distinctions between the adoration due to God alone (*latria*), the honor due the saints (*dulia*), and the special honor due to Mary as Mother of God (*hyperdulia*). Regarding the question of necessity, the authors usually restricted themselves to the statement that the veneration of the saints does not fall under a positive precept and is not necessary for salvation. A typical statement is that of the 1913 manual by C. Pesch: "We ought absolutely to pray to God; it is not absolutely necessary to invoke the saints, but it is respectable and beneficial to do so."[9] To this teaching the author ascribes the theological note *de fide,* thus giving it the strongest weight of doctrinal authority possible. In other words, regarding calling upon the saints, it is absolutely certain that one absolutely does not have to do this.

Post-Vatican II Theologians

In the ecumenical climate after the council, the question of the necessity of veneration of the saints and Mary has been addressed with more frequency and directness. Karl Rahner's position is typical of that of many other theologians. The church as a whole in its official life and prayer must venerate the saints, he writes, in order thereby to proclaim the victory of God's grace not just as an ideal or possibility but as a reality in concrete persons. Individuals should not radically and explicitly dissociate themselves from such veneration, especially as it is carried out in the liturgy, in which the church witnesses that the grace of God actually does win out over sin. But insofar as private prayer is concerned, "the veneration of the saints is not in itself laid as an absolute duty upon the individual Christian."[10] Conscious of the mood of many committed Catholic Christians who find such veneration out of synch with their piety, he writes:

Christians of today should certainly not feel bound by a sense of traditionalism to include the veneration of saints as a matter of course in their religious practice. They should feel free to say that although they are prepared to acknowledge the historical significance, and to a certain extent also the example of the major Christian figures, both past and present, they nevertheless do not think that the individual feast days, pilgrimages, new canonizations, exhortations to pray to the saints (especially Mary) and so on, have any relevance for them.[11]

In the clearest possible terms he draws out the implication of conciliar teaching: "The dictum of the Council of Trent that it is 'good and beneficial' to invoke the help of the saints does not however impose on Christians any duty to do so. Rather, it is intended...to give them a measure of freedom in their spiritual lives; they are free to pray to the saints — or not — if they wish."[12]

Herbert Vorgrimler agrees with this position, writing that "the veneration of the saints is licit and useful (Trent), but the church does not teach that it is a duty for the individual."[13] Devoting an entire section of his book on the saints to the issue of necessity, Paul Molinari attests that the public life of the church should include their veneration but that the private prayer of the individual does not require any reference to the saints, all the while arguing that even for the individual, veneration of the saints is a great help toward holiness of life.[14] George Tavard adds another note when he observes, "Apart from joining in this prayer when it occurs liturgically, the Christian faithful have no obligation to pray to specific saints, although in practice many do so, in keeping with their personal devotion. There is no reason to believe that specific saints ought to be invoked for specific purposes, as in the case of the Fourteen Auxiliary Saints of late medieval piety."[15] On the specific question of invocation, Michael Schmaus in his handbook of Catholic dogmatics states that it is a "theologically indefensible exaggeration" to hold that the invocation of Mary is necessary for salvation and that to omit such a practice would be the occasion for not being saved.[16] And on it goes. A recent handbook of Catholic theology expresses the consensus this way: "For the church the veneration of saints is entirely legitimate and important. For individual Christians, however, it is neither a duty nor a necessity for salvation, but it is part of the freedom of individual piety."[17]

After intensive conversation, the theologians of the Lutheran-Catholic dialogue in the United States came to a similar conclusion, all the more noteworthy since this was one of the defining issues over which the church in the West split up. Lutherans queried with some concern as to whether they would be expected to join in invoking the saints if unity with the Catholic Church became a more present reality. The dialogue's "Common Statement" assures them that divergence on this subject need not be church-dividing:

> Precisely because the church regards the invocation of the saints and Mary as "good and beneficial," the individual Catholic is strongly encouraged to make use of, and participate in, such prayers. Many Catholics continue to respond to this encouragement with enthusiasm. But there is no reason for thinking that a person who refrained from personally invoking saints would forfeit full communion with the Catholic Church. This freedom now enjoyed by Catholics would certainly be enjoyed also by Lutherans should a greater degree of communion between the respective churches be achieved.[18]

Papal Teaching

There is an illuminating statement near the end of Paul VI's apostolic letter on Marian veneration that may stand as a summary of the whole tradition on the question of obligation. Setting forth principles for renewing devotion to Mary in the wake of Vatican II, the pope himself gives strong encouragement to the devotional practice of saying the rosary. In paragraph after paragraph he explains and extols the christocentric nature of this prayer, its beauty, its ability to calm the mind, its value for growth in attentiveness to the Spirit, and its potential for integration into family life. In conclusion, the pope recommends that people say the rosary but then cautions that it not be promoted in a way that could be interpreted as one-sided or exclusive. Rather, the nature of the prayer itself should exercise its own attraction: "The Rosary is an excellent prayer, but the faithful should feel serenely free toward it. Its intrinsic appeal should draw them to calm recitation."[19] Serenely free: even here, in a papal exhortation toward veneration of the Mother of God, respect for the individual conscience is paramount.

The same holds true for the voluminous sermons and writings of John Paul II on Mary, chief among them the meditative encyclical

"Mother of the Redeemer" issued to herald a Marian year. Speaking here not only of doctrine but also of spirituality, the pope takes pleased note of new manifestations of love for the mother of the Redeemer emerging in our time and recommends this piety to all. After limning a dramatic vision of Mary present to help in the midst of the constant struggle between good and evil in history, the encyclical ends with a fervent wish: "I hope with all my heart that the reflections contained in the present encyclical will also serve to renew this vision in the hearts of all believers."[20] This again is the rhetoric of persuasion, seeking to move hearts and minds to share a certain outlook judged to be theologically valuable and pastorally effective. In keeping with tradition, however, there is no suggestion that this vision is mandatory for full participation in the life of faith.

To sum up, a survey of traditional sources shows that venerating the saints and Mary is an element in the public witness of the church in which individual persons de facto share by their involvement in liturgical worship. While also encouraged to honor the saints and Mary in their personal prayer and nonliturgical communal rituals, individuals are free to do so or not, as they are led by the Spirit. No one is ever required to do so privately either as a necessary act in order to be saved or as a particular requirement for membership in the church. This conclusion is supported by conciliar and papal teaching, canon law, and traditional and contemporary theology.

The intent of this survey has not been to advocate abandoning veneration of the saints and Mary. In light of misunderstandings of the subject, however, it is important to be clear about just how wide the zone of freedom of individual conscience extends. If a particular climate of spirituality tilts a local church into an orbit where a certain diminishment occurs, such as has happened in communities within modern/postmodern culture, this does not necessarily mean that something is amiss. It can indicate a lack of fit between the contemporary quest for God and the religious forms of another cultural era, which are quietly laid aside in favor of a concentration on essential matters in accord with biblical patterns of faith amid the struggles of history. By such nonpractice persons are exercising a freedom of conscience which is appropriately theirs, according to the temper of their own time and place. Precisely here, though, the situation is also ripe for the creation of new approaches to the communion of saints and consequent theologizing. For what account does the present generation give of the struggle, creativity, and fidelity, by the grace of

God, of those who have gone before them? The answer contains an implicit evaluation of the worth of its own life as a community of faith.

Pray for Us

In our exploration into the question of requirement, the practice of invoking the saints, that is, calling upon them for their prayer on our behalf, was used with regular frequency as an example of venerating the saints. In fact, invocation has traditionally been such an outstanding characteristic of devotion to the saints in the patronage model, which by nature requires petition in order for the relationship to be actualized, that its absence could be equated with lack of belief in the communion of saints. This is not the case, as liturgical remembrance of the saints makes clear; there, the community names the saints in prayer that is addressed to the holy God in gratitude for their lives and in hope of sharing their destiny. But asking the saints for their prayer or even for direct favors has marked customary usage for centuries.

At least three serious criticisms have been brought to bear against this practice. The classic Protestant critique judges that its danger lies in transferring the heart's trust from Jesus Christ who alone is the merciful Savior to other persons who are needed to bridge the gulf between unworthy sinners and the just Judge. But this is to distort the basic structure of Christian faith, in which the heart clings to God's mercy freely and abundantly poured out through the cross, without need of other intercessors. In addition, the basic feminist critique of dominant-subordinate relationships finds in this practice an instance of just such a bond, typically relating as it does a dependent petitioner to powerful patron. Not only does this imply the distance of a monarchical God to whom access is limited except for the privileged few, but within a patronage model it also robs women of a sense of their own sacred power, giving them a borrowed power at best, thus oppressing rather than liberating them in the Spirit. Thirdly, modern/postmodern Christian reflection, intensely aware of the unknown character of what lies beyond death and cognizant that there can be no direct communication between the living and the dead, sees the practice of invocation as spiritually deficient in yet another way. With a kind of naive imagination this practice seems to assume a relationship with a host of invisible persons who are cognizant of what people on earth are doing and saying; but this is precisely what we are unable to know. Silence is the more respectful stance.

In the face of these critiques, should the practice be totally abandoned? Or is there any sense in which calling on the saints in prayer could be meaningful, even within ecumenical, feminist, and modern/postmodern Christian consciousness? The clue to an answer is found in the original pattern of relationship between the living and the dead as a companionship in grace.

Recall that Scripture encourages persons to pray for all human beings and for specific needs and is replete with examples of people praying for each other. Paul ends one letter with "brothers and sisters, pray for us";[21] in another he assures them "I always pray for you."[22] Such prayer functions as a key way of expressing love and concern for others in what pertains to their earthly well-being and ultimate salvation. Nor is this person-for-person intercession among the living in conflict with the prayer of Jesus Christ who, having drawn near to God, "always lives to make intercession for them";[23] rather, it is called into being by God's grace as a way of participating in that prayer of Christ. Recall further that building on this underlying sense of things, the age of the martyrs extended prayer for each other on earth into heaven with the idea that the martyrs joined with their risen Savior in continuing to pray for those still struggling on the way to their joy. Cemetery graffiti inscribing a request for their prayer — "Vincent, you are in Christ, pray for Phoebe," "Januaria... pray for us" — are but one expression of a strong sense of connection in a community of mutual regard. Here we come to the nub of the question of meaning. If living persons can and do ask each other for the encouragement of prayer, must that stop when persons die?

If we understand relationship between the living and the dead embraced in God's life to be structured along the lines of the companionship model, then saints in heaven are not situated *between* believers and Christ in a hierarchy of patronage, but are *with* their companions on earth in one community of grace. Then calling on a saint in heaven to "pray for us" is one particular, limited, concrete expression of this solidarity in the Spirit, through the ages and across various modes of human existence. We remember these friends of God and prophets definitively with Christ and ask them to remember before God their sisters and brothers who are still on the way: thus the bond of *koinonia* is activated. In this act, living disciples are simultaneously encouraged to struggle on in hope and strengthened in their relationship of immediacy with God.

This sense of how invocation "works" was captured by the nineteenth-century American philosopher Orestes Brownson, who decided to join the Catholic Church in his adult years. In a revealing passage, this thinker formed in the Reformation tradition describes how insight into the intelligibility of this practice first struck him:

> What we ask of the saints in glory is only what we may and do ask of one another while living in the flesh. Many years ago, before I had the happiness of being received into the communion of the Catholic Church, I was, as most Protestants who retain some respect for religion are, in the habit of frequently closing my letters to my friends with the words, "pray for me." One day, writing to a very dear friend, but one who was not precisely a saint, I concluded [in this very same way]. I did so from the force of habit, but I had no sooner written the words than a sudden thought struck me, and I exclaimed to myself: "There is the justification of the Catholic practice of invocation of the saints. Here I am asking a sinful mortal to pray for me; how much rather should I ask the prayers of a beatified saint in heaven, always in the presence of God." From that moment to this I have had no difficulty with the invocation of saints, nor hesitated to ask them to pray for me.[24]

Noting that we do not invoke the saints because they are nearer to us than God is, or more compassionate, or more disposed to aid us — indeed, how could they be, for in God alone we live and move and have our being — Brownson goes on to attempt a positive formulation of what goes on in this act of piety:

> We do not ask the saints, not even the blessed Mary, for pardon, for mercy, for grace, or blessings of any sort, as things in their power to grant. We simply ask them to aid us by their prayers, or to intercede to obtain these things for us from God from whom comes every good and perfect gift. . . . What we ask of them is their intercession, or simply their prayers, as human beings united with us in one and the same communion.[25]

United with us in one and the same communion — here is the logic of solidarity undergirding the practice of invocation in the companionship model.

An example of invocation universally if occasionally used in the Catholic Church may serve to illustrate how this works in practice. The litany of the saints is prayed every year during the Easter Vigil as part of the liturgy of baptism. The litany opens with a threefold invocation to Jesus Christ to "have mercy on us." Then follows a roll call of saints; after each name is called, the people respond, "pray for us." First named is Mary, Mother of God; next, Michael and the angels of God; then, a number of biblical holy people such as John the Baptist, Joseph, Peter and Paul, and Mary Magdalene; martyrs such as Ignatius, Perpetua, and Felicity; doctors of the church such as Athanasius, Augustine, Catherine, and Teresa; preachers such as Francis and Dominic; other saints whom a local congregation would find appropriate to name; and finally "all holy men and women." The litany continues with a series of petitions directed to Christ to deliver the people from all evil, sin, and death, and to save them by his death, resurrection, and gift of the Holy Spirit. It concludes with a global petition: "Christ, hear us; Lord Jesus, hear our prayer."

Singing one's way through this litany on the festal occasion of Easter night gives rise to the realization that the church is much more universal than this particular congregation gathered at this particular time. Our ancestors in the faith, all of whom had their hearts set on Christ, form a great cloud of witnesses that widens our assembly. Now forever with God, their lives and prayer are of benefit for us who are still on the journey. Summoning the memory of particular ones by name out of the unnumbered multitude and asking them to "pray for us" has the effect of strengthening bonds of persons today with the whole holy people of God throughout time, thereby deepening union with God in Christ. As the movement of the litany from Christ to the saints and back to Christ implies, it is not a matter of the saints functioning as intermediary patrons but of everyone connected in mutual regard in the great company of the friends of God and prophets: "we rejoice for them, they pray for us.... Yet do we all serve one Lord, ... follow after the one love."[26]

Interpreting invocation of the saints within the companionship model of the communion of saints allows a measure of response to the criticisms rightly levied against its practice in the patronage model. To Reformation commitment that Christ not be overshadowed: the saints are not petitioned as intermediaries with a judgmental Christ but addressed as codisciples in a small act that strengthens bonds of fellowship in grace across the generations. To feminist passion for relationships of mutuality: rather than casting one into the dependent, subordinate position of petitioner typical of patriarchal elitism, invocation activates mutual regard and provides a vehicle for leaning on and being supported by the saving solidarity among all the friends of God and prophets. To postmodern spiritual agnosticism: read as symbolic rather than literal address, calling the other by name with a request for prayer is a concrete act by which we join our lives with the prayer of all who have gone before us in common yearning for God. Within the companionship model, invocation of any saint, in Rahner's luminous words, "is always the invocation of *all* the saints, i.e., an act by which we take refuge in faith in the all-enfolding community of all the redeemed."[27] We dive into the whole company of saints through a single categorical deed.

Keeping in mind the freedom that exists with regard to any individual devotional practice, we conclude that invoking the saints is but one way to honor the saints, certainly not the most important way, not even essential. When enacted within the logic of solidarity in a community of grace, it is a prayer form that activates the bonds of companionship between wayfarers and saints in heaven. In the world of grace as in nature, everyone depends on everyone else, and the courage, witness, and love of one person affects the whole body, as indeed does everyone's apathy and sin. Calling on this cloud of witnesses for their prayer recognizes and actualizes this affiliation between our lives in a spirit of appreciation. In turn, the dynamism of this mutual *koinonia,* called into being by the work of life-giving Spirit-Sophia, far from being a distraction, deepens our communion with the mystery of God in Christ. Apart from this the practice becomes deeply problematic; in this perspective, it has a modicum of meaning.

Final Gleanings

In canvassing the Christian heritage of the saints we have culled a number of insights useful for contemporary understanding. It is most interesting to observe how two worldviews have remained in tension throughout the history of the tradition. On the one hand is the idea of the equality in diversity of all the disciples of Jesus through the grace-filled blessing of the Spirit. On the other hand are the social and mental structures of patriarchal hierarchy that skew the circle of companions into a pyramid of dominant-subordinate relations. These two patterns of recognizing and structuring the communion of saints have consistently contended, with the patriarchal model most often emerging as officially endorsed, yet frequently in danger of being subverted by the rediscovery of sacredness "from below."

Gleanings from Scripture and tradition yield the following elements.

• The biblical conception of the holy people of God, based on a central affirmation of the Jewish tradition, is fundamentally egalitarian. Through sharing in the bread and cup of salvation, all the members of the Christian community are saints, participating in the holiness of God now experienced through the life, death, and resurrection of Jesus Christ. Those who have died form a cloud of witnesses in whose company the living find encouragement to run the race. A good case can be made that this equality before God has social and political implications for life together.

• The age of the martyrs added new names to the biblical list of witnesses. In this setting, particular persons whose life and death distilled the central values of the community in concrete and accessible form are remembered with joy and gratitude. From them the living community gains lessons of encouragement and inspiring example; together they form a company of companions in hope.

• Inculturation of the church within the Roman system of patronage led to a fundamental shift in the people's relationship to saints in heaven according to the same model. Sanctity is now attributed less to the church as a whole and more to exceptional personalities. Saints become a religiously defined human elite among the dead, an exception rather than the rule, with power to mediate the presence and healing work of God. In theology and piety they are seen as advocates pleading their clients' causes before a stern, divine judge, and as mediators who bring divine presence closer to unworthy, needy people. Saints evolve from witnesses to intercessors.

Thus were created two categories of Christians, the one morally superior and capable of miraculous powers, the other their needy clients, far from the sacred. Lest painting history in too bold a stroke should produce caricature, it should be remembered that even early in the age of the martyrs, when companionship was the norm, the holy dead were asked to "pray for" those still on the way, though this did not imply patronage; and even as the patronage model waxed and grew strong, it continued to cast saints as invisible friends who supported those who were struggling. But the model had in fact radically shifted. The result cast the biblical and early Christian vision, fundamentally egalitarian and inclusive, into deep shadow and in the course of time rendered it virtually unintelligible to great numbers of people.

• The interplay of the companionship and patronage models forms the warp and woof of subsequent centuries. The addition of the term *communio sanctorum* into the Apostles' Creed and the celebration of a festival day honoring All Saints encodes the companionship model into official teaching. The creedal term holds a fruitful ambiguity inasmuch as it can refer to a communion in sacred things as well as among holy people. The feast itself is subversive of elitism, proclaiming the victory of grace in the lives of innumerable anonymous ancestors. Meanwhile the process of canonization makes saints into an exceptional group that increasingly resembled an aristocratic class of patrons, most often male and clerical.

• Hewing to Scripture alone as a theological method, the Reformation rediscovers the abundant mercy of God in Christ and consequently the church as the holy people of God. Although saints are honored for their witness as examples of the grace of God, invocation is forbidden for it transfers trust to saints that belongs to Christ alone.

• Returning to ancient sources, the Second Vatican Council likewise rediscovers the church as a people universally called to holiness thanks to the grace of God in Christ. In the wake of this theology, saints are seen once again as companions in hope and appreciated for their example, their witness, and their prayer. In a unique theocentric interpretation, they are said to reveal God's face, voice, and presence. In their company the church worships God.

• At no time has veneration of the saints been compulsory in the private prayer or spiritual practice of individuals or groups. Insofar as the liturgy commemorates saints, persons do so also as part of the praying community; for the rest, they are led by the Spirit who blows where she wills. Invocation of the saints, so linked with patronage, can find a renewed if limited meaning when practiced within a *koinonia* of equal disciples.

◆ ◆ ◆

The fruit of this search through the Christian heritage of the saints fills our basket with insights and possibilities for reinterpretation. In our assessment through the lens of feminist theology, one idea stands out unmistakably and surprisingly clearly (I did not expect this at the outset of my research), namely, the existence of two contrasting models of relationship between the living and the dead in Christ, either companions together or patrons-petitioners. Although it has predominated throughout history, the patronage model is inadequate, even counterproductive, for use in a contemporary reading of the communion of saints, given its intrinsic link with patriarchal hierarchy in image, theory, and practice. It overlooks the basic gift of holiness given by the Spirit to the community as a whole, including and especially women; it eviscerates women's sense of their spiritual dignity and power before God, casting them into the role of needy petitioners; it constitutes an element in the ecclesiastical oppression of women, modeling male-defined holiness and feminine virtues conducive to subordination.

But a scan of tradition shows that this is not the only option. In rereading the communion of saints feminist theology does not have to make something up out of whole cloth, for a different, egalitarian understanding also exists and awaits retrieval. Present in Scripture, the experience of the early martyrs, creed, liturgy, reformation, and council, the belief runs through the Christian churches, however strongly or weakly, that there is an interlocking community of equal companions in grace that extends across the world and beyond death. It is a kinship in hope that demonstrates the continuous movement of the Spirit of God in all times and places and peoples and cultures; a *koinonia* that demonstrates that the creed is not an abstraction but comes to birth in a continuous river of holy lives; a company of the friends of God and prophets today, in the past, and in the future. How, then, to make contemporary theological meaning of this?

Part III

Theology of the Friends of God and Prophets

– Chapter 8 –

Women's Practices of Memory

Dialogue with history has given us light to steer by as we explore a contemporary meaning of the doctrinal symbol of the communion of saints. We seek an interpretation, first of all, that includes all God-seekers living today as friends of God and prophets and, since this is a specifically Christian symbol, the whole community of the church as sharing in this calling in a Christian way. In the context of secular culture that eschews relationship with the dead, our interpretation also quests for vital links that will connect the living and the dead without embarrassment, so that past generations now alive in God can be included. In both instances, we track a core relationship among the living and between the living and the dead that is one of companionship rather than any kind of dominant-subordinate pattern. And our horizon of interpretation expands beyond the human world to include the natural world in the community of what is holy and blessed by the Spirit of God. Our reading of the communion of saints, finally, searches for a liberating and nourishing outcome, empowering women in the struggle for their own freedom and dignity, inspiring the *ekklesia* to grow as a living community of memory and hope, and promoting the transformation of church and society in accord with God's compassionate justice and care.

Among these interpretive goals, the vector of the relationship between the living and those who have died calls for particular attention, given secular culture's alienation from the realm of the afterlife. Critical thought in this culture precludes a naive imagination regarding the status of the dead, but relationship in the Spirit with previous generations can still be established and maintained through memory and hope. As already indicated when framing the question in chapter 2, I find it a distinct and intriguing possibility that the current resurgence of historical research focused on women and the reception of this scholarship in women's lives might provide a limited but valuable key to one avenue of connection, that of memory. Accordingly, this chapter begins a systematic interpretation of the communion of saints by using this key, exploring four examples of women's practices of memory. As these practices recover lost memory, rectify distortion, reassess value, and respeak the silence surrounding women's lives before God, the fruitfulness of the connection between feminist scholarship and the communion of saints begins to be evident.

Recovering Lost Memory: Hagar

The story of Hagar, recounted in the first book of the Hebrew Scriptures and used as an analogy in the Christian Scriptures, has long been overlooked in preaching and teaching because it does not fit neatly into themes of divine liberation and covenant. It is no accident that contemporary recovery of her memory proceeds from the perspective of women who are poor, outsiders, and objects of repression even by other women. Hagar is an Egyptian slave-woman far from home.[1] Pressed into service as Sarah's maid, she mothers Ishmael, Abraham's first child. Twice she is driven into the desert by Sarah's harsh abuse; the first time, an experience of theophany leads her to return so that the child with whom she is pregnant will survive; the second time, near death, both she and her child are rescued with a divine word of promise for their future. In terms of divine-human encounter, Hagar's exchanges are paradigmatic. To her the voice of God pledges: "I will so greatly multiply your offspring that they cannot be counted for multitude,"[2] and later, "Do not be afraid."[3] In turn, she is the first woman in the Bible to dare to name the Holy One: "So she named the Lord who spoke to her, 'You are El-roi' [the God who sees, or the Living One who sees me]; for she said, 'Have I really seen God and remained alive...?"[4] The last we see of Hagar she is finding a wife for her free and defiant son from among her own people, thus ensuring a burgeoning of divine promise in the continuity of her line. The ambiguity of divine blessing is obvious even here, however, as the biblical narrative identifies Sarah's son Isaac as alone the bearer of the promise of the covenant.

From the first, Christian interpretation spun her story to the periphery of interest. During the circumcision fight, Paul developed an allegory that contrasted Hagar's progeny with Sarah's offspring, identifying Hagar with subjection to the law and the flesh while Sarah corresponds to freedom and the spirit. His conclusion, "we are children not of the slave but of the free woman,"[5] buttresses the theological argument against Christian continuation of the Jewish practice of circumcision. This reinterpretation of Hagar's symbolic significance traditionally removes any impulse of the community to identify with her narrative. But how different the result when these texts are read from the social location of poor and oppressed women.

Hagar's condition of being enslaved far from her own culture and people, her miserable treatment at the hands of her mistress, the textual fact that both their stories are satellite to the "great man" around whom the story revolves, her life-threatening sojourns in the wilderness, and her will to survive despite it all create an immediate resonance among women whose lives are similarly laden with social and economic suffering. But far from her narrative being pressed into service as a law-gospel allegory, it is read to bring the injustice of her situation and the strength of her character to light.

Almost invariably, African-American women's haunting interpretations of this story evoke the painful history of race relations between black and white women. Entitling this story "A Mistress, a Maid, and No Mercy," Renita Weems writes that "for black women, Hagar's story is peculiarly familiar. It is as if we know it by heart.... The truth is, very few black women manage to make it through adulthood without a footlocker of hurtful memories of encounters with white women.... We must remember this story for its piercing portrayal of one woman's exploitation of another woman."[6] The devastating effects of economic and class stratification coupled with the prejudice of race relations, both embedded in the tensions erupting between women in patriarchal society where ruling men and the begetting of their sons are of prime importance, make this a story whose sorrow cannot be denied. In and through all of this pain, Delores Williams argues, the result of Hagar's first encounter with God is precisely *not* liberation. The appalling instruction from the angel of the Lord to "return to your mistress and submit to her"[7] indicates a strategy for sheer survival amid desperate circumstances; nothing more, but also nothing less. In Hagar's second encounter, God gives her new vision to see resources for survival where she had seen none before: a well of water in the desert for herself and her wailing, dying child to drink. In both instances she was not rescued from her environment, as the Hebrew slaves were later to be liberated from Egypt. Rather, through encountering the Holy One she found ways to survive and create a future even as the oppressive situation persisted. In a litany of pain and strength, Delores Williams points out that while chattel slavery in the United States has ended, thus removing the situation where black women served as surrogates for the physical and reproductive labor of white women, even today, "most of Hagar's situation is congruent with many African-American women's predicament of poverty, sexual and economic exploitation, surrogacy, domestic violence, homelessness, rape, motherhood, single-parenting, ethnicity and meetings with God. Many black women have testified that 'God helped them make a way out of no way.' "[8] Rather than conclude that God has abandoned them if liberation does not arrive, their sense that God is here with them "nevertheless" grounds the strength and wits needed to survive and build a better quality of life in the midst of dire circumstances. Such is the lens Hagar's narrative offers to the journey of black women still in the wilderness.

Women in other political and social circumstances of oppression also find this narrative a prime instance of women's gritty experience and religious determination amid the interlocking of sexism, racism, and classism that continues to affect their own lives. In Latin America, the situation of Hagar's poverty and servitude, the struggle she mounts as a single mother abandoned by her husband, and the hope against hope inspired by her encounters with God cause poor women to cherish her memory.[9] In Africa, the social structure of polygamy sheds light on the Hagar-Sarah rivalry, which in turn illuminates the exploitation of a subordinate woman by a privileged woman in the shadow of the great man; the story encourages women whose lives are played out on the same confining grid of patriarchal structures.[10] Asian women identify with Hagar's struggle as a foreign domestic servant, ill-used and far from home, and with her efforts to maintain her cultural identity despite enslavement. In Judith Gallares's reading, Hagar today is the Filipina domestic servant thrown out of the house by her mistress because she bears a child by her master whom she was powerless to resist; taken as an object, discarded as an object, she is the thousands of Pakistani girls working in rich or middle-class homes who end up abused and exploited by the men of these houses, their male children taken as sons but their female children often suffocated; she is the Asian woman in an Arab household working to send economic relief to the family in poverty back home but suffering sexual assault and physical abuse along the way.[11] Asian theologian Kwok Pui-Lan neatly summarizes the situation: "It seems that African-Americans focus on Hagar as a slave woman, the Latin Americans stress that she was poor, the Africans underscore the fate of Hagar in polygamy, and Asians emphasize the loss of cultural identity. Each group observes a certain analogy between the oppression of Hagar and their own situation."[12]

It is obvious that these parallels emerge when the narrative is told from the underside of history through the faithful intelligence of women struggling to survive. The analogy between their experience and the social relationships in the biblical text opens up new insight into the way divine purpose might be effective in the world. Women and men of privileged races and classes, hearing this story of an oppressed and rejected woman who nevertheless is an extraordinary figure in the history of faith, hear a summons to radical conversion of heart and mind. For the story with all of its strickenness continues in every foreign worker deprived of personal power, every woman oppressed by another, every outsider to a religious tradition who nevertheless seeks a life with her God.

Most terrible of all, there is no neat religious solution. Phyllis Trible concludes her telling of the desolation of Hagar with the insight that she is a contrasting, mirror image of Israel's pilgrimage of faith: "As a maid in bondage she flees from suffering. Yet she experiences exodus without liberation, revelation without salvation, wilderness without covenant, wanderings without land, promise without fulfillment, and unmerited exile without return."[13] True, she is a pivotal figure in biblical theology, hearing an annunciation about the conception of her child, receiving a divine promise of descendants, and daring to name the deity. Despite her torment, she keeps on making a way where there is no way. But in the text she is the consummate outsider, suffering so that a religiously privileged couple can succeed, and in subsequent tradition her extraordinary role in the story of faith has been marginalized beyond general recognition. "All we who are heirs of Sarah and Abraham, by flesh and spirit," writes Trible, "must answer for the terror in Hagar's story. To neglect the theological challenge she presents is to falsify faith."[14]

This example of Hagar illustrates one front on which women's practices of memory are working. Hagar is certainly in the biblical text; her suffering is profound; her wits are keen; her encounters with the divine are groundbreaking. Yet the prevailing voice of interpretation has made her virtually invisible. Recovering the lost memory of her creative striving to survive interrupts dominant discourse. It demands that the corporate memory of the *ekklesia* make room for the female, the foreigner, the one in servitude, the religious stranger — and the person who is all four — as a vital player in the history of humanity with

God. By bringing Hagar visibly into the cloud of witnesses, it lifts up a source of lament and resistance as well as strength and inspiration for all who remember her name.

Rectifying the Distorted Story: Mary Magdalene

Feminist interpretation of the story of Miriam of Magdala demonstrates another practice of memory that operates to set the record straight. Recounted in all four canonical gospels and in later extrabiblical texts such as the "Gospel of Mary," the contributions of this woman to the ministry of Jesus, her fidelity during his crucifixion, and her leadership as first apostolic witness to the resurrection place her in a pivotal role at the foundation of the *ekklesia*. Yet centuries of patriarchal construal in literature, art, and preaching have depicted Magdalene primarily as a repentant sinner, most likely a prostitute, forgiven by Jesus for sins of a sexual nature. There is an ethical issue here, for the distortion that shifts the story of a leading apostolic woman into someone remembered mainly as a sexual transgressor is a deep untruth. A powerful religious leader is turned into a beautiful, pliant sinner, symbol of female sexuality redeemed. Like all lies, this robs her of the integrity of her own life. It cheats women out of the dangerous memory of her discipleship, leaving them bereft of a key piece of history on which to build resistance to ecclesial male dominance. And it deprives the church as a whole of the prophetic power of the memory of women's leadership.

Rereading the texts, feminist scholarship discerns a different contour to her story.[15] This Mary is among the band of Galilean women who leave their homes to follow Jesus in his itinerant ministry. Luke's gospel describes the situation:

> Soon afterwards he went on through cities and villages, proclaiming and bringing the good news of the kingdom of God. The twelve were with him, as well as some women who had been cured of evil spirits and infirmities: Mary called Magdalene, from whom seven demons had gone out, and Joanna, the wife of Herod's steward Chuza, and Susanna, and many others, who provided for them out of their resources.[16]

In biblical usage the presence of evil spirits most often indicates that a person is ill, perhaps with epilepsy, more likely with mental illness.

Mary Magdalene is evidently a woman in ill health whose interaction with Jesus issues in new vitality; she then joins his ministry as a faithful friend and influential, provident disciple. The position of her name, always listed first among the women in Jesus' company, suggests her leadership function.

This comes clearly to the fore when, the men disciples having gone into hiding, the Galilean women disciples form the moving point of continuity in the narrative of Jesus' death, burial, and resurrection. The way Matthew tells it, together they keep vigil at the cross: "Many women were also there, looking on from a distance; they had followed Jesus from Galilee and had provided for him. Among them were Mary Magdalene, and Mary the mother of James and Joseph, and the mother of the sons of Zebedee."[17] Together they attend Jesus' burial: "[Joseph] then rolled a great stone to the door of the tomb and went away. Mary Magdalene and the other Mary were there, sitting opposite the tomb."[18] And together they discover the empty tomb: "After the sabbath, as the first day of the week was dawning, Mary Magdalene and the other Mary went to see the tomb. And suddenly there was a great earthquake."[19] To them the risen Christ entrusts the experience of his new life: "So they left the tomb quickly with fear and great joy, and ran to tell his disciples. Suddenly Jesus met them and said, 'Greetings.' "[20] And to them Christ conveys the apostolic commission to witness the good news to the eleven and the rest: "Do not be afraid; go and tell my brothers."[21] Luke affirms that "Now it was Mary Magdalene, Joanna, Mary the mother of James, and the other women with them who told this."[22] John singles Magdalene out and paints the encounter between the risen Christ and this beloved disciple in loving detail: "Early on the first day of the week, while it was still dark, Mary Magdalene came to the tomb and saw that the stone had been removed"; following the experience of profound recognition between the weeping woman and the gardener — "Mary," "Rabbouni" — she moves into high apostolic gear: "Mary Magdalene went and announced to the disciples, 'I have seen the Lord'; and she told them that he had said these things to her."[23] Mark synthesizes the result: "Now after he rose early on the first day of the week, he appeared first to Mary Magdalene, from whom he had cast out seven demons. She went out and told those who had been with him, while they were mourning and weeping. But when they heard that he was alive and had been seen by her, they would not believe it."[24]

Remove the witness of the women from the narrative of Jesus' death and resurrection, and the story falls apart. Led by Mary Magdalene, they are the disciples who operate publicly to maintain connections between all segments of this momentous event as well as between Jesus and the men disciples, sequestered in fear and shame. Led by Mary Magdalene, they discover beyond tragedy a new coming of the Spirit and commit their considerable energies to bringing about the resulting vision of a new world.

Extrabiblical writings such as the "Dialogue of the Savior," the "Gospel of Philip," the "Gospel of Thomas," and the "Gospel of Mary" carry this tradition forward in accounts of rivalry between the male disciples and Magdalene over her right to such a leadership position.[25] Elaine Pagels's study of gnostic use of Mary Magdalene, for example, explores the incident in the "Gospel of Mary" when the disciples, terrified by the death of Jesus, encourage Mary Magdalene to help them by relating what things the Lord has taught her. She teaches them assiduously until Peter interrupts in anger, asking, "Did he really speak privately with a woman and not openly to us? Are we to turn about and all listen to her? Did he prefer her to us?" Troubled at his disparagement of her witness and her relationship to Christ, Mary responds, "My brother Peter, what do you think? Do you think that I thought this up myself in my heart, or that I am lying about the Savior?" At this point Levi breaks in to mediate the dispute, consigning Peter to the league of evil powers but defending Mary's role: "Peter, you have always been hot-tempered. Now I see you contending against the woman like the adversaries. But if the Savior made her worthy, who are you, indeed, to reject her? Surely the Lord knew her very well. That is why he loved her more than us."[26] The result of this intervention is that the others agree to accept Mary Magdalene's teaching and, encouraged by her words, they themselves go out to preach. In a widely accepted interpretation, Pagels suggests that such second- and third-century writings use the figure of Mary Magdalene as a symbol for women's activity in ministry that was challenging male efforts, symbolized by Peter, to suppress visionaries and female leadership in the developing orthodox ecclesial community.

Taken together, the biblical texts and their trajectory in later gnostic literature carry the memory of Mary Magdalene as a powerfully faithful disciple of Jesus and courageous witness to his life and destiny, a founding church mother, wise woman, revealer and teacher, interpreter of Jesus' message in the early church, a woman friend of God. Early on she is honored with the moniker "apostle to the apostles" for the strength of her witnessing word; the gnostic texts describe her as Jesus' most intimate companion, a symbol of divine Wisdom, and worthy of praise because "she spoke as a woman who knew the All."[27] How then, to cite Jane Schaberg's framing of the question, did the first apostolic witness become a whore?[28]

Technically, it happened when male preachers and biblical interpreters conflated the stories of several different women in the New Testament. There is Luke's account of an unnamed "woman of the city" who dares to enter a private dinner to anoint Jesus' feet with her tears and her fragrant oil; against the objections of the host, Jesus forgives her sins because she showed such great love.[29] In addition to the woman taken in adultery whom Jesus saves from stoning, John tells the story of another anointing of Jesus' feet with costly, fragrant perfume, this time by Mary of Bethany, sister of Martha and Lazarus, whom Jesus had raised back to life.[30] There is also Mark's account of an unnamed woman disciple who anoints Jesus not on the feet but on his head with costly ointment of nard, thereby prophetically commissioning him to his messianic destiny on the cross; she is the one about whom Jesus declares that wherever the gospel is preached, what she has done should be told "in memory of her."[31] These are all different women and none of them is Mary Magdalene. In truth, there is no biblical story that depicts Mary Magdalene as a prostitute or any other kind of sinner, and none that shows her either anointing Jesus or being forgiven her sins. Yet these various stories were coalesced under her name, with the result that by medieval times she becomes a sinner repenting her ways in the sex trade.

Refusing to attribute this to an innocent mistake, feminist analysis judges this to be a stunning example of what results when theology and religious symbols are crafted almost exclusively by men in a patriarchal framework. Then the power of the male gaze, which shapes women into beings that satisfy the needs of the male psyche rather than seeing women whole in their own integrity, has full sway. Wittingly or not, generations of male interpreters constructed the Magdalene portrait out of their own dream of love and sexual guilt, with elements of *eros* and *agape* intertwined. The fantasy of relationship with an unmarried, beautiful woman has driven artistic depictions of her, with innumerable paintings that feature voluptuous breasts, long, curly hair, and disheveled clothing, while the need to justify this fantasy casts her gaze toward a skull or a cross. What comes to the fore is "woman" as attractive, unattainable object of desire or as symbol of sorrow for sin. But woman as creative leader chosen by Christ? Not likely.

Feminist strategies of interpretation correct this distortion by bringing a different and clearly more authentic chronicle to light. In essence, Miriam of Magdala is a first-century Jewish woman who speaks and acts in the power of Spirit-Sophia. A faithful disciple of Jesus during his ministry, first witness of the risen Christ, on fire with the Spirit of Pentecost, she is an apostolic leader who helps develop the gospel message and continues Jesus' preaching once he is gone. In all texts where she appears she acts as a wisdom figure with the personal autonomy of her own stance before God, a freedom always related to the circle of women and men disciples in whose stories her own is illuminatingly embedded. In a feminist midrash on the gospels Rosemary Radford Ruether envisions Mary Magdalene, after Peter and the others reject her witness to the risen Christ and continue arguing about who should be first in the kingdom, slipping away to a quiet place outside the city and sitting under the shade of a tree. "She knew that she had glimpsed a momentous new thing, the key to the whole mystery of the world to come that had eluded them all through Jesus' lifetime." He had tried to teach the uselessness of fantasies of power and revenge and the wrongness of relationships of domination-subjugation, even in the name of God. His death had shown that God was no heavenly Ruler in whose name men on earth could lord it over others, but a God whose blood was poured out on the earth in order to create a new heart in us. But now Peter and those who thought like him were busy trying to fill the throne again, making even Jesus into a new Lord and Master in whose name they could rule, howsoever humbly(!). "Mary shuddered. 'Is there any way to rend this fabric, to let the light of this other world shine through? Perhaps some of this vision will still get through the distortion. Other people, even women like myself, will glimpse something of the true vision, and they will recognize me as their sister.' "[32] Correcting the distortion of the historical memory of Mary Magdalene, this "dear friend of God,"[33] women find a companion whose memory cheers them with a dynamic flash of faithful friendship, spiritual insight, and self-confident leadership, and challenges them with a cautionary tale of how even the most outstanding witness can be bent by the pressures of patriarchal dominance.

Reassessing Value: The Virgin Martyrs

Both the Jewish and Christian Scriptures carry women's stories that like Hagar's and Mary Magdalene's can be pieced together, glimpsed through their traces in the male-centered narrative, or discerned through the silences. Feminist interpretation uses these texts to reconfigure the memory of the history of salvation to include women as full players with men in the shaping of tradition. Work in this field offers a stunning enhancement of the cloud of witnesses in ways that empower women and challenge the dominant social-political patriarchal world. A third example of women's practices of memory takes us into subsequent centuries of persecution when women and men were put to a tortured death for their Christian witness. One subset of these martyrs honored by the early church is comprised of young women, girls really, who were also perceived as virgins: Agatha, Agnes, Lucy, Cecilia, Anastasia, and others. Scholarly interpretation of their story today takes the form of thesis, antithesis, and a yet further antithesis to the antithesis, bringing a needed reassessment to the value of martyrdom itself.

Traditional ecclesial interpretation presents female physical virginity as a phenomenon of the highest spiritual value. To protect their virginity from contamination by marriage, usually to a Roman nobleman, these young women resist advances to the point where their intended husbands betray their stubborn Christian commitment to a magistrate, thus ensuring their death. They are remembered because they defended their virginity and because they suffered for it. At least, that is how the stories have been told by the church for centuries, underscoring the values of virginity and suffering as ways of perfection for women. The current edition of the Roman breviary praises the virgin martyr Cecilia for being "the most perfect model of the Christian woman because of her virginity and the martyrdom which she suffered for love of Christ."[34] In her commentary on the passion of Perpetua and Felicity, Maureen Tilley points out that even these two obviously sexually active young women, one a nursing mother and the other who had just given birth, were turned into virgins in the course of tradition, with liturgical texts and prayers transforming their sexuality and maternity into virginity up until the Vatican II reforms.[35] The not so subtle message conveyed by this cache of stories is that women who exercise or enjoy their sexuality, or who do not suffer enough, belong on a plane of lesser holiness for precisely these reasons.

This pattern persists into the present. Witness the twentieth-century promotion of Maria Goretti who received a death blow in the course of resisting rape and died with forgiveness in her heart, but was canonized primarily as a "martyr of purity." Or the more recent canonization of Marie Clementine Anwarite, a vowed religious in Zaire, who chose to be killed rather than yield her virginity; according to the citation, she demonstrated the "primordial value accorded to virginity." Drawing on Valerie Saiving's by now classic critique of ideals of virtue,[36] Anne Patrick argues that the official hagiography of these virgin martyrs undermines the validity of women's choice for their own physical life as a moral value. Instead of these narratives of fading power, which in any event women today intuitively dismiss, there is need for ideals of wholeness of body and spirit: "what women in patriarchal society need are not exhortations to humility and self-sacrifice, or stories of saints who preferred death to rape. Women need instead new models for virtue and new stories that communicate them."[37]

But if inherited construals of the virgin martyrs are damaging to women's empowerment, reflecting as they do a male-centered appraisal of women's bodies, new readings uncover a different message. Kathleen Norris signals the arrival of an antithesis when she notes the uneasy message the young early Christian women convey:

> They die, horribly, at the hands of imperial authorities. They are sanctified by church authorities, who eventually betray them by turning their struggle and their witness into pious cliché, fudging the causes of their martyrdom to such an extent that many contemporary Catholics, if they're aware of the virgin martyrs at all, consider them an embarrassment, a throwback to nineteenth century piety; the less said, the better. It's enough to make one wonder if the virgin martyrs merely witness to a sad truth: that whatever they do or don't do, girls can't win.[38]

Placing these stories within the context of Roman society, however, brings to light the bold political nature of the acts of the virgin martyrs. In addition to the standard patriarchal controls over women and their fertility, the need for a constant supply of young men to replenish its far-flung legions led Rome to demand that women marry and reproduce as a duty to the state. Marriage and the family were functions of the *imperium*. In this context, these young women, deeply attracted by the word of God, presume to have a life, a body, an identity apart from the patriarchal state's definitions of what constitutes their humanity. Their refusal of marriage defies the conventions of "feminine" behavior, witnessing to a wild power of self-definition even in young girls. Finding their center of gravity in relationship to Christ, they break through the restrictions of patriarchal Roman society to claim their own truth in an astonishingly radical way. Maureen Tilley notes the movement from dependence to independence in the prison diary of Perpetua as she shucks off a self-definition previously achieved through her relationship to men: "Her father lost control of her. She disengaged herself from her infant son who could have controlled her when he grew up. Her power determined the eternal repose of her brother. Even her judge could not frighten her for her sentence was not to the beasts but to heaven. Her executioner could not perform his job without her assent and physical assistance."[39] Like this young married woman, the virgin martyrs regard the disposition of their physical body as a mark of their self-determination deeply intertwined with their spiritual integrity. They take control of their own life. How fierce a young girl's sense of honor can be! How this has always been feared and repudiated by male authorities! And this is a defiance infused with the mystery of holiness. Kathleen Norris muses, "The virgin martyrs make me wonder if the very idea of girls *having* honor is a scandal, if this is a key to the power that their stories still have to shock us, and even more important to subvert authority, which now as in the ancient world rests largely in the hands of males."[40] Given the oppressive context, rebellion against the conventions of feminine behavior in growth toward ownership of the young woman-self results in bloody death.

These martyr stories reveal women to be supremely capable of self-definition and courageously committed to faith in God as the ground of their wholeness despite the ultimate cost of their lives. Rejecting androcentric descriptions that would have these martyrs exercising male-like strength, feminist interpretation sees each one of them exercising the strength of precisely one woman. It is this dedicated, defiant aspect running through the early Christian women martyr stories that so inspired certain medieval women whose pathway to sanctity involved a bid for liberation from the prison of sex-role stereotyping and patriarchal marriage.[41] It also motivated the nineteenth-century African-American "sister of the Spirit" Maria Stewart to put martyrdom at the head of her proud list of achievements women have accomplished by the Spirit of God; she writes: "The religious spirit which has animated women in all ages...has made them, by turns, martyrs, apostles, warriors, and concluded in making them divines and scholars."[42]

Women's self-defining commitment in the face of danger continues to elicit intense, critical appreciation as brutal instances of martyrdom do not cease to occur. In 1980 four North American churchwomen, Ita Ford, Maura Clark, Dorothy Kazel, and Jean Donovan, consciously chose to remain in El Salvador because of their passion for God which flowed into love for suffering women and children, awash in an ocean of tears. As a result they were raped and murdered. True, they were not hauled before a tribunal and asked to deny Christ, offer incense to the emperor's statue, or marry a noble Roman. But, as Karl Rahner among other theologians argues, the essence of the act of martyrdom is there when death is foreseen as a possible consequence of witnessing to the gospel and the courageous choice is made to continue, nevertheless. Like Jesus, who fell in the struggle for the reign of God against religious and political authorities of his time, in our day the death of the martyr "can be a consequence of an active struggle for social justice and other Christian values"[43] against oppressive powers. Clearly these women opted in the face of threat to share the lot of victimized people in the interest of offering spiritual sustenance and material support; they did so out of a profound, self-defining compassion nourished by Christian faith; clearly, too, the right-wing death squad that rubbed them out functioned in the name of a repressive state. As the Bretts write of these and other U.S. missionaries martyred in Central America, the hope that they offer benefitted not only the struggling people with whom they ministered but "like a relentless breeze, has crossed international borders and returned home to refresh North Americans as well. Thousands have been heartened by the witness that these women...have given to the vitality of Christianity in a tormented century when secular and religious institutions alike have often fomented injustice."[44]

The stories of women martyrs, and in particular of the early Christian virgin martyrs, can be read in such a way that the vitality of women's self-definition can be strengthened, not sapped. But now an ambiguity in interpreting these stories begins to emerge. "If anything," writes Kathleen Norris, "our era has made us more fully aware of the psychological dynamic of sexual violence against women that these stories express so unconsciously in raw form."[45] The female body with its beauty, its vulnerability, its reproductive strength, has long been a country where male resentment and authority have been enacted. Under fierce pressure to submit, the young women martyrs of old chose to define themselves in relation to God rather than husband; their choice brought them face to face with male violence because their refusal to submit raised a challenge to patriarchal rule. Within the rigid limits of the situation and attracted by the mystery of God, they seized the opportunity to be protagonists in their own history. And in that moment they meant something dear for the hope and self-understanding of their fellow Christians. But why should death be the only option for women seeking self-definition? Holding this up as *the* ideal in all situations implicitly glorifies the torture and the murder while undermining women's motivation to resist male predation. Here a second antithesis begins to operate, arguing that the destruction of women through the ruination of their female bodiliness occurs too readily in the course of history, and needs to be resisted.

The whole edifice of theological legitimation of suffering is at stake in this feminist metacritique of unjust suffering known by women, by poor people, by victims of racial prejudice, by all those who feel the boot of the oppressor on their neck. In alliance with the God of life, the *ekklesia* is called to resist rather than justify such suffering. If in the process life is taken, then the critical narrative of the struggle, far from promoting passivity, releases hope that energizes continuing resistance on the part of others. But terrible death need not be the only nor even the ideal road to salvation. Bringing a woman's perspective to bear on what happens to women's bodies in martyrdom, Maureen Tilley intriguingly suggests, keeping our eyes on the actual torture and graphic suffering, can challenge and "expose the community of discourse which offers death as the only option for women's self-definition."[46] At the end of this twentieth century drenched in blood, our hope dreams for a world where such death is no longer necessary, neither for women, for poor people, for anyone.

By contrast, feminist theorists posit, as with Hagar, survival to be a holy choice. Thinkers from the region where the ethos of martyrdom is strong make this point with eloquence. "Too often the revolutionary legacy of the women of Central America is martyrdom," writes Renny Golden; by contrast, women villagers left with the care of children and the elderly, and women refugees who construct the social fabric of life in the camps even as violence looms, all these women, "tenacious as the forgotten wildflowers clinging in the rocky crevices of the highlands,...are the blooming presence of God in the blood-drenched earth."[47] Spinning out strategies to keep death at bay, such women make present the redemptive possibilities of life in the concrete. "Women's salvation rises in the songs they sing to their children while hiding in holes as napalm bombs are dropping. It surges as God hovers over them with each tortilla made over open fires in the camps. Salvation is possible only because these women embrace all children as their own and nourish them at the breast, on the run, even in death."[48] Like Jesus of Nazareth, these women face death as the price for refusing to abandon their radical activity of protective love; like the virgin martyrs, they commit self-defining acts. But "as martyrs of survival, these women do not advocate self-abnegation."[49] Rather, participating with the God of life they pass on and sustain life, maintain the community, and deepen possibilities for future healing and rebuilding. Not victims of history but holy survivors, they make choices that spell life in the concrete for those dependent upon them. In this, women reveal an efficacy that challenges martyrdom as traditionally understood. Living for the faith is as crucial a witness as dying for the faith. Resisting death is as much a way of holiness as is sacrificing one's life. The memory of the virgin martyrs as self-defining women on fire with the Spirit is contextualized within the wider memory of women's courageous and compassionate fight for survival for themselves and others. In the words of the poet Julia Esquivel:

> O Mother of mine, Mother of the People
> buried with a woman's pains, and a thousand times redeemed
> in every debased woman who rises in dignity.... [50]

Reclaiming the Silence: Anonymous

Reference to the many unnamed women who have sustained life in the face of death already illuminates a fourth example of women's practices of memory. In addition to searching for women whose names and stories are preserved, however partially, in the tradition, women call to mind the generations upon generations of women whose bold mettle, touched with the grace of the Spirit, created and bequeathed life, warmth, beauty, skill, artistry, justice, insight, and goodness to the world, and whose pain and degradation leaves terrifying memories that awaken the will to resist. Feminist interpretation reclaims from the silence and the invisibility of history those labeled "anonymous."

These are women of every tongue and culture who bore and birthed, farmed and harvested, fetched and fed, cleaned and mended, taught and protected little ones, related to husbands, poured forth unending labor, pondered and prayed, sought their own space and exercised their wits in a patriarchal world, finding their connections to the sacred in the midst of myriad daily sufferings and joys. Their circle is as wide as the earth, including women from our own family trees and women of different races, classes, and ethnic cultures; women from the recent past and women long distant in time; struggling, poor, artistic, prophetic, quiet, shouting, funny, loving, suffering, self-defining, seeking, defiant, scared, subtle, sexy, gutsy women of all ages. Here we do not search out the singularly heroic. While most women have not been simply male appendages, neither have they been elite women who are exceptions to the rule, outstanding for their public contributions such as fighting against multiple obstacles for their oppressed people. Instead, as Adrienne Rich points out, in seeking strength from our heritage we need to look above all for the greatness and sanity of ordinary women and how, day in and day out, these women collectively waged resistance. "In searching that territory," she writes, "we find something better than individual heroines: the astonishing continuity of women's imagination of survival, persisting through the great and little deaths of daily life."[51] While these foresisters remain unknown, the very act of remembering that they existed empowers women in the struggle for their dignity and freedom by connecting them with the flesh and blood, the eyes and hands, the sexuality and minds, the dreams and defeats and victories of women through the ages.

Among this company, we also remember the innumerable women who suffered violence unto death, or at least to the diminishment of their bodies and their spirits. Women who were beaten by husband or lover, the men protected by law; women raped and sodomized; women brutalized by war; women murdered. A trail of bloody and violated bodies runs through the communion of saints. Shameful is the persecution of tens of thousands of women hunted down and gruesomely tortured as witches by the male leadership of the ecclesial Inquisition; reprehensible too is the scholarly erasure of this holocaust of women from historical memory, so that barely a book or course on European or church history traditionally makes mention of it.[52] Abominable is the enslavement of African women by their new world Christian masters. Because the ownership of these female bodies with their productive and reproductive power belonged to their masters by right sanctioned by church and state, atrocious the violence these men must needs use to keep the slave women of unbroken spirit in subjection.[53] Horrendous the violation of tens of thousands of Korean Comfort Women, many of them teenagers, designated as "military supplies" on Japanese manifests and forcibly shipped from battlefront to mining camp to factory town as sexual slaves to soldiers — a not uncommon story of war. When artist Mona Higuchi visualizes these lost lives in a gallery-size structure, each woman is a shimmering golden square trapped in a little bamboo cell, thousands of them building a giant cage to the ceiling, with the Buddhist female deity of compassion, Kuan-yin, over all.[54] Remembering these and other women who suffered violence gives rise to deep lament and hot outrage; the injustice done to them is unrequited. It also carries a liberating impulse: never again, we say; and damned be the male state, church, and military establishments that had such power over the lives of women; and how shall we mobilize to prevent, deflect, and stop this violence against women even today?

The tradition of "anonymous" is made up of individual stories that cannot be universalized. Behind each is a face, a voice, a mind, and heart of a woman who created and struggled in her own way. In all their quirky uniqueness, they left an imprint in the wide tradition of human history in the Spirit that we inhabit. Their ongoing influence is beautifully captured in the concluding lines of the novel *Middlemarch*. Here the author reflects on how the deeds of her character, the generous Dorothea, will be poorly remembered after this figure's death but spins off a judgment about the worth of her life *nevertheless*:

> For there is no creature whose inward being is so strong that it is not greatly determined by what lies outside it. A new Theresa will hardly have the opportunity of reforming a conventual life, any more than a new Antigone will spend her heroic piety in daring all for the sake of a brother's burial: the medium in which their ardent deeds took shape is for ever gone. But we insignificant people with our daily words and acts are preparing the lives of many Dorotheas, some of which may present a far sadder sacrifice than that of the Dorothea whose story we know.
>
> Her finely touched spirit had still its fine issues, though they were not widely visible. Her full nature, like that of the river of

which Cyrus broke the strength, spent itself in channels which had no great name on the earth. But the effect of her being on those around her was incalculably diffusive. For the growing good of the world is partly dependent on unhistoric acts; and that things are not so ill with you and me as they might have been is half owing to the number who lived faithfully a hidden life, and rest in unvisited tombs.[55]

Choosing to remember the vast heritage of unremarked women, what Adrienne Rich names as "the particularity and commonality of this vast turbulence of female becoming which is continually being erased or generalized,"[56] releases strength today in the struggle for a living future. Faithful amid countless hardships, hungry yet committing acts of untold existential courage, denied a voice, excluded from official circles of power and yet clinging to their God — these women have nourished the goodness that is the legacy of the world and the church today. Remembering them gives rise to a surge of awareness, grief, gratitude, and hope. Untold "anonymous" ones of today form part of this great historical company. Warmed and warned by their memory and empowered by the same Spirit, women are inspired to add to this legacy and send it into the future.

Strategies for a New Vision of History

Never before have so many women been equipped with the necessary tools to undertake historical research; never before has there been such impetus for this research from the perspective of women's spiritual hunger for a sustaining heritage. The examples of women's practices of memory given here are but outflying sparks from the explosion of contemporary feminist historical scholarship that is working to recover, retell, reassess, and reclaim the critical memory of women's victories and defeats as a vital part of the Christian tradition. This work uses a variety of research methods, which ensures that even the same figure or group will receive diverse readings.[57] Using the biblical image of a parent who knows how to feed a child with bread rather than stone, Elisabeth Schüssler Fiorenza offers one schema of the methods used by herself and many others to deliver nourishing fare to women's spirits from the hard rock of patriarchal biblical texts; these methods also work well to interpret later tradition.[58] Her analysis is particularly helpful in enabling the reader to understand and then practice strategies that, by calling women out of the shadows, bring a new wholeness to inherited memories.

The first strategy, ideological suspicion, is necessary because of the androcentric nature of most biblical and historical texts. Since the narrative is written from a male point of view within a patriarchal context, the fact that it casts women into subordinate roles or erases their memory altogether cannot be taken at face value. Working like a detective, the interpreter must question the apparent way things are presented in order to glimpse a different reality at play. Critical analysis suspects that women were not all that silent and invisible, not all that passive and compliant, not totally the simple objects into which the male gaze would shape them. Furthermore, the meaning assigned to women's action or suffering by the dominant male voice in a narrative does not necessarily equate with the meaning that emerges when texts are read from the perspective of women's struggle for equal human dignity. Thus the work of interpretation begins by questioning the text's narrative line and traditional spin.

With the second strategy, historical reconstruction, the stories of women and marginalized men submerged in the biblical and historical texts are located and brought to light. Finding an implication here, a glancing reference there, the interpreter acts like a quilt-maker stitching these disparate patches into a new design of biblical history, one that highlights what androcentric composition has overlooked. One tactic pursues the idea that if women are mentioned in the text at all, how much more important must have been their original contribution, since the story simply could not be told without it, e.g., Mary Magdalene and the women disciples from Galilee at the resurrection. Again, if women are not mentioned, that does not necessarily indicate their absence, given how marginalized persons are overlooked by a dominant gaze; their presence may be ascertained by other means, e.g., the participation of women in the Last Supper. Interpreters read women into generic words like prophet and apostle, and understand that prescriptive commands restricting women's behavior actually describe what women are doing that men find offensive, e.g., preaching in the church's public assembly. With these and other strategies the text can be unlocked to release a wealth of insight into women's initiatives.

A third strategy assesses the ethical quality of texts in terms of their capacity to engender oppression or liberation and wholeness in the community today, especially when read in liturgical assembly. It makes the judgment that some texts should cease being read aloud and announced as the word of God when the church is assembled for public prayer, e.g., texts that call for wives to be submissive to their husbands.

Finally, a celebrative strategy receives texts in communal gatherings, making present in ritual and story the reimagining of the sufferings, struggles, and victories of biblical foresisters and foremothers accomplished by the previous methods. Here the critical memory of women becomes bread for the ongoing journey as prayers of praise and lament bring specific examples and the enormity of women's striving into the heart. Not necessarily exercised sequentially, these interpretive strategies of a hermeneutics of suspicion, of remembrance, of proclamation, and of celebration interact with each other and with women's struggle to bless the gift of themselves before God and to transform social and political structures that subordinate them.

It is crucial to note that these strategies do not focus on a study of women in the biblical or some other period as a topic distinct from a wider history. Doing so would merely keep patriarchal structures in place and add women to the picture. The result might appear more inclusive, but in fact would remain as inimical to the memory of women's historical agency as before. Instead, these strategies seek to construe the whole story differently, locating women's historic role not just at the margins but also at the center of the community's relations and insights. In the process, men's stories also become reconceptualized. For example, the founding story of the Exodus is usually told from beginning to end with a focus on Moses. But starting the story with Exodus 1, the story of the courageous and cunning Hebrew midwives named Shifrah and Puah who defied the Pharaoh to let the male babies live, and with Exodus 2, the partnership of the mother of Moses, his sister Miriam, and the daughter of Pharaoh, a female collaboration that cuts across barriers of class, ethnicity, and age, makes clear that without all these women Moses would never have stood a chance to live, let alone to grow to adulthood, let alone to become, along with Miriam and others, a leader of the struggle for liberation.[59] Telling the story of the Exodus as the story of a lone male heroic figure rather than the story of a community of women and men struggling for freedom reflects and promotes androcentric interests. Reconceptualizing the whole makes room for women to exist as subjects of history, now as then.

The result of this pioneering scholarship is a growing treasury of memory with which women today can connect and, finding their rootedness in a heritage of female holiness, be empowered in their struggle for full human dignity in transformed communities. The subversive power of the remembered past acts like a leaven, raising the flat dough of despair and preparing a nourishing future.

Chapter 9

Companions in Memory

An Interpretive Template

The creedal symbol of the communion of saints expresses the understanding that a community of faithful God-seekers exists around the
earth and across time itself, through the life-giving communion of
Spirit-Sophia who forever weaves links of kinship throughout the
world. When interpreted theologically, current practices of women's
remembering that restore a heritage of religious power to a disen-
franchised group, one that ultimately involves half the human race,
also serve to revive the significance of this relatively dormant Christian belief, the one effect not separable from the other. By searching
for the lost heritage of women's tough and joyful lives in relation to
the mystery of God, by reading history from the margins rather than
the center of power, by naming names and pointing to the nameless,
by connecting to generations who have walked faithfully on this earth
until now, women find a place to stand from which they can challenge the interconnected biases that continue to press down on their
lives in church and society. When practiced as part of a living faith,
this kind of remembering contributes to a spiritual event at the very
heart of the gospel: the coming into being of suppressed selves, newly
energized with the fire of the Spirit to bless, to work for justice, to
follow Christ by forging new paths of discipleship. In the process, the
experience so ringingly conveyed in Hebrews becomes a living reality: a great cloud of witnesses comes into view in whose company the
ekklesia runs the race.

The intriguing possibility begins to take shape. Recognizing the play
of grace in the lives of other women, women gain a more anchored
appreciation of their own blessedness. Conversely, acknowledging
themselves to be sacred, in the very image of God, women become
empowered to name and celebrate the holiness of other women. Tracing the effect of grace in women's will to survive, power to lead, wit
to defy, the sheer good and evil of daily life, awakens women to new

possibilities of their own contribution to the world. Conversely, their own walking and wrestling with divine mystery at this moment enables women to cherish the journeys others have taken with their God. This experience offers a paradigm for retrieving the communion of saints not as a static doctrine but as a dynamic symbol of the company of friends of God and prophets, thanks to the vivifying work of the Spirit. Rich connection to the past functions as a source of religious energy for struggle now and also as a pointer to a different future in view of God's promise, tested and witnessed to in so many lives.

To analyze more deeply what is going on in women's practices of memory, we employ the template "narrative memory in solidarity." Developed by contemporary political theologies concerned with the systemic, practical ramifications of belief for person's lives, this notion braids together three realities, memory, narrative, and solidarity, into one working tool for understanding. In a series of incisive essays, Johann Baptist Metz, one of the key shapers of this template, argues that these are not decorative notions brought in to adorn the Christian proclamation which can be better understood by more abstract thought processes. Rather, they are basic categories of a fundamental theology that seeks to interpret the love of God in the midst of a conflictual world.[1] Rooted in Scripture and liturgy, the three are indissolubly connected. Memory and narrative provide cognitive content while solidarity propels the community toward action, thus ensuring a practical character to belief. Taken together, these categories prevent theology from becoming an act of *hubris* that sails away in abstractions, pleased with its own cleverness, while the suffering of the world goes on unabated. Rather, they enable a grasp of faith inseparable from active discipleship, so that the community of memory and hope becomes through its prayer a community that struggles for justice, peace, and the well-being of the earth. Teasing apart these three elements and examining each in detail will enable us to grasp just how strongly the communion of saints can function as a matrix of the healing, redeeming, and liberating grace of the gospel.

Subversive Memory

In a most basic sense, memory is necessary for personal and communal identity. Amnesia suffered by an individual robs that person of an irreplaceable sense of who she or he is. Similarly, without a shared memory, no community, whether a small local church or a large nation, can long survive. To reduce a whole group to the status of nonpersons, keeping them quietly in bondage, a dominating power must take away the memory of their heritage, ancestors, and traditions. The histories of human oppression reveal that destruction of memory is a typical maneuver of totalitarian rule. Only official history is allowed, and this tells the story of those who have triumphed and conquered while the story of the defeated ones is repressed. By contrast, personal and corporate identity is formed when suppressed memory is aroused. Witness the fact that every protest and rebellion is fed by the subversive power of remembered sufferings and freedoms. Thus, memory is a practice that serves to rescue threatened or lost identity.

Obviously, only a certain kind of memory functions this way. By refusing to engage the hard edges of suffering and struggle, memory that is simply nostalgia, bathing the past in a sentimental light, or memory that works as an anesthetic, bringing the challenge of the past into reconciling harmony with the misery of the present, loses its transforming power. But memory that dares to connect with the pain, the beauty, the defeat, the victory of love and freedom, and the unfinished agenda of those who went before acts like an incalculable visitation from the past that energizes persons. It interrupts the omnipotence of the present moment with the dream, however fleeting, that something else might indeed be possible. Consequently, instead of keeping attention pinned in the past, this kind of memory turns mind and heart to the future. If the times are fat and comfortable, it calls present banalities into question, saying: there is more to life than the acquisition of things and the search for the latest entertainment. If the times are lean and tough, it calls present oppression into question, saying: many have struggled before you, and, you can resist the course of things. By evoking the sufferings and victories of the past it startles those who are bored or despondent into movement. By lifting up the unfulfilled promise of past suffering it galvanizes an unquenchable hope that new possibilities coming out of the past can be realized now, at last. By bringing "something more" into view, it awakens protest and resistance. In these ways it operates as a practical, critical, liberating force that helps to forge deep historical identity. Metz calls this type of remembrance "eschatological memory" for the surplus of meaning carried in this act of remembering makes a different future possible.

Examples from different cultural groups elucidate how this subversive memory works.

• Speaking from the faith perspective of desperately poor, hungry people, Gustavo Gutiérrez writes, "Human history has been written by a white hand, a male hand, from the dominating social class. The perspective of the defeated in history is different. Attempts have been made to wipe from their minds the memory of their struggles. This is to deprive them of a source of energy, of an historical will to rebellion."[2] Revivifying that memory awakens the impulse to change the situation and sustains efforts to do so.

• The mothers and grandmothers of Argentina's Plaza de Mayo used their own bodies as a living symbol of this power. In a situation of state-sponsored terror, citizens survived by *not* seeing. Before piles of unidentified bodies, disappeared people, and tales of unspeakable torture, forgetting became a self-protective way of life. Many grew used to this dehumanizing anonymity, but these women refused to accept injustice as the final word. Their response to the savage butchery was to assert the power of their relationships. "The laws command amnesia, lifelong, as a price of survival... but the mothers remember."[3] By their public, literally dangerous remembering, they help to create a different reality.

• African-American philosopher bell hooks recalls her grandmother and great-grandmother, both dedicated quilt-makers, and utters their name in full: Sarah Hooks Oldham, daughter of Bell Blair Hooks. "I call their names in resistance, to oppose the erasure of black women — that historical mark of racist and sexist oppression."[4] To reclaim their history by stating their particulars is to gather and share an inheritance too easily rubbed out. And remembering black women, their service to the white community as domestic servants and nannies which often left them with little time or energy for their own lives and families, has a very definite effect. It honors their history of service, thereby giving their descendants a "homeplace" in which to find themselves, even while it criticizes the racism and sexism that oppressed their lives. "The act of remembrance," she writes, "is a conscious gesture honoring their struggle, their effort to keep something for their own. I want us to respect and understand that this effort has been and continues to be a radically subversive political gesture."[5]

• Collecting the writings of poets, rabbis, journal keepers, and others who poured out their thoughts in the midst of the Nazi holocaust, Jewish scholar Albert Friedlander sees their words as signals of truth and love sent out of night toward the dawn: "Many of the Dawn Riders who instruct us did not get to this part of the road, but sent their messages ahead of them, out of the darkness, towards the light. They depend upon being heard. We, the remembrancers, will carry their lives along and mourn the darkness which destroyed them, to celebrate the goodness which endures."[6] The imperative against genocide, "Never Again," stays alive with the memory of all the dead, while the messages of the dawn riders keep a glimmer of hope alive. In these and every other instance, the struggle for justice is sparked by a struggle of memory against forgetting.

• North American poet and essayist Adrienne Rich, in her acute observations on the moral responsibility to resist amnesia, which starves the imagination, and to fast from nostalgia, which is no more than a sugar rush leaving depression in its wake, notes that it is nothing new to say that history is an account of events told by the conqueror: "Even the dominators acknowledge this. What has more feelingly and pragmatically been said by people of color, by white women, by lesbians and gay men, by people with roots in the industrial or rural working class is that without our history we are unable to imagine a future because we are deprived of the precious resource of knowing where we come from: the valor and waverings, the visions and defeats of those who went before us."[7]

Because this kind of remembering challenges the absolute power of the present and brings to mind a future that is still outstanding, a certain measure of danger is connected with it. Certainly there is danger for those who dominate and thus benefit from the status quo, for when inklings of "what was" and "what if" dawn upon the marginalized, unjust arrangements are called radically into question. There is also danger for those oppressed who become empowered by memory, for when they shuck their suffering passivity, the ensuing struggle for the future can be costly and even life-threatening. Among the complacent, memory acts as a trigger that shocks persons into awareness of the compromises they have made with the prevailing trends and banalities of society, shaking them out of apathy. For all groups, remembrance of suffering and of historically realized freedom breaks the stranglehold of what is currently held to be plausible. Memory's danger lies precisely in its ability to detach people from the grip of a given situation, if only for an instant, and by bringing to light new possibilities, to empower hope for a different future.

This kind of eschatological memory that functions so powerfully to create and sustain a liberating identity in social and political situations also functions at the core of Christian faith. At the heart of biblical and liturgical proclamation is the *memoria passionis, mortis, et resurrectionis Jesu Christi*, a very definite memory of concrete suffering, injustice, violence, and death, and through this of God's victory over evil and death that grounds the promise of future freedom for all the world. The effective power of this memory with its hope of a future, promised but unknown, sustains the community's efforts to live faithfully and compassionately in the world even now. As with any critical memory, remembrance of the crucified and risen Jesus Christ is dangerous in a very particular way.[8] Since he was put to death because of his ministry, his compassionate and liberating preaching and behavior enter into the meaning of his destiny in death and beyond death. For those in developed nations, the memory of the passion and death of Jesus Christ interrupts the triumphant pride of modern society and its callous, bourgeois complacency, consciously making room for heartfelt compassion, joyful connection, and the reality of sorrow and death. In that light the dominant image of the all-competent human being in perfect control, superficially comfortable, ruling everything, is challenged and provoked, while importance is given to those who struggle and are defeated or lost. Given the particularity of the cross, the memory of the passion summons up in a special way the concrete crosses of so many historical victims vanquished by injustice, persons defined by dominant voices as unimportant, while hope in the resurrection anticipates a liberating future precisely for them. Consequently, memory of the defeated prophet raised to life by the power of the Spirit, the crucified one who is God with us, aligns the church precisely with those multitudes of people who today drink the cup of unjust suffering and presses it toward transformative action that will overcome such torment. The capacity to remember in this way creates a social force that breaks the spell of history as a history of the victors; it propels the *ekklesia* out of passivity into active engagement against all that wrecks the glory of God in the world.

Woven into the paradigmatically dangerous memory of Jesus the Christ are the lives of all disciples and seekers in the Spirit, persons who reveal the face of God disfigured with suffering, alive with resistance, compassionate to heal — in creedal parlance, all saints, in one communion. The pallid state into which the roster of saints has fallen can be measured by the degree to which the official memory of this company now fails to function in this dangerous and life-giving way. But the feminist work of remembering in the church, conducted with clear consciousness of historic disenfranchisement and advocacy for the fullness of women's human and Christian birthright, is one living instance of how memory of the saints can serve a new justice.

Created in the image of God, redeemed by Christ, blessedly graced by the Holy Spirit, the whole cloud of female witnesses forms a company whose memory is truly and rightly subversive. Existentially it subverts the inculturated tendency to self-effacement in women, for in celebrating that Spirit-Sophia has graciously made generations of women into little miracles and masterpieces full of unexpected blessedness, women begin to recognize and own the wonder of their own selves. One does not even need words or images for this encouragement to take hold. The silent memory of the whole raft of female friends of God and prophets has the power to buoy up self-identity and spark resistance to self-denigration. Working its power in women's lives, this remembrance is also subversive in calling the collective memory of the whole church to a greater amplitude of inclusiveness. The challenge here is to reshape the church's memory so as to transform community structures and practices. Writing of this same struggle in Judaism, Judith Plaskow makes the point well: "When women, with our own history and spirituality and attitudes and experiences, demand equality in a community that will allow itself to be changed by our differences, when we ask that our memories become part of Jewish memory and that our presence change the present, then we make a demand that is radical and transforming."[9] Practices of memory then release hope for women *as a group* by breaking the patriarchal silence about the vast heritage of female witness, a speaking that becomes an element in reclaiming the center for women as well as men.

While the erasure of the memory of women in patriarchal religious tradition is a serious tool of continued subjugation, the sheer fact of negating this erasure by bringing to mind generations upon generations of women touched with the grace of the Spirit in all struggle and hope connects women to a powerful past from which they can draw strength for present commitments. In Hebrews the cloud of witnesses is not a handicap to the runners, weighing them down, but rather a dynamic help that sustains their efforts, helping them run faster. So too the memory of all these lives is not an antithesis to women's spiritual growth and involvement in the world but a presence that bolsters and encourages their efforts. Remembering the great crowd of female friends of God and prophets opens up possibilities for the future; their lives bespeak an unfinished agenda that is now in our hands; their memory is a challenge to action; their companionship points the way.

Such a fully realized memory of the history of women's involvement with God issues in an irresistible call for conversion, away from the marginalization of women and their gifts in church and society and toward full recognition and equal participation. In effect, the summons to remember and to act because of the lives cherished in memory resounds as an integral part of contemporary women's spiritual journey and as a liberating paradigm for the *ekklesia* as a whole.

Critical Narrative

Memory has an intrinsically narrative structure. In the widest sense, life itself has the character of a story, and human experience is brought to expression through narrative in a way impossible to more abstract thought. The story mode of discourse gives human beings a way to discover how the world works and what their role within it calls for, helps them to shape and make sense of things, enables them to articulate order in the fathomless mystery of their lives and to maintain it in the face of the unexpected. Especially in moments of crisis, narrative gives sharp focus to the questions that arise and empowers energy to survive and resist. All this is accomplished through the power of the telling of the tale itself. One cannot sift out the moral of the story and relay it, flat and colorless, and hope to have the same impact. Rather, the disclosive and transformative power of the story is grasped only through the dynamic of the narrative itself, through the interrelations between the story, the storyteller, and the listeners. When a story carries a dangerous memory, it expands its existential significance to become a critical narrative at the service of human dignity.[10]

Probing the vitality of narrative more deeply makes clear that its power to transform lives results from multiple aspects at play. There is, first of all, a self-involving aspect. By telling and listening to stories, persons locate themselves in a cultural, historical, or religious tradition and allow its insights and challenge to shape their identity as human subjects. The stories become woven into their lives, and they join the plot of their own lives to the ongoing tale. Perhaps nothing illustrates this more keenly than Martin Buber's famous and often told tale:

A rabbi, whose grandfather had been a disciple of the Baal Schem, was asked to tell a story. "A story," he said, "must be told in such a way that it constitutes help in itself." And he tells: "My grandfather was lame. Once they asked him to tell a story about his teacher. And he related how the holy Baal Schem used to hop and dance while he prayed. My grandfather rose as he spoke, and he was so swept away by his story that he himself began to hop and dance to show how the master had done. From that hour on he was cured of his lameness. That's the way to tell a story!"[11]

The self-involving aspect of narrative ensures that when rightly told, people become what they tell precisely in the telling, with practical effects.

Closely related to the self-involving dimension, narrative also has a performative aspect. By its inner dynamic it has the power to change the persons who hear it and lure them into certain attitudes and behaviors as part of a larger community and its tradition. This uniquely compelling power of narrative to influence ways people understand their experience and consequently behave is starkly illustrated by the case of the martyr stories in the popular Catholicism of El Salvador in the 1980s. Battered by poverty and struggle, the death of a beloved archbishop, the violent deaths of loved ones, and ongoing suffering, people found in the paradigmatic story of Jesus' life, death, and resurrection both an interpretation and a spur to action. As Rosa, a resident of a working-class *barrio*, described it, "Now we're in the times of the Romans...with the same spying and vigilance....It's the same now as in the early church."[12] If Jesus and his early disciples were persecuted, so are his followers now; if the resurrection shows the ultimate victory of God's cause, so too may people now hope. Here the story of Jesus is not simply told but inhabited, lived in. Its unique, self-involving dynamic issues a summons to emulate his own actions, which contemporary martyrs do and which those who tell their stories may soon do. Writes Anna Peterson in a sensitive study, "As a paradigmatic story or master narrative, the passion grounded ideas about the necessity of sacrifice, the fruits of sacrifice, and resurrection, which in turn served as the foundation for a coherent and powerful understanding of repression, martyrdom, and rebirth. These ideas helped people make sense of both personal experiences and national events and spurred a wide range of opposition activities."[13] The performative aspect of narrative is here writ large as local communities connect with the Christian tradition and become the story they tell.

As this example shows, narrative also functions at a social-political level. In addition to being used to support the status quo, which it can do, it can also be the language of the interruption of the system. The power of oppressors rests on being able to create a master narrative that erases subversive memory, thus giving justification to present domination. As the philosopher Walter Benjamin graphically put it, "Whoever has emerged victorious participates to this day in the triumphal procession in which the present rulers step over those who are lying prostrate."[14] But telling stories that bear liberating impulses enables persons to resist manipulation, glimpse a different reality that features them as subjects of their own history, and turn toward innovative praxis in the social order. African-American author Toni Cade Bambara expresses this aspect with lilting cadence when she emphasizes how her stories of transformation and renewal serve the continuing need of her community for resistance to ignorance and evil:

> Stories are important. They keep us afloat. In the ships, in the camps, in the quarters, fields, prisons, on the road, on the run, underground, under siege, in the throes, on the verge — the storyteller snatches us back from the edge to hear the next chapter. In which we are the subjects. We, the hero of the tales. Our lives preserved. How it was, how it be. Passing it along in the relay. That is what I work to do: to produce stories that save our lives.[15]

It is not for private, individual good only that stories function, but to sustain the identity of groups under threat, an eminently political act.

Narrative, finally, has an inevitable ontological or religious aspect, however implicit, being a medium that communicates the experience of meaning before the mystery of the universe and the experience of salvation within the historical experience of suffering and struggle. When intense joy or intense pain seeks expression, abstract words alone do not suffice. A description of the method of Holocaust survivor and witness Elie Wiesel puts this rhetorically:

> You want to know about the kingdom of night? There is no way to describe the kingdom of night. But let me tell you a story.... You want to know about the condition of the human heart? There is no way to describe the condition of the human heart. But let me tell you a story.... You want a description of

the indescribable? There is no way to describe the indescribable. But let me tell you a story.[16]

Rational argument breaks down in face of the surd of excessive human suffering, whereas story enables the touch of grace present in such experience to be thematized. This is not done in such a way, however, as to bring intelligibility to the suffering or to deliver a premature sense of how it will all work out. In the classic tradition the experience of suffering generates an awareness of the apophatic dimension of faith: there are no reasons and silence becomes a suitable response. Refusing to trivialize tragedy, narrative finds its home in this dimension, birthing at least glimmers of light in the midst of darkness.

The power of narrative to effect personal identity, communal behavior, political justice, and meaningfulness in all areas of life is on full display in the story that is central to Christian faith, the life, death, and resurrection of Jesus the Christ. Told daily in the Eucharist's insistence on remembering what happened "on the night before he died" and elaborated in detail in the gospels, this narrative points toward the arrival of God's reign in and through this person and his words and deeds. It is a story of healings and exorcisms, of intimate prayer to the God of Israel and prophetic insistence on openness to the poor and outcast; a story of scandalous table community with tax collectors and sinners and confrontation with the superficially secure and self-righteous; a story filled with Jesus' own imaginative telling of stories to tease and usher the hearer into the coming mystery; a story of joy for sinners but filled with outsider criticisms that this man is a drunk and a glutton, a despiser of sabbath and tradition, a flouter of decency and social convention. Above all it is a story of passion and godforsaken death, and of new experience in the Spirit giving assurance that his death issues in new life in God. The Christian proclamation of this story takes place against an eschatological horizon: only when all the living and the dead and the whole world itself are consummated in God will the promise of the narrative be fulfilled. In the meantime, the story of Jesus now experienced as the Christ — a story of prophetic vision, active compassion, real suffering, and unimaginable new life — remains the dangerous and subversive narrative by means of which the Christian community commits its life and enacts its hope.

The revolutionary character of this narrative is brought to the fore by René Girard's thesis that through telling a story that presents an innocent victim of religious and state power as the one with whom

God sided, Christian faith overturns the sacred character historically granted to the exercise of violence. It uproots the sacred myth that grants legitimacy to official powers that deal out death: "This is where critique of accounts of persecution from the persecutor's standpoint begins."[17] This did not stop violence in the world; the institutional church itself became a persecutor once it became powerful. But since the Christian story took shape, the Spirit of truth revealed through the gospel has been working in history to remove the deceit that would see innocent people as guilty, despite the authorization of violent administrations. Persecutors may try to bury all the slain by telling the story from their own standpoint, but the memory of the dead, led by the crucified Christ, bears luminous testimony against them. "That is the reason," writes Girard, "why we still go on using the term *martyr* — meaning witness — for all the innocent victims, irrespective of differences of belief or doctrines, just as the gospels themselves proclaim.... In popular usage the term *martyr* goes further than scholarly interpretations and suggests to theology things it does not yet know."[18] Thus, remembering the dead, telling their stories, making lists, creating art, reciting martyrologies, keeping memorial days, tolling bells, crafting litanies, all strike a blow against oppression. Narrative remembrance refuses to grant it legitimacy.

Woven into the story of Jesus are the stories of all those who throughout history have responded to the call of the Spirit in suffering and joy: all saints. Few traditionally told lives of the saints, however, function with anything near the full potential of critical narrative, enabling hearers to leap about and dance, to risk their lives, to stay afloat, to survive evil. The stories women are telling today, however, offer one instance of how the communion of saints can have just such an impact. Crafted in affirmation of the blessedness of being female and with a passion for mutuality, these narratives undermine the sacred validation of male rule and female subordination. In resistance to patriarchy, they tell the story of victimized and marginalized persons with whom God, as always, sides. They also hold up the agency, participation, and leadership of women who resisted and stepped out of their male-defined, less-than-fully human, less-than-fully spiritual place. In the process, the dynamic power of the communion of saints to aid and abet spiritual growth and social-political transformation takes wing.

For historical women could and did subvert the ideal picture of virtue prescribed for them by patriarchy. Women have been Spirit-filled leaders, healers, spiritual guides. Friends of God and prophets in their own right, they have known spiritual power coming to them from God out of the struggles of their own life. They have expressed this power in fights for self-worth, in wide and deep hospitality, in unremitting service with and to the poor, in struggles for justice, in tongues touched with fire that announce the Holy Spirit, in continuous assertive patterns of compassionate ministry. They have also been consistently silenced, suppressed, abused by violence, and unjustly killed. Telling of their defeat and accomplishment in the Spirit becomes a self-involving, performative, political, and mystical narrative that God-seeking women today inhabit in the struggle for equal human dignity. Since in its broadest contours this narrative is structured according to a companionship model in which women and men are fully equal partners in the community, it sounds a call to conversion to the *ekklesia* as a whole to interrupt its own master narrative of patriarchal rule and live by the gospel narrative of the excluded, crucified one who was, in the end, the beloved of God. The critical narrative of the cloud of witnesses functions then as a verbal sacrament of the vivifying, redeeming work of the Spirit, helping women stay afloat and issuing a challenge for transformation.

Solidarity in Difference

Narrative memory reaches its saving, practical outcome when it is exercised in solidarity. This category does not signify just a generic relationship of togetherness, a simple association with others like ourselves automatically entered into because of similarity in race, class, gender, or interest. Nor does being in solidarity with others signify conformity of outlook, loss of self or of one's own unique history. Rather, it connotes a vital union of interests in a group, a genuine community of desires, expectations, and goals, issuing in action and social cohesion, usually in the face of opposition. Solidarity is a type of communion in which deep connection with others is forged in such a way that their sufferings and joys become part of one's own personal concern and a spur to transformative action. It entails a movement out of a selfish seclusion and into relationship where people bear one another up in mutual giving and receiving. It is inseparable from liberating praxis for the common good.[19]

In situations of tremendous injustice, solidarity among the victims themselves is expressed in initiatives mutually taken to resist, to hope, and to celebrate even in the midst of suffering. For those not directly affected by the particular victimization, solidarity is expressed in conversion toward those who suffer, not just being affected emotionally by their pain but choosing to love by taking it as one's own, joining the struggle for life for all. When engaged in as a practice of faith, solidarity ushers both groups, those whose life is being destroyed but who are resisting and those who accompany them, asymptotically toward the mystery of God.

A fascinating aspect of solidarity as it functions in an emancipatory way in the social-political sphere is that it includes not only community among the living but also alliance with the dead, especially those who have been overcome and defeated in history. If the struggle is to continue, it must be pervaded by this larger historical solidarity with the dead whose future is still outstanding. Otherwise, disregarding the dignity of the fallen, the movement for justice turns into a vicious march of progress that just piles up more victims. The narrative memory of the dead creates a solidarity backward through time that emphasizes the common character of human destiny and its unfulfilled promise. It is thus a category of help, support, and togetherness by means of which the dead can be affirmed as significant in their lives, and the living who are struggling are succored and encouraged by their memory. This historical anamnetic solidarity between the living and the dead breaks the grip of dominating forces and empowers transformative praxis toward a fulfilling future for *all,* guaranteed only when the value of the most insignificant and despised is assured.

The pivotal reality witnessed to by Christian faith is God's own commitment to incarnate solidarity with the world, worked out through the life and death of the risen Jesus and the ongoing presence of the living Spirit. Called to share in this solidarity, the community of disciples becomes increasingly configured to God's own loving ways. Consequently, they begin to partner and advocate for those most in need who are struggling for life in the face of oppression and death. This is solidarity, which "breaks the bonds of isolated individuality and forgetfulness — the bondage of sin — and enables the creation of community and conversion to the other."[20] Then the struggle is engaged to make concretely real in history what faith declares is true of God's intent for human beings and the world: salvation and ultimate well-being for all. In turn, growth from isolation with its attendant apathy to connectedness with its active and political loving brings new interpretations of theological and spiritual themes. As Dorothee Soelle highlights, "Solidarity asks that we change the image of God from that of a power-dispensing father to one of a liberating and unifying force, that we cease to be objects and become subjects involved in this process of change, that we learn cooperation rather than wait for things to come to us from on high."[21] Enabling the church to participate in God's own energy, the dynamism inherent in solidarity directs Christian life into the midst of the world.

The communion of saints is a symbol of this solidarity that transcends time in a graced connection of witness and care. The broken links between heaven and earth typical of postmodern culture coupled with the traditional patriarchal structure of this communion, however, leave the symbol heavy with lassitude and unable to communicate its innate power of connection. Reading inherited narratives against the grain of assumptions of male rule while struggling for equal human dignity, women who are subjects of their own religious history newly understand the connections between their own lives and the women who have gone before them. Diverse as situations are, parallel experiences of suffering and power under civil and ecclesial patriarchy link women of different generations once their stories are heard. "Mary Magdalene went and announced to the disciples, 'I have seen the Lord'; and she told them that he had said these things to her";[22] "Mary McLeod Bethune, with $1.50 and a prayer, started a school for girls in Daytona"[23] — these are memories with the seed of the future in them, for they galvanize response. This solidarity with the saints, intuitively and consciously grasped, strengthens, consoles, sparks determination, sustains hope, and sets example for the whole *ekklesia*. No atrophied connection, this, but a touching of spirit that empowers and blesses in the face of strong gender prejudice.

Precisely here, however, a deep ambiguity in the working of solidarity comes to light, one that affects our reading of the symbol of the communion of saints in unexpected ways. *Mujerista* theologian Ada María Isasi-Díaz criticizes how fashionable the usage of the term "solidarity" has become, "how easily it rolls off the tongues of all sorts of speakers, how unthreatening it is. If the true meaning of solidarity were understood and intended, visible radical change would be happening in the lives of those who endorse it with their applause."[24] Far from a comforting community of interest, solidarity requires critical analysis of how oppressions interlock with one another and commitment to praxis in the teeth of opposition. Womanist theologian M. Shawn Copeland calls the consciences of white women to account on this same score: "Focus on solidarity calls for an end to facile adoption of the rhetoric of solidarity by Celtic-, Anglo-, European-American feminists, while they ignore and, sometimes, consume the experiences and voices of the marginalized and oppressed, while, ever adroitly, dodging the penitential call to conversion — to authenticity in word and in deed."[25] These critiques are leveled at the tendency of women in the majority race and class, white, educated, middle-class women, to overlook differences among women, projecting their own experience as universal and folding others into their own dominant voice and experience. Thus they ignore the complex relations of power between privileged and nonprivileged women and privileged women's complicity in the fierce stereotyping of men of oppressed groups. Thus, too, they foster unequal relationships under the guise of sisterhood to the detriment of each other's insights and creative energy. From the standpoint of women in poor, marginalized, and oppressed communities, a universal, nonproblematic solidarity is tantamount to a stifling and manipulation of their truth while racism and classism perdure uncontested in the hearts of their white, middle-class sisters. Thanks to this critique, and despite some backsliding, feminist theologies now hold themselves accountable to differences among women's situations and practical concerns worldwide, appreciating the fact that for the sake of both truth and justice, in Lisa Cahill's words, "the experience of privileged, educated women, those with a voice in politics or the academy, should not merely be projected onto the lives of other women who differ by class, race, ethnicity, or even historical era."[26] The challenge now becomes how to respect the full play of women's diversity, summed up in the notion of difference, a concept that is an intense focus of contemporary feminist theorizing.

Copeland notes how the term "difference" rings with negative connotations in our culture, where it points to those to be avoided or treated with suspicion and disdain and implies the presence of a factor disruptive to the harmony of a community. But feminist critical theory maintains that difference is an existential principle that honors the integrity of the person by giving full play to her historical concreteness. There is no ideal, archetypal "woman"; there are only real women whose lives are embedded in various combinations of bodily, relational, economic, political, and social structures in historical times and geographic places, for better or worse. When admitted within a relationship of solidarity, moreover, difference, rather than being a regrettable obstacle to community, can contribute as a creative, enriching, community-shaping force. For genuine community is not the result of suppression of differences but of respecting and celebrating them within multiple larger narratives and liberating praxis. The poet Audre Lorde evokes this truth with her koan-like words: "Difference is raw and powerful connection."[27]

Only intense listening, imagination, and openness of heart can accomplish this in practice, however lucid the theory. Because most of us assume the correctness of our own way of being in the world, acknowledging difference with appreciation rather than with negative judgment requires the most profound and difficult change of heart. Furthermore, granting essentially equal worth to other persons in all of their concrete human difference rather than construing their otherness in a hierarchical rank of better and worse is a practice so beyond humanity's traditional ken as to be a genuinely graced achievement.[28] But it is precisely the boundlessly varied combination of personal differences that occasions the rich, radiant reality of women, as well as of men and children, as *imago Dei*. When this is respected, a new type of community appears in the world. As Shawn Copeland urges us to see, honoring difference carries forward the "struggle for life in its uniqueness, variation, and fullness"; it "is a celebrative option for life in all its integrity, in all its distinctiveness."[29]

With this understanding, we add one more nuance to a feminist reading of the communion of saints. As women connect with this great historical company, we do not try to erase differences, even with the dead. What each woman suffered and accomplished, what each one meant for the hope and self-understanding of others in her world and in the *ekklesia* of the past, cannot be repeated and may even strike us as strange. Likewise, the present situation with its possibilities and terrors has never existed before. The category of solidarity in difference works to prevent memory from making women of old into merely mirror images of ourselves, as well as to promote appreciation rather than rejection of the otherness of their ways. Creative action in the Spirit then springs from this deep, nonviolent connectedness. As Elisabeth Schüssler Fiorenza writes, "We participate in the same struggle as our biblical foresisters against the oppression of patriarchy and for survival and freedom from it. . . . We are not called to empathize or identify with *their* struggles and hopes but to continue *our* struggle in solidarity with them."[30] Bearing connectedness in its very definition, the communion of saints becomes yet more critical when understood as a solidarity in difference. Then it "moves us onto something larger than yet constitutive of ourselves,"[31] a great cloud of witnesses of the most amazing diversity who surround us in all our differences with courage and hope.

The template "narrative memory in solidarity" serves to unlock a strongly practical-spiritual interpretation of the communion of saints. Women's practices of narrative memory in solidarity with the vast witness of generations of women offers one striking example of the strength of this symbol to empower and challenge the *ekklesia* on the path of discipleship today. These practices restore a rich heritage of holy lives, women who kept faith with the mystery of God through the thick and thin of history, through all the vagaries, conflicts, and victories of daily or dramatic events. Read from a feminist perspective their memory is subversive, their narrative empowering, and solidarity with them in all difference encouraging in the quest for wisdom and the struggle to transform unjust, violent structures that dehumanize persons. Then the doctrine is retrieved as a source of comfort and joy for the heart, of grief for resistance, and of strength for the struggle. Then the doctrine is practiced less as a cult of the saints and more as a discipline or way of remembering and connecting that brings life. Then the communion of saints becomes the cloud of witnesses, surrounding those who cry for justice with encouragement and blessing, lending the support of their own witness for personal and social transformation.

Chapter 10

The Darkness of Death

Vivit!

The power surging from the subversive memory of the cloud of witnesses who contended in the past generates a certain moral energy for current efforts to heal, redeem, and liberate the world here and now. As the present generation alive in the world remembers them in grief and gratitude, the communion of saints become companions in memory who support the struggle for life and justice even now. But the question inevitably arises: do the dead live on only in the memory of the living or, in some unimaginable way, do they themselves also live anew by the power of the vivifying Spirit of God? From the beginning this has been the Christian affirmation, rooted in late Jewish belief in resurrection sealed in the Easter experiences. It is a belief captured in Martin Marty's dictum about what he would like to see engraved on his tombstone: "What should the stone above the buried ashes say? *Vivit* would do better than *Hic Jacet* or *Rest in Peace*, since I hope to live and not to lie or rest."[1] Indeed, in the course of Christian tradition the communion of saints itself developed as part of the vocabulary of this hope, shifting our gaze beyond death to the promise of eternal communion in the life of God.

Giving an account of this hope in the current era is no easy matter. Modernity's empirical orientation has led to numerous intellectual and ethical criticisms of belief in "life after death"; widespread existential experience that the dead disappear from this world has removed a foundation from which thinking traditionally set out; and theology's renewed awareness that the symbols and ideas of eschatology are not even remotely literal has introduced a certain ambiguity to the religious imagination.[2] In this chapter and the next we explore the communion of saints as a symbol of hope, taking account of these difficulties.

A cardinal rule that governs this exploration is that language about what happens after death can never be taken literally because the human mind simply cannot conceive existence that is set beyond the dimensions of time and space. Listening in on a funeral, Gerard Sloyan pens a voice-over that makes this point. The pastor eulogizes the deceased: "Surely your dear mother is enjoying the presence of God at this very moment." Well, yes. The congregation sings the hymn "Amazing Grace": "When we've been there ten thousand years / bright shining as the sun." Well, yes. But quite literally we know not whereof we speak, for "this very moment" and being "there" have no reference points after death. The question of how to articulate existence for creatures whose medium up to then has been time and change, space and movement, becomes an immense problem. "We can attach a name to that state but we cannot understand it," he writes, "only say that it is not the divine eternity and is not the human sequence of moments marking change."[3]

We do not know in any detail what the ultimate future has in store, either for the individual or for the world as a whole. It is beyond our experience and imagining. In the face of this ignorance, everyone, including those who hold to Christian faith, are rightly agnostic. Although some persons report near-death experiences that give great consolation, no one has ever definitively died and been able to report the aftermath back to the living. Nor, bound as we are to the parameters of time and space, would we understand even if anyone did. At this edge, theology casts its words forward with hope into profound and utter darkness. Scripture is replete with this awareness: "Eye has not seen nor ear heard, neither has it entered into the human heart, what things God has prepared for those who love him."[4] The very nature of life's journey is that "we walk by faith, not by sight";[5] and "we hope for what we do not see."[6] These salient texts underscore how deeply a legitimate agnosticism reaches, even in Scripture. Eschatological events partake of the character of ultimate mystery. What will be will be surprising, coming from the overflowing wellspring of life, the incomprehensible mystery of God. Thus theological language about whatever follows death is of necessity indirect, like language about God, proceeding by way of analogy, metaphor, or symbol, and knowing that no similarity can be affirmed but that the dissimilarity is always ever greater. With this understanding, we begin exploring the communion of saints as a symbol of hope by examining the intellectual and ethical critiques brought against traditional eschatological beliefs by the modern age.

A Disappearing Heaven

In the early Christian centuries, hope for eternal life expressed itself in a great variety of images, theological constructions, and practices of popular piety, creating a heritage of almost unmanageable complexity. In his study of the first six centuries entitled *The Hope of the Early Church*, Brian Daley concludes that the book's title should actually broadcast the *hopes* of the early church, so wide is the range of ideas in which early Christian writers expressed their expectations of the future of the planet and the individual. Yet at bottom all shared a common assumption that "the Christian can look forward to the resurrection of his or her own body, to a merciful judgment, and to a lasting, transforming and utterly fulfilling union with God, because he or she is part of a community that believes Jesus is risen, reigns in glory, has sent forth his Spirit and will come again as judge of history."[7]

Theological consensus in East and West gradually tamed the diversity of eschatological expression into more systematic order, though differences in regions and individual theologians continued. The form in which this ever-evolving tradition arrived in the twentieth century was pruned by the late medieval synthesis. Knit closely together were the doctrine of the four last things, death, judgment, heaven, and hell, with the addition of purgatory as an intermediate state of purification and limbo for unbaptized babies and other innocents. Focusing mainly on the individual's destiny, these doctrinal symbols were augmented by corporate and cosmic symbols of the last day "when" all the dead will be assembled for a final, general judgment and the summing up of the world in a new heaven and a new earth. These symbols each had their place chronologically within in a kind of master narrative of the afterlife, undergirded by anthropological assumptions of the immortality of the soul and the resurrection of the body. In the popular imagination and much Christian art, the story was carried by vivid images of pearly gates, heavenly white robes, crowns, golden streets, fluffy white clouds, and the music of harps, to say nothing of monstrous demons, pitchforks, and blazing hellfire.

The culture and faith experience of people in advanced industrial societies, fortified for Catholics by biblical study and changes in the funeral liturgy, have shaken loose the hegemony of this neo-scholastic vision of afterlife. Advances in science and philosophy have rendered the premodern master narrative, supporting concepts, and popular images of eschatology increasingly implausible, while in response eschatological talk for more than a century has been subjected to radical critique and restatement.[8] To speak about hope in God for the life of the dead in these circumstances, one has to recognize that the inherited map of the afterlife has become intellectually quaint and existentially inadequate, like the drawings of sixteenth-century cartographers. Problems with the traditional construal fall roughly into two sets of criticisms, namely, those that find its content no longer rationally intelligible, and those that censure the way it has functioned to oppose rather than promote earthly well-being.

Intellectual Problems

The first cluster of criticisms points toward the inadequacy of the underlying concepts used by eschatology.

• Philosophy has long rejected the dualism inherent in the classical model of the human person composed of two separate elements, a material body and an immaterial soul, mated for a time on earth and destined for a life together on the last day, but with the ontologically higher soul able to exist separately on its own in the interim. Instead, the grounding intuition of contemporary thought about the human being is the unity of the person who is spirit-in-the-world or body-spirit interconnected with the community of life in the whole material universe.[9] Rather than being discrete pieces of the self, body and soul (if such language must still be used) refer to the whole person in her or his total historical reality, under distinct but related aspects. It is not thinkable that they can endure separation.

• Contemporary scientific insight into the origins and workings of consciousness underscores this unity-in-distinction. The universe is composed of dynamic, self-organizing systems by means of which, at least in the case of planet Earth, matter becomes increasingly complexified to the point where it emerges into consciousness. Spirit and matter are not two essentially different substances but two forms of the same phenomenon, even though once spirit emerges it is not simply reducible to the workings of matter. Spirit evolves from matter and the two are profoundly interdependent. In basic terms: no human mind without a physical brain; the human mind needs the body for its operations. In death, therefore, it is not the case that the body decomposes while the conscious mind marches on, intact in its own functions. The whole functioning human unit dies and arrives at a historical conclusion. How then to conceive of a disembodied soul with faculties of mind and will, consciousness and freedom? This anthropological construal loses its compelling force as an adequate conception of the future of the individual beyond death.

Science also renders the physicality of the resurrected body unthinkable. It always has been so: the first Christian writing on this subject stretched language to the breaking point when Paul, pointing out the difference of fur, feathers, fins, and skin of earthly bodies and the different glorious bodies of sun, moon, and stars, coined the evocative oxymoron "a spiritual body" to indicate the contrast between weakness and power, between the perishable and imperishable body.[10] In addition to his example of the seed growing into the finished plant, there is also the much used illustration of the difference between the caterpillar and the butterfly, certainly the same physical animal but in radically different form. Casting even these analogies into darkness as suitable for the earthly body/risen body difference, however, scientific studies demonstrate the interchange of matter through all life systems. The molecules that once belonged to a certain living body are recycled after that body's death, passing as nutrients into the bodies of others. Even during life the body is constantly replenishing itself, daily taking in and giving off material and replacing its cells with a regular rhythm.[11] What then would constitute the resurrection of a person's body, let alone all the bodies of the world? The impossibility of simultaneously existing bodies with shared molecules would seem to make the demise of literalism complete.

The same scientific checkmate also stops literal thinking about the end of the world. The apocalyptic scenarios of trumpets blowing, sun and moon falling, persons going up to meet Christ in the air, or a bloody Armageddon are biblical symbols pointing to a final future. But one day the end of the world in the sense of the end of this planet Earth will occur in reality. Our planet will most likely perish from heat death in the sun's old age; it will turn into a small dark cinder, no longer blue, all species extinct, circling a dead star whose fire has gone out. What would a new heaven and a new earth mean then?

Ethical Problems

A second set of criticisms rejects eschatology for its practical role in undermining passion for social justice for the poor, women's liberation, and care of the earth.

• Arching over all is the ethical criticism that religious interest in life after death has been so otherworldly that it has robbed the earth of intrinsic value, cut the moral nerve in the face of injustice, and sapped energy needed for the struggle for life over death here and now. Especially where oppressed peoples are counseled to put up with their suffering in light of a future reward, heaven functions as a tool of oppressive earthly rule. It is true that the classic nineteenth-century Marxist form of this critique, religion as opiate of the people, has met its match in liberation theology, which practices eschatological hope as a critical and creative force in society.[12] Yet the lingering legitimacy of this critique cannot be denied.

• In feminist theological analysis this criticism receives an added impulse in view of the deleterious effects of patriarchal dualism. The traditional concept of an immortal soul inhabiting a corruptible body functions to disparage women, their female bodies, and their creative bodily functions of birthing and mothering, these being identified with the lower, messy, physical order from which one ascends to the heavenly, masculine realm of spirit. Extremely anxious about bodily change and decay, patriarchal thought splits off this "dark," material side of men's experience and projects it onto women, whom they can then attempt to control. The notion of the disembodied soul at peace in the domain of light promotes a damaging fantasy, that by escaping the so-called feminine realm of sexuality and procreation, one can also free oneself from finitude and mortality. The result is that both women and the body are profoundly disvalued.[13]

• The global ecological crisis adds still another sharp nuance. By focusing on life to come in a distant place that is considered our true home, eschatology displaces our identity as "earthlings" and undermines care for this planet, the only home we and future generations as living, historical beings actually have. The human race grew from this earth; we are responsible for its well-being in a wholistic community of life; to set our sights elsewhere and to pour our energies into getting there is nothing less than what Catherine Keller sharply calls a "trivial pursuit."[14] Instead of focusing so intensely on the hereafter, our minds and hearts need to be converted to this earth. It is not that there can be no responsible sense of life after death; indeed, as Keller herself points out, most of the indigenous peoples who live sustainably with the earth also honor the living spirits of their ancestors. But to be responsible in this moment of earth's crisis, eschatology needs to become green. Hope for the new creation, in other words, must alert us to the power of the Spirit flowing as the holy life force through all living things here and now, calling us to cherish the earth rather than to flee it for a higher world.[15]

To summarize: These criticisms alone or in some combination have percolated through the spirit of the modern/postmodern age to the point where the traditional model and appeal of afterlife has thoroughly folded, even among those committed to the Christian faith. In seeking to give an account of hope, theology has responded in at least three ways, reinterpreting traditional symbols, providing critical mediations of those symbols from the point of view of philosophical anthropology, and weaving these ideas into new scenarios of what happens at death.

Reinterpreting Symbols

In this critical culture, rigorous interpretive work is being done to deconstruct the naive sense attached to eschatological symbols and retrieve them anew in forms that are both intellectually credible, bearing the community's hope in a recognizable and engaging way, and ethically productive, capable of promoting just and mutual relations in the social order, between women and men, and among human beings and the earth. Without such acts of creative, faithful interpretation, as Paul Ricoeur argues, symbols cannot be dealt with today in a believing way at all: "we can believe only by interpreting ... it is by interpreting that we can hear again," at once an expression of modernity's distress and a cure for that distress.[16] The classic symbols of purgatory, heaven, and hell, which focus mainly on the fate of the individual, receive interesting nuance as a result.

Purgatory

Rejected by the Reformers because of its connection with indulgences and other practices that seemed to infringe on the centrality of salvation in Christ alone, belief in an intermediate state after death where a person is purified has now also fallen from the view of many Catholics, to the point where theologians speak about "the disappearance of a doctrine."[17] In an interesting analysis of the last thirty years of Catholic life, Robert Schreiter attributes the slippage partly to the liturgical renewal after Vatican II, which replaced the funeral rite's medieval focus on the wrath to come with revised prayers that highlight rising to new life in Christ, symbolized by the change from black to white vestments. Furthermore, the renewal of theology, recovering themes of the boundless love and mercy of God, altered the Catholic notion of sin, moving it from legalist to personalist categories as signified in the name change of the sacrament of forgiveness from Penance to Reconciliation. Rather than talk of making satisfaction for the temporal punishment due to sin, preaching now speaks of healing broken relationships with God and neighbor. In ritual and thought, purgatory becomes less comprehensible.

But while the literal image of the doctrine disappears, religious scholars find it newly meaningful to think that human development is perhaps not frozen at death but that maturity is a continuing possibility. Some have linked purgatory analogously with the Hindu belief in reincarnation, both doctrines trying to keep open the possibility that persons may yet achieve an integrity that they fell short of in their current passage through life.[18] Other contemporary interpretations of the symbol of purgatory tend to follow the basic idea that it signifies a purification that takes place "instantaneously" after death in the searing light of divine truth and love. Sensitive to human interdependence, Schreiter intriguingly suggests that we cannot undo the repercussions of wrong we have done, which remain as "vapor trails" in the communities through which we pass and in the trajectory of our own existence. These consequences must be dealt with as part of coming into communion with God after death. Purgatory points to this cleansing action of God, "the source of life, who purifies the dead of the consequences they have created. That purification is done through an intensification of communion."[19]

One imaginative construal of how this cleansing might be accomplished was offered by Walter Rauschenbusch, the American theologian of the social gospel, who thought that heaven itself might offer the opportunity for personal repentance and reparation:

> Suppose that a stockholder has taken large dividends out of a mill town, leaving only the bare minimum to the workers and stripping their lives of what could humanize them. He followed the custom of his day, and the point of view of his social class hid the injustice from his conscience.... Would not justice demand that in the other world he serve their souls until they grow beyond the ways he has retarded them? Suppose that a man sent a child into life without accepting the duties of fatherhood, breaking the spirit of a girl and her family, and leaving his child to be submerged in poverty and vice. Would it not be just and Christian to require that he serve the soul of his child until it becomes

what it might have been? Such labor and expiation might well keep us busy for some part of eternity, and in doing it, relationships of love and service would be formed which would make us fit to live closer to the Source of Love.[20]

The notion of "serving the souls" of those one has harmed is a profoundly relational way of thinking about the debt of satisfaction carried in the traditional doctrine of purgatory. In the end, however, Rauschenbusch admits that these images are but the play of personal imagination about a fascinating subject. Moved by the passionate conviction that the good of the whole human race in general could not compensate for the defeat of the poor in the concrete, he suggests that the images be put away in favor of the few things we can know with assurance: namely, that the love of God forever goes out, especially to the neediest; that a God-inspired personality is forever growing; and that the law of love and solidarity will be even more effective in the life of heaven than on earth. This is more than enough, he figures, to sustain our hope.

In contemporary interpretation, purgatory signifies a full ripening of the whole person as communion with God pervades all dimensions of a person's reality. Perhaps the artist says it best. In one of her short stories, Flannery O'Connor offers a stunning insight into purgatory as an act of mercy:

> Mr. Head stood very still and felt the action of mercy touch him again, but this time he knew that there were no words in the world that could name it. He understood that it grew out of agony. . . . He understood it was all a man could carry into death to give his Maker, and he suddenly burned with shame that he had so little of it to take with him. He stood appalled, judging himself with the thoroughness of God, while the action of mercy covered his pride like a flame and consumed it. . . . He saw that no sin was too monstrous for him to claim as his own, and since God loved in proportion as He forgave, he felt ready at that instant to enter Paradise.[21]

Heaven

The notion of a static state of happiness has long plagued this symbol, robbing it of its vital attractiveness. Even in the hands of great literary artists such as Dante and Milton, the *inferno* seems a much more interesting and exciting place than the *paradiso*. Noting how difficult it is to speak adequately about what will happen at death when we meet the grace, friendship, and beauty of God, Ladislaus Boros comments, "Our theology expresses the essential nature of heaven by the term beatific vision of God. Some theologians manage to make a masterpiece of boredom of this."[22] It is as if we will be locked into a position of staring at an eternal television set which gives rise to nothing less than the strong desire to turn it off and get moving with life. Walter Rauschenbusch also observed this problem. He wrote that as we think of ourselves someday beholding the face of God in glory, made perfect in a fixed condition of holiness forever, the static quality of heaven "is so unlike any life we know and so contradictory of our aspirations that our imagination stands still before a tedious sameness of bliss."[23]

And yet, the scriptural images of final fulfillment are corporate, cosmic, and filled with joy. The vision of God itself entails "knowing" in the biblical, experiential sense, relating intimately to the unfathomable mystery of another in deeply mutual regard. And analogues in the human experiences of loving in freedom, enjoying beauty, pursuing truth, and interacting in community have an absorbing and life-giving character that is the opposite of stasis. At root, heaven is the symbol of a community of love sharing the life of God. This entails forever exploring the absolute mystery of the Other with new discoveries forever abounding; it also involves being deeply related to all other creatures in the free embrace of the one God. As Zachary Hayes has persuasively argued, "This life-giving relation with God is intrinsically bound to our relations with other human beings in a communion of saints. Our final state will be one of pleasure in the entire created and fulfilled world of God." Nevertheless, "we must admit that we know very little of what this means in detail," apart from intimations of eternity in our experiences of loving here and now.[24] There is unimaginable plenitude of life ahead. Heaven, the symbol, codes this expectation into the language of faith.

Hell

Even more than heaven, the symbol of hell meets with outright criticism in the contemporary mind. Apart from the pictorial details, an interesting spillover from the besetting theodicy question holds that it is unworthy of God's fundamental and infinite goodness to condemn persons to an eternity of anguish. If God is all good and God is all powerful, then whence a suffering that never ends? Edward Schillebeeckx expresses this dilemma when he writes, "It is an unimaginable scenario for me as a Christian, familiar with the gospel, that while there is said to be joy among the heavenly ones, right next to heaven people are supposed to be lying forever, gasping for breath and suffering the pain of hell forever, however you imagine this, physically or spiritually."[25] Most theologians today hold that God condemns no one to hell; rather it is a punishing choice persons themselves make when they opt to shut love for God and neighbor out of their lives and pursue a genuinely evil course. In this sense, hell is a symbol of self-chosen isolation, a torment of loneliness. They also tend to agree that heaven and hell are asymmetrical as human possibilities, the former being that toward which human beings are called by the divine offer of grace and therefore more likely to be the destiny of the majority. Still, the possibility exists that some persons definitively choose evil, in which case hell's very existence for all eternity seems an affront to the universal saving will of God. Thus there is lively debate today about whether hell exists forever.

One option, taken by Schillebeeckx among others, is to surmise that hardened sinners, since they have destroyed the foundation of eternal life which is communion with God, will simply cease to exist: "Their death is in fact the end of everything; they have excluded themselves from God and the community of the good."[26] Rather than a shadow kingdom of pain next to the bliss of heaven, wickedness by the weight of its own logic disappears into emptiness. Utter evil has no future. In the purging of death, argues Gordon Graham, "those whose hearts are fixed on evil, the false and the ephemeral, will fade into nothing. They will, in short, be annihilated. In this way eternal death comes about, not as an act of vengeance or even retribution, but through the actions of a God who wills only the good."[27] However, annihilation may also be judged an evil on a par with perpetual torment. And so others query whether hell need indeed be eternal, or whether in fact, though hell might "exist," whether any person is actually "there." Basing his thought on the universal saving will of God made known in Christ which will not be thwarted, Hans Urs von Balthasar has vigorously argued that we are permitted to hope for the possibility of universal salvation. At the center of his proposal is the notion of the harrowing of hell: on Holy Saturday the crucified Jesus descends into hell and shows his wounds simply and humbly to all the damned. The sight of such love willing to go so far for them melts the heart of even the most hardened sinners. The human heart is not designed to withstand such love and so, as Jesus rises from the dead, all hell empties out with him. This salvific power continues to rescue those newly shriveling in the lowest depths of hell — at least, we may dare to hope.[28] Supporters of this modern version of *apokatastasis* find it interesting to note that while the Roman Catholic Church canonizes people, declaring the names of certain ones who are in heaven, it has never presumed to do the opposite and declare that certain people are forever damned. We do not know but that God will yet have mercy. Yet hell, like the other eschatological symbols, signifies that human moral choices have lasting consequences. There remains a chance that some may decide deeply and irrevocably to shut themselves off from the heart of the universe and plunge in isolation into outer darkness. Hell, the symbol, codes this terrible possibility into the language of faith.

It is an open question whether these reinterpretations of traditional symbols, creative and intelligible though they be, can rescue the symbols for use in modern/postmodern ecclesial communities, given the centuries-long practice that has sedimented them into the imagination in a literal way. Realizing that at bottom these symbols signal the hope at the heart of Christian faith and alert people to the seriousness of how they take up their life here and now may still allow them to function with some suppleness in the community's language of faith. Even when reinterpreted, the traditional imagery and its explication in theology now create a sense that the future after death is more open, more of a mystery, than we had imagined. "When people cease to represent reality by picturing," David Power rightly sees, "and so differentiate between images and symbols, not only their world of conceived meaning is touched but also their affective relationships, their dispositions of belonging, awe, and respect and their sense of personal wholeness and oneness with the world."[29] Thus the future is felt to be much darker, in the sense of the truly unknown.

Critical Mediations

Underlying the effective use of these eschatological symbols is the presumption that, with the possible exception of persons who damn themselves to hell and are possibly annihilated, persons continue to exist in some fashion as themselves after death, finding definitive fulfillment in God. In the face of contemporary philosophical and scientific insights that undercut the dualistic body-soul model of the person, precisely how this is accomplished becomes difficult to explain.

This question, too, is tackled by some theologians who attempt a critical mediation of eschatological symbols through a core assessment of
the human person. The value of this work lies in stretching imaginations to envision in what direction life after death might be thinkable
in terms of anthropological elements, though by unanimous agreement
it is unimaginable.

Working with categories of transcendental Thomism, the early Karl
Rahner conjectured that since the soul is profoundly united to the
body, it clearly has a relation through the body to the whole material
universe of which the body is a part. In death, when the immediate relation with the body and its space-time location is severed, the soul is
freed not to become acosmic, totally transcending the world, but pancosmic, more deeply and intimately related to the ground of the world.
This occurs because the soul by its own intrinsic dynamism essentially
belongs to the world, despite the persistent influence of Neoplatonism
that mistakenly argues "as though lack of relation to matter and nearness to God must increase in direct ratio."[30] But if during its life the
soul-animated body is an open system in relation to the world so that
it is not so easy to regard the human body as ending at the skin, and
if the soul through its embodiment is never a closed monad without
windows but is in principle always open to communication with the
world, and if consummation in God brings a person into the flow of
God's own love which is always toward the material world, then such
a pancosmic relation to the world is not totally inconceivable. In fact,
such a relation of the soul to the world "might imply that the soul,
by surrendering its limited bodily structure in death, becomes open towards the universe, and, in some ways, a codetermining factor of the
universe precisely in the latter's character as the ground of the personal
life of other spiritual corporeal beings."[31]

A more prevalent approach among thinkers today is the move to
assess persons as relational beings and to posit eternal life from that
perspective. That persons and indeed all reality have a profoundly
social and relational character is emphasized by contemporary psychology, sociology, political theory, science, philosophy, and theology,
and in a particular way by feminist theology and ethics.[32] The Carte-
sian model of the self isolated from the rest of the world has come
to seem ever more inadequate in view of discoveries of the way that
basic connections with the surrounding social and physical environment form personal reality. Persons don't just have relations but are
constituted by them, so that to be an isolated person is a contradiction

in terms. This insight extends in theology to the reality of the triune God whose very essence is understood to be relational, existing in a communion of love, and to the concept of human persons, women and men, as icons of divine nature precisely in their being ineffably, concretely, and interdependently relational. Catherine LaCugna captures this dynamic connection when she writes, "The doctrine of the Trinity stresses the relational character of personhood over and against the reduction of personhood to individual self-consciousness, and also emphasizes the uniqueness and integrity of personhood over and against the reduction of personhood to a product of social relations."[33]

In this context, the terms of the problem of the survival of the person after death are shifted, from the question of how an individual self-consciousness can be preserved apart from its physical embodiment, to the question of how death transposes the relational structure of the person into a new form of communion with God. Based on a relational ontology, for example, John Zizioulas concludes that once persons come into existence, each a unique, unrepeatable *hypostasis* formed by the love of God and destined for communion with God, they overcome even in death because they share by their very being-a-person in the love that grounds all reality. "The life of God is eternal because it is personal, that is to say it is realized as an expression of free communion, as love. Life and love are identified in the person: the person does not die only because it is loved and loves."[34] In other words, since a person is essentially constituted by relation to God, then even in the shattering of death one is held in communion by this relation of Love, which always and everywhere creates new being. Love is the voice of eternity in our heart.

A quite different hypothesis is ventured by Wolfhart Pannenberg, whose attempt to develop a notion about continuing self-awareness after death coherent with both scientific knowledge and Christian faith uses what can plausibly be said about the effect of being in the presence of God. "If our life remains present to God," he writes,

> is it not conceivable that God could restore its ability of relating to itself, a form of self-awareness, though different from self-consciousness in the present world, because it would not occur in a succession of perishing instants of time, but in the eternal present and therefore could relate to the simultaneous whole of one's life? Such a possibility would be different from the continuance of a disembodied consciousness, because it is rather the

totality of our bodily life, as preserved in the presence of God, that would recover self-awareness.... The realization of such a possibility would come close to the act of creation.[35]

The tentative nature of this hypothesis is underscored by its presentation as a question; we simply do not know. Its connection with creation is also important, for it posits that the discontinuity caused by death requires a new divine act, virtually *ex nihilo,* to preserve personhood.

These and other theological construals that attempt to think critically about the anthropological underpinnings of eternal life and thus mediate a measure of thoughtful meaning carry out the legitimate task of giving an account of Christian hope. At the same time, their speculative and diverse character shows that the questions put to Christian imagination by contemporary culture are far from resolved. Eternal life, made perhaps more thinkable, remains shrouded in darkness.

Narrative Scenarios

For centuries people lived by the expectation that when they died, they would appear before the judgment seat of God to receive an assessment of their life and then enter into a state of damnation, purgation, or bliss according to their just deserts and the mercy of God, there to await the final day of general judgment and eternal settling in. The power of narrative itself assured that this story of what was to come was one of the most effective ways imaginable for passing on the community's eschatological hope. In face of current criticisms that make such a scenario less than credible, theology today responds by constructing new scenarios about what happens in death and beyond death. In these scenarios as in the traditional one, fundamental beliefs about the relationships among human beings, the world, and God are synthesized Since they flow like little narratives of our own future, they elicit concentrated attention.

The Recycling Scenario

An ecological sense of peace and wholeness pervades Rosemary Radford Ruether's proposal that death be accepted as a natural part of the life cycle, a moment that reveals our deep connectedness to the universe. Profoundly committed to healing relationships between women and men, nations and classes, humans and the earth, and the world and the divine so that they nurture rather than destroy the living planet, her basic move is to cast eschatology on a horizontal, historical plane rather than allow it to point vertically to what comes "beyond" or "after" history. In this context, she challenges the usefulness of the concept of an immortal, eternal future both for the world as a whole and for the individual.

With respect to the whole world, Ruether contends that any vision of a final end point of history, whether biblical or those of modern revolutionary movements, whether within history or beyond it, distracts us from our present responsibility in the world with the hope that something will one day be achieved once-for-all. But women's work of nurturing and maintaining life shows that nothing is ever done once-for-all. Rather, it has to be continuously renewed. As adults, our task is not to long for some promised future but to get on with the work of creating a just and peaceable society on this planet to hand on to our children. And we need to do this over and over again, in every generation with its different challenges. A future, definitive eschatology only undermines our mature commitment to this, our main responsibility in this life.

Regarding personal immortality, especially in the face of so many people who endure a life of miserable toil, pinched development, and unjust, untimely death, we need to acknowledge the tragic dimension of life, Ruether believes, and quietly practice an honest agnosticism. For the concern to affirm individual immortality is a symptom of the basically patriarchal attempt to transcend mortality, an egotistic effort to absolutize oneself over against the total community of being. It causes us to deny the radical ambiguity of material existence, which involves coming to be and passing away in continuous change up to and including the radical finality of death. Rather than hold out for personal immortality, we should envision that in death we abandon our individuated ego to the great Matrix of being. Matrix here is a cognate of matter and mother, and refers to the power at the heart of the universe, the total self which contains us all. This self-abandonment is quite literal. We relinquish our body so that its material becomes food for new beings, just as our body was itself composed of substances that were once part of other people, animals, and plants. And we give up what has flowered in us as consciousness, allowing it to flow back into the great Thou from whom all small centers of personal being continuously emerge in new forms. Ruether's act of faith as she contemplates her own self-being extinguished is breathtaking: "Like bread tossed on the water, we can be confident that our creative work will be nourishing to the community of life, even as we relinquish our small self back into the great Self. Our final gesture, as we surrender ourselves into the Matrix of life, then can become a prayer of ultimate trust: 'Mother, into your hands I commend my spirit. Use me as you will in your infinite creativity.' "[36] Being recycled into the universe of being is our ultimate self-gift to the world.

In this scenario, Ruether's ecological analysis of the deleterious effects of eschatological dualism and her commendably strong sense of responsibility to this world conclude to a solely immanentist outcome for personal and cosmic life. The emphasis is on the value of history and divine immanence within it to the exclusion of any transcendence, whether divine, cosmic, or human. While I agree that patriarchal eschatology undoubtedly overemphasizes transcendence in a dualistic way that links hope with otherworldiness and disparages female bodiliness and care for the earth, and while I applaud Ruether's emphasis on the importance of ecological consciousness for a living planet, I suggest that a solely immanentist end is not the only conceivable possibility, even within an ecological and feminist perspective. Without doubt, the focus of hope needs to be on bringing about the reign of God in peace, justice, and the integrity of creation on this earth here and now. But the experience especially of poor women articulated in third world feminist liberation theologies suggests that hope for life with God after death for human persons and the whole earth not only does not cut the nerve for action on behalf of justice but actually sustains it, especially in violent situations. Furthermore, such transcendent hope, when cast into a nondualistic framework, functions critically and creatively to promote care for the earth precisely because it sees that this world has an eternal value. Instead of contending with patriarchal dualism by opting exclusively for an immanentist end, thus emphasizing what has been neglected but maintaining rather than healing the split, the meaning of eschatological hope would be better served by being directed toward a goal that is both immanent and transcendent in dynamic interaction.

Neither of the next two narratives are perfect examples of this dynamic balance. But each in its own way tells a story of what happens in death that expresses hope for a future for the person and the world precisely as themselves. The contrast between them reveals that even within this commitment there is room for radically different imaginations.

The Fruition Scenario

In accord with the tenets of transcendental anthropology that pervade his theological system, the later Rahner develops a story of how the passage through death achieves fruition, the permanent, redeemed, final, and definitive validity of each concrete human existence by God and in the presence of God. This is incomprehensible and known only in hope. It is true that this hope seems to be contradicted by empirical observation, which knows that the human metabolism which previously existed to maintain an individual life is now redirected in order to replenish the biological system of the earth. But in addition to this metabolism, he writes, "a few other things also existed previously: a person with love, fidelity, pain, responsibility, freedom. By what right really does one maintain that everything is over? Why should it really be over? Because we do not notice anything anymore? This argument seems a little weak!"[37] In analogy with modern physics, which thinks of particles existing without being able to imagine this, we should affirm that due to the nature of freedom in history, death, while it truly marks an end for the whole body-spirit, nevertheless shapes human beings into grace-filled, living, completely achieved ones in all dimensions of their existence.

Key to this scenario is a critical sense of the meaning of eternity. Theological and popular language makes use of words like "after" and "beyond" which imply some sort of continuation of personal action and experience when life on earth is over. We imagine persons existing, however transformed, in a succession of endless days. But at the very least, death means that time ends. Consequently, everything as we know it ends. It is not as if we simply change horses and ride on.[38] After death there is no newness in a temporal sense, no movement through space, no rectilinear continuation of empirical reality. One day, we shall have had our life.

In place of eternity as endless time, Rahner proposes to think of it as the definitive fulfillment of freedom achieved through historical acts in time. Eternal life is a fruition: the abiding plenitude of what has transpired in time, the final and definitive state of a personal history brought to its fullness in freedom, the end point of a life brought to completion in immediacy before God. "Anyone who has ever made a morally good decision in a matter of life and death, radically and uncompromisingly, so that absolutely nothing redounds to him from it except the presumed goodness of this decision, has already experienced in this decision the eternity we mean here."[39] This approach credits the work of the Spirit who blows over all life to quicken and to bless and who, in the case of the human embodied spirit, draws forth the fruit of eternity. Savoring this pneumatological nuance, Rahner explains that "eternal life is not the 'other side' so far as our personal history is concerned, but rather the radical interiority, now liberated and brought to full self-realization, of that personal history of freedom of ours which we are living through even now and which, once it has been brought to birth in death, can no longer be lost."[40] What has transpired during a person's history does not vanish into nothingness as if the person went extinct, but neither does it continue on in another time-like state. Rather, as an intrinsic moment in death itself, persons sum themselves up in a free self-affirmation, a radical endorsement of their lives' fundamental option, and so come to completion in God. Eternity then emerges from time as the blessed consummation of the free history of the spirit.

Ultimately this blessing of eternity involves the person's body as well as the matter of the universe in all its forms, for God creates both matter and spirit for the same end, and because in the incarnation the matter of the earth truly became forever the body of God, not to be shucked off forever but to be redeemed. With regard to the fulfillment of both the person and the universe, it remains the case that "we are totally incapable of forming any conception whatever of the mode of existence of matter in the consummation of the free history of the spirit."[41] We understand neither bodily nor mental existence in eternity. But due to the working of freedom, persons come to fruition as the definitively redeemed ones enfolded into the incomprehensible mystery of the living God: "Through death there comes to be the final and definitive validity of human existence which has been achieved and has come to maturity in freedom."[42]

The Dissolution Scenario

In a blazing critique, Bartholomew Collopy accuses Rahner and others of like mind of pusillanimity in the face of death. Facing the human cadaver, he tries to face the fact that death is truly terrible and destructive. For too long theology has tried to mitigate this reality, denying what is toxic in the experience. For traditional eschatology based on the dualism of body and soul, death presents no basic problem since the soul survives in a disembodied state. Likewise, theorizing about a final option which the person makes in death, while it does admit to death's darkness, makes the dying person active in a free decision that is personally fulfilling and ultimately casts death as an integration. These and other theological strategies all try to mitigate the fact that death cuts us to shreds. It finishes us so that there is nothing left. Instead of offering benign diagnoses and deep secrets about death, Collopy argues, theology in our age should practice a conceptual asceticism, being reticent in what it claims and willing to admit that death reveals no intelligibility working away beneath its surface obscurity. Instead of the soul surviving, death breaks the whole person. Instead of death being acceptable, it is profoundly unnatural in its sundering of life's patterns. Instead of the moment for a fundamental option, death is optionless, taking no notice of human choice and freedom and reducing the self to silence. "From beginning to end a dark model would present death as relentless and implacable, a breaking of the whole human person, an unacceptable and repugnant event, disintegration rather than achievement, a final fall into the weakness of being human — a fall even for religious faith and theological articulation."[43] For this is the basic truth about death: it is ultimately untheological. It harrows all religious categories, mounting the most elemental case against God.

In the face of this radical negation, theology needs to grieve, to lament, to wrestle with nothingness. Then will emerge the only possible response: faith in its rawest form. Taking the risk that God will be there; leaping over the wide gap of collapse; clinging to absolute mystery in the darkness; holding to the promise of God beyond all logic or empirical evidence — this is not faith as sweet assurance but as sheer commitment, profound risk. Collopy grounds this risk on a christological mystery, the cross of Jesus. This was a hard human death, robbed of all comfort, godforsaken, bringing the life of this prophet to a blank halt. In stunning boldness Christian faith dares to affirm that the mystery of God is found even here, in the ragged unraveling of death. It is quite literally inconceivable and inexplicable but is the very heart of faith, that "the promise of God is bound to what is empirically the end of all promise."[44] The resurrection of the crucified then appears as no natural fruit of death, but as a counterclaim that radically rebuts death while yet leaving it empirically unaltered. In this approach, there is no survival of death that would not be based on the most creative act of God. About what life beyond death might consist in, we quite literally have no idea.

Whereas Rahner gives evidence of an analogical imagination at work, Collopy exemplifies a dialectical imagination, although both ultimately hope for eternal life for the person. The power of their scenarios, along with Ruether's, lies in their searching honesty about the truly unknown character of the future, their unflinching acknowledgment of death as a genuine end to historical life, and their willingness to resolve the issue in the only way possible, not with rational argument but ultimately with an existential act of radical trust in God, whether Matrix of the universe or Absolute Mystery or One who did not forsake Jesus in death. This is where every modern/postmodern discussion of eschatology, its symbols, critical mediations, and scenarios, finally comes down. Empirically, the darkness of death is unconquerable. Regarding its outcome, we literally have no information nor adequate conceptions. We do not know, in the literal sense, but we hope. In the end, everything depends upon the character of God.

Chapter 11

Companions in Hope

Questions about death and life "after" death are ultimately questions about God. This is the case because death places such an absolute empirical limit on what human beings can know that thinking beyond it on the basis of cosmological and anthropological convictions reaches only a short distance into the darkness. Whether human thought envisions a destiny of being recycled into the great cosmos or living eternally in communion with divine life, and whether, in the latter case, it affirms a continuity of some substratum of the person as such through death or accepts a total discontinuity and subsequent reassembly of the person, it offers no finally satisfying explanations. At this point philosophical anthropology reaches its limit. Whatever is to be said needs to be grounded elsewhere than the fragility and finitude of the human condition. The language of faith urges that the only foundation able to bear up thought about "after death" is an interpretation of the ultimate power and love of God in whose presence even death is a creature.

In the context of modern/postmodern culture, where faith takes the mind beyond death yet respects the limits of our ability to understand, even those who affirm the destiny of eternal life learn to be at home in an emptiness of mind without definitive conceptual anthropological models. Their affirmation of eternal life does not stem from clear concepts but from a sense of reliance on God who can be trusted to keep faith with the human being in death and beyond death. This situation brings to sharp existential expression the biblical exhortation that "your faith and hope, then, are centered in God," with its bolder variant "your faith is hope in God."[1] Sharing this hope and what it portends for eternal life, Christians may try to explicate it in some way; but knowing that there are no explanations that could do justice to this mystery, the community reiterates this hope mainly through liturgical ritual and preaching. In effect, the community says: we hope for what we do not know but we are trusting that the future, like the past, will come from God freely as a gracious gift.

The language of this radical hope is inevitably symbolic. Seeking understanding of the communion of saints as part of the vocabulary of Christian hope, this chapter argues for the eternal life of persons who have died on the basis of God's typical ways of acting. Our starting point is the biblical structure of hope, which offers a paradigm for the pattern of this reasoning.

The Biblical Dynamism of Hope

In phenomenological terms hope is a firm expectation of something good to come, closely linked with the experience of yearning and desire for it. So too in the Scriptures; hope is typically the expectation that something good will come from God, coupled with longing for this good. It refers the community to what God will do. According to Bultmann's analysis, biblical hope is not necessarily aimed at anything specific but consists in "general confidence in God's protection and help. It may thus be said that God is the hope or confidence of the righteous."[2] In times of peace and blessing, hope gives thanks and expects further good. In times of affliction and distress hope, still directed toward God, longs for deliverance. The dynamic of this relation is paradoxical, even contrarian, for genuine hope grows in strength as a situation grows more desperate, becoming a "hope against hope"[3] that refuses to give trouble the last word because ultimately God's mercy will encompass it with care and new life.

For Israel, the ground of this hope lies in the Exodus narrative of passing over from slavery to freedom and a covenanted life. At first, prophetic interpretation focused expectation on a good and blessed state of affairs that would arrive within history and on this earth. Later, the terribleness of present sufferings drove this hope beyond history to an apocalyptic vision of the community's final vindication after death. In both cases, the future was expected to be a blessed one because the community knew that the Holy One had once already seen their misery, heard their cries under their taskmasters, known well what they were suffering, and therefore had come down to deliver them.[4] For the Christian community, the bedrock of hope, similarly directed toward God, became the paschal narrative of the death and resurrection of Jesus Christ. Here, too, hope oscillates between the arrival of the good in this world and expectation of a future for the living, the dead, and the whole cosmos in the glory of God. Chaos, injustice, suffering, meaninglessness, death — both these major religious narratives embrace it all and bear a vital hope that is hope only because they take all this into account. Looking slavery, exile, and death in the face, biblical hope draws on the tradition of what God has already done to trust that God will be there even and especially when all other sources of help have dried up.

The language that carries this hope is richly symbolic. Most of the images that dream a blessed future are corporate and cosmic in scope, from Ezekiel's vision of the dry bones reconnecting and being enfleshed to Revelation's vision of a new heaven and a new earth where crying is no more.[5] Some few also attend to the future of individuals. In the oldest and only undisputed reference to the resurrection of the dead in the Hebrew Bible, the apocalyptic Book of Daniel describes the end of time: "Many of those who sleep in the dust of the earth shall awake, some to everlasting life and some to shame and everlasting contempt. Those who are wise shall shine like the brightness of the sky, and those who lead many to righteousness, like the stars forever and ever."[6] The Greek Old Testament, the Septuagint, also employs beautiful metaphor, the Book of Wisdom advising, "the souls of the just are in the hand of God, and no torment shall touch them. They seemed in the eyes of the foolish to have died, and their going out a disaster, and their going forth from us to be their destruction, but they are at peace.... At the time of their visitation they will shine forth, and will run like sparks through the stubble."[7] The martyrdom account of the seven Maccabean brothers and their mother declares quite directly that God will rescue them from eternal death. With his last breath the second brother exclaims, "You accursed wretch, you dismiss us from this present life but the King of the world will raise us up to live again forever, because we have died for his laws."[8] The mother, meanwhile, filled with a noble spirit, compares God's vindication of her children to her own creative experience of giving them birth from her womb: "The Creator of the world, who shaped the beginning of humankind and presided over the origin of all things, will in his mercy give you back both breath and life."[9] To her youngest son she recalls God's creation of the world out of nothing and then encourages: "Do not fear this butcher, but prove yourself worthy of your brothers. Make death welcome so that in God's mercy I may get you back again along with your brothers."[10]

This array of images cannot be reconciled nor synthesized into a coherent whole. Each one carries the community's hope about the future, promised but unknown. Falling into the great, warm hands of God, shining like bright stars, waking up from sleep, sparking a grand conflagration in a hayfield, being raised up to life, being born anew, entering into peace, joining a family reunion — all point symbolically to a destiny that the community hopes awaits those who have been persecuted. The symbols attempt to articulate the depth of belief that holds: death is not the end because God is faithful.

In the New Testament the images multiply in light of the new belief that this promised future has already begun in the risen life poured out on the crucified Jesus, the first fruit harvested from the dead by the power of the Spirit. There will be judgment and it will be terrible; there will also be divine compassion more superabounding than judgment. The reign of God will come. There will be merry feasting, nuptials, homecoming, sowing ripened to bounteous harvest, riches inherited, rest and peace, communion of all in bliss, day without night, a chorus of praise, a jeweled city, wrongs righted, tears wiped away. These images of joy, mutuality, and abundance arise for the most part in the midst of pain and suffering. The bleakness is borne and resisted with a sense that there is yet more, that present devastation even unto death will yield to a fullness of life. It is clear that everything hinges on the plenitude of God's mercy, who "has given us a new birth into a living hope through the resurrection of Jesus Christ from the dead."[11]

On the one hand, biblical texts are reticent to predict or describe literally what happens after death. On the other hand, they are brimming with images drawn from the happiness of earth that point to what may be hoped, for the individual and the world. Obviously, the one does not negate the other. For these texts are not meant to be interpreted literally, as if they provided a blueprint or a script for what is to come. Rather, they operate as symbols of hope, pointing beyond themselves to the incomprehensibly transcendent mystery of God and connecting the heart of the people to this mystery. No other language is possible in view of the unknown character of the future.

An influential account of the inner dynamics of this kind of talk is provided by Karl Rahner, who proposes that religious language about the future is meaningful as an extension of a community's experience of grace in the present. If in the present the Christian community knows the compassionate, healing, saving love of God poured forth through Jesus Christ by the power of the Spirit, then it can hope for a future when this same gracious mercy will be victorious, even amid the dissolution of death. Statements about the future affirm the futurity of the graced present. This is not to say that something genuinely new cannot appear. But the newness will lie in the direction of what has already been experienced in Christ. "We may say that biblical eschatology must always be read as an assertion based on the revealed present and pointing towards the genuine future, but not as an assertion pointing back from an anticipated future into the present."[12] In this view, the biblical language of hope is not mere projection driven by wishes for immortality in the face of death. Rather, it is an interpretation arising out of present experience of the Spirit's effects that dares to call them foretastes, on the way to fulfillment. The Bible has no anticipatory report of what will happen at the end of life or of time, whether to persons or the world. The Jewish and Christian communities have only their living tradition and the experience of divine graciousness in the present, which they boldly conjugate into the future tense.

This is a pattern of reasoning that can continue to serve present efforts to think about the destiny of human beings in the face of the darkness of death. Attesting that God graciously creates, redeems, and makes holy the world, the living Christian tradition can give grounds for talk about a future that maintains personal identity even while acknowledging the radical difference that death makes. What this paradigm drives into sharp relief is the character of the God in whom human beings place their trust, for affirming the way God typically acts grounds the daring move that tracks present faith experience into the future and expects new life in and through death.

The Character of God

Of the many ways this idea can be worked out — through a theology of God in relation to the world, through trinitarian theology in the economy of salvation, through christology — an approach through pneumatology has received less attention and yet can prove very fruitful. Not one power among others but the all-embracing matrix that makes all else possible, the Spirit is the creating, redeeming, sanctifying God always and everywhere present and active in the world, drawing near and passing by to bring life and resist evil. Three ways that the Spirit acts in particular can feed the pattern of thinking that leads to eschatological hope. In the beginning and ever since, the Creator Spirit breathes and births the world into ongoing being; the resurrection of the crucified Jesus from the dead into glory is the work of the Spirit of God; and the indwelling Spirit surrounds the world and the human heart with the offer of God's own self-communication in grace. Examining the effect of these divine actions on the world in general and the creature in particular gives grounds for the trust that the future is destined to be not reabsorption but eternal communion.

Creation

In the act of creation, the Creator Spirit brings into being the world which up until this instant of creation has not existed. In doing so She Who Is freely enters into relationship with the world, becoming the unfathomable source, support, and goal of all that is. The models of God as mother, lover, and friend of this world render this relationship in more appropriate fashion than that of a monarch ruling over his kingdom, for they emphasize that the world dwells in God, in whom we live and move and have our being, while the Creator Spirit moves over all, through all, and in all as the matrix of the world's dynamic existence.[13] Whether in this panentheistic pattern of relation or the more traditional theism, God is at the same time totally, creatively transcendent and totally, creatively immanent as the primal ground, sustaining power, and ultimate destiny of the whole universe.

From the side of creation this relation can be interpreted as one of participation. This is an awesome concept, suggesting an intrinsic, ever present, ongoing relationship of the world with the very wellspring of being, with the sheer livingness of the living God, who in overflowing graciousness quickens all things. Exemplifying the Catholic imagination at work, Aquinas works with a fine analogy to explain this.[14] God's presence among creatures awakens them to life the way fire ignites what it brushes against. We know that fire is present when something catches on fire. Just so, all that exists does so by participation in the fire of divine being. Everything that acts does so by participation in divine act. Anything that brings something else into being does so by sharing, according to its own created nature, in divine creative power. As the dynamic ground of all that exists in past, present, and future, the Spirit, Lord and giver of life, vivifies the whole community of existence and, when it is damaged or violated, works continuously to renew the face of the earth in its cosmic, social, and personal dimensions.

The intimate and unbreakable relationship of the world to God, rather than crushing creation by the overpowering presence of the divine, serves to set the world up in its own integrity. Spinning out the fire metaphor, Rahner writes that God is a blazing flame whose drawing near does not burn everything else to a crisp but gives it its own reality and authentic value: "We must understand that in this infinite sea of measureless flame everything else is not destroyed; on the contrary, only in this flame does all else become truly alive."[15] This is a genuinely noncompetitive view of God and the world. According to its dynamism, nearness to God and genuine autonomy grow in direct rather than inverse proportion. That is, God is not threatened by the active independence of the creature nor enhanced by its diminishment but is glorified by the creature's flourishing in the fullness of its powers. The nature of created participation in divine being is such that it grants creatures their own integrity, without reserve.[16]

Scientific perspectives add a further nuance. In the beginning, Creator Spirit brings the world into being. Thenceforth it evolves and develops into ever new complexities according to the interplay of its own inner dynamics of law and chance, which themselves are sustained by divine essence, power, and presence. Reading the book of nature to discern in the free play of its indeterminate and agential forces the direction of God's intent, we see that the whole drive of evolution is in the direction of greater and greater distinctiveness-in-community as galaxies self-organize from formlessness, as life ignites from nonorganic matter, and as species and ultimately human persons emerge from previous forms. This did not happen according to a pre-established blueprint, but nevertheless it has happened. The creating work of the Spirit who loves the world into ever more diverse forms of being gives grounds for thinking that in and through loving the whole, God cherishes each human person in the community of life, such creatures being the most distinctively unique, self-conscious, freely acting results of the evolutionary process that we know of. When death returns them to the earth whence they came and natural processes dissolve their body-spirit, is that the absolute finish of the person or does the same Creator Spirit creatively preserve each person's distinctiveness in a communion of life with God, so that not one gets lost? Such an outcome, far from being unseemly, actually coheres with the typical action of the Spirit in creating the world and guiding it in the direction of greater complexity-consciousness, since persons are not reducible simply to the working of the matter that comprises them.[17] Note that such a line of thinking provides no proof of eternal life. It simply shows grounds for eschatological hope in the typical actions of the Creator Spirit vivifying and renewing the world.

Resurrection of the Crucified

Although counted among those who hope in history, dreaming of justice and healing for all, Jesus was cruelly, unjustly, and in an untimely manner killed. This death was a real death, casting him into the unknown darkness beyond the time and space of this world. It violently tore apart his whole life; no piece of him slipped through its mesh. He died. This historical event cannot be reversed. In the face of this destruction, the Easter message proclaims that the Creator Spirit has her way even with death. For Jesus the true dissolution of death is met by (and here words speaking of a sequence are inadequate) a new and wholly different brilliance of life. The crucified one does not die into nothingness; he dies into the absolute mystery of the glory of God. At the decisive frontier he is taken into the hidden, ultimate reality which is the innermost heart of the universe and quickened to new life surpassing all imagination. Starting with Mary Magdalene, the disciples proclaim *Vivit*: the godforsaken one lives forever with God as pledge of the future of all the world.

How to imagine this? Not at all. For the crucified Jesus there is no more time or space, rhythms of the physical body or thought processes of the embodied mind, nothing that we can envision similar to what we know but that the dissimilarity is always ever profoundly greater. Resurrection and rising up are themselves metaphorical terms. But the Easter proclamation affirms that through the compassionate initiative of Creator Spirit which is known only through faith and yet is not the product of faith, Jesus lives again. This is not a kind of physiological miracle that intervenes in history to redirect the laws of nature, but an act that takes place when the laws of nature and human evil have done their worst and played themselves out and finished his life. The point where everything is at an end from the historical point of view then becomes the point where the glory of God takes the crucified into the circle of divine life hidden from historical observation. "What happened is not nothing," Hans Küng explains, "but what happened bursts through and goes beyond the bounds of history. It is a transcendental happening out of human death into the all-embracing dimension of God."[18]

As with all those who have died, there is no more direct, sensate, mutual communication between Jesus and the circle of women and men who knew and loved him during his life, nor with those who follow him in later centuries. As the narratives of the Easter appearances make clear, henceforth he is present through the power of the Spirit in word and sacrament, dwelling wherever two or three gather in his name, encountered as a stranger explaining the Scriptures as he walks along the road, recognized in the breaking of the bread, present where human wounds are touched and healed and, in a special way, served where the hungry receive bread, the thirsty drink, and the naked clothing. But — and this is the critical point for faith — while known through historical memory made present and active through the power of the Spirit, the crucified Jesus is yet more than a memory. The heart of the good news proclaims that, while utterly unimaginable, in his whole person and in all dimensions of his historical existence the crucified one lives forever with God.[19]

There is a close connection between the action of God that creates the world and the action of the same Spirit that raises Jesus to new life. Indeed, the context of original belief in Jesus' resurrection was late Jewish expectation of the universal resurrection of the dead. In itself this was not some esoteric idea but a consequence of belief in God as Creator of the world. If the compassionate power of God could bring about the existence of the world in the beginning, and if the living God as encountered in the history of Israel is unshakably faithful, then that same compassionate power can be trusted not to let created persons perish into oblivion but to engage in an act of new creation at the end. In this perspective, faith in the creating God gave rise to the conviction that the Creator Spirit keeps faith with the beloved creature even in death. The One who begins life and continuously sustains it is the same One who will complete it. The wellspring of creation and saving power at the heart of the struggle for being is also the fulfillment of the whole groaning creation, including the human race.

In its own historical context, the proclamation that Jesus is risen simply adds the astounding twist that what Israel is expecting to happen on the last day has already begun in the case of this crucified prophet from Nazareth. And it has begun not only as his individual destiny but as a divine pledge of a future for all the dead: "If the Spirit of God who raised Jesus from the dead dwells in you, then he who raised Christ from the dead will give life to your mortal bodies also through the Spirit that dwells in you."[20] The future will be on a cosmic scale what has already happened in Christ. What awaits the world is not nothing but the vivifying touch of the Creator Spirit. The view of God as the One who "gives life to the dead and calls into existence the things that do not exist"[21] becomes practically the designation of the Christian God.

The Nicene Creed follows the logic of this late Jewish/early Christian pattern of belief when it starts with faith in God the maker of heaven and earth, moves through the story of the death and resurrection of Jesus Christ, and ends with an affirmation of the resurrection of the dead and the life of the world to come. For hope in eternal life is not some unverifiable curiosity tacked on as an appendage to faith but is faith in the living, creating God carried to its radical depth. It is faith in God that does not stop halfway but follows the road consistently to the end, trusting that the One who calls things from nothingness into being, can, and in fidelity does, call them also from death to new life. It is faith in which human beings rely the God of their beginning to be also the God of their end, not only Alpha but also Omega. It is faith that trusts the Spirit of God to have the last word in our regard as indeed she had the first: let there be life. As Küng writes, "Resurrection means the real conquest of death by God the Creator to whom the believer entrusts everything, even the ultimate.... The almighty Creator who calls things from nothingness into being can also call human beings from death into life."[22]

In the real dissolution of death, when the body returns to nourish the flow of life in the world and human consciousness within history ceases to function, the action of God who raised Jesus from the dead grounds hope that what ultimately awaits is not nothing but the All who is the living God and in whose embrace a new future is offered to persons in an unimaginable way. In this light, the law of the conservation of energy governs everything empirical; but it does not have the final word. Again, this is not an attempt to prove eternal life. But it is an argument based on the resurrection of the crucified by the power of the Spirit that finds a foundation in this divine way of acting for eschatological hope that persons are not lost in death but in and through this process are found anew in the presence of God. Nor can this divine act be separated from the destiny of the whole human race and the world, which coincide in ultimate communion.

Self-Communication in Grace

The hope that the Creator Spirit's typical ways of acting in creating the world and raising the crucified Jesus point to an eternal future for persons rather than to total assimilation back into the universe finds further support in the way God gives human persons a share in divine life through the gift of grace. This gift, which is not some third thing between God and a person but a gracious offer to participate in the very life of trinitarian communion, heals, redeems, and liberates a person when it is received and responded to from the depths of one's heart. As with the creating relation between God and the world that enhances rather than diminishes creaturely integrity, this justifying and sanctifying relation in grace, much more deeply personal, restores a person to one's own true self: thanks to amazing grace "I once was lost but now I'm found, was blind but now I see." A growing integrity comes from living in coherence with rather than against the grain of the true ground of one's being, the living God. Such would not be the case if God were in competition with the world; then receiving the gift of grace would wipe out a person's individuality and independence, putting on pressure to be other or less than who one is. However, the experience of the most wholesomely holy persons gives evidence that the effect of responding to grace is just the opposite. For the Creator Spirit who *is* God's self-communication is not a vampire who sucks the proper reality out of persons to feed its own life force but the Life-giver who has a vested interest in seeing creatures flourish. Hence God's drawing near in saving grace is a blessing that strengthens one's personal reality. Finding its most intense expression in the genuine, free, loving humanity of Jesus Christ, the graced synergy between God and human persons comes to expression in Rahner's inimitable axioms: "Nearness to God and genuine human autonomy grow in direct and not inverse proportion";[23] or otherwise stated, "The nearer one comes to God, the more real one becomes; the more God grows in and before oneself, the more independent one becomes oneself"; and again "The closeness of God's self-bestowal and the unique personality of the creature grow in equal and not converse measure."[24]

If this be the principle that governs the gift of the Spirit in grace, then there is a certain logic to hoping that it continues to hold in the darkness of death. With the emergence of consciousness and freedom something new appears in history, something not reducible to the marvelous interplay of biological and chemical forces that regulate its embodiment. There is precisely a person here, capable of great love and also of great baseness, a relational subject with the suffering, joy, responsibility, yearning, failure, freedom, and much more besides that being human entails. Is this all dissolved in death, recycled back into the flow of history, or has something come to be in time and space that can never be absolutely erased? Something, in fact, that arrives at its own autonomy and fulfillment in the measure that it comes nearer to the mystery of God, which the event of death makes unavoidable? In view of the direct proportion, thanks to God's own graciousness, between divine closeness and the creature's integrity, there are grounds for hope that as death breaks apart the historical existence of the whole person, the mystery of persons' human identity grows ever more authentic through profound presence to God. They become alive as themselves in a radically transformed, unimaginable sense.

A corollary to this line of thinking is the idea that communion requires distinction. Divine being itself has the nature of communion, being a mystery of profound trinitarian relatedness. For the future to be the fullness of communion between God and the beloved world, something that seems indicated in virtue of the Creator Spirit having created a world in the first place, then persons need to retain in some transcendent sense their own individual differentiation. If all finite distinctions were to disappear in an ocean of universal substance, then the very condition for interrelationship would be missing. But rather than allowing persons to collapse into an indistinct mass, the typical graciousness of God who creates, redeems, and makes holy the world can preserve persons in their own uniqueness in order to make possible a new and eternal communion.

◆　◆　◆

To sum up: the language of hope, encoded in biblical symbols, is ultimately grounded on the character of God. To put the matter starkly: does God want everyone to merge back into the whole? Based on an interpretation of divine action in creating the world, raising the crucified, and self-communicating in grace, this argument transposes the same blessed ways of acting into the future and trusts that God will be there in typical fashion. In full awareness of the destructive power of death, no piece of us escaping and time absolutely coming to an end for our life, faith can affirm a great nevertheless: there is yet more. Rather than persons being assimilated, mystically absorbed, or fused with the divine matrix, they will be quickened into new, inconceivable life in the communion of saints as God wipes away all tears. This flies in the face of sense experience and we cannot conceive it, but it is not an unreasonable hope. Because of the creative, redeeming mercy of God, as Georgia Harkness eloquently writes, "It is the Christian hope that whether death comes early or late, no life is fruitless, no personality prized by God as an infinitely precious creation is snuffed out like a candle in the dark."[25]

Companions in Hope

Our exploration of eschatology, both the darkness of death and the reasons for hope, has been aimed at examining whether that sector of the communion of saints comprised of those who have lived before us can be interpreted not only as a company of friends whose memory stirs our action in loving care and the struggle for justice, but also as a company of friends whose destiny shines as a beacon of hope. Totally agnostic as to the *how* of personal continuity in and through death, we have arrived at a position that nevertheless affirms a personal future thanks to the action of God. Because each unique life does not just sink into the emptiness of the void or merge with the All, then we do not simply acknowledge them as those who have lived and made possible our own history. Instead, trust in the Creator Spirit who keeps faith with the creature gives rise to the hope that the dead, whether famous or unknown, whether distant in time or our own beloved ones, are enfolded into the absolute mystery of the gracious, compassionate being of God which to us is darkness but which to them is the fulfillment of their lives in the sphere of the Spirit. Their destiny signals the future toward which we the living are headed.

If we ask about these persons where they are to be found, the only possible answer, since they do not belong to the empirical world around us, is that they abide in God. It is quite impossible to picture this definitive fulfillment of persons in eternity. In fact, the more the artistic imagination succeeds at envisioning heaven and the more literally this picture is absorbed, the less truly do we intuit the reality toward which hope directs our lives. All the biblical images of light, banquet, harvest, rest, singing, homecoming, reunion, tears wiped away, seeing face to face, and knowing as we are known point to a deep, living communion in God's own life. We know nothing more of this than that the dead, silenced by death, have fallen not into nothingness but into the embrace of God. All we know in hope is that they exist as those who have been finally awakened into the unfathomable mystery of love at the heart of the universe. And that is enough.

If we seek to relate to these persons by a remembering that not only makes present the power flowing from their memory but also delivers a hopeful existential connection in the present, then we must look for them in the only possible direction in which they may be found: "They are found in our experience where God is."[26] Since their existence is now embedded by death in the incomprehensible ground of all being, there can be no direct, sensate communication such as was possible when they were alive in time. Even if we try to summon them and transpose them into our concrete world, something that is attempted in spiritualist seances or manipulative pieties, they could only appear as we are, earthbound, and not as they are, embraced in the light of absolute mystery. But they have passed from our circle into the hidden, silent life of God, and their silence, taken into ourselves, becomes a constitutive part of our relation with them. In Rahner's careful words,

> We meet the living dead, even when they are those loved by us, in faith, hope, and love, that is, when we open our hearts to the silent calm of God's own self, in which they live; not by calling them back to where we are, but by descending into the silent eternity of our own hearts, and through faith in the risen Lord, creating in time the eternity which they have brought forth forever."[27]

We meet them not by reducing their reality to our own imaginative size but by going forth to where they dwell as the beginning of the new heaven and the new earth in the mystery of the living God.

Our solidarity with those who have died consists not only in a common history, origin, and goal, but in the same Spirit who flows through and enlivens all. But insofar as we are aware of the limits of our capacity to know or speak in any detail about their status, we confide them to God's mercy, respecting the difference that death makes. Their status in our memory is that of a great cloud of witnesses whose efforts, defeats, and victories empower us for the struggle of our own lives to do justice, love kindness, and walk humbly with our God.[28] Their status in our hope is that of a great cloud of witnesses whose destiny encourages our hearts and charges us to care for the world and its flourishing. Their status in themselves is that of the utterly transformed ones who have entered upon the consummation of their life in close communion with the mystery of the living God. Beyond that there is not much we can say. But the symbol of the communion of saints bears the pledge that in and through the wrenching of death, terrible at times, an ever so quiet "Alleluia" can be heard. Having arrived at their destiny, the living dead become our companions in hope.

Hope in History

The question remains whether the hope generated by the communion of saints provides an escape from responsibility for this world or whether it promotes practical activity for the benefit of human beings and the earth. At certain points in history what was taken for hope did indeed provide an analgesic for pain, a too easy consolation, a distraction from the moral imperative to act against injustice. But alerted to the deficiencies of dualism that divides soul from body and heaven from earth, we seek to understand how hope for a destiny of life with God does not destroy the impetus for human action in the present but actually energizes persons toward social and ecological commitment. The key lies in returning the future blessedness of the world to the present as both a gift and a task.[29]

Since the world is not going forward toward ultimate nothingness but toward fullness of life, and since that fullness is not a replacement of this world but is precisely this world transformed, then present time and space, all manner of bodies and spirits, institutions, habitats — this world itself — is of irreplaceable worth. It would be of irreplaceable worth in any event, but the promise of a blessed, God-given future precisely as "vertical" and not only "horizontal" underscores the lasting importance of what transpires here and now. In the light of the promised future, radical hope then functions not as a lulling opiate but as a critical and creative power for the transformation of history in its personal, social, and cosmic dimensions. It propels all who seek God into cocreative and coredeeming partnership with the Creator Spirit to ensure that the promised well-being begins to arrive even here, even now, despite antagonistic powers that seek to mar and destroy. In the face of brokenness and oppression, in the midst of the rape of peoples and the earth, this hope breeds a certain defiant toughness far different from either optimism or pessimism, for it nourishes passion to see blessing come about precisely because the world in its own integrity has a future in God. What is excluded is despair.

Critical Power

The poignant words of the martyred priest Rutilio Grande preaching on eternal life to desperately poor peasants in El Salvador ring with an evocative assurance: "We see a common table, with a broad tablecloth, and set for everyone, as at this Eucharist. A chair for everyone. No one left out. Napkins and place settings for everyone."[30] This imagery captures and catalyzes the spirit of an oppressed people precisely by ascribing intrinsic value to the things of this earth. In the light of this utopian vision of a heaven where the poor are included in all dignity, they become stubborn with resistance against the economic and political structures that deprive them and their children of that dignity: everyone deserves a place at the table, even now.

Thus does transcendent hope work critically in the service of social justice. The final, God-given, blessed future provides a point of reference to which present injustices stand in sharp contrast and can be named for the abominations they truly are. Historical depths of negativity stand opposed to hope's vision, and this very antagonism, for those who hope in God, generates prophetic criticism aimed at transformation and healing. Rather than be immobilized by the dead weight of suffering, or by apathetic indifference before the pain of others, or by discouragement over the long haul yet to be made, those who live with transcendent hope drink from an unquenchable source of power, the promise of God that *nevertheless* something else will be possible. Then they are inspired so to struggle that fragments of well-being become embodied in the world, real if transitory anticipations of the coming well-being even here, even now.

Creative Power

In a positive vein, radical hope inspires people to put the imprint of hope on personal relationships, social structures, and ecological communities. Working with the biblical symbol of the "new creation," Sallie McFague offers a beautiful insight into this creative function of hope. This symbol expresses the belief that the direction of the world is toward salvation, that is, toward the honor and fulfillment of the body of the world through the liberating, healing, inclusive love of God. Not just the individual and not just the human race, but the whole natural world is included in this hope: "beyond even suffering we live with the hope against hope that defeat and death are not the last word, but that the least body in the universe, the most insignificant, most vulnerable, most outcast one will participate in the resurrection of the body,"[31] which is the gracious gift of God. Goaded and lured by this hope, human beings turn toward this world (where else?) to partner God in fulfilling the basic bodily needs of all creatures, a godly task. The ecological eschatological vision of the new creation, then, is a powerful resource for human solidarity with the oppressed who comprise not only humanity but also nature which, in McFague's powerful expression, we have made the new poor. Precisely because the body of the world is destined for a blessed future, we have a sublime and formidable vocation to bond with all life forms in ways that will create a rich, sustainable, and satisfying world for every particular body here and now.

Eschatology is not opposed to ethics. The Marxist point that religion's promise of heaven is opiate for those who suffer injustice, and the Ruetherian assessment that transcendent eschatology distracts attention from ecological responsibility, both telling critiques in a dualistic, patriarchal framework, become muted when hope is set free within a panentheistic paradigm. Then hope in God who creates, redeems, and blesses with a view to a living future operates with critical and productive power to quicken love for this world and energy to see it thrive.[32]

To conclude: hope is a dynamic at work in a community, first of all. Finding expression in a community's imagery, rituals, and stories, it arises in individuals insofar as they partake of this social reality. In the Christian community, a shared attitude of trustful hope is directed toward the gracious reality of God who in making and sustaining the world, raising Jesus from the dead, and gifting human beings with grace pledges unconquerable fidelity to all of creation. The communion of saints forms part of the vocabulary of this hope. Because the God of love who holds the world in being still embraces the dead, they can be affirmed as being alive in communion with the living God, thus signaling the destiny that awaits all. With these companions in hope the church cries out to God amid the beauty and suffering of history, "You are my hope,"[33] and sets itself to the task of making an earth where life with dignity is possible for all creatures.

– Chapter 12 –

Communion of Saints: Friends of God and Prophets

We have been exploring at length one vector of the relationship signified by the *communio sanctorum,* namely, the connection between living persons and those who have died. Typically overlooked in the worldview of advanced industrialized nations, this relationship comes to life under the rubrics of memory and hope. Remembering the women friends of God and prophets of previous generations who have been marginalized and ignored by an exclusive history challenges patriarchal bias and promotes the transformation of the church into a more just and liberating community. Hoping for life for the whole company of women and men who have died, out of radical trust in the creating God who gives life to the dead, sets free the energies of critical and creative hope amid the sufferings of the world. With this vector firmly in view, we return to a systematic interpretation of the symbol as a whole.

The *communio sanctorum* is a most relational symbol. From age to age, the same Spirit who vivifies and renews the natural world enters into holy souls, and not so holy ones, and makes them friends of God and prophets. Guided by this core vision, we follow the symbol of the communion of saints into the thought to which it gives rise, seeking to understand the fullness of relationship it means to convey. Our interpretation parses the communion of saints into five rudimentary elements: the community of living, ordinary persons as "all saints," in particular as this designation is used to characterize members of the Christian community and their relationship to the triune God; their working out of holiness through creative fidelity in ordinary time; their relation to the circle of companions who have run the race before, who are now embraced in the life of God and accessed through memory and hope; the paradigmatic figures among them; and the relation of this community, living and dead, to the whole community of the natural world. Taken together these five elements formulate a contemporary systematic articulation of this doctrinal symbol and render it rife with intellectual and practical consequences.

1. All Saints

In the first place, the communion of saints comprises all living persons of truth and love. The point to emphasize is "all": all Christians as well as all persons of good will. While the term itself springs from the experience of grace within the church, the communion of saints does not limit divine blessing to its own circle. Within human cultures everywhere, Spirit-Sophia calls every human being to fidelity and love, awakening knowledge of the truth and inspiring deeds of compassion and justice. The friends of God and prophets are found in every nation and tongue, culture and religion, and even among religion's cultured despisers. Indeed, where human participation in divine holiness disappears the opposite appears — barbarity, cruelty, murder, and unspeakable despair. At its most elemental, then, the communion of saints embraces all women and men who hear Holy Wisdom's call and follow her path of righteousness: "whoever finds me finds life."[1]

Too often theology has squeezed this meaning dry, eliminating first those who are not baptized and then most of the baptized themselves. Many a theologian begins discussion of the subject by acknowledging that even though the New Testament refers to the whole Christian community as saints, this will be set aside in order to consider paradigmatic figures, who then become in practice if not in theory the real saints. But this strategy woefully shortchanges the breadth and depth of Wisdom's strategy which is to lead all peoples on the path to life. Recovering a sense of the holiness of the ordinary person is a first step in unleashing the symbol to its full, comprehensive scope.

This global framework serves to keep the symbol inclusive when applied to the specific religious tradition in which it primarily functions. The term originates as a particular linguistic practice that reflects the Christian community's sense of the blessing being worked in its midst by the gracious power of God: where sin did abound, grace did superabound; there is now no more condemnation for those who are in Christ Jesus.[2] The whole community of redeemed sinners becomes a locus of God's saving intent and action. Thus, in a foundational way, the communion of saints is an evocative symbol of the nature of the Christian church.[3]

The Pentecost story as told in the Acts of the Apostles beautifully conveys this idea that participating in the holiness of God is a
matter of identity for the whole Christian *ekklesia.* Gathered in the
upper room in Jerusalem are the male apostles, "together with certain
women, including Mary the mother of Jesus, as well as his brothers,"[4]
all devoting themselves to prayer. Presumably the "certain women"
include those already named in Luke's gospel as being among Jesus'
followers: Mary Magdalene, Joanna, Susanna, the other women who
had stood by the cross and tended to Jesus' burial, and Mary the
mother of James who with them had announced the Easter message.[5]
Together "the crowd numbered about one hundred twenty persons,"[6]
women and men, disciples, friends, and relatives of the crucified and
risen Jesus, the nucleus of the church. The narrative goes on:

> When the day of Pentecost had come, they were all together in
> one place. And suddenly from heaven there came a sound like
> the rush of a violent wind, and it filled the entire house where
> they were sitting. Divided tongues, as of fire, appeared among
> them, and a tongue rested on each of them. All of them were
> filled with the Holy Spirit and began to speak in other languages,
> as the Spirit gave them ability.[7]

Responding to the amazement and criticism of devout Jews from every
nation under heaven who had traveled to Jerusalem for the feast but
could not make heads or tails out of the exuberant witness of the
women and men, Peter explains the meaning of what was going on:

> Indeed these are not drunk, as you suppose, for it is only nine
> o'clock in the morning. No, this is what was spoken through the
> prophet Joel: "In the last days it will be, God declares, that I will
> pour out my Spirit upon all flesh, and your sons and your daugh-
> ters shall prophesy, and your young men shall see visions, and
> your old men shall dream dreams. Even upon my slaves, both
> men and women, in those days I will pour out my Spirit; and
> they shall prophesy."[8]

The gift of the Spirit to *all flesh,* and not just to chosen individuals, is
a mark of the messianic age. Even the lowest of the low, slave women,
will find their voice and speak in the name of God. And this prophecy
now comes alive as "all of them," the women and men of the crucified
prophet's circle, receive the Holy Spirit and, as "all of them," a tongue
of fire on each head and burning in each heart, begin to speak in their

own voices in diverse tongues. They testify to the mighty and transformative ways of the living God who raises up the crucified, thereby
making possible a new kind of hope in the teeth of human injustice
and sinfulness. The whole community receives the gift of the Spirit for
the sake of the world.

This same intuition surfaces, in a less dramatic, more didactic fashion, in the Second Vatican Council's teaching on the call of the whole
church to holiness. Through baptism persons are justified in Christ
and, receiving the Spirit, become sharers in the divine nature. "In this
way they are really made holy."[9] This same holiness, furthermore, is
essentially the same for all insofar as it is a gift of participation in divine life. There are not different types of holiness, one for lay persons
and another for those in religious life or ordained ministry. There is
not one kind of indwelling of the Spirit for officeholders or public personages in the church and another for unnoticed, faithful members.
Rather, "in the various types and duties of life, one and the same holiness is cultivated by all who are moved by the Spirit of God."[10] One
and the same holiness: the church is not divided into saints and nonsaints. Because of Wisdom's generous work, all are called to be holy,
to be saints; the vocation of being friends of God and prophets shapes
the life of everyone in the community.

The communion of saints is comprised first of all of the current
generation of living Christians who respond to the promptings of the
Spirit and follow the way of Jesus in the world. In the circumstances
of their own historical time and place, these women and men try to
be faithful friends and courageous prophets, taking seriously the invitation to love God and neighbor and pouring good purpose into their
lives. Some work anonymously in fidelity to duty; others speak loudly
in the assembly; some risk the wrath of the powerful by engaging in
structural analysis and action on behalf of justice, for the poor and
for women; others are the powerful converted to their responsibility;
still others perform miracles of nonviolence in bringing about peace;
some bountifully nurture and nourish young life; others show the way
in nurturing and healing the oppressed self; still others lead the way
in caring for the earth; some compassionately tend the sick and the
dying; others are artisans of new visions, new images, new designs for
society; some know the pleasures of sexual expression; others experience their sexuality as the locus of violation; some fulfill a particular
mission or office in the church; many more live "ordinary lives," growing in love through the complex interactions of their work, play, and

relationships; some are well-off; many more are numbered among the poor who struggle for bread; some know success; many others are broken by suffering, both personal and political; some clearly make God attractive; others wrestle with demons that obscure the immediacy of divine presence. Any combination of the above situations is possible; the diversity of circumstances is amazing.

This *communio sanctorum* participates in the holiness of Sophia-God, whose kindly, people-loving spirit fills the world, pervading everything and holding all things together. The symbol itself originates when Christians recognize this corporate sharing in grace that marks themselves and others, and rise up in appreciation of the blessing. Since for Christian faith the one God graciously relates to the world in a triune gift of self-communication through incarnation and grace, we use this threefold pattern to describe the foundational relation to the Holy One without which there would be no communion of saints.

God beyond the World: Unoriginate, Source of All

The mystery of the incomprehensible God, whom no one has seen or can see, is made present and active through created things in their own integrity that disclose something of divine quality. This relation of participation is traditionally articulated as the sacramental principle, a postulate that governs the spiritual meaning of things far beyond the concrete seven sacraments. The world itself is the primordial sacrament, reflecting the glory of God and speaking a revelatory word; human beings are made to the image and likeness of God; and religious words and rituals in turn make explicit the gracious, compassionate ways of the divine with the world known through concrete revelatory events.

Affirming that the presence of God in the world is rendered visible in the saints, Vatican II applies this sacramental principle of relationship in extraordinarily bold language. In the lives of holy people, the council writes, God "vividly manifests" both the divine "presence" and also the divine "face." Not only that, but God "speaks to us in them," thus also making audible the divine voice. These persons are nothing less than a gift from God, given as signs who point in their own human ways to the coming of God's reign, "to which we are powerfully drawn, surrounded as we are by so many witnesses (Heb 12:1), and having such an argument for the truth of the gospel."[11] In context, the language of this text veers back and forth between a focus on paradigmatic figures and on the great community of faithful ones who share in the same Spirit and who in various ways "all partake in the same love for God and neighbor, and all sing the same hymn of glory to our God."[12] Interpreting the communion of saints in the broad sense of including all who respond to grace, we find here a powerful restatement of the ancient idea of the church's identity in relation to God, namely, that it is a veritable sacrament of the divine in the world. This dignity characterizes first and foremost not institutional accoutrements but the community of persons following Jesus in the Spirit.

Each person makes God present; each face reveals God's face; each voice resounds with God's word.[13] This conciliar restatement of the *imago Dei* doctrine is replete with historical dynamism. In classical theology the image of God in persons is understood as both a present state and a capacity. By our gifted nature we already reflect the divine and, although the image is historically marred by sin, we can grow more clearly transparent to the Light through deeper knowledge and love in response to the offer of grace. The closer we get to the goal of image restoration, the more we perceive ourselves not as enslaved servants but as friends of God, so enamored that we are compelled to go out into the world with compassion.[14] The council's metaphors of presence, face, and voice press this idea into a most concrete mold, saying in effect that in the communion of saints every woman, man, and child, of whatever race, class, ethnicity, sexual persuasion, or any other marker that at once identifies and divides human beings, is a sacrament of the presence, face, and voice of the unseen, unknowable mystery of God. When, grounded in memory and hope, the church goes forth to care for the world, the presence of the mystery of divine otherness is as close as the nearest smiling face or the nearest ravaged face, as audible as the inspiring, comforting, crying, or challenging word of the nearest neighbor.

Such is the relation to God of the saint, of all saints. Reclaiming this teaching in the perspective of feminist theology, we see that such is the relation to God of that host of human persons who are women. Every woman seeking divine truth and responding to grace in her life vividly manifests God's presence. Her face reveals the face of God. Her voice bespeaks the word of God. Her embodied witness precisely as female attracts and encourages others toward the reign of justice and peace. In light of this historic and continuing witness rendered by persons largely officially silenced and invisible, it is not superficial wordplay but an expression of the deepest truth to gloss the council's exclusive language and say: in all graced women "God vividly manifests to human beings Her presence and Her face. She speaks to us in them, and gives us a sign of Her reign, to which we are powerfully drawn, surrounded as we are by so many witnesses (Heb 12:1), and having such an argument for the truth of the gospel."

God with the World: Wisdom Made Flesh in History

For the Christian community, participating in the holiness of God comes about through being disciples of Jesus, the one in whom God showed and enacted divine solidarity with all people, especially the humble of the earth and those crucified. By following Jesus, taking our bearings from his story, opening ourselves to the inspiration of his Spirit, sharing in his intense experience of God and his compassion for the least of his sisters and brothers, and entrusting our own destiny to God in the darkness of death, as Edward Schillebeeckx has written, "we allow the history of Jesus, the living one, to continue in history as a piece of living christology, the work of the Spirit among us, the Spirit of God and the Spirit of Christus.... Therefore we can only speak of the history of Jesus in terms of the story of the Christian community which follows Jesus.... The living community is the only real reliquary of Jesus."[15] In the same passage where it affirms God's face and voice manifest in the saints, Vatican II also takes note of this basic relation of the community to Jesus as a piece of living christology, writing of all members of the church that they "belong to Christ" and of paradigmatic figures in particular that they are sharers in the human condition who "were transformed into especially successful images of Christ."[16]

The core relation to Jesus, begun in baptism and kept alive through spiritual practices of memory and hope and practical actions of following, does not mean that the communion of saints copies Jesus' life in exact detail. People live in different times and places, which have different needs; they have different temperaments, face different sufferings, delight in different joys. Being disciples means that they strike out on their own, transpose, innovate, as the Spirit creates something fresh while still in accord with the compassionate direction of his life and teaching. This is not only a theoretical following but a practical one as well, one that calls on reserves of integrity and discernment. It results in there being not just one life of Jesus set down in the gospels, but a continuous biography of Christ in all fullness in the lives of all saints, complete with liberating ministry, passion narratives, and hints of resurrection. The more they are "transformed into successful images of Christ," the more they together bring to light ever new aspects of the truth and love incarnate in the gospel.

Women of all races and economic classes share equally in the process of being "transformed into especially successful images of Christ." Precisely as female persons they form a piece of living christology in the myriad circumstances of history. In keeping with traditional and conciliar teaching about the theological identity of all the saints as images of Christ, but in contrast to current official statements in the ordination debate locating the *imago Christi* in the male body, feminist theological understanding insists that insofar as the human race is a distinct species, natural resemblance to Christ is enjoyed by graced human beings precisely as human. In terms of theological identity, it is not naive physicalism but transformation through the power of the Spirit; not sexual similarity to the human man Jesus but coherence with the narrative shape of his compassionate, liberating life in the world; not male genes but congruity with Christ-Sophia's friend-making and prophetic power; not specificity of embodiment, essential as that is for personal identity, but participation in the living and dying and rising of Christ, that makes the community and its members christomorphic. African-American theologian Kelly Brown Douglas gets this precisely right when she observes:

> A womanist portrayal of the Black Christ avails itself of a diversity of symbols and icons, living symbols and icons as Christ is a living Christ.... These portrayals of Christ suggest, for instance, that Christ can be seen in the face of a Sojourner Truth, a Harriet Tubman, or a Fannie Lou Hamer, as each one struggled to help the entire Black community survive and become whole. Seeing Christ in the faces of those who were and are actively committed to the wholeness of the Black community suggests several things...that it was not who Jesus was, particularly as a male, that made him Christ, but what he did. Essentially, Christ's biological characteristics have little significance for discerning Christ's sustaining, liberating, and prophetic presence. ...[We] consistently lift up the presence of Christ in the faces of the poorest Black women.[17]

The theory that would deny the christic identity of such women, of all women, is so skewed by *scotosis,* blind prejudice, that it verges on a heretical subverting of the gospel itself. Scholarly research has abundantly shown the shortcomings of this ideology as well as alternatives in accord with the gospel, to no avail in the Roman Catholic Church.[18] Perhaps it is time for humor. A classic incident in American feminism occurred when Gloria Steinem, youthful feminist leader and editor of *Ms.* magazine, reached a significant birthday. In surprise, a reporter objected, "But you don't look forty." Her retort, perfect for its assumption of authority and rejection of stereotyping, was, "*This* is what forty looks like." Similarly, women friends of God and prophets in the communion of saints today can simply declare of themselves, "*This* is what Christ looks like," affirming in this way their deepest affiliation and resisting its denial until the heart of officialdom is converted.

God within the World: Indwelling Fire of Divine Love

Being related to the Spirit immerses the community in a deep spring of creative and re-creative power; in a very real sense the Spirit *is* the energy of relation, even within God's own being. Boundlessly vivifying, flaming, blowing, outpouring, healing, birthing, making green and fertile, uniting, resisting, indwelling, luring, hidden but glimmering in every act of truth and beauty, Spirit-Sophia makes all alive at the deepest level. Here is the source of the *koinonia* with God and one another that is the very heart of the communion of saints. Here is the source of holiness which means nothing more or less than belonging to God. Here is the wellspring of creativity that leads to risk-taking for the gospel in the face of injustice and the threat of death. Here is the source of the power of memory and the encouragement of hope.

Women share equally in this life-giving relationship to the Spirit. In our day epiphanies of the working of grace are newly embodied in their acts of self-confidence and self-love, courage for autonomy, holy impatience, bold speech, organizing, resisting, struggling for justice and the relief of suffering, blessing their own bodiliness, and being a blessing for the liberation of others, in addition to the more traditionally affirmed holy acts of women. Bearing the power of creation and new creation in the bright nooks and dark crannies of history and in the event of death itself, the Spirit shapes their very being into a sacrament of the presence of God.

In an intriguing thesis ripe with ecumenical implications, Herman Wegman suggests that the Spirit's presence can be seen to the degree that holiness wells up in people, and that furthermore this *successio sanctorum,* or Spirit-inspired continuation of gospel witnesses, is as intrinsic to the church's identity as is apostolic succession, and in fact validates the lasting significance of the latter. Without the succession of women and men saints, a global phenomenon, the apostolic tradition would be as a sounding bell or tinkling cymbal, an extrinsic handing on of office without ultimate spiritual substance. But if holy people keep appearing, ordinary people in ordinary time, they give living witness that the Spirit has not abandoned the church and thus grace continues more powerful than evil in every age. He writes:

> That the church is a community of sinners is verifiable, but that it can nonetheless be characterized as holy is not only a hopeful prospect, directed toward the *eschaton*, but also a confession based upon the actual and realized experience of holiness by so many men and women in all the periods of church history. The creedal confession of the holy church is no free-floating pronouncement, but is filled with the life stories of people who have been sanctified and graced by God through the ages.[19]

This not only ensures gospel meaning to apostolic office but provides a ground for church communion across institutional divides where the succession of office is disputed even now, for "the walls of division do not reach up to heaven." In a similar vein, philosopher Patrick Sherry argues that if there were no more saints, then this would count tellingly against the truth of Christian belief, because the doctrine of the Holy Spirit requires that people be transformed by God.[20] Considered both as an institution and as a people, the historical church is a sinful church, on the way, always in need of reform, sometimes very obviously lost. But the community of sinful yet redeemed women and men, vivified by grace, *is* the church and testifies, in a historically tangible manner, that the Spirit still moves in history, creating a flowing river of holy lives.

Some few of this multitude out of every race and tongue and nation are known by name beyond their own immediate circle. Most are not. But all know in some way the pull of the power, joy, shock, and challenge of Wisdom's gracious action in their lives. And none stop seeking the living God, clinging to divine mercy in the face of sin, oppression, depression, and death. This is the communion of all saints. The center of gravity for reflection becomes not extraordinary personalities or heroes but the extraordinary status of simple human women and men in the image and likeness of God, trying to find their way, called and gifted by grace. In a community of companionship in the Spirit that circles the globe, they make their own contribution and then pass on through the nothingness of death into the life-giving hands of God, to be followed by a new generation of the fresh young faces of all saints.

2. Creative Fidelity in Everyday Life

From this first rudiment of interpretation there follows a second, namely, that the arena where holiness flourishes is everyday life which itself has a sacred character. The term "heroic sanctity," used in official church language as a criterion for those whose cases are tested for canonization, reflects a value given to a certain kind of spiritual achievement, attained by intrepid acts and buttressed by miracle. It customarily points to such deeds as witnessing to the point of bloody martyrdom, or engaging in the white martyrdom of stringent asceticism, or experiencing a radical conversion from which one does not turn back, renouncing family and worldly possessions, or pouring out lifelong dedication to the sick, the poor, the imprisoned. Traditional "lives of the saints" are filled with such titanic acts. Noble they may be, but their telling within a tradition of holiness interpreted along lines of hierarchical dualism serves to reinforce the "unsaintliness" of those who do not measure up to these epic proportions. Reading the communion of saints as a company of the friends of God and prophets reclaims the ordinary milieu of virtue and the nobility of struggle despite failure and defeat, locating holiness not only or even chiefly in mighty, ideal deeds but in creative fidelity in the midst of everyday life.

Feminist analysis sheds an unexpectedly helpful light on this point. The very ideal of the heroic, upon closer inspection, shows itself to be more a creation of the male psyche under patriarchy than the female, and more reflective of the situation of elite men in positions of privilege even at that. Caroline Walker Bynum's sympathetic critique of Victor Turner's assessment of medieval religiosity is a case in point. Turner gives great play to the notion of liminality, defined as a transitional situation in human life when normal cultural roles are suspended (e.g., going on pilgrimage), which sets up a condition in which one can freely explore an alternative identity. Being in this unusual space, persons are at times moved to a radical conversion of heart accompanied by a freely chosen reversal of social status. Bynum notes how this notion is not germane to medieval religiosity in general, as Turner writes, but is indeed applicable to men. Medieval men's religious stories and symbols are replete with images of full social reversals, such as wealthy men renouncing riches or power-ful men adopting humble positions in order to follow the poor and crucified Jesus. Such a pattern of discipleship, however, reflects these men's status in society where they are the elites; having much, one must be emptied. The stories and symbols of medieval women, by contrast, opt not for reversal of status but for continuous and deep-ening relationship. The eucharistic devotion of female mystics, for example, did not move them either to celebrate Christ's triumphant reversal of the power of sinful flesh or to renounce their own sta-tus, but restored them to themselves through deep intimacy with his love. "Christ on the cross was not victory or humility but 'humanity,'" writes Bynum. "And in eating and loving that 'humanness' one became more fully oneself. What women's images and stories expressed most fundamentally was neither reversal nor elevation but continuity."[21]

Bynum's discovery of continuity of the self in medieval women's religious experiences coheres with a wealth of contemporary insight. Contemporary studies of women's spiritualities underscore the ways in which women's experience of the sacred typically involves a whole-ness rather than a disjunction, a oneness with God comprised not of solitary achievement but of interdependence and the power that comes from connectedness, of care for those outside the pale of official inter-est, of the sensuality of their embodied, sexual selves, of creative links with the natural world, and of repetitive life rituals.[22] My point here is that Bynum's and similar studies are not intended to set up new, universally applicable stereotypes of the feminine, and certainly not to imply that women do not reverse course, break boundaries, or accom-plish heroic deeds. But it is to highlight that the disjunctive, solitary, dramatic achievement, and in that sense the heroic, is characteristic of only some people's way to God and has traditionally reflected the experience of male elites. As research continues to reveal underlying male/female historical differences in experience of the sacred, resulting from inculturated experience of the embodied self in a given society, it becomes ever more clear how women's exclusion from the church's public culture has led to one-sided definitions of exemplary charac-ter, holiness, and spiritual paths. The result is an official ideal that disvalues the different paths to holiness taken by all saints.

Creative fidelity in everyday life takes different forms in different eras. "Today, it is not nearly enough merely to be a saint, but we must have the saintliness demanded by the present moment, a new saintliness, itself also without precedent."[23] Simone Weil, who penned these lines, envisioned that in the modern age of divine eclipse, holiness might well take the form of waiting determinedly and passionately for God. Saints may not necessarily be persons who have found God; in fact, they may experience in a profound way the absence of God. Yet they try to walk with others faithfully even in the darkness and their restless hearts do not stop seeking. In Theresa Sanders's engaging view, this holiness entails not so much an accomplishment as being on fire with desire, saints being those whose hunger and thirst for God is insatiable.[24] In our day too, the arena for holy action stretches from the personal sphere to the farthest reaches of the political, with asceticism suffered not for its good effect on one's personal spiritual standing but as an inevitable by-product of struggling for the well-being of the dear neighbor. Religious attention shifts away from miraculous deeds that defy the laws of nature to deeds of friendship and prophecy that defy the weight of systemic power and privilege. Spiritual value is given to action on behalf of justice and against racism, sexism, classism; to endeavors of active nonviolent resistance for peace; to measures that promote meaning among the young and dignity among the old; to efforts to cultivate kinship with the earth and protect it from harm; to works of building communities of mutuality; and to acts of shucking off denigrating self-images, refusing victimization, blessing the body, finding one's voice, and speaking the truth in all boldness.

In an interesting thought experiment, Rembert Weakland invites us to imagine what such spiritual passion would look like in the year 2100. His candidate for sainthood is one Ellen Piasecki, married, mother of three children, worker in a local brewery, accidentally killed at the age of forty-five when she was called out to help a neighbor being brutalized by domestic violence. She had already wrestled with the vagaries of life, including breast cancer and the stresses of an unemployed husband. But through a slow process of spiritual growth fed by the Scriptures, the sacraments, and relationships with her family, co-workers, and other people, especially the poor, she became a deeply peaceful person rooted in God. Through an almost imperceptible process of maturing, she was purified from childhood expectations:

> She did not seek a God of magic, a *deus ex machina* that could be turned off and on as needed, nor a schoolmaster to discipline society, nor a policeman to keep it in line, but she came to seek rather a God who was a lover, a friend, a transcendent other — bigger than she but not distant from her. Once she had discov-

ered that God was a companion, she seemed able to relax in that transcendent presence that was so real and so close to her.[25]

No goody-goody, she worked on her relationship with her husband and reared her children with the usual ups and downs. Her family, co-workers, fellow parishioners, and citizens of Milwaukee, where she served on a reconciliation commission, found her more and more to be a caring woman with a listening ear, a compassionate heart, and a passion for peacemaking, not taken with herself but radiating a spiritual depth that was crucial to their own growth in faith. In the end, she protected a wife and kids from a raging husband, becoming caught in the crossfire herself. In this typically American midwestern setting, Ellen was an example in death as in life: "she mirrored Christ to us...taught us how to relate to God in a new way...how to be a practitioner of peace like Jesus," and one hundred years later her memory continues to inspire. Yes, Weakland concludes, her goodness and giftedness became famous because of the notoriety surrounding her death. But "how many others are there out there who do not become famous?"[26]

This imaginative narrative elucidates in a novel and enlightening way the presence of grace in a life caught up in an average American existence that seeks the face of God. Not the search for the heroic but creative fidelity within a network of relationships marks Ellen's story of growth in the Spirit. From a feminist point of view I myself would want to know more about Ellen's relationship with other women and also how she dealt with the patriarchy of the church; very few women of her age and experience in this country are not troubled by this issue at least to some degree, as the archbishop himself has made clear on other occasions. Even more ambiguous is her death, which, though its starkness does make her noteworthy, plays into traditional hagiography's tendency to see that the good woman is one who suffers. But this effort to imagine a holy life in a secular culture is a worthy one, and succeeds in breaking through outdated and unrealistic notions of what it means to respond to the gift of Spirit-Sophia in everyday life.

Wisdom's community of friends of God and prophets includes all persons who respond to the Spirit; they do so through lives that move in the direction of truth and love in the midst of ordinary time, seeking, even if often failing, to be faithful. The third rudiment of understanding is this: the community also includes all such persons who have died.

3. Cloud of Witnesses through Time

The communion of saints is not restricted to persons who live and breathe at the present moment, but embraces those who have gone through the shattering of death into eternal life. Only the hope that God is trustworthy can ground this interpretation, for death truly ends life as we know it. What follows is unimaginable, and no pictorial description of saints in heaven is ever remotely adequate. What Christian faith affirms of persons who lived and died trying to respond to the Spirit, even in their failure, is simply and radically this: *Vivit!* — by the mercy of God. As George Tavard has succinctly written, this "is not the fruit of works or the reward of individual merit, but it is entirely God's gift. All the faithful on earth are saints in the biblical sense of the term. All those who die in Christ are saints in heaven."[27] And both groups are linked by their communion with the living God who pervades and transcends the boundaries of time itself.

The company of saints in heaven beggars description. While some few are remembered by name, it enfolds millions upon anonymous millions of people whom we will never know. In different times and places their imagination and initiatives brought compassion alive in their own corner of life and comforted, healed, and challenged the world in ways that we can never imagine. "By passing along the narrow road they widened it, and while they went along, trampling on the rough ways, they went ahead of us,"[28] as Augustine preached. Their pioneering faith, replete with hope in divine mercy over sinfulness, and the patterns of goodness they traced in history make our life possible. Bearers of our past, they also signify our future.

Among these saints, known and mostly unknown, are counted those untimely dead, killed in godforsaken incidents of terror, war, and mass death, their life's projects cut down in mid-stride. Having drunk so deeply of the cup of crucifixion, they call forth special mention in anguish and lament. Among these saints are also numbered some whom we knew personally. Their number increases as we get older: grandparents, mother and father, sisters and brothers, beloved spouses and life partners, children, teachers, students, patients, clients, friends and colleagues, relatives and neighbors, spiritual guides and religious leaders. Their good lives, complete with fault and failure, have reached journey's end. Gone from us, they have arrived home in unspeakable, unimaginable life within the embrace of God. To say of all these people that they form with us the company of the redeemed is to give grief a direction, affirming that in the dialogue between God and the human race the last word is the gracious word of life. In instances where persons have wrought real and lasting damage by their actions, faith holds out the possibility that at their deepest core they did not concur in diabolical evil. The church's prayer is that God will be more merciful toward them than they have been to others. On their behalf, at least we may hope.

Cheered on by this great, richly varied cloud of witnesses, learning their "lessons of encouragement,"[29] protesting their pain, catching their hope, standing on their shoulders, the church today takes its own steps on the path of discipleship as legacy for future generations. Orthodox theologian Kallistos Ware spins out a beautiful metaphor of this relationship when he writes, "The saints in each generation, joined to those who have gone before, and filled like them with light, become a golden chain in which each saint is a separate link, united to the next by faith, works, and love. So in the One God they form a single chain which cannot quickly be broken."[30]

Saints on earth have access to the company of saints in heaven through memory and hope. Memory is meant here in the sense of *anamnesis*, an effective remembering that makes something genuinely past to be present and active in the community today. A remembered event becomes a living force in history when it is recalled and narrated; in the very retelling power comes forth to change the horizon of our days and offer new possibilities of existence. The primary *anamnesis* of the Christian community occurs in the sacramental action of the Eucharist, where the community makes memorial of Jesus' death and resurrection in such a way that it becomes a living, transforming reality in the lives of those who celebrate it.[31] Christian remembrance of the saints is linked to this action, making present the creative struggle and witness of so many who themselves participated in this paschal mystery. Retelling their story brings the subversive, encouraging, and liberating power of their love and witness into the present generation.

Lamentably, the exclusion of women from the public culture of the church has resulted in an official memory that has erased a good part of the history of women's discipleship, giving to the communion of saints a largely male face both in heaven and on earth. This erasure has never been wholly effective, however, and feminist hermeneutical methods now bring to light women and the contributions they have made in licit and illicit ways. For ecclesial practices of memory to be liberating to women, to poor women, to women of color, to lay women, to married women everywhere, deliberate attention must be turned to their stories. Their absence must be noticed, missed, criticized, and corrected. It is not just a matter of adding women to what remains a patriarchal master narrative. The challenge, rather, is to reshape the church's memory so as to reclaim an equal share in the center for women and thereby transform the community.

The prevailing relationship among members of this company of the living and the dead that crosses centuries is fundamentally mutual and egalitarian. This interpretation retrieves the biblical insight that the people as a whole are holy, as well as its affirmation of each person's equal standing in a political as well as spiritual sense: "There is no longer Jew or Greek, there is no longer slave or free, there is no longer male and female; for all of you are one in Christ Jesus."[32] It also reclaims the intuition of the early Christian centuries that the martyrs are splendid companions in the following of Christ. This relational pattern runs counter to the later image of a spiritual hierarchy of patrons and petitioners, with saints in heaven in the role of powerful intercessors and nonsaints on earth asking for their aid. Shaped according to the Roman system of patronage, this construal understands God to be a powerful monarch whom a little person dares not approach directly. Saints dwell in the heavenly court, some closer to the throne than others, and can present the needs of their devotees with greater certainty of success. This patronage model has been rendered moot by deep theological shifts, not least the gospel depiction of Jesus' ministry to the poor and marginalized that embodies divine compassion for the most godforsaken with an overwhelming freedom and graciousness, calling all to a place around the table. It also falters in the light of feminist theological analysis that reveals it to be a projection of patriarchal structures into heaven. By contrast, the saints alive in God are sisters and brothers who accompany the current generation on the path of discipleship. In this companionship paradigm, differences between persons are not erased but neither are they the occasion for relating as superior to inferior. Rather, because each person is truly called to the one holiness and gifted by the Spirit with a unique talent, all come together as companions along the way. As Augustine preached on one feast of the martyrs Perpetua and Felicity: "If we are not capable of following them in action, let us follow in affection; if not in glory, then certainly in joy and gladness; if not in merit, then in desire; if not in suffering, then in fellow feeling; if not in excellence, then in our close relationship with them."[33] A lively sense of friendly appreciation, with room for these young women's unique witness, does not undermine but strengthens the common vocation of all to the same discipleship; all interrelate as companions following after the one love. The words of Vatican II underscore this dynamic even more clearly: "Just as Christian communion among wayfarers brings us closer to Christ, so our companionship with the saints joins us to Christ, from whom as from their fountain and head issue every grace and the life of God's people itself."[34] Rather than be caught in an elitist structure, the saints in heaven and on earth become partners in memory and hope.

4. Paradigmatic Figures

Within this great cloud of witnesses, different times and places will see the emergence of particular persons who focus the energies of the Spirit for a local community in its own unique circumstances. When these persons are recognized by the common spiritual sense of the community, they become publicly significant for the lives of others. These are the persons traditionally and all too narrowly called saints in the customary parlance of Christian tradition. Using this sense of the term, Lawrence Cunningham's definition captures this vector of the communion of saints well: "A saint is a person so grasped by a religious vision that it becomes central to his or her life in a way that radically changes the person and leads others to glimpse the value of that vision."[35]

Theologically these particular persons have no essential spiritual advantage over the rest of their community who are saints in the biblical sense. All are touched by the fire of the Spirit and called to a life of prophecy and friendship with God, which renders holiness a general and constant phenomenon in the sinful church. But the confluence of historical conditions with their own unique giftedness and initiative gives them a beneficial function in the wider circle of their fellow pilgrims. Canonized or not, their names are remembered as a benediction, as an act of resistance, as a call to action, as a spur to fidelity. In addition to persons involved in the life and ministry of Jesus and the beginnings of the *ekklesia,* and in addition to the early martyrs, each age including the present one knows such persons: "the fountain is still flowing, it hasn't dried up."[36]

In an intriguing thesis, Karl Rahner has proposed that particular saints stand out because they are the initiators and creative models of a path of holiness right for their particular age.[37] Holiness is not a generic ideal but a historically shaped participation in the friendship of God; it takes different forms according to the needs and possibilities of time and place. In fact, such is the novelty of history, never to be underestimated, that what counts concretely for virtue in one period may indicate its opposite in another. It is not always clear or self-evident what the following of Christ calls for in new circumstances. Empowered by the Spirit, certain persons take risks in discerning a way. They embark on an adventure of the spirit to embody the *novum* of the gospel in new circumstances. The response of the community affirms that their wager paid off in creating a new possibility that many others can now benefit by adopting. Like the phenomenon of all saints in general, the flare of these successful risk-takers does not originate with the hierarchy but belongs to the realm of noninstitutional charisms where the Spirit blows freely. These friends of God and prophets come along unexpectedly, their creativity being a free gift and challenge to the church. Rahner's thesis needs to be emended insofar as he used it to explain why only a few people are canonized by the church. There obviously cannot be hundreds of new ways of life developed and recognized in a given historical era, so the current multitudes being canonized escape the understanding that he delineates. However, his analysis holds insofar as it pinpoints the dynamic at work in the lives of those particular saints who have captured and held the Christian imagination over centuries and, with the shock of the new, even today.

One can be a paradigmatic figure and still be an untamed individual. However, the process of the community's recognition of an outstanding saint makes it clear such persons are saints by and for others; they belong to and reflect the community that engenders them. In this sense, they are a social construal. In her study of saints and postmodernism, Edith Wyschogrod effectively uses a musical analogy to describe how this recognition of the holiness of a particular saint happens in the community. Grasping the compelling presence of grace in another person is less like being convinced by a rational argument and more like understanding a musical theme. One has to begin with some notion of the theme, such as its author, relation to other works, and so on, or there can be no move to deep insight. Then, one attends to performance, seeking to appreciate how expression, gesture, and interpretation cast light on what the theme might mean. "Now something happens to the listener. As the theme is experienced intensely, it points to something beyond itself connecting up with the total fabric of music — music's rhythmic, harmonic, and melodic capacities, its emotional power, and its previous literature."[38]

So it is with appreciation of a particular person's giftedness in the Spirit. There has to be some awareness of the sacred dimension of the community's own life and understanding of the gospel to begin with. Then we encounter the narrative memory, the artistic icon, or the living presence of the person herself or himself. In the encounter, something happens to the "listeners." They recognize the light of divine goodness refracted in this vivid, real, concrete life in a way that is compellingly attractive. They realize that their own lives are interwoven with a story larger than their own hearts. The world becomes leavened with divine presence, gifting the community but also claiming its response amid the struggles of history. This process of recognition is not irrational, but it transpires at a level of sensibility that is not exhausted by explanations: it is a discernment in the Spirit. Just as the charism of a particular saint is a gift of the Spirit, so too is noticing a saint the fruit of the Spirit's moving in the intuition of the community, which realizes in this paradigmatic figure its own best impulses.

Unique friends of God and prophets emerge in the dynamic context of ongoing history fraught with suffering and disaster and filled with temptations to infidelity to the core vocation to holiness. Paradigmatic saints then correct or enlarge the community's moral vision, challenging the hardening of heart and loss of creative response. In this instance, they may certainly be ignored or, even worse, domesticated. But if people participate in recognizing saintly character even in the judgment coming to meet them, they are opening themselves up to a new working of grace. Writes David Matzko:

> In the naming of a prophetic saint, a community offers itself to be transformed.... Good communities, open histories, faithful traditions are not secure. They cannot be sustained easily. It is difficult to be open to prophetic voices; it is difficult for judgment to be heard. But faithfulness cannot be sustained by good theories or static traditions. It takes faithful people. So when a faithful one rises up among us and we are able to hear and recognize the

goodness of this person's judgment upon us, we call this extraordinary person a saint and the miraculous transformation in us the work of God.[39]

By so naming saints, the community itself catches the vision of a world made whole and becomes itself, a little more, an advocate for peaceable community throughout the earth, a counterforce against violence and domination. The living tradition then grows anew.

Like all saints but in a more public way, paradigmatic figures who emerge in the course of history are like a Milky Way thrown down from heaven to earth, to use Peter Brown's lovely metaphor, a shining river of stars spiraling out from the center of the galaxy, the still point of the turning world who is God alone, to light a path through the darkness. They are women and men who shine like the sun with the shimmer of divinity, showing the community the face of Christ in their own time and place.[40] They distill the central values of the living tradition in a concrete and accessible form. The direct force of their example acts as a catalyst in the community, galvanizing recognition that yes, this is what we are called to be. Because Christianity is a way of life, their concreteness leavens and nurtures the moral environment, drawing others to pursue their own creative fidelity. The strange wholeness and integrity of these persons lures the community ever more into the encompassing logic of a life for God and in God, in the process strengthening the network of relationships among all. Their religious passion fuels the community's forward movement. In the light of their memory all are encouraged to walk the path of life: "one fire kindles another."[41]

Paradigmatic saints are one vector of the larger reality of the communion of saints. To interpret them in such a way that their memory liberates rather than diminishes the discipleship of others, we must return them to the whole company of the friends of God and prophets. By the power of Spirit-Sophia generations upon generations of good, sinful, but redeemed persons are joined in a living tradition of friendship with God and compassion toward the world. No one of them alone or no one group can monopolize what it means to be holy. "The definition is never complete," writes David Matzko of sainthood. "A single, a few, a dozen lives of the saints will not complete what it means to love God and neighbor or to be in the community of heaven. The definition can be given only by the whole communion of saints."[42]

5. All Creation

The fifth rudiment of understanding the communion of saints amplifies its scope to include other living creatures, ecosystems, and the whole natural world itself. On the face of it, the symbol appears to have a rather complete anthropological interest, focused as it has traditionally been on human persons and their companionship in the Spirit throughout space and time. As scientific discovery and ecological concern reposition the human race in relation to the natural world, however, the realization dawns that the greatest community of all is the world itself which has spawned the human race and which sustains its life at every moment. In a physical and biological sense, interrelationship is not an appendage to the natural order but its very lifeblood. Everything is connected to everything else, and it all flourishes or withers together. In a theological sense, the same divine creativity that fuels the vitality of all creation also lights the fire of the saint. The communion of holy people is intrinsically connected to the community of holy creation, and they stand or fall together.[43]

This connectedness, as with all unity, is a gift of the Creator Spirit. In Jürgen Moltmann's beautiful description, "If the Holy Spirit is poured out on the whole creation, then [the Spirit] creates the community of all created things with God and with each other, making it that fellowship of creation in which all created things communicate with one another and with God, each in its own way. The existence, the life, and the warp and weft of interrelationships subsists in the Spirit," for it is in God that all things live and move and have their being. Therefore, he continues, "nothing in the world exists, lives, and moves *of itself*. Everything exists, lives, and moves *in others,* in one another, with one another, for one another, in the cosmic interrelations of the divine Spirit. So it is only the community of creation in the Spirit itself that can be called fundamental."[44] This many-faceted community, which includes human beings, is the primordial *communio sanctorum* by the power of the Spirit.

Central biblical themes are alive with this inclusion. The world is Sophia-God's good creation and dwelling-place and is replete with her generosity, beauty, playfulness, and power. Far from being a mere backdrop to the salvation history of humankind, it is intrinsically bound to covenant and jubilee, to sin and the resulting devastation, and to the messianic promise of future peace and fruitfulness. Biblical hope embraces the entirety of cosmic occurrence as part of its promise, for the whole world is moving toward a goal which is not simply annihilation. Despite later Christian suppression of bodiliness, the christological story affirms the union of God with the very flesh of this world and the resurrection of that same flesh from the dead so radically that it too entails a cosmic vision. All creation groans, waiting for redemption, while the good news is that Christ, the "firstborn from the dead," is primordially the "firstborn of all creation."[45] The community of the redeemed will include the whole world in glory.

These provocatively inclusive themes of creation, covenant, messianic promise, incarnation, death-resurrection, and eschatological hope make clear that the natural world does not just form a context for the communion of saints but is itself included in the community. Recall that a fascinating ambiguity in the original Latin term *communio sanctorum* supports this understanding, *sanctorum* referring to holy persons (the *sancti*) and also to holy things (the *sancta*). The latter idea, especially in view of the importance of eucharistic communion, played an important role in shaping the original meaning of this doctrine and its medieval interpretation. The *communio sanctorum* signifies a "communion in the holy": holy people and holy things in interrelationship. Thus from within the symbol itself a way opens to include all beings, sacred bread and wine, certainly, but also the primordial sacrament, the sacred earth itself. The communion of saints has an ecological, cosmic dimension.

Including the natural world in the communion of the holy sets up an interesting dynamic between human hope for the dead on the one hand and hope for the natural world on the other. The two become intertwined in ways that affect understanding and ethics. Human hope that neither we nor the world are to be ground into nothingness but rather are included in the promise of the new creation can be seen to embody the hope of the universe itself. "Billions of years before our appearance in evolution," explains John Haught, the cosmos "was already seeded with promise. Our own religious longing for future fulfillment, therefore, is not a violation but a blossoming of this promise. Human hoping is not simply our own constructs of imaginary ideals projected onto an indifferent universe, as much modern and postmodern thought maintains. Rather, it is the faithful carrying on of the universe's perennial orientation toward the unknown future."[46] If the universe is on an adventurous journey toward the complexity and beauty of a future perfection, then hope for all the dead, encoded in the symbol of the communion of holy ones, can be interpreted as an expression of the world's own powerful impulse toward the future.

At the same time, breaking connections with the memory of the dead and losing hope for them can have deleterious effects on our ecological responsibility. It is important to ponder that those native peoples whom contemporary thinkers admire for their kinship with the land and its creatures also honor the spirits of their ancestors present upon the land. While such wisdom cannot be adapted without revision in urban and suburban communities, there is a link here that needs to be understood. John Haught explores this further with his idea that much current indifference to the cause of conservation stems not so much from hope for another world to which we flee at death, as was true in a previous age, but from the secular assumption that there is an unbridgeable gap between the dead and ourselves. This "broken connection" robs us of convincing reasons to care for the earth and saps our moral energy to do so. Focusing on the modern inability to imagine our connection with other generations, he writes:

If we are unable to symbolize immortality in one way or another, we lose any sense of relatedness to the vast world that has gone before us, as well as to the generations of living beings that may follow. In breaking our connection with other generations, we understandably forfeit our responsibility to them. Stranded in a meaninglessly brief life span, and severed from communion with the perished past or the promised future, we grow ethically impotent."[47]

Consigning the dead to utter extinction undermines the basis for an ecological ethic, he argues, while healing the broken connection provides sustenance for our moral commitment to care for the earth. This intriguing insight, promising in the integrity it portends for a community that remembers and hopes, is deserving of wide study. Set within the life-giving history of God with the world, which is not simply an anthropocentric event, the *communio sanctorum* ultimately reaches out to signify the community of all creation, past, present, and to come, sharing in the flow of life in the Spirit: holy people and a sacred earth together.

To sum up: A foundational shift in the theological interpretation of the communion of saints results from the rediscovery of this company as an inclusive community of friends of God and prophets in contrast to a spiritual hierarchy of patrons and petitioners. From this flow several other key interpretive changes: from emphasis on the dead alone to the whole living community as all saints; from emphasis on heroic virtue and the miraculous to everyday struggle and creative fidelity; from canonized saints alone to the whole company of the dead, embraced in the life of God and accessed through memory and hope; from paradigmatic figures as elite practitioners of virtue to these same persons as comrades cherished for their witness and the encouragement it gives; and from a purely anthropocentric circle to a community of the whole natural world imbued with God's blessing. As the symbol of the communion of saints is retrieved in these ways, it discloses the boundless creativity of Spirit-Sophia who continuously moves in all times and places, cultures, contexts, and peoples to awaken an amplitude of response to amazing grace. Together the living form with the dead one community of memory and hope, a holy people touched with the fire of the Spirit, summoned to go forth as companions bringing the face of divine compassion into everyday life and the great struggles of history, wrestling with evil, and delighting even now when fragments of justice, peace, and healing gain however small a foothold. When they are seen together with the whole natural world as a dynamic, sacred community of the most amazing richness and complexity, then the symbol of the communion of saints reaches its fullness as a symbol of effective presence and action of Holy Wisdom herself.

– Chapter 13 –

To Let the Symbol Sing Again

Practices of Memory and Hope

We have been thinking with the symbol of the communion of saints, tracking it through the power of memory and the radical challenge of hope to a set of theological insights to which it gives rise. In its plenitude, the symbol signifies that those who seek the face of the living God today belong to a great historical company, an intergenerational band of the friends of God and prophets that includes the living and the dead, joined in community with the cosmic world, all connected in the gracious, compassionate love of Holy Wisdom who, in the midst of historical struggle, sin, and defeat, continuously renews her gift of saving, healing grace. It remains for us to see how this doctrinal symbol can appear concretely in prayer and piety to nourish the vitality of the *ekklesia*. One fire kindles another — but how are the sparks to fly? What practices can release the liberating power of the heritage of all saints to stir the affections and motivate action?

Under the traditional patronage model of the saints, a vast set of devotions grew up known collectively as the *cultus sanctorum,* or cult of the saints. Living persons established relations with the holy ones in heaven in numerous ways such as pilgrimages, novenas, veneration of relics, the use of medals, and many other devotional practices designed to facilitate protection and help in the trials of life. It is this pattern of veneration that has so diminished in postconciliar, postcritical culture, with its realignment of the counter-Reformation religious paradigm on the one hand and its anonymous social pressures that destroy society's feeling of community with the dead on the other. But as Scripture and the early age of the martyrs show, a patronage model is not the only possibility available for the practice of the communion of saints. The companionship model calls forth its own concrete expressions, many still in the process of being shaped in the current age as different groups devise forms of keeping memory.

Given the apophatic character of contemporary belief, practices that allow the symbol to sing again in religious piety engage the community in acts of remembrance and hope rather than imaginations of direct presence. These practices, furthermore, by their own internal dynamism, turn persons toward the social, political world with increased commitment to resist the cruelties of history and to build toward healing and well-being for all. While these practices do not address the saints as patrons who can supply our needs, they are nevertheless a form of prayer. "Remembering the dead," writes Rahner, "becomes a prayer even if it does not contain a specific petition to the 'saints,' a plea for their intercession,"[1] for it ultimately leads the mind and heart into the mystery of God. In modern and postmodern culture, such prayer through acts of remembrance and hope awakens consciousness and revitalizes the spirit. It contributes to building the church into a living community of memory and hope with "habits of the heart" that make the life of discipleship an attractive option. In its cultural setting, hopeful remembrance in fact is an act of resistance to banality, to debasement of persons and the earth, to consumerism, to individual isolation, to personal drift and apathy, to hopelessness and resignation. Practiced with concern for the poor and those who suffer violence, such acts galvanize the struggle for justice and peace. Practiced with concern for the marginalization of women, they strengthen resistance to patriarchy in both church and society. Practiced with concern for the earth, they awaken bonds of kinship that promote ethical care. On all fronts, remembrance in hope functions as a source that renews the church's expectation and turns it to political, social, and ecological responsibility.

After examining the basic prayer forms appropriate to these acts of remembrance and hope, this chapter describes two examples of the companionship model of the communion of saints in action, namely, the annual celebration of All Saints Day and various forms of litanies being used in the churches. Since to be truly effective this symbol needs concrete expression, we conclude with a host of other contemporary examples, noting the need for ongoing creativity.

Praise and Lament

Instead of the prayer of petition which has had pride of place in traditional devotion to the saints, the prayer of praise and thanks to God and the prayer of lament characterize the companionship model. It is not that explicit petition is never made, but such asking assumes a different character when set within a relationship of mutuality rather than a structure of elitism. Prayer for help also diminishes in importance in the context of the larger impulses of imbibing encouragement from the saints' witness and praying in profound gratitude for their lives and in lament over their destruction. While thanking God for the witness of the saints is part of the liturgical heritage, complaint to God over the historical treatment suffered by many of them has not customarily been associated with this symbol. Both forms flow today in practices of hopeful remembrance.

Thanks

With the belief that every good gift comes from the generous hand of the One who creates and saves the world, hearty thanks to the Giver characterizes Jewish and Christian prayer from the beginning. People bless God for the wonders of creation, the gift of a plentiful harvest, safe delivery in childbirth, relationships healed, peace established, justice attained, health recovered, and for the transforming gifts of divine mercy and redeeming grace. Indeed, the whole orientation of liturgical prayer is in this direction. The subversive memory of the cloud of witnesses leads in this same direction of gratitude and praise when their historical reality is appreciated in light of its deepest truth, their ever so individual response to amazing grace. As an example of the prayer of thanks, the *Oxford Book of Prayer* cites the following:

> We thank thee, O God, for the saints of all ages; for those who in times of darkness kept the lamp of faith burning; for the great souls who saw visions of larger truth and dared to declare it; for the multitude of quiet and gracious souls whose presence has purified and sanctified the world; and for those known and loved by us, who have passed from this earthly fellowship into the fuller light of life with thee.[2]

Profound gratitude to God for these women and men who are our honor recognizes that what makes them remarkable, both those known and those unknown, stems from the power of the Spirit who has had a greening effect on their lives, to use Hildegard of Bingen's metaphor, keeping them from being dried out sticks and filling them with the juice of life. The prayer also implies that the community to-day is similarly gifted. People still keep faith burning in the darkness, speak truth to power, and live gracefully in this world; loved ones still die and go forth with our hope clinging to them. Thanking God for these lives is a theocentric way of expressing the phenomenon of connectedness in the Spirit.

The dynamism of thanks that flows from remembrance presses the community at every step to go and do likewise. A prayer composed by the insightful, committed Walter Rauschenbusch traces this connection with clear vigor:

> We praise thee, Almighty God, for thine elect, the prophets and martyrs of humanity, who gave their thoughts and prayers and agonies for the truth of God and the freedom of the people. We praise thee that amid loneliness and contempt, in poverty and imprisonment, when they were condemned by the laws of the mighty and buffeted on the scaffold, thou didst uphold them by thy spirit.... Our hearts burn within us as we follow the bleeding feet of thy Christ down the centuries and count the calvaries of anguish on which he is crucified anew in these prophets.... Help us to forgive those who did it, for some truly thought they were serving thee when they suppressed thy light, but oh, save us from the same mistake! Grant us an unerring instinct for what is right and true, and a swift sympathy to divine those who truly love and serve the people. Suffer us not by thought-less condemnation or selfish opposition to weaken the arm and chill the spirit of those who strive.... Grant us rather that we too may be counted... with these pathfinders of humanity. And if we must suffer loss and drink of the bitter pool of scorn, uphold us by thy spirit in steadfastness and joy because we are found worthy to share in the work and the reward of Jesus and all the saints.[3]

Thanking God for the friends of God and prophets who form the community's heritage sets feet today on a certain path. Their witness and the encouragement it gives serve as a vehicle for the same Spirit who inspired them to kindle the sacred fire in our own lives.

Lament

Reclaiming the communion of saints as all saints, however, brings another aspect to the fore, one suggested by the pain in the Rauschenbusch prayer but in fact quite different: the senseless, terrified, anonymous, tragic deaths of too many whose destruction does not even have the saving grace of witnessing to a cause which they held dear. Human death by famine, torture, war, genocide, and one-on-one violence and the death of living creatures and earth's life-systems by human cruelty and greed disrupt the harmony of one generation's witness to the next. Such victimization introduces unmitigated evil into the picture. It cries to heaven for justice, for relief, at least for explanation, which is never forthcoming. The ancient prayer of lament, flung in outrage and grief to God, arises from remembrance of these things. Well attested by the psalms, Hagar's complaint, Jeremiah's lamentations, the tears of the companions of the daughter of Jephthah, Job's challenge to heaven, and Jesus' god-forsaken cry from the cross, lament is curiously lacking from Christian practices of prayer, especially liturgical prayer. But the powerful memory of those who died senseless deaths deprived of dignity demands that the praise of God be suffused with their tragedy. In the process, as we gather them into our common memory and hope, they become something more than faceless, forgotten individuals but enter into a living history as an impetus to forge a different future for others.

In North American civil society, forms of remembrance such as the wall of the Vietnam Veterans Memorial in Washington, D.C., the AIDS quilt, and the ringing of church bells on August 6 defy the tendency to reduce victims to statistics and, by creatively preserving the identity of the dead, allow for ceremonies of grief that ultimately awaken resistance to the cause of their deaths. These public symbols make the dead and the events by which they died part of the living cultural memory of a people. In so doing, they keep alive the potential of remembrance to forge new life. The same dynamic needs to pervade Christian remembrance of those defeated by the frightful evils of history. "There is no future possible in this world or in eternity," David Power writes, "without inclusion of those whose disappearing was without sense, even made deliberately senseless since they were counted dispensable."[4] In remembering all saints with this imperative in mind, the church is called to look tragedy in the face. It must recognize the massive, anonymous dead as individual sisters and brothers. It needs to repent of a trivializing or benumbed response to such suffering or even of being complicitous in it through its own acts of violence or silence. It should give voice to the dead, as John

Paul II did so dramatically while visiting the Nazi concentration camp in Mauthausen, Austria:

> You people who have experienced fearful tortures.... What is your last word? ... You people of yesterday, and you people of today, if the system of extermination camps continues somewhere in the world even today, tell us ... in our great hurry, haven't we forgotten your hell? ... Tell us, what direction should Europe and humanity take "after Auschwitz...." Speak, you have the right to do so — you who have suffered and lost your lives. We have the duty to listen to your testimony.[5]

In face of this suffering, the church needs to lament, ringing out complaint to God's face, wrestling with the holy name, dethroning traditional pat answers, and looking anew amid the defeated for God.

The direction of such remembering, while it disorients our inherited sureties, is back toward praise of God, unreasonable as that may seem. A striking instance of this faith dynamic is found in the Jewish prayer said in the face of death, the Kaddish. Hallowed by centuries of faithful use even in the most terrible of circumstances, the prayer begins: "Magnified and sanctified be the great name of God throughout the world," continues with yearning that the reign of God be speedily established, and ends with the response, "May God's great name be blessed forever and ever."[6] One mourns the dead by praising God who created the world and will ultimately establish righteousness and justice. Similarly, when the tragically dead are remembered in the context of Christian faith, the cross of Jesus introduces a hope that transforms these raw depths of unreason and suffering into doxology, only now the praise is forever imbued with the knowledge of unimaginable pain and the darkness of hope against hope. That which is remembered in grief can be redeemed, made whole, through the promise of the Spirit's new creation. And so we affirm a future for all the nameless dead in the hands of the living God.

The challenge of this prayer is not simply to commend the victims of murderous death to heavenly blessedness, however, but to give their memory a place in the making of a just society and a compassionate world here and now. The disorientation of lament has a critical edge. By the way the church remembers, it allows the past of all the dead to function as raw material for a future of promise. It commits itself to seeing, as Power writes, "that out of their lives on earth, out of the apparent absurdity of their death, a future comes that belongs to the realization of covenant justice here on earth."[7] The prayer of lament — unreserved protest, sadness, impassioned questioning, strong cry against suffering, and tenderness for the defeated — becomes a social force confronting unjust ideologies and structures. It calls us out of passivity into active engagement against all premature death caused by human beings. Along with the prayer of praise, it shifts our responsibility to praxis.

All Saints Day

The reality of the communion of saints comes consciously to the fore with the annual celebration of All Saints Day observed on the Sunday after Pentecost in the East, on November 1 in the West, or, wisely, on the nearest Sunday to this in many Protestant churches. This is the day when the church recalls the great tribe out of every nation and people, proclaims the following of Jesus according to the beatitudes, and allows the subversive memory of the friends of God and prophets of all ages and the hope of our communion with them to take center stage. This is a feast of the greatest solidarity, a fundamentally joyous day that takes note of historical suffering within the overarching theme that the last word belongs to divine love. The Preface for the feast prays in a mood of thanksgiving: "Around your throne the saints, our brothers and sisters, sing your praise forever. Their glory fills us with joy, and their communion with us in your church gives us inspiration and strength as we hasten on our pilgrimage of faith, eager to meet them. With their great company and all the angels we praise your glory as we cry out with one voice: Holy, Holy, Holy...." As Rahner has reflected, this day makes us realize that "in the course of the world's history an innumerable multitude has already been drawn into the eternity of God before us, so that we are the late-comers. And the realization of this should generate hope and consolation in us, courage and trust."[8] The companionship model of the communion of saints allows multiple aspects of the meaning of this feast to be uncovered.

In a particular way this is a day that celebrates the great host of "anonymous" whom the world counts as nobodies and whom the church, too, has lost track of but who are held in the embrace of God who loses not one. Canonized saints have their day on the calendar, but this is the day for everyone. "When we celebrate All Saints," writes Rahner, "we have in mind chiefly those saints who are anonymous, the unknown saints who...lived quietly in the land, the poor and the little ones who were great only in God's eyes, those who go unacclaimed in any of the rolls of honour belonging to the Church or to world history."[9] To his list of qualities I would add those nameless saints who raised a little hell in defense of the vulnerable and the growth of justice. All are celebrated in this remembrance of the generations of God-seekers. For, as Rahner continues, "what this festival is saying to us is: Where there is not actually the most profound guilt, where there is not diabolical evil, there, ultimately speaking, there are no minor or intermediary degrees of goodness at the end, but only saints."[10]

In a particular way, this day that remembers persons whose lives made a difference but who are otherwise not officially remarked becomes a day of celebration of women. It is not facetious but merely brings the present state of affairs to its logical conclusion to point out that since the official roster of saints names mostly men, simple arithmetic indicates that the majority of those celebrated on All Saints Day are women. Even without this mathematical accounting, the forgotten memory and distorted narrative of generations of women meets redress in this celebration of female friends of God and prophets who lived faithfully and creatively but are not officially remembered. A community that remembers in this way allies itself with the struggle for women's equal human dignity even now.

This day also lifts up victims of injustice crushed by historical evils, and in this way this feast is subversive. For while the murderers may have triumphed over their victims on earth, this remembrance of the suffering of those without a name affirms a future for the defeated, thereby writing a different kind of history from that done from the perspective of unjust victors. The suffering is not erased, but noted and commended to God's care. A community that remembers in this way puts itself in alliance with the oppressed even now.

On this day we also remember those whom our hearts have personally known and loved, those who nourished and created us as human beings and those who helped us through rough times. This is our immediate cloud of witnesses, beloved faces held in living memory. Their errors and failings may have affected us in deep ways; their goodness, too, is intertwined with the fabric of our loves, leaving a deep imprint on the way we now vie for life in all its wholeness. If their death is recent, grief is fresh. But we dare to trust that Holy Wisdom has not allowed them to perish but has received them into unimaginable life forever. Entrusted to God's mercy, these are *our* saints. A community that remembers in this way underscores the dignity and importance of every one of its members.

Remembering the dead, this feast of "all saints" also honors the mystery of divine grace that pervades the lives of people living today. Someday each one of us will be included among the company of the dead, and we hope that this day will celebrate our lives too, even if anonymously. But the grace that brings people to fulfillment in God is already operative here and now. The living church is itself a communion of saints because amid the joys and tears of history, God's compassion has already gained a foothold. If we do not cherish this power in ourselves, how can we appreciate it in those who have died? If we cannot recognize the grace of God in our neighbor, how can we praise it in saints beyond history? As a festival of the victory of grace, All Saints is our festival day too, even now. A community that remembers in this way praises the merciful grace of God and supports the rightful self-affirmation of all its saints, and of its marginalized ones including women most of all.

In view of the cosmos's participation in the "communion of the holy," this day, finally, remembers with gratitude the complex community of life in which the human race is embedded, the vast array of life given in nourishment for the life of others, and the systems of earth, air, and water that sustain the whole. We lament the waste of this bounty through human greed and ignorance, and the species that have gone extinct. The whole earth groans even now, and is included in the hope that ultimately "all will be well, and all manner of thing will be well."[11] A community that remembers in this way aligns itself with the earth under threat and begins to act with ethical responsibility for all creatures who share in the communion of the holy.

None of these dimensions of the feast of All Saints stands alone; they intertwine with each other as do the meanings of any rich symbol. The presenting image is of the blessed dead, but its implications include ourselves and the whole community of life held in the powerful care of Sophia God. In a sermon on the great cloud of witnesses, Barbara Brown Taylor preached:

Call their names and hear them answer "Present." On All Saints Day they belong to us and we to them, and as their ranks swell so do the possibilities that open up in our own lives. Because of them and because of one another and because of the God who binds us all together, we can do more than any of us had dreamed to do alone.[12]

A community that keeps festival in this way unleashes liberating forces by the power of the Spirit to critical and practical effect.

Lists of Names: Litanies

Outside of this major feast, the company of the friends of God and prophets can enter into spiritual practice in a variety of ways. Naming the names is one such practice. This occurs in rhythmic cadence in the litany, a flexible form of common prayer that energizes the connections between the living and the dead. Originating in Eastern Christianity in the fourth century as a prayer form of the laity rather than the clergy, the litany has proved itself capable of endless variation and deep effectiveness.[13]

• At the annual Easter Vigil, the procession to the baptismal font is accompanied by the traditional "Litany of the Saints" set to the tones of ancient or contemporary chant. Summoning particular saints by name out of the unnumbered multitude of the redeemed brings the memory and hope of their lives before our eyes while repeated reference to "all" stretches the cloud of witnesses to the horizon. By joining together the saints on earth with those in heaven, the litany creates a welcoming community around those about to be baptized and gives to the church an energetic self-presence before God.

• A variation of this litany, set to contemporary music and inclusive of names suitable to a group's purpose, has a similar vivifying effect.[14] On the occasion of the fiftieth anniversary of the Catholic Theological Society of America, for example, the litany extended the list of biblical and traditional saints with Hildegard of Bingen and Julian of Norwich; Martin Luther, John Calvin, and John Wesley; Gertrude of Helfta, Mechthild of Magdeburg, and other beguines; John Henry Newman and Romano Guardini; Sarah and Angelina Grimké and Georgia Harkness; Dietrich Bonhoeffer and Teilhard de Chardin; Karl Rahner and Karl Barth; Dorothy Day and Thomas Merton, among other crafters of theology. In addition, as the refrain "All you holy men and women pray for us" repeated in rhythmic cadences, hundreds of participants came forward bearing a lighted candle and spoke the name of a deceased theologian who had influenced them and inspired them to this ministry in the church. An amplitude of spirit resulted as the present workers in the vineyard were bonded through the act of living remembrance with others who had labored through the centuries to befriend and prophesy the word of God.

• In addition to the refrain "pray for us," other responses are appropriate. "Pray with us," or "Be with us" or "To you, O God, with N. we pray" give clearer expression to the reality of mutual companionship. In Latin America the custom has grown of responding to the name of the martyrs with the affirmation *Presente,* a multivalent term asking that the saint be present, implying that the saint is present, and most basically, affirming the power of the resurrection which makes it possible for the saint to be present. It is a powerful response that commits the community to honor their memory by emulating their lives.

On the anniversary of the murder of the archbishop of San Salvador, a group gathered in a North American urban church to keep memorial. After Scripture readings from the prophet Isaiah and a gospel passion narrative, excerpts were read from the writings of some church members killed in El Salvador.

From Oscar Romero himself:

I am a shepherd who with his people has begun to learn a beautiful and difficult truth: our Christian faith requires that we submerge ourselves in this world. The course taken by the Church has always had political repercussions. The problem is how to direct that influence so that it will be in accord with the faith....My life has been threatened many times. I have to confess that as a Christian, I don't believe in death without resurrection. If they kill me, I will rise again in the Salvadoran people....Better, of course, that they realize they will be wasting their time. A bishop will die, but God's church which is the people will never perish.[15]

From Maura Clarke:

I am beginning to see death in a new way, dearest Katie....There are so many deaths everywhere that it is incredible. It is an atmosphere of death. The work is really what Bishop Romero called *acompañamiento* [accompanying the people], as well as searching for ways to help....We are on the road continually, bringing women and children to refugee centers. Keep us in your heart and prayers, especially the poor forsaken people.[16]

From Ignacio Ellacuría:

Our intellectual analysis finds that our historical reality, the reality of the Third Word, is fundamentally characterized by the effective predominance of injustice over justice, poverty over abundance.... We ask ourselves what to do about it in a university way. We answer first from an ethical standpoint: we must transform it, do all we can to ensure that good predominates over evil, truth over falsehood.... If a university does not decide to make this commitment, we do not understand the validity it has as a university, much less as a Christian-inspired university.... But in a world where falsehood, injustice, and oppression reign, a university that fights for truth, justice, and freedom cannot fail to be persecuted.[17]

From Jean Donovan:

And so the Peace Corps left today, and my heart sank low. The danger is extreme and they are right to leave, but it seems that the more help is needed, the less is available. Now I must assess my own position, because I am not up for suicide. Several times I have decided to leave — I almost could, except for the children, the poor, bruised victims of adult lunacy. Who would care for them? Whose heart would be so staunch as to favor the reasonable thing in a sea of their tears and loneliness? Not mine, dear friend, not mine.[18]

And then began the litany:

Oscar Romero? *Presente!*

Maura Clarke, Ita Ford, Dorothy Kazel, Jean Donovan? *Presente!*

Ignacio Ellacuría, Ignacio Martín-Baró, Juan Ramón Moreno, Amando López, Segundo Montes, Joaquin López y López? *Presente!*

Elba Ramos and Celina Ramos? *Presente!*

All you young catechists, laborers, community workers, religious leaders of the *pueblos* murdered for the justice of Christ? *Presente!*

Here the devotion of memory, giving expression to deep Christian belief in the communion of saints, has a clearly critical impact. The living memory of the seventy-five thousand men, women, and children who died during El Salvador's decade of violence, supported by American arms and training, and the voices of those who ministered to and with them shake the complacency of the mostly privileged persons in the assembly. They are challenged to be converted and act on behalf of justice toward their sisters and brothers who are poor and oppressed, which situation continues in untold places even today.

• The litany's ability to be endlessly adaptable recommends it for use by women in the churches. Ann Heidkamp, a member of the Presbyterian Church (USA), created "A Litany of Women's Power" to buoy up flagging spirits. It prays in part,

> Spirit of Life, we remember the women, named and unnamed, who throughout time have used the gifts you gave them to change the world. We call upon these foremothers to help us discover within ourselves your power — and the ways to use it to bring about the reign of justice and peace.
>
> We remember Esther and Deborah, whose acts of courage saved their nation....
> We remember Mary Magdalen and the other women who followed Jesus....
> We remember Phoebe, Priscilla, and the other women leaders of the early church....
> We remember the Abbesses of the Middle Ages who kept faith and knowledge alive....
> We remember Teresa of Avila and Catherine of Siena, who challenged the corruption of the church during the Renaissance....
> We remember our own mothers and grandmothers whose lives shaped ours....
> And we pray for the women who are victims of violence in their homes....
> We pray for those women who face a life of poverty and malnutrition....
> We pray for those women who are "firsts" in their fields....
> We pray for our daughters and granddaughters....

Oration: We have celebrated the power of many women past and present. It is now time to celebrate ourselves. Within each of us is that same life and light and love. Within each of us lie the seeds of power and glory. Our bodies can touch with love; our hearts can heal; our minds can seek out faith and truth and justice. Spirit of Life, be with us in our quest. Amen."[19]

In a similar way, Roman Catholic Joan Chittister has shaped "A Litany of Women for the Church." It begins, "Dear God, creator of women in your own image, born of a woman in the midst of a world half women, ... made known by women to all the children of the earth, give to the women of our time the strength to persevere, the courage to speak out, the faith to believe in you beyond all systems and institutions"; it proceeds by remembering the holy women who went before us,

> Saint Elizabeth of Judea, who recognized the value of another woman...
> Saint Mary Magdalene, minister of Jesus, first evangelist of the Christ...
> Saint Hildegard, who suffered interdict for the doing of right...
> Saint Julian of Norwich, who proclaimed for all of us the motherhood of God...
> Saint Dorothy Day, who led the church to a new sense of justice...;

and it ends with remembrance of Mary, mother of Jesus,

> who heard the call of God and answered...
> Who drew strength from the woman Elizabeth...
> Who turned the Spirit of God into the body and blood of Christ...."[20]

Making these acts of remembrance in connection with today's daunting struggle for the human dignity of all women energizes those who pray at the deepest level possible.

Women-church groups associate Halloween with the hosts of women tortured and executed as witches by the Inquisition. In this orgy of the murder of women, anywhere from thirty thousand to one million women were annihilated by the powerful religious institution of the church in the name of God, an event largely erased from standard histories of the Enlightenment.[21] In the tradition of sorrowing witness, the names of the dead are read in a litany of remembrance:

Margaret Jones, midwife, hanged 1648.

Joan Peterson, veterinarian, hanged 1652.

Isobel Insch Taylor, herbalist, burned 1618.

Mother Lakeland, healer, burned 1645...

Anna Rausch, burned 1628, twelve years old.

Emerzianne Pichler, tortured and burned together with her two children, 1679....

Frau Dumler, boiled to death in hot oil while pregnant, 1630.[22]

Realizing that on the stage of world history this particular litany is practically endless and could be extended to include all the women throughout the generations who have been beaten, raped, killed, or ruined by male misogyny, the response takes the form of lament: "What have they done to you.... What have they done to us?" With incense, flowers, and harvest fruits, those who keep memory are summoned to resist this ongoing harm to women and girls.

• The litany can also be crafted to celebrate anniversaries or milestones of particular church bodies. Commemorating seventy-five years of existence, the American Baptist Convention held a worship session at its annual meeting that included this litany:

Let us recall the works of God in the American Baptist family — 75 years as pilgrims in grace in Long Beach, Fargo, Philadelphia, Matadi, Bangalore, and Shanghai...praying, planning, struggling, working together.

Response: We remember the faithful paths of our mothers and fathers, sisters and brothers, the people of God, pilgrims in grace....

Through multiple wars, economic crises, times of apathy and upheaval, we have ministered to each other by sharing common resources and gifts as pilgrims in grace.... In a broken world we have sought to unite yellow, red, black, and white in justice and reconciliation, in peace and security, in strength and dignity....

Response: We sense God's Spirit among us, pilgrims in grace.

As did our forebears, Helen Montgomery, Henry Morehouse, Luther Wesley Smith, Martin Luther King, Jr., and Isabel Crawford, we continue to be faithful to our mission, to act boldly and prophetically, to dare to be pilgrims in grace.

Response: Let us, O God, become anew the people of God, pilgrims in grace.

Continue to call thy people, O God, to a recommitment to our
historic principles of soul liberty and new life in Christ. Continue
to lead us, thy pilgrims in grace, lest we miss your Kingdom's
goal. In the name of Jesus Christ the author and finisher of our
faith. Amen.[23]

In another example, a Consultation of the Episcopal Church prayed
a litany that drew on members of the community only recently
deceased and still remembered by many:

Carol Davis, who quietly demonstrated what a woman could do
in full-time parish ministry... Bill Gray, who proved that a dioce-
san newspaper did not have to be dull, irrelevant, and trivial...
William Lawrence, for years the only consistent voice for peace in
the House of Bishops... Chuck Packard, who in a short life...
energized... tired cynics in the Diocese of Newark... Jeannette
Piccard, who in a long and full life lifted our vision up to the
stratosphere and broke not only the gender but the age barrier
... Betsy and Bob Rodenmayer, who together showed the church
a vision of marriage and team ministry that broke the traditional stereotypes... Vida Scudder, who constantly reminded us
that justice and peace are linked, and that both are deeply rooted
in our peculiar Anglican tradition... God, send us anywhere you
would have us go, only go with us. Place any burden upon us,
only stand beside us. Use the ties that bind us together to bind
us closer to you. And may your peace, O creator, redeemer, and
sustainer, be always with us. Amen.[24]

Church communities praying in this way draw on the heritage of their
own cloud of witnesses in such a way that it cheers their hearts and
directs their energies in the same direction. The past becomes effective
prologue.

• In her stunning address at the opening of the 1991 World Council
of Churches Assembly in Canberra, Korean theologian Chung Hyun
Kyung expanded the litany in a feminist, Third World, and Asian
direction to include those for whom lament goes forth. She called
upon the Holy Spirit through the spirits of the oppressed, imploring
(in part):

With humble heart and body, let us listen to the cries of creation
and the cries of the Spirit within it:

Come. The spirit of Hagar, Egyptian, black slave woman exploited and abandoned...

Come. The spirit of Uriah, loyal soldier sent and killed in the battlefield...

Come. The spirit of Jephthah's daughter, the victim of her father's faith...

Come. The spirit of male babies killed by the soldiers of king Herod...

Come. The spirit of indigenous people of the earth, victims of genocide...

Come. The spirit of Jewish people killed in the gas chambers...

Come. The spirit of people killed in Hiroshima and Nagasaki...

Come. The spirit of Korean women in the Japanese "prostitution army..."

Come. The spirit of the Amazon rain forest now being murdered every day...

Come. The spirit of earth, air, and water, raped...exploited by human greed for money...

Come. The Spirit of the Liberator, our brother Jesus, tortured and killed on the cross...

Dear sisters and brothers, with the energy of the Holy Spirit let us tear apart all walls of division and the "culture of death" that separate us. And let us participate in the Holy Spirit's political economy of life, fighting for our life on this earth in solidarity with all living beings, and building communities for justice, peace, and the integrity of creation. Wild wind of the Holy Spirit, blow to us. Let us welcome her, letting ourselves go in her wild rhythm of life. Come, Holy Spirit, Renew the Whole Creation. Amen![25]

Whatever form it takes, the litany surrounds the *ekklesia* with the cloud of witnesses, in light of which people struggling today are inspired and encouraged to their own creative fidelity.

The litany is but one of a variety of expressions by which people today can put the communion of saints into practice according to the companionship pattern to build a responsible community ethic and spirituality. I could also cite a multitude of other examples from church architecture, martyr chapels, stained-glass windows, home altars, contemporary icons and sculpture, newly crafted lives of the saints of all faiths, races, and nationalities and both genders, newly compiled calendars of holy people, hymns of companionship and accompaniment, movies, tapes of live addresses of paradigmatic figures, and gatherings on anniversary days, to name some of the more salient. Two particular examples serve to illustrate the wider possibilities. A "Calendar of Holy Women" compiled annually with a different woman remembered on each day includes Thea Bowman (1938–90), "joyous black American Franciscan & evangelist," Komyo (701–60), "Buddhist founder of hospices for the suffering at Nara, Japan," and A'isha Bint Abi Bakr (613–78), "Sunni Muslim religious teacher in Arabia," among countless others.[26] A statue of St. Mary Magdalen sculpted by Luis Tapia depicts the raven-haired apostle with a small figurine of the risen Christ in her outstretched hand, graphically imaging the historic vulnerability of the Easter message and the church's debt to her preaching. It is found in a niche in the church of Our Lady of the Most Holy Rosary parish in Albuquerque, New Mexico. In the design of this church, "aside from the adobe-like wall behind the altar, perhaps the most unusual interior feature is the ambulatory which surrounds the main worship space and serves as a rounded aisle. Parents often use it during Mass to walk and calm their crying infants. Along the ambulatory wall are twelve *nichos,* each housing the image of a saint, created by New Mexican artists. Thus, the communion of saints surrounds all who gather in worship."[27]

These and other contemporary examples are in essence practices of simple, sober, subversive remembrance before the face of God. They make the symbol of the communion of saints sing again in praise and lament to God and in encouragement to persons to live in solidarity with divine compassion. In keeping with tradition, everyone may feel serenely free to engage any of these expressions or not. The power of remembrance, though, amid the struggle of history, has a profoundly liberating and hopeful effect. In the fifth century the theologian Jerome defended the practice of simple people who lighted candles to the martyrs, refuting the charge that they were engaging in idolatry. We can take a page from his advocacy. In the teeth of death and destruction, amid marginalization and continued systemic oppression, before apathy, banality, and spiritual deafness, against all sin in human hearts, with gratitude for the lives of one another, and with radical hope in the living God who is faithful, we remember the company of the friends of God and prophets. "We do this not to dispel the darkness, but as a sign of our joy."[28]

Conclusion

The great Spirit of God, Holy Wisdom herself, forges bonds of connectedness throughout the universe. In all of its dazzling variety the world enjoys a profound unity; in all of its evolving, unpredictable change it rides forward with an intrinsic continuity tying the eras together. The underlying interrelatedness of this one world is the gift of the life-giving Spirit-Sophia who calls the community of creation into being and dwells within the world to repair the breaches that disrupt community, all the while luring it into a renewed future. Because Holy Wisdom is above all and through all and in all, the world itself is a community that shares a common origin, history, and destiny. The religious symbols of creation, sin and redemption, and eschatology express this unitary, relational view of reality in biblical tradition. The communion of saints is another such symbol, developed in Christian usage to express the experience of persons connected to one another in virtue of being connected to the sacred mystery at the heart of the world. Potentially it is a most inclusive symbol for it not only relates disparate cultural groups around the world at any one time, and women with men, and the most socially marginalized with the powerful, all within an egalitarian community of grace, but also the living with the dead and the yet to be born, all seekers of the divine, in a circle around the eucharistic table, the body of Christ which encompasses the earth itself. Remembering in hope that we are part of this great cloud of witnesses turns the living community today toward historical praxis that adds to rather than subtracts from the measure of compassion and justice in the world that the next generation will inherit. Thus we participate in the great work of redemption. "From generation to generation she passes into holy souls and makes them friends of God and prophets,"[29] an unceasing work of love and challenge whereby Holy Wisdom marks the world as her own.

Notes

Introduction

1. Marina Warner, *Alone of All Her Sex: The Myth and Cult of the Virgin Mary* (New York: Knopf, 1976).

2. Rosemary R. Ruether, "Mistress of Heaven: The Meaning of Mariology," in her *New Woman, New Earth: Sexist Ideologies and Human Liberation* (San Francisco: Harper & Row, 1975), 36–62, and "Mariology as Symbolic Ecclesiology: Repression or Liberation?" in her *Sexism and God-Talk: Toward A Feminist Theology* (Boston: Beacon, 1983), 139–58; Elisabeth Moltmann-Wendel, "Motherhood or Friendship?" in *Mary in the Churches,* ed. Hans Küng and Jürgen Moltmann (New York: Seabury, 1983), 17–22.

3. Wis 7:27. All biblical citations are from the New Revised Standard Version (New York: Oxford University Press, 1991).

4. Elizabeth A. Johnson, *She Who Is: The Mystery of God in Feminist Theological Discourse* (New York: Crossroad, 1992).

5. The Verrazano-Narrows is a huge steel bridge that spans the inner mouth of New York Harbor.

Chapter 1: A Sleeping Symbol

1. Chung Hyun Kyung, "Welcome the Spirit, Hear Her Cries: The Holy Spirit, Creation, and the Culture of Life," *Christianity and Crisis* 51 (July 15, 1991): 220–23.

2. Third Eucharistic Prayer of the Roman liturgy.

3. Rev 7:2–4, 9–14, first reading of the feast, at verse 9.

4. Rev 7:17, a continuation of the text.

5. 1 Jn 3:1–3, second reading of the feast, at verse 2.

6. Mt 5:1–12, gospel for the feast. Thanks to the common lectionary, these passages receive wide ecumenical use on this day.

7. Insightful exceptions that prove the rule are Michael Perham, *The Communion of Saints* (London: Alcuin Club / SPCK, 1980); Pierre-Yves Emery (brother of Taizé), *L'unité des croyants au ciel et sur la terre, Verbum Caro – Supplement* 16 (1962): 1–240; and Romano Guardini, *The Saints in Christian Life* (Philadelphia: Chilton Books, 1966).

8. Full text in *Canons and Decrees of the Council of Trent,* trans. H. J. Schroeder (St. Louis: Herder, 1941), 214–17. See Carl J. Peter, "The Communion of Saints in the Final Days of the Council of Trent," in *The One Mediator,*

the Saints, and Mary: Lutherans and Catholics in Dialogue VIII, ed. George Anderson et al. (Minneapolis: Augsburg Fortress, 1992), 219–33.

9. The council's teaching, entitled "The Eschatological Nature of the Pilgrim Church and Her Union with the Heavenly Church," appears as chapter 7 of the Dogmatic Constitution on the Church (Latin: *Lumen Gentium*); in Walter Abbott, ed., *The Documents of Vatican II* (New York: America Press, 1966), 78–85.

10. Studies by Lawrence Cunningham, *The Meaning of Saints* (New York: Harper & Row, 1980), and William Thompson, *Fire and Light: The Saints and Theology* (New York: Paulist, 1987), are exemplary.

11. René Latourelle, ed., *Vatican II: Assessment and Perspectives, Twenty-Five Years After (1962–1987)*, 3 vols. (New York: Paulist, 1989).

12. The lack of an integrated approach is noted with regret by Paul Molinari, *Saints: Their Place in the Church*, trans. Dominic Maruca (New York: Sheed and Ward, 1965), 8, 32–35, 232 n. 173; and Karl Rahner, "The Church of the Saints," *Theological Investigations* 3, trans. Karl-H. and Boniface Kruger (New York: Seabury, 1974), 91–92, among others. Lawrence Cunningham, "A Decade of Research on the Saints: 1980–1990," *Theological Studies* 53 (1992): 517–33, bears out the ad hoc nature of investigation with his essay's subheadings which reveal new lines of inquiry but little synthesis going on: "Who or What Is a Saint?" "Saints as Resources for Theological Inquiry," and "Saints and Comparative Studies." The French journal *La vie spirituelle* published its five issues in 1989 on the saints and sanctity (vol. 69, nos. 683–87), probing new ideas that might revitalize doctrine and practice but again, with little synthesis.

13. Outstanding examples are Peter Brown, *The Cult of the Saints: Its Rise and Function in Latin Christianity* (Chicago: University of Chicago Press, 1981); Donald Weinstein and Rudolph Bell, *Saints and Society* (Chicago: University of Chicago Press, 1982); Stephen Wilson, ed., *Saints and Their Cults: Studies in Religious Sociology, Folklore, and History* (London and New York: Cambridge University Press, 1983), with an excellent introductory essay by the editor (1–41) and extended bibliography; and Richard Kieckhefer, *Unquiet Souls: Fourteenth Century Saints and Their Religious Milieus* (Chicago: University of Chicago Press, 1984).

14. For example: Jane Tibbetts Schulenburg, "Saints' Lives as a Source for the History of Women, 500–1100," in *Medieval Women and the Sources of Medieval History*, ed. Joel Rosenthal (Athens: University of Georgia Press, 1990), 285–320, with extended bibliography; and the study of the relation between image and social reality by Clarissa Atkinson, Constance Buchanan, and Margaret R. Miles, eds., *Immaculate and Powerful: The Female in Sacred Image and Social Reality* (Boston: Beacon, 1985).

15. Prime examples are John Stratton Hawley, ed., *Saints and Virtues* (Berkeley: University of California Press, 1987), with the editor's introductory essay (xi–xxiv) and a helpful bibliography; Richard Kieckhefer and George Bond, eds., *Sainthood: Its Manifestation in World Religions* (Berkeley: University of California Press, 1988); and Jacques Marx, ed., *Sainteté et martyre dans les religions du Livre* (Brussels: Éditions de l'Université de Bruxelles, 1989).

16. See Patrick Sherry, *Spirit, Saints, Immortality* (Albany: State University of New York Press, 1984); and Edith Wyschogrod, *Saints and Postmodernism: Re-visioning Moral Philosophy* (Chicago: University of Chicago Press, 1990), with analysis and counterproposal by David Matzko, "Postmodernism, Saints and Scoundrels," *Modern Theology* 9 (1993): 19–36.

17. For example, W. W. Meissner, *Ignatius of Loyola: The Psychology of a Saint* (New Haven: Yale University Press, 1992).

18. Robert Orsi, *Thank You, St. Jude: Women's Devotion to the Patron Saint of Hopeless Causes* (New Haven: Yale University Press, 1996). See also the illuminating essays in Thomas Kselman, ed., *Belief in History: Innovative Approaches to European and American Religion* (Notre Dame, Ind.: University of Notre Dame Press, 1991).

19. Karl Rahner, "Why and How Can We Venerate the Saints?" *Theological Investigations* 8, trans. David Bourke (New York: Seabury, 1977), 5.

20. M. Searle and D. Leege, "Of Piety and Planning: Liturgy, the Parishioners, and the Professionals," *Notre Dame Study of Catholic Parish Life*, Report 6 (Notre Dame, Ind.: University of Notre Dame Press, 1985), 6–7; see also J. Gremillion and D. Leege, "Post-Vatican II Parish Life in the United States," *NDS*, Report 15.

21. James Wallace, *Preaching through the Saints* (Collegeville, Minn.: Liturgical Press, 1982), 26.

22. June Macklin and Luise Margolies, "Saints, Near-Saints, and Society," *Journal of Latin American Lore* 14, no. 1 (1988): 9–10; this whole issue carries papers from a symposium on popular religion in Latin America.

23. Ibid. See also the sympathetic, trenchant assessment of popular Marian devotion by Ivone Gebara and Maria Clara Bingemer, *Mary: Mother of God, Mother of the Poor*, trans. Phillip Berryman (Maryknoll, N.Y.: Orbis, 1989), 128–58.

24. Leonardo Boff, *Saint Francis: A Model for Human Liberation*, trans. John Diercksmeier (New York: Crossroad, 1982).

25. Leonardo Boff, "The Need for Political Saints," *Cross Currents* 30, no. 4 (1980–81): 369–76; Jon Sobrino, "Political Holiness: A Profile," in *Martyrdom Today* (*Concilium* 163), ed. J. B. Metz and E. Schillebeeckx (New York: Seabury, 1983), 18–23; and Eduardo Hoornaert, "Models of Holiness among the People," in *Models of Holiness* (*Concilium* 129), ed. C. Duquoc and C. Floristan (New York: Seabury, 1979), 36–45.

26. Luke 1:46–55. See Gebara and Bingemer, *Mary, Mother of God, Mother of the Poor*, 159–71; Leonardo Boff, "Mary, Prophetic Woman of Liberation," *The Maternal Face of God: The Feminine and Its Religious Expressions*, trans. Robert Barr and John Diercksmeier (San Francisco: Harper & Row, 1987), 188–203; and Virgil Elizondo, "Our Lady of Guadalupe as a Cultural Symbol: The Power of the Powerless," in *Liturgy and Cultural Religious Traditions* (*Concilium* 102), ed. H. Schmidt and D. Power (New York: Seabury, 1977), 25–33.

27. See Edward Fasholé-Luke, "Ancestor Veneration and the Communion of Saints," in *New Testament Christianity for Africa and the World*, ed. M. Glasswell and E. Fasholé-Luke (London: SPCK, 1974), 209–21; Ephraim

Mosothoane, "Communio Sanctorum in Afrika," in *Zwischen Kultur und Politik,* ed. Theo Sundermeier (Hamburg: Lutherisches Verlaghaus, 1978), 62–77; Aylward Shorter, "Eschatology in the Ethnic Religions of Africa," *Studia Missionalia* 32 (1983): 1–24; and Jack Partain, "Christians and Their Ancestors: A Dilemma of African Theology," *Christian Century* 103 (November 26, 1986): 1066–69.

28. This is the key insight in the controverted work by Tissa Balasuriya, *Mary and Human Liberation* (Colombo, Sri Lanka: Centre for Society and Religion, 1990); see also the Singapore Conference, "Summary Statement on Feminist Mariology," in *Feminist Theology from the Third World: A Reader,* ed. Ursula King (London: SPCK and Maryknoll, N.Y.: Orbis, 1994), 271–75; and Chung Hyun Kyung, "Who Is Mary for Asian Women?" in her *Struggle to Be the Sun Again* (Maryknoll, N.Y.: Orbis, 1990), 74–84.

29. René Laurentin analyzes this temperament, different in tone from that of northern Europe, in *La Vierge au Concile* (Paris: Lethielleux, 1965), 21–22; however, William Christian, *Person and God in a Spanish Valley* (New York: Macmillan, 1972), 88–93, demonstrates that popular veneration of the saints is no longer universal even in these regions.

30. Quoted in Timothy Kallistos Ware, "The Communion of Saints," in *The Orthodox Ethos,* ed. A. J. Philippou (Oxford, England: Holywell Press, 1964), 140. See also John Meyendorff, *Byzantine Theology: Historical Trends and Doctrinal Themes* (New York: Fordham University Press, 1974), 170–76.

31. Weinstein and Bell, *Saints and Society,* 161.

32. Cunningham, *The Meaning of Saints,* 3.

33. John Coleman, "Conclusion: After Sainthood?" in *Saints and Virtues,* ed. J. Hawley, 206; Alasdair McIntyre, *After Virtue* (Notre Dame, Ind.: University of Notre Dame Press, 1981).

34. John Howe, "Saintly Statistics," *Catholic Historical Review* 70 (1984): 82.

35. For example, Regis Duffy, "*Devotio Futura:* The Need for Post-Conciliar Devotions?" in *A Promise of Presence,* ed. Michael Downey and Richard Fragomeni (Washington, D.C.: Pastoral Press, 1992), 163–83.

36. Richard Mazziotta, "When the Saints Went Marching Out," *Commonweal* 119 (October 23, 1992): 14–16.

37. Charles Morris gives a lucid rendition of this change in a chapter entitled "The End of the Catholic Culture," *American Catholic* (New York: Random House, 1997), 255–81; see also Mark Massa, "A Catholic for President?: John F. Kennedy and the 'Secular' Theology of the Houston Speech, 1960," *Journal of Church and State* 39 (1997): 297–317. For extended background, see Jay Dolan, *The American Catholic Experience* (Garden City, N.Y.: Doubleday, 1985); and Joseph Chinnici, *Living Stones: The History and Structure of Catholic Spiritual Life in the United States* (New York: Macmillan, 1989).

38. Edward Farley, *Deep Symbols: Their Postmodern Effacement and Reclamation* (Valley Forge, Pa.: Trinity Press International, 1996), 9. Discussion of postmodernism forms a vast and complex literature. I have found particularly helpful the concise description of the state of affairs by David Tracy, "On Naming the Present," in his *On Naming the Present: God, Hermeneu-*

tics, and Church (Maryknoll, N.Y.: Orbis, 1994), 3–24; and also David Griffin, ed., *Spirituality and Society: Postmodern Visions* (Albany: State University of New York Press, 1988), especially his "Introduction: Postmodern Spirituality and Society," 1–31; David Griffin, ed., *God and Religion in the Postmodern World* (Albany: State University of New York Press, 1989); Frederic Burnham, ed., *Postmodern Theology: Christian Faith in a Pluralist World* (San Francisco: Harper & Row, 1989); Sheila Greeve Davaney, ed., *Theology at the End of Modernity* (Philadelphia: Trinity Press International, 1991); and Terrence Tilley, ed., *Postmodern Theologies: The Challenge of Religious Diversity* (Maryknoll, N.Y.: Orbis, 1995).

39. David Power, "The Church's Calendar: Are the Saints Neglected or Misrepresented?" in his *Worship: Culture and Theology* (Washington, D.C.: Pastoral Press, 1990), 145.

40. Susan Rabe, "Veneration of the Saints in Western Christianity: An Ecumenical Issue in Historical Perspective," *Journal of Ecumenical Studies* 28 (Winter 1991): 60.

41. Rahner, "Why and How Can We Venerate the Saints?" 7, emended for inclusivity.

42. See Michael Buckley, "Atheism and Contemplation," *Theological Studies* 40 (1979): 680–99.

43. Perham, *The Communion of Saints,* 93.

44. Rahner, "Why and How Can We Venerate the Saints?" 7.

45. Ibid.

46. Orlando Espín, "Tradition and Popular Religion: An Understanding of the *Sensus Fidelium,*" in *Frontiers of Hispanic Theology in the United States,* ed. Allan Figueroa Deck (Maryknoll, N.Y.: Orbis, 1992), 62–87; an enlightening collection. See also the *Journal of Hispanic/Latino Theology,* as well as works such as Gilbert Romero, *Hispanic Devotional Piety: Tracing Biblical Roots* (Maryknoll, N.Y.: Orbis, 1991); Roberto Goizueta, ed., *We Are a People! Initiatives in Hispanic American Theology* (Minneapolis: Fortress, 1992); Ada María Isasi-Díaz, *En la Lucha / In the Struggle: Elaborating a Mujerista Theology* (Minneapolis: Fortress, 1993); María Pilar Aquino, *Our Cry for Life,* trans. Dinah Livingstone (Maryknoll, N.Y.: Orbis, 1993); and Orlando Espín, *The Faith of the People: Theological Reflections on Popular Catholicism* (Maryknoll, N.Y.: Orbis, 1997).

47. Elizabeth Dreyer, *Manifestations of Grace* (Wilmington, Del.: Michael Glazier, 1990), 5.

48. Robert Bellah, Richard Madsen, William Sullivan, Ann Swidler, and Steven Tipton, *Habits of the Heart: Individualism and Commitment in American Life* (San Francisco: Harper & Row, 1985), 153.

49. Ibid.

50. Ibid., 154.

51. Paul Tillich, *Dynamics of Faith* (New York: Harper & Row, 1957), 41–48, and his "The Meaning and Justification of Religious Symbols," 3–11, as well as "The Religious Symbol," 301–21, in *Religious Experience and Truth,* ed. Sidney Hook (New York: New York University Press, 1961). See also Karl Rahner, "The Theology of the Symbol," *Theological Investigations* 4, trans. Kevin

Smyth (New York: Seabury, 1974), 221–52. A helpful description of the dying of symbols is given by Langdon Gilkey in "Symbols, Meaning and the Divine Presence," *Theological Studies* 35 (1974): 252.

52. Wis 7:27.

Chapter 2: Christian Feminism

1. Keri Hulme, *The Bone People* (New York: Penguin Books, 1983), 4.

2. Pastoral Constitution on the Church in the Modern World (*Gaudium et Spes*), no. 29, in Abbott, *The Documents of Vatican II* (see ch. 1, n. 9). The full text reads: "Nevertheless, with respect to the fundamental rights of the person, every type of discrimination, whether social or cultural, whether based on sex, race, color, social condition, language, or religion, is to be overcome and eradicated as contrary to God's intent."

3. This principle is enunciated by Ruether, *Sexism and God-Talk*, 18–20, at 19 (see Intro., n. 2). For basic definitions, see the paradigmatic essay by Elisabeth Schüssler Fiorenza, "Feminist Theology as a Critical Theology of Liberation," *Theological Studies* 36 (1975): 606–26; and the recent essay by Susan Ross and Mary Catherine Hilkert, "Feminist Theology: A Review of Literature," *Theological Studies* 56 (1995): 327–52.

4. Pierre Delooz, "The Social Function of the Canonisation of Saints," in *Models of Holiness*, 14–24 (see ch. 1, n. 25); see further references in chapter 5 ahead.

5. Shawn Madigan, "Models of Holiness Derived from the Saints of Universal Significance in the Roman Calendar: Exposition and Theological Critique," Ph.D. dissertation, Catholic University of America, 1984; Regina Boisclair, "Amnesia in the Catholic Sunday Lectionary: Women Silenced from the Memories of Salvation History," in *Women and Theology*, College Theology Society 40, ed. Mary Ann Hinsdale and Phyllis Kaminski (Maryknoll, N.Y.: Orbis, 1995), 109–35; and Marjorie Proctor-Smith, "Images of Women in the Lectionary," in *The Power of Naming: A Concilium Reader in Feminist Liberation Theology*, ed. Schüssler Fiorenza (Maryknoll, N.Y.: Orbis, 1996), 175–86.

6. Adrienne Rich, "Resisting Amnesia: History and Personal Life," in *Blood, Bread, and Poetry: Selected Poems 1979–1985* (New York: Norton, 1986), 155.

7. Elisabeth Schüssler Fiorenza, "Saints Alive Yesterday and Today," in her *Discipleship of Equals: A Critical Feminist Ekklesia-logy of Liberation* (London: SCM Press, 1993), 40.

8. Anne Patrick, "Narrative and the Social Dynamics of Virtue," in *Changing Values and Virtues* (*Concilium* 191), ed. D. Mieth and J. Pohier (Edinburgh: T & T Clark, 1987), 74.

9. Mt 14:21.

10. The literature is vast; for exemplary introduction, see Rosemary R. Ruether and Eleanor McLaughlin, eds., *Women of Spirit: Female Leadership in the Jewish and Christian Traditions* (New York: Simon and Schuster, 1979).

11. For midwives see Ex 1:15–21; for Miriam, Ex 2:1–10 and 15:19–21; Num 12 and 20:1–2; Deut 24:8–9; 1 Chr 6:1–3; and Mic 6:3–4.

12. Judges 19:1–30; Phyllis Trible, *Texts of Terror: Literary-Feminist Readings of Biblical Narratives* (Philadelphia: Fortress, 1984), 65.

13. Judges 11:29–40; Renita Weems, *Just a Sister Away: A Womanist Vision of Women's Relationships in the Bible* (San Diego: LuraMedia, 1988), 66–67; see also Trible, *Texts of Terror*, 92–116; Cheryl Exum, *Fragmented Women: Feminist (Sub)versions of Biblical Narratives* (Valley Forge, Pa.: Trinity Press International, 1993), 16–41; and Jo Ann Hackett, "In the Days of Jael: Reclaiming the History of Women in Ancient Israel," in Atkinson, *Immaculate and Powerful*, 15–38 (see ch. 1, n. 14).

14. The paradigmatic study is Elisabeth Schüssler Fiorenza, *In Memory of Her: A Feminist Theological Reconstruction of Christian Origins* (New York: Crossroad, 1983); for Mary Magdalene, see ch. 8 ahead in this book; for Martha, consult Elisabeth Moltmann-Wendel, *The Women around Jesus*, trans. John Bowden (New York: Crossroad, 1986), 15–48; and Raymond Brown, "Roles of Women in the Fourth Gospel," *Theological Studies* 36 (1975): 688–99.

15. See Bernadette Brooten, *Women Leaders in the Ancient Synagogue: Inscriptional Evidence and Background Issues* (Chico, Calif.: Scholars Press, 1983); Judith Romney Wegner, *Chattel or Person?: The Status of Women in the Mishnah* (New York: Oxford University Press, 1988); Karen Jo Torjesen, *When Women Were Priests* (San Francisco: HarperCollins, 1993); Elizabeth Clark, "Early Christian Women: Sources and Interpretation," in *That Gentle Strength: Historical Perspectives on Women in Christianity,* ed. Lynda Coon, Katherine Haldane, and Elisabeth Sommer (Charlottesville, Va.: University Press of Virginia, 1990), 19–35; and Susan Ashbrook Harvey, "Women in Early Byzantine Hagiography: Reversing the Story," ibid., 36–59. A theoretical analysis of questions this scholarship raises is found in Rosemary R. Ruether, ed., *Religion and Sexism: Images of Woman in the Jewish and Christian Traditions* (New York: Simon and Schuster, 1974); and Ursula King, ed., *Religion and Gender* (Oxford: Blackwell, 1995).

16. Hildegard of Bingen, *Scivias,* trans. Mother Columba Hart and Jane Bishop (New York: Paulist, 1990), and Barbara Newman, *Sister of Wisdom: Saint Hildegard's Theology of the Feminine* (Berkeley: University of California Press, 1987); Julian of Norwich, *Showings,* trans. Edmund Colledge and James Walsh (New York: Paulist, 1978), and Joan Nuth, *Wisdom's Daughter: The Theology of Julian of Norwich* (New York: Crossroad, 1991).

17. Carolyn Walker Bynum, *Holy Feasts and Holy Fast: The Religious Significance of Food to Medieval Women* (Berkeley: University of California Press, 1987), and Clarissa Atkinson, *Mystic and Pilgrim: The Book and World of Margery Kempe* (Ithaca, N.Y.: Cornell University Press, 1981); Anne Llewellyn Barstow, *Witchcraze: A New History of the European Witch Hunts* (San Francisco: HarperCollins, 1994); Jo Ann McNamara, *Sisters in Arms: Catholic Nuns through Two Millennia* (Cambridge, Mass.: Harvard University Press, 1996); Brenda Meehan, *Holy Women of Russia* (San Francisco: HarperCollins,

1993); Delores Williams, *Sisters in the Wilderness: The Challenge of Womanist God-Talk* (Maryknoll, N.Y.: Orbis, 1993).

18. Mary Collins, "Daughters of the Church: The Four Theresa's," in Schüssler Fiorenza, *The Power of Naming,* 232–41. For Catherine, see her letter "To Three Italian Cardinals," in *Saint Catherine of Siena as Seen in Her Letters,* trans. and ed. Vida Scudder (New York: Dutton, 1905), 278, with modern translation in Gilbert Markus, ed., *The Radical Tradition: Saints in the Struggle for Justice and Peace* (London: Darton, Longman & Todd, 1992), 53; for Teresa of Avila, see *The Complete Works of Saint Teresa of Jesus,* vol. 2, trans. E Allison Peers (London: Sheed and Ward, 1946), 13; for Thérèse of Lisieux, see Joann Wolski Conn, "Thérèse of Lisieux from a Feminist Perspective," in *Women's Spirituality: Resources for Christian Development,* ed. idem (New York: Paulist, 1986), 317–25, and Barbara Corrado Pope, "A Heroine without Heroics: The Little Flower of Jesus and Her Times," *Church History* 57 (1988): 46–60.

19. Andrew Kadel, *Matrology: A Bibliography of Writings by Christian Women from the First to the Fifteenth Centuries* (New York: Continuum, 1995); Patricia Wilson-Kastner et al., *A Lost Tradition: Women Writers of the Early Church* (Lanham, Md.: University Press of America, 1981); Marla Selvidge, *Notorious Voices: Feminist Biblical Interpretation 1500–1920* (New York: Continuum, 1996); Rosemary R. Ruether and Rosemary Skinner Keller, *In Our Own Voices: Four Centuries of American Women's Religious Writing* (San Francisco: HarperCollins, 1995).

20. Rich, "Resisting Amnesia," 146.

21. Heb 12:1.

22. Augustine, *The Works of Saint Augustine: A Translation for the 21st Century,* part 3: *Sermons,* 10 vols., ed. John Rotelle, trans. and notes by Edmund Hill (Hyde Park, N.Y.: New City Press, 1990–95): Sermon 273.2 (8:17).

23. Sandra Schneiders, *Beyond Patching: Faith and Feminism in the Catholic Church* (New York: Paulist, 1991), 15, with commentary 15–31; see the definitions in the magisterial work by Gerda Lerner, *The Creation of Patriarchy* (New York: Oxford University Press, 1986), 231–43.

24. Margaret Brackenbury Crook, *Women and Religion* (Boston: Beacon, 1964), 1, 5; as quoted in Carolyn De Swarte Gifford, "American Women and the Bible," in *Feminist Perspectives on Biblical Scholarship,* ed. Adela Yarbro Collins (Chico, Calif.: Scholars Press, 1985), 11–33. All religious traditions are subject to this critique; see Paula Cooey, William Eakin, and Jay McDaniel, eds., *After Patriarchy: Feminist Transformations of the World Religions* (Maryknoll, N.Y.: Orbis, 1993).

25. Rita Nakashima Brock, *Journeys by Heart: A Christology of Erotic Power* (New York: Crossroad, 1988).

26. Schüssler Fiorenza, *In Memory of Her,* 97–241.

27. Anne Carr, *Transforming Grace: Women's Experience and Christian Tradition* (San Francisco: Harper & Row, 1988).

28. John XXIII, *Pacem in Terris,* no. 41, in *The Gospel of Peace and Justice,* ed. Joseph Gremillion (Maryknoll, N.Y.: Orbis, 1976), 209–10.

29. *The Beijing Declaration and Platform for Action,* Fourth World Conference on Women (New York: United Nations, 1996), 2.

30. Letty Russell and Shannon Clarkson, eds., *Dictionary of Feminist Theologies* (Louisville, Ky.: Westminster John Knox, 1996), 100–120. The following collections, published during the past decade, reveal something of the scope of this work:

Africa, Asia, and Latin America: Virginia Fabella and Mercy Amba Oduyoye, eds., *With Passion and Compassion: Third World Women Doing Theology* (Maryknoll, N.Y.: Orbis, 1988); and Ursula King, ed., *Feminist Theology from the Third World: A Reader* (Maryknoll, N.Y.: Orbis, 1994);

Africa: Denise Ackermann et al., *Women Hold Up Half the Sky* (Pietermaritzburg, South Africa: Cluster Pub., 1991);

Asia: Prasanna Kumari, ed., *A Reader in Feminist Theology* (Gurukul, Madras, India: 1993);

Latin America: Elsa Tamez, *Through Her Eyes: Women's Theology from Latin America* (Maryknoll, N.Y.: Orbis, 1989);

Australia: Mary Ann Confoy, Dorothy Lee, and Joan Nowotny, eds., *Freedom and Entrapment: Women Thinking Theology* (North Blackburn, Victoria: HarperCollins Australia, 1995);

Europe: Teresa Elwes, ed., *Women's Voices: Essays in Contemporary Feminist Theology* (London: HarperCollins, 1992); and A. Esser and L. Schottroff, eds., *Yearbook of the European Society of Women in Theological Research* 1 (Kampen, Netherlands: Kok Pharos, 1993);

North America: Judith Plaskow and Carol Christ, eds., *Weaving the Visions: New Patterns in Feminist Spirituality* (San Francisco: Harper & Row, 1989); Emilie Townes, ed., *A Troubling in My Soul: Womanist Perspectives on Evil and Suffering* (Maryknoll, N.Y.: Orbis, 1993); and Catherine LaCugna, ed., *Freeing Theology: The Essentials of Theology in Feminist Perspective* (San Francisco: HarperCollins, 1993).

31. Shawn Copeland, "Toward a Critical Christian Feminist Theology of Solidarity," in Hinsdale and Kaminski, *Women and Theology,* 10.

32. See the spirited defense of the appeal to women's experience as a hermeneutical and not an ontological practice by Sharon Welch, "Sporting Power: American Feminism, French Feminisms, and an Ethic of Conflict," in *Transfigurations: Theology and the French Feminists,* ed. Maggie Kim, Susan St. Ville, and Susan Simonaitis (Minneapolis: Augsburg Fortress, 1993), 171–98.

33. Lisa Sowle Cahill, *Sex, Gender, and Christian Ethics* (Cambridge: Cambridge University Press, 1996), 28–29.

34. See the discussions of geographical, religious, and theoretical difference in Elisabeth Schüssler Fiorenza and M. Shawn Copeland, eds., *Feminist Theology in Different Contexts* (London: SCM Press and Maryknoll, N.Y.: Orbis, 1996); the pair of articles by Seattle colleagues Susan Secker, "Women's Experience in Feminist Theology: The 'Problem' or the 'Truth' of Difference," *Journal*

of Hispanic/Latino Theology 1 (1993): 56–67, and Jeannette Rodriguez, "Experience as a Resource for Feminist Thought," ibid., 68–76. An important trigger for this consciousness is the work of Audre Lorde, *Sister Outsider* (Freedom, Calif.: The Crossing Press, 1984), especially "An Open Letter to Mary Daly," 66–71, and "Age, Race, Class, and Sex: Women Redefining Difference," 114–23.

35. Prov 8:35. For background on Wisdom/Sophia see *"sophia"* in *Theological Dictionary of the New Testament,* ed. Gerhard Kittel, trans. Geoffrey Bromiley (Grand Rapids, Mich.: Eerdmans, 1964). 7:465–528; and Johnson, *She Who Is,* 86–100 (see Intro., n. 4).

36. Wis 7:27.

37. Jas 2:23; see also 2 Chron 20:7 and Isa 41:8.

38. See Prov. 27:19, 9.

39. For a superb analysis of God as friend, see Sallie McFague, *Models of God: Theology for an Ecological, Nuclear Age* (Philadelphia: Fortress, 1987), 157–80; for the dynamics of friendship among women, see Mary Hunt, *Fierce Tenderness: A Feminist Theology of Friendship* (New York: Crossroad, 1991).

40. Isa 61:1–2; Lk 4:18–19.

41. For excellent analysis of the prophetic vocation, see Abraham Heschel, *The Prophets* (New York: Harper & Row, 1962); and Walter Brueggemann, *The Prophetic Imagination* (Philadelphia: Fortress, 1978).

42. Prov 8:20.

43. See James Dunn, *Christology in the Making* (Philadelphia: Westminster, 1980), 163–212; James Robinson, "Jesus as Sophos and Sophia: Wisdom Tradition and the Gospels," in *Aspects of Wisdom in Judaism and Early Christianity,* ed. Robert Wilkens (Notre Dame, Ind.: University of Notre Dame Press, 1975), 1–16; Celia Deutsch, "Wisdom in Matthew: Transformation of a Symbol," *Novum Testamentum* 32 (1990): 13–47; Raymond Brown, *The Gospel according to John, I–XII* (Garden City, N.Y.: Doubleday, 1966), cxxii–cxxviii, 3–37, 519–24; Elizabeth A. Johnson, "Jesus the Wisdom of God: A Biblical Basis for Non-Androcentric Christology," *Ephemerides Theologicae Lovaniensis* 61 (1985): 261–94; and idem, "Wisdom Was Made Flesh and Pitched Her Tent among Us," in *Reconstructing the Christ Symbol,* ed. Maryanne Stevens (New York: Paulist, 1993), 95–117.

44. Jn 14:6.

45. Mt 11:19.

46. Jn 15:15.

47. David Tracy, *The Analogical Imagination: Christian Theology and the Culture of Pluralism* (New York: Crossroad, 1981), 193–229.

Chapter 3: A Holy Nation, a People Belonging to God

1. Lk 7:33–34.
2. Lk 7:35.

3. Edward Schillebeeckx, *Jesus: An Experiment in Christology,* trans. Hubert Hoskins (New York: Seabury, 1979), 200–218.

4. Isa 12:6; also Num 16:5, Job 6:10, Prov 9:10, Ps 89:19, Isa 12:6; see analysis and description of *hagios* in *Theological Dictionary of the New Testament,* 1:88–115 (see ch. 2, n. 35).

5. Phrase from Rudolf Otto, *The Idea of the Holy,* trans. John Harvey (London and Oxford: Oxford University Press, 1923/1950).

6. Claus Westermann, "Sacré et sainteté de Dieu dans la Bible," *La vie spirituelle* 143 (January 1989): 13.

7. Ex 15:11, the song as led by Moses; see v. 20, the song as led by Miriam.

8. Abraham Heschel, *The Prophets* (New York: Harper & Row, 1962), 227.

9. Isa 6:3.

10. For what follows, see *"doxa"* in *Theological Dictionary of the New Testament,* 2:232–55.

11. Ps 19:1.

12. Wis 10:15, 17–18.

13. Isa 40:5.

14. Ps 85:9; Ps 72:19; and Ezek 43.

15. Wis 7:25; 7:26; and 7:29–30. For detailed discussion of spirit, wisdom, and *shekinah* as female metaphors of the divine, see Johnson, *She Who Is,* 76–103 (see Intro. n. 4).

16. It is interesting to note that in his discussion of creation, Thomas Aquinas uses this same metaphor to describe God's work on the fourth, fifth, and sixth days. Speaking of the stars, the birds and fishes, and the earth animals, he writes: "so the work of adornment is set forth by the production of things having movement in the heavens and upon the earth" (*Summa theologiae* 1 [New York: Benziger Bros., 1946], q. 70, a. 1).

17. Mt 11:5.

18. 2 Cor 3:18.

19. Rom 8:21.

20. Col 1:27.

21. Ex 19:4–6.

22. Deut 7: 7–8.

23. Lev 11:45.

24. Deut 7:6; also Ex 19:6 and Lev 20:7. See Michel Buit, "La sainteté du peuple dans l'Ancien Testament," *La vie spirituelle* 143 (1989): 25–37; and Hans Hermann Henrix, "Von der Nachahmung Gottes: Heiligkeit und Heiligsein im biblischen und judischen Denken," *Erbe und Auftrag* 65 (1989): 177–87.

25. Judith Plaskow, *Standing Again at Sinai: Judaism from a Feminist Perspective* (San Francisco: HarperCollins, 1990), 96; see also Dvorah Setel, "Feminist Reflections on Separation and Unity in Jewish Theology," *Journal of Feminist Studies in Religion* 2, no. 1 (1986): 113–18.

26. Plaskow, *Standing Again at Sinai,* 82; see also 170–210, where this author develops a theology of women's sexuality as sacred and a fitting image of the divine.

27. Ibid., 107.

28. Hos 11:9.

29. 1 Cor 10:16–17.

30. 2 Cor 13:14.

31. Irenaeus, *Adversus Haereses* Book 3, chap. 17:2; cited in *The Holy Spirit,* ed. J. Patout Burns and Gerald Fagin (Wilmington, Del.: Michael Glazier, 1984), 34–35.

32. See Eduard Schweizer, *The Holy Spirit,* trans. Reginald and Ilse Fuller (Philadelphia: Fortress, 1980), 73–75.

33. For examples of these three referents, see sequentially 1 Thess 3:13; Mt 27:52; Rev 18:24.

34. The term appears in Dan 7 verses 18, 22, 25, and 27. See Stephen Woodward, "The Provenance of the Term 'Saints': A *Religionsgeschichte* Study," *Journal of the Evangelical Theological Society* 24 (1981): 107–16; D. W. B. Robinson, "Who Were the Saints?" *Reformed Theological Review* 22 (1963): 45–53; L. Dequeker, "The Saints of the Most High in Qumran and Daniel," in *Oudtestamentische Studien* 18 (Leiden: Brill, 1973), 108–87; and Hugues Cousin, "A tous les saints qui sont à Corinthe," *La vie spirituelle* 143 (January 1989): 39–43.

35. Rom 1:7.

36. Phil 1:1

37. 1 Cor 1:2; see also 6:2, 16:1, 15.

38. 2 Cor 13:12–13; see also 1:1, 8:4, 9:1.

39. Owen Evans, "New Wine in Old Wineskins: The Saints," *Expository Times* 86 (1974–75): 198.

40. Gal 3:27–28.

41. Two versions of Joseph Fitzmyer's commentary on Gal 3:28, separated by twenty years, vividly makes this point. In the 1968 edition of the *Jerome Biblical Commentary,* Fitzmyer judges this text to mean that "secondary differences vanish through the effects of this incorporation of Christians into Christ's body through 'one Spirit. . . .' This verse is really the climax of Paul's letter." In the 1988 edition, however, after the sentence about secondary differences vanishing, he drops the line about this being the climax of Paul's letter and adds: "Such unity in Christ does not imply *political* equality in church or society" (emphasis in the original). There is not a shred of evidence adduced for this interpretation. One can only wonder at the switch of concluding sentences (is Gal 3:28 no longer to be considered the climax of Paul's letter?), and ponder why a scholar who would not dream of interpreting philological meanings without all the apparatus of scholarship makes such a sweeping and emphatic statement without any textual support. See "The Letter to the Galatians," in *The Jerome Biblical Commentary,* ed. Raymond Brown, Joseph Fitzmyer, and Roland Murphy (Englewood Cliffs, N.J.: Prentice-Hall, 1968), 243, and *The New Jerome Biblical Commentary,* ed. idem (Englewood Cliffs, N.J.: Prentice-Hall, 1988), 787.

42. Elisabeth Schüssler Fiorenza, "Justified by All Her Children: Struggle, Memory, Vision," in *The Power of Naming,* ed. Schüssler Fiorenza, 350 (see ch. 2, n. 5); see detailed analysis of this text in this same author's *In Memory of Her,* 205–41 (ch. 2, n. 14); and commentary by Sheila Briggs, "Galatians,"

in *Searching the Scriptures: A Feminist Commentary,* ed. Elisabeth Schüssler Fiorenza (New York: Crossroad, 1994), 2:218–36.

43. Schüssler Fiorenza, "Justified by All Her Children," 351.

44. Ibid.

45. 1 Cor 12:4, 7.

46. See Heb 2:17.

47. 1 Pet 2:9. "Au risque de surprendre, je dirai de façon paradoxale que la sainteté chrétienne est essentiellement 'laïque'!"("At the risk of surprising you, I would say in paradoxical fashion that Christian holiness is essentially 'lay'!") (Bernard Rey, "La sainteté reçue, vécue, et partageé par Jésus Christ," *La vie spirituelle* 143 (January 1989): 44–52); see illuminating discussion of the priesthood of all believers by Hans Küng, *The Church,* trans. Ray and Rosaleen Ockenden (New York: Sheed and Ward, 1967), 370–87.

48. 4 Macc 17:9–10; see 4 Macc 5–18, and 2 Macc 6–7. See Robert Doran, "The Martyr: A Synoptic View of the Mother and Her Seven Sons," in *Ideal Figures in Ancient Judaism: Profiles and Paradigms,* ed. John Collins and George Nickelsburg (Chico, Calif.: Scholars Press, 1980), 189–221.

49. Mt 23:29. For detailed discussion see Joseph Fitzmyer, "Biblical Data on the Veneration, Intercession, and Invocation of Holy People," in Anderson, *The One Mediator, the Saints, and Mary,* 135–47 (see ch. 1, n. 8).

50. Rom 8:35–39.

51. 1 Cor 15:20–23.

52. Rom 4:17.

53. Rom 14:7–9.

54. Rev 8:14.

55. Rev 14:13.

56. Heb 11:1–12:2; translation from NRSV, using the variant of verse 11 about Sarah provided in note g. See commentary by Cynthia Briggs Kittredge, "Hebrews," in *Searching the Scriptures,* 2:428–52, who makes the case, first suggested by Adolf Harnack, for female authorship of this letter, a likely candidate being Priscilla.

Chapter 4: Patterns in the Age of the Martyrs

1. The literature on the martyrs is vast. See W. H. C. Frend, *Martyrdom and Persecution in the Early Church: A Study of a Conflict from the Maccabees to Donatus* (Garden City, N.Y.: Doubleday, 1967), with extended bibliography. A general survey of Christian interpretation of the martyrs is conducted by Robin Lane Fox, *Pagans and Christians* (New York: Knopf, 1987), 419–92; background on the term itself is given in *"martus"* in *Theological Dictionary of the New Testament,* 4:474–514 (see ch. 2, n. 35), and by Christoph Burchard, "Kerygma and Martyria in the New Testament," in *Christian Witness and the Jewish People,* ed. Arne Sovik (Geneva: Lutheran World Federation, 1976), 10–25; studies in archaeology, social history, and popular religion are com-

piled by M. Lamberigts and P. van Deun, eds., *Martyrium in Multidisciplinary Perspective* (Leuven: Leuven University Press, 1995).

2. Lawrence Cunningham, *The Catholic Heritage* (New York: Crossroad, 1983), 17.

3. Maureen Tilley, "The Ascetic Body and the (Un)Making of the World of the Martyr," *Journal of the American Academy of Religion* 65 (1991): 467.

4. Ibid., 474.

5. Ibid., 475.

6. Brian McNeil, "Suffering and Martyrdom in the Odes of Solomon," 136–42, and William Horbury, "Suffering and Messianism in Yose ben Yose," 143–82, in *Suffering and Martyrdom in the New Testament*, ed. William Horbury and Brian McNeil (Cambridge: Cambridge University Press, 1981); and J. W. van Henten, "The Martyrs as Heroes of the Christian People: Some Remarks on the Continuity between Jewish and Christian Martyrology, with Pagan Analogies," in *Martyrium in Multidisciplinary Perspective*, 303–22.

7. Herbert Musurillo, ed., *The Acts of the Pagan Martyrs: Acta Alexandrianorum* (Oxford: Oxford University Press, 1954); and his "Christian and Political Martyrs in the Early Roman Empire: A Reconsideration," in *Assimilation et résistance à la culture Greco-Romaine dans le monde ancien*, ed. D. Pippidi (Paris: Société D'Édition, 1976), 333–42.

8. This literature is collected in Herbert Musurillo, ed., *The Acts of the Christian Martyrs* (Oxford: Oxford University Press, 1972). Christel Butterweck, *Martyriumssucht in der Alten Kirche?: Studien zur Darstellung und Deutung frühchristlicher Martyrien* (Tübingen: J. C. B. Mohr, 1995), explores the spirituality conveyed in the way the stories are presented.

9. Rev 1:5 and 3:14; see John Downing, "Jesus and Martyrdom," *Journal of Theological Studies* 14 (1963): 279–93; and Brian Beck, "*Imitatio Christi* and the Lucan Passion Narrative," in *Suffering and Martyrdom in the New Testament*, 28–47.

10. "The Martyrdom of Perpetua and Felicity" 1, trans. Rosemary Rader, in Wilson-Kastner, *A Lost Tradition*, 19 (see ch. 2, n. 19).

11. "The Letter of the Churches of Lyons and Vienne" I.17–19, 37–38, 41–42, 53–56, in Musurillo, *The Acts of the Christian Martyrs*, 67, 73–75, 79–81.

12. Stuart Hall, "Women among the Early Martyrs," in *Martyrs and Martyrologies*, ed. Diana Wood (Oxford and Cambridge, Mass.: Blackwell, 1993), 16.

13. Peter Brown, *The Body and Society: Men, Women and Sexual Renunciation in Early Christianity* (New York: Columbia Press, 1988), 142.

14. The classic description is given by Hippolyte Delehaye, *Les origines du culte des martyrs* (Brussels: Bureaux de la Société des Bollandistes, 1912); see also Josef Jungmann, "The Veneration of the Martyrs," in his *The Early Liturgy to the Time of Gregory the Great*, trans. Francis Brunner (Notre Dame, Ind.: University of Notre Dame Press, 1959), 175–87; W. Rodorf, "Aux origines du culte des martyrs," *Irenikon* 46 (1972): 315–31; and J. B. Ward-Perkins, "Memoria, Martyr's Tomb, and Martyr's Church," *Journal of Theological Studies* 17 (1966): 20–37. Parallels with the practice of Shiite Muslims are described by Mahmoud Ayoub, "Martyrdom in Christianity and Islam," in *Religious Resurgence: Contemporary Cases in Islam, Christianity, and Judaism*, ed.

Richard Antoun and Mary Hegland (Syracuse, N.Y.: Syracuse University Press, 1987), 67–77.

15. "The Martyrdom of Polycarp" 18, in Musurillo, *The Acts of the Christian Martyrs,* 17.

16. First three citations from Delehaye, *Les origines du culte des martyrs,* 123, 124, 125; next from Jungmann, "The Veneration of the Martyrs," 182; last from Charles McGinnis, *The Communion of Saints* (St. Louis: B. Herder, 1912), 54.

17. See P. Séjourné, "Saints (culte des)," *Dictionnaire de théologie catholique* 14/1 (Paris: Librarie Letouzey et Ané, 1939), 870–978; and Hippolyte Delehaye, *The Legends of the Saints,* trans. V. Crawford (Notre Dame, Ind.: University of Notre Dame Press, 1961).

18. Rom 8:1.

19. "The Martyrdom of Polycarp" 17, in Musurillo, *Acts of the Christian Martyrs,* 16–17.

20. Augustine, Sermon 280.4, 6; this translation by W. H. Schewring, *The Passion of Perpetua and Felicity, together with the Sermons of St. Augustine upon these Saints* (London: Sheed and Ward, 1931), 49–51.

21. For an overview with Latin texts, see Robert Eno, *Saint Augustine and the Saints* (Villanova, Pa.: Villanova University Press, 1989). Augustine's late shift to interest in miracles shows up in the last book of the *City of God;* Eno dispenses with the idea that it was due to advancing old age, arguing instead that the emphasis was due to Augustine's desire to promote belief in the bodily resurrection of Christ, in light of which bodies are and remain important. See T. J. van Bavl, "The Cult of the Martyrs in St. Augustine: Theology vs. Popular Religion?" in Lamberigts, *Martyrium in Multidisciplinary Perspective,* 351–61.

22. All of the following quotations of Augustine's sermons are taken from the Hill translation (see ch. 2, n. 22); this citation is from Sermon 332.1 (vol. 9:194).

23. Sermon 227.1 (6:254).

24. S. 53.13 (2:73).

25. S. 137.15 (4:382).

26. S. 273.2 (8:17).

27. S. 302.7 (8:304).

28. S. 325.1 (9:167).

29. S. 314.2 (9:127).

30. S. 315.8 (9:133).

31. See S. 94a.2 (4:19–20); and S. 286.7 (8:105).

32. S. 81.1 (8:78).

33. S. 64a.3 (3:190).

34. See the textual study by Kari Elisabeth Børresen, *Subordination and Equivalence: The Nature and Role of Women in Augustine and Thomas Aquinas* (Lanham, Md.: University Press of America, 1981); and the more psychologically oriented study linking Augustine's writings with his personal and cultural experience by Kim Power, *Veiled Desire: Augustine on Women* (New York: Continuum, 1996).

35. S. 273.9 (8:21).

36. Ibid.

37. S. 273.3 (8:18).

38. S. 306c.1 (9:36–37).

39. Ibid.

40. S. 306.10 (9:24).

41. See Jean-Yves Tilliette, ed., *Les Fonctions des saints dans le monde occidental (IIIe–XIIIe siècle)* (Rome: École française de Rome, 1991), especially Charles Pietri, "L'Évolution du culte des saints aux premiers siècles chrétiens: du témoin à l'intercesseur," 15–36.

42. Wilson, "Introduction," *Saints and Their Cults,* 23 (see ch. 1, n. 13).

43. Carl Landé, "Introduction," in *Friends, Followers, and Factions,* ed. Steffen Schmidt, Laura Guasti, Carl Landé, and James C. Scott (Berkeley: University of California Press, 1977), xx.

44. Ibid., xxi. This volume contains a helpful bibliographic essay by James C. Scott, "Political Clientelism," 483–505; and another definition of terms by Anthony Hall, "Patron-Client Relations: Concepts and Terms," 510–12. In S. N. Eisenstadt and Luis Roniger, *Patrons, Clients and Friends: Interpersonal Relations and the Structure of Trust in Society* (London and New York: Cambridge University Press, 1984), the patronage system is studied in societies as diverse as the Muslim Middle East and southeast Asia. While it is noted that the United States is the first modern polity based on premises of equality, participation, and equal access of citizens to centers of power, the example of nineteenth-century urban bosses with their political machines demonstrates that under certain conditions patronage can emerge even in such a society, although the basic values of democratic society tend to provide a countervailing and reforming force.

45. See T. F. Carney, *The Shape of the Past: Models and Antiquity* (Lawrence, Kans.: Coronado Press, 1975), 137–234, with bibliography 371–81; and John Duncan Powell, "Peasant Society and Clientist Politics," in Schmidt, *Friends, Followers, and Factions,* 147–61.

46. John Dominic Crossan, *The Historical Jesus: The Life of a Mediterranean Jewish Peasant* (San Francisco: HarperCollins, 1991). Although Crossan's major interest lay elsewhere, I am indebted to this work for the background on patronage it provided for my thinking about this paradigm of the communion of saints.

47. See Richard Saller, *Personal Patronage under the Early Empire* (Cambridge: Cambridge University Press, 1982), with bibliography 209–16.

48. G. E. M. de Ste. Croix, "Suffragium: From Vote to Patronage," *British Journal of Sociology* 5 (1954): 46.

49. Brown, *The Cult of the Saints,* 61 (see ch. 1, n. 13).

50. Ibid., 65.

51. Ibid., 38.

52. Ibid., 127; Brown also proposes that the same structure of patronage in late antiquity drove the phenomenon of the holy man, patron par excellence in the East: "The Rise and Function of the Holy Man in Late Antiquity," in his *Society and the Holy in Late Antiquity* (Berkeley: University of California Press, 1982), 103–52.

53. See astute analysis of the monarchical model of deity by McFague, *Models of God,* 63–69 (see ch. 2, n. 39); and Brian Wren's seriously humorous descrip-

tion of the KINGAFAP model (King-God-Almighty-Father-Protector) from the perspective of an alien anthropologist in his *What Language Shall I Borrow?: God-Talk in Worship — A Male Response to Feminist Theology* (New York: Crossroad, 1989), 115–36.

54. It is important to note that in the context of the growing popular cult of the saints increasingly expressed in the use of icons, and of its strong criticizers, the last ecumenical council to occur before the split between East and West found it necessary to make clear the distinction between honoring God and honoring the saints. Nicea II in 787 taught that God alone is worshiped and adored (*latria*), while to the saints simple respect and veneration is given (*dulia*).

55. Brown, *The Cult of the Saints*, 64, and *passim*.

56. Jeremy Boissevain, in *Patrons and Clients in Mediterranean Societies*, ed. Ernest Gellner and John Waterbury (London: Duckworth, 1977), 94; cited in Crossan, *The Historical Jesus*, 68.

57. Ibid.

58. Gerda Lerner, *The Creation of Patriarchy* (New York: Oxford University Press, 1986), 228.

Chapter 5: Institutional Settling

1. The debate over the origin and meaning of the phrase is traced in J. N. D. Kelly, *Early Christian Creeds*, 3d edition (London: Longman, 1972), 388–97. I found these resources helpful in sorting out the vocabulary issue: Émilien Lamirande, "The History of a Formula," in *The Communion of Saints*, trans. A. Manson (New York: Hawthorn Books, 1963), 15–38; Wilhelm Breuning, "Communion of Saints," in *Sacramentum Mundi*, ed. Karl Rahner (New York: Herder & Herder, 1968), 1:391–94; Wolfhart Pannenberg, *The Apostles' Creed*, trans. Margaret Kohl (Philadelphia: Westminster, 1972), 144–59; Kenan Osborne, "Communion of Saints," in *The New Dictionary of Theology*, ed. Joseph Komanchak, Mary Collins, Dermot Lane (Collegeville, Minn.: Liturgical Press, 1987), 213–16; and Heinz Kruse, "Gemeinschaft der Heiligen: Herkunft und Bedeutung des Glaubensartikels," *Vigiliae Christianae* 47, no. 3 (1993): 246–59.

2. Kelly, *Early Christian Creeds*, 389–90.

3. Cited in ibid., 391; emended for inclusivity.

4. Cited in ibid., 394.

5. Berard Marthaler, *The Creed* (Mystic, Conn.: Twenty-Third Pub., 1987), 347–68; see also his "Interpreting the Communion of Saints," *Liturgy: With All the Saints 5*, no. 2 (Fall 1985): 89–93. The symbolic nature of the creed also permits multilevel reading; see Nicholas Ayo, *The Creed as Symbol* (Notre Dame, Ind.: University of Notre Dame Press, 1989).

6. Mary Ann Fatula, "Communion of Saints," in *The Modern Catholic Encyclopedia*, ed. Michael Glazier and Monika Hellwig (Collegeville, Minn.: Liturgical Press, 1994), 187, who refers to *Gaudium et Spes* and *Unitatis Redintegratio*, both in Abbott, *The Documents of Vatican II* (see ch. 1, n. 9).

7. See Thomas Berry with Thomas Clarke, *Befriending the Earth* (Mystic, Conn.: Twenty-Third Pub., 1992); Rosemary R. Ruether, *Gaia and God: An Ecofeminist Theology of Earth Healing* (San Francisco: HarperCollins, 1992); Carol J. Adams, ed., *Ecofeminism and the Sacred* (New York: Continuum, 1993); and David Hallman, ed., *Ecotheology: Voices from South and North* (Maryknoll, N.Y.: Orbis, 1994).

8. Thomas Talley, "The Evolution of a Feast," *Liturgy: With All the Saints* 5, no.2 (Fall 1985): 48.

9. Cunningham, *The Meaning of Saints*, 45 (see ch. 1, n. 10).

10. Kenneth Woodward, *Making Saints: How the Catholic Church Determines Who Becomes a Saint, Who Doesn't, and Why* (New York: Simon and Schuster, 1990), 67; this book is a thorough and readable account of the history of canonization and its current workings.

11. Key work has been done by Pierre Delooz, *Sociologie et canonisations* (The Hague: M. Nijhoff, 1969). See also the important contributions to this developing field of research by André Vauchez, *La Sainteté en Occident aux derniers siècles du moyen âge* (Rome: École française de Rome, 1981); Michael Goodich, "The Politics of Canonization in the Thirteenth Century: Lay and Mendicant Saints," in Wilson, *Saints and Their Cults,* 169–87 (see ch. 1, n. 13); and Aviad Kleinberg, "Proving Sanctity: Selection and Authentication of Saints in the Later Middle Ages," *Viator: Medieval and Renaissance Studies* 20 (Berkeley: University of California Press, 1989), 183–205.

12. Pierre Delooz, "Towards a Sociological Study of Canonized Sainthood in the Catholic Church," in Wilson, *Saints and Their Cults,* 189–216, at 199; this essay poses an enormous number of questions that need further research.

13. Cunningham, *The Meaning of Saints*, 59.

14. For a contemporary presentation of the current roster of saints, see *Butler's Lives of the Saints,* general ed. Paul Burns (Collegeville, Minn.: Liturgical Press, 1996–), 12 volumes.

15. Jane Tibbetts Schulenburg, "Female Sanctity: Public and Private Roles, ca. 500–1100," in *Women and Power in the Middle Ages,* ed. Mary Erler and Maryanne Kowaleski (Athens and London: University of Georgia Press, 1988), 103; the basic research is reported in this same author's essay entitled "Sexism and the Celestial Gynaeceum — From 500 to 1200," *Journal of Medieval History* 4 (1978): 117–33.

16. Delooz, "The Social Function of the Canonisation of Saints," 21 (see ch. 2, n. 4). An extended set of "saintly statistics" categorizing the canonized according to family status, occupation, charitable activity, asceticism, and gender is presented in Weinstein and Bell, *Saints and Society,* 220–38 (see ch. 1, n. 13).

17. According to an often quoted statistic, John Paul II canonized more saints in the first ten years of his pontificate than all of his successors taken together back to Benedict XIV in 1746 — a span of 232 years. See the list compiled by Jean Evenou, "Les Saints et Bienheureux proclamés par Jean Paul II (1978–1988)," *Esprit et vie* 99 (1989): 200–207. As of this writing (1998) the number of saints this pope has canonized and beatified has long passed the one thousand

mark. According to projections, if the current rate continues until 2001, he will have canonized more people than all the popes in history added together.

18. Woodward, *Making Saints,* 337.

19. Cunningham, *The Meaning of Saints,* 49.

20. Michael Perham, *The Communion of Saints,* 114–19 (see ch. 1, n. 7), develops a set of suggested criteria for the Anglican Church; Craig Erickson, "Reformed Theology and the Sanctoral Cycle," *Liturgy: With All the Saints 5,* no. 2 (Fall 1985): 83–87, proposes criteria for the Presbyterian Church.

21. Power, "The Church's Calendar: Are the Saints Neglected or Misrepresented?" 151 (see ch. 1, n. 39).

Chapter 6: Movements for Reform

1. For historical analysis, see Jaroslav Pelikan, *The Growth of Medieval Theology* (Chicago: University of Chicago Press, 1978), 158–84; and Heiko Oberman, *The Harvest of Medieval Theology* (Cambridge, Mass.: Harvard University Press, 1963), 281–322.

2. Martin Luther, *Large Catechism,* in *The Book of Concord,* ed. Theodore Tappert (Philadelphia: Fortress Press, 1959), 366.

3. The most thorough theological discussion of the issue to date is Anderson, *The One Mediator, The Saints, and Mary* (see ch. 1, n. 8), the fruit of an eight-year discussion by the Lutheran/Catholic Dialogue in the United States; this book contains a careful statement of common ground and still disputed issues, along with supporting papers. It concludes that the remaining differences need not be church-dividing.

4. Luther, *Large Catechism,* 366.

5. Luther, *Smalcald Articles* 2:28, in *The Book of Concord,* 297.

6. *Augsburg Confession* 21:2, in *The Book of Concord,* 46–47; see analysis by Georg Kretschmer and René Laurentin, "The Cult of the Saints," in *Confessing One Faith: A Joint Commentary on the Augsburg Confession by Lutheran and Catholic Theologians,* ed. George Forell and James McCue (Minneapolis: Augsburg, 1982), 262–85.

7. *Apology of the Augsburg Confession* 21:8–9, in *The Book of Concord,* 229–30; this text was also written by Melanchthon in 1531.

8. Robert Kolb, *For All the Saints: Changing Perceptions of Martyrdom and Sainthood in the Lutheran Reformation* (Macon, Ga.: Mercer University Press, 1987), especially chapter 4, "Saint Martin of Wittenberg," 103–38; see also idem, "Festivals of the Saints in Late Reformation Lutheran Preaching," *Historian* 52 (1990): 613–26.

9. See Vilmos Vajta, "Die Kirche als geistlich-sakramentale communio mit Christus und seinen Heiligen bei Luther," *Lutherjahrbuch* 51 (1984): 10–62; the clear summation in Marc Lienhard, "La sainteté et les saints chez Luther," *La vie spirituelle* 143 (1989): 521–31; and the creative work by Robert Bertram, "A Constructive Lutheran Theology of the Saints," *Dialogue* 31 (1992): 265–71.

10. John Calvin, *Institutes of the Christian Religion,* ed. John McNeill (Philadelphia: Westminster, 1960), III.xx.21, p. 879; see also III.xx.24, p.883.

11. Ibid., III.xx.27, p. 887.

12. Ibid., IV.i.3, p. 1014.

13. Ibid., IV.i.2, p. 1013.

14. *II Helvetic Confession,* in *Book of Confessions* (New York: Office of the General Assembly of the United Presbyterian Church USA, 1970), 5.026; cited in Erickson, "Reformed Theology and the Sanctoral Cycle" (see ch. 5, n. 20).

15. See documentation in ch. 1, n. 8.

16. John Wesley, "Letter to a Roman Catholic," cited in Geoffrey Wainwright, "Wesley and the Communion of Saints," *One in Christ* 27 (1991): 334.

17. John Wesley, *Journals,* ed. Nehemiah Curnock (London: Epworth Press, 1938), 4:190.

18. Ibid., 5:236.

19. Ibid., 5:237.

20. *Book of Common Prayer* (New York: Seabury, 1979), 194.

21. Wainwright, "Wesley and the Communion of Saints," 339.

22. J. Wesley, *Journals,* 5:191.

23. *Hymns and Psalms* (London: Methodist Pub. House, 1983), no. 812; see the selection of Charles Wesley's hymns in *John and Charles Wesley,* Classics in Western Spirituality, ed. Frank Whaling (New York: Paulist, 1981), 175–295.

24. See Angel Antón, "Postconciliar Ecclesiology: Expectations, Results, and Prospects for the Future," in Latourelle, *Vatican II: Assessment and Perspectives* 1:407–38 (see ch. 1, n. 11), who details the debates and traces them back to compromises embedded in the conciliar documents.

25. Joseph Komanchak, "Concepts of Communion, Past and Present," *Cristianes nella storia* 16 (1995): 339–40; I am indebted to this essay for the above analysis.

26. See exegesis of *Lumen Gentium* in *Commentary on the Documents of Vatican II,* ed. Herbert Vorgrimler (New York: Herder & Herder, 1967), especially Gerard Philips, "History of the Constitution," 1:105–37; also Jean Tillard, "The Church of God Is a Communion: The Ecclesiology of Vatican II," *One in Christ* 17 (1981): 117–31.

27. Cited by Antón, "Postconciliar Ecclesiology," 413.

28. *Lumen Gentium,* no. 17, in Abbott, *Documents of Vatican II* (see ch. 1, n. 9).

29. Ibid., no. 32. Piero Bonnet, "The *Christifidelis* Restored to His [sic] Role as Human Protagonist in the Church," 1:552–53, in Latourelle, *Vatican II: Assessment and Perspectives,* explores further this strong affirmation of equality in the church.

30. Friedrich Wulf, "Chapter V," in Vorgrimler, *Commentary,* 1:261.

31. *Lumen Gentium,* no. 40.

32. Ibid., no. 41; italics mine.

33. Ibid.; italics mine.

34. Ibid., no. 50; see Otto Semmelroth, "Chapter VII," in Vorgrimler, *Commentary,* 1:280–84.

35. *Lumen Gentium,* no. 48.

36. Ibid., no. 49.

37. Ibid., no. 50, citing 2 Thess 1:10.

38. Ibid.

39. Ibid., no. 51.

40. Constitution on the Sacred Liturgy (*Sacrosanctum Concilium*) nos. 102–11 and no. 13, in Abbott, *The Documents of Vatican II.*

41. *Lumen Gentium,* no. 50.

42. Ibid., no. 51.

43. Geoffrey Wainwright, "Wesley and the Communion of Saints," cites the calendars in the North American *Lutheran Book of Worship* (1978), the *Book of Common Prayer of the Episcopal Church USA* (1979), and *Uniting in Worship,* the prayer book for the Reformed and Methodist churches uniting in Australia. See John F. Johnson, "Mary and the Saints in Contemporary Lutheran Worship," in Anderson, *The One Mediator, the Saints, and Mary,* 305–10; Patricia Fort, "For All the Saints," *Reformed Liturgy and Music* 25 (1991): 41; and Susan Schweiter Garrett, "I Sing a Song of the Saints of God: The Celebration of Saints in a United Methodist Church," D.Min. thesis, Wesley Theological Seminary, Washington, D.C., 1987, which builds on suggestions in *Handbook of the Christian Year,* ed. H. Hickman et al. (Nashville: Abingdon, 1986).

44. An excellent exploration of the issue is George Tavard, "The Veneration of Saints as an Ecumenical Question," *One in Christ* 26 (1990): 40–50; from the liturgical point of view, see Michael Whelan, "Saints and Their Feasts: An Ecumenical Exploration," *Worship* 63 (1989): 194–209; arguing that the walls of division do not reach up to heaven; Grigorios Larentzakis, "Heiligenverehrung in der Orthodoxen Kirche," *Catholica* 42 (1988): 56–75, offers an inviting vision of how veneration of the saints can promote not only ecumenical harmony between the churches but also justice and peace on earth.

Chapter 7: Serenely Free

1. In *Canons and Decrees of the Council of Trent,* 146 (see ch. 1, n. 8).

2. "...*bonum atque utile esse suppliciter eos invocare*"; ibid., Latin text 483–85; English text 215–17, at 215.

3. Kretschmer and Laurentin, *Confessing One Faith,* 273 (see ch. 6, n. 6).

4. "*Summopere ergo decet...,*" *Lumen Gentium,* no. 50, in Abbott, *The Documents of Vatican II* (see ch. 1, n. 9).

5. *Sacrosanctum Concilium,* no. 13, in ibid.

6. *Lumen Gentium,* no. 67.

7. *Codex Iuris Canonici* (Vatican City: Typis Polyglottis Vaticanis, 1974; orig. 1917), canon 1276.

8. *The Code of Canon Law,* trans. Canon Law Society of Great Britain and Ireland (Grand Rapids, Mich.: Eerdmans, 1983), canon 1186.

9. Christian Pesch, *Compendium theologiae dogmaticae* (Freiburg: Herder, 1913), 3:114. See also, among widely used manuals, J. Pohle and J. Gummersbach, *Lehrbuch der Dogmatik* (Paderborn: F. Schöningh, 1956; orig. 1903),

2:466; Ludwig Ott, *Fundamentals of Catholic Dogma,* trans. Patrick Lynch (Cork, Ireland: Mercer Press, 1955), 318; and Joseph de Aldama et al., *Sacrae theologiae summa* (Madrid: Biblioteca de Autores Cristianos, 1956), 3:477–84.

10. Rahner, "Why and How Can We Venerate the Saints?" 22 (see ch. 1, n. 19).

11. Karl Rahner and J. B. Metz, *The Courage to Pray,* trans. Sarah O'Brien Twohig (New York: Crossroad, 1981), 35.

12. Ibid., 33–34.

13. In Karl Rahner and Herbert Vorgrimler, *Theological Dictionary,* trans. Richard Strachan (New York: Herder & Herder, 1965), 479.

14. Molinari, *Saints, Their Place in the Church,* 95–104 (see ch. 1, n. 12).

15. Tavard, "The Veneration of Saints as an Ecumenical Question," 50 (see ch. 6, n. 44).

16. Michael Schmaus, *Der Glaube der Kirche: Handbuch katholischer Dogmatik* (Munich: Max Hueber, 1970), 2:694.

17. Georg Kraus, "Saints: Holiness, Sanctification," in *Handbook of Catholic Theology,* ed. Wolfgang Beinert and Francis Schüssler Fiorenza (New York: Crossroad, 1995), 638–39.

18. Anderson, *The One Mediator, the Saints, and Mary,* no. 95, p. 57 (see ch. 1, n. 8). See essays in the same volume by John Reumann, "How Do We Interpret 1 Timothy 2:1–5 (and Related Passages)?" 149–57; and Gerhard Forde, "Is Invocation of Saints an Adiaphoron?" 327–38.

19. Paul VI, *Marialis Cultus,* E.T. *Devotion to the Blessed Virgin Mary* (Washington, D.C.: United States Catholic Conference, 1974), no. 55.

20. John Paul II, *Redemptoris Mater, Origins* 16, no. 43 (April 9, 1987), no. 52.

21. 1 Thess 5:25; rendering *adelphoi* in inclusive language.

22. 2 Thess 1:11.

23. Heb 7:25.

24. Orestes Brownson, *Saint Worship. The Worship of Mary,* ed. Thomas Ryan (Paterson, N.J.: St. Anthony Guild Press, 1963), 39–40.

25. Ibid., 28.

26. Augustine, Sermon 280.4, 6 (see ch. 2, n. 22). See further discussion in Elizabeth A. Johnson, "May We Invoke the Saints?" *Theology Today* 44 (April 1987): 32–52, and in chapter 13 below.

27. Rahner, "Why and How Can We Venerate the Saints?" 23.

Chapter 8: Women's Practices of Memory

1. For Hagar, read Gen 16:1–16; 17:18–27; 21:1–21; 25:12–18; the narrative is stitched together by Miriam Therese Winter, *WomanWisdom: A Feminist Lectionary and Psalter* (New York: Crossroad, 1991), 1:36–43.

2. Gen 16:10; see Cheryl Exum, "Mothers in Israel," in *Feminist Interpretation of the Bible,* ed. Letty Russell (Philadelphia: Westminster, 1985), 76–77.

3. Gen 21:17.

4. Gen 16:13.

5. Gal 4:31; see Sheila Briggs, "Galatians," in Schüssler Fiorenza, *Searching the Scriptures*, 2:223–25 (see ch. 3, n. 42).

6. Weems, *Just a Sister Away,* 1, 8, 14 (see ch. 2, n. 13). For analysis of the racism within white feminism, see Barbara Andolsen, *Daughters of Jefferson, Daughters of Bootblacks: Racism and American Feminism* (Macon, Ga.: Mercer University Press, 1986).

7. Gen 16:9.

8. Williams, *Sisters in the Wilderness,* 15–33 at 5–6 (see ch. 2, n. 17). For a probing use of this symbolism, see Diana Hayes, *Hagar's Daughters: Womanist Ways of Being in the World* (New York: Paulist, 1995).

9. Elsa Tamez, "The Woman Who Complicated the History of Salvation," in *New Eyes for Reading: Biblical and Theological Reflections by Women from the Third World,* ed. John Pobee and Bärbel von Wartenberg-Potter (Oak Park, Ill.: Meyer-Stone, 1987), 5–17.

10. Musimbi Kanyoro, "Interpreting Old Testament Polygamy through African Eyes," in *The Will to Arise: Women, Tradition, and the Church in Africa,* ed. Mercy Amba Oduyoye and Musimbi Kanyoro (Maryknoll, N.Y.: Orbis, 1992), 95.

11. Judith Gallares, *Images of Faith: Spirituality of Women in the Old Testament* (Maryknoll, N.Y.: Orbis, 1992), 7–33.

12. Kwok Pui-Lan, "Racism and Ethnocentrism in Feminist Biblical Interpretation," in Schüssler Fiorenza, *Searching the Scriptures*, 1:106.

13. Trible, *Texts of Terror,* 28 (see ch. 2, n. 12).

14. Ibid., 28–29.

15. For Mary Magdalene, read Mk 15:40–41, 47 and 16:1–11; Mt 27:55–56, 61 and 28:1–10; Lk 8:1–3 plus 23:49, 55–56 and 24:1–11; Jn 19:25 and 20:1–18; for synthesis see M. T. Winter, *WomanWord: A Feminist Lectionary and Psalter* (New York: Crossroad, 1990), 156–62. Detailed studies include Carla Ricci, *Mary Magdalen and Many Others: Women Who Followed Jesus* (Minneapolis: Augsburg Fortress, 1994); Mary Thompson, *Mary of Magdala: Apostle and Leader* (New York: Paulist, 1995); Moltmann-Wendel, *The Women around Jesus,* 60–90 (see ch. 2, n. 14); and Regina Coll, *Christianity and Feminism in Conversation* (Mystic, Conn.: Twenty-Third Pub., 1994), 155–73.

16. Lk 8:1–3.

17. Mt 27:55–56.

18. Mt 27:59–61.

19. Mt 28:1–2.

20. Mt 28:8–9.

21. Mt 28:10.

22. Lk 24:10

23. Jn 20:1, 16, 18.

24. Mk 16:9–11.

25. Texts appear in *New Testament Apocrypha* vols. 1 and 2, ed. Edgar Hennecke and Wilhelm Schneemelcher, trans. R. Wilson (Philadelphia: Westminster, 1963, 1966). For Mary Magdalene in the extrabiblical literature, see Elaine

Pagels, *The Gnostic Gospels* (New York: Random House, 1979), esp. 76–81; Karen King, "The Gospel of Mary Magdalene," in Schüssler Fiorenza, *Searching the Scriptures,* 2:601–34; and Gail Paterson Corrington, *Her Image of Salvation: Female Savior Figures and Formative Christianity* (Louisville: Westminster/John Knox, 1992), *passim.*

26. "Gospel of Mary," 17.18–18.15; cited in Pagels, *The Gnostic Gospels,* 77–78.

27. "Dialogue of the Savior" 139.12–13; cited in ibid., 77.

28. Jane Schaberg, "How Mary Magdalene Became a Whore," *Bible Review* 8, no. 5 (1992): 30–37. The deleterious ethical implications of the iconography of Magdalene as penitent prostitute are traced in the master's thesis of Dina Cormick, "The Visual Portrayal of Mary Magdalene: A Case Study in Feminist Ethical Issues," University of South Africa, Cape Town, 1992. Contemporary interpretations with an eye to the effect on women's spirituality include Susan Haskins, *Mary Magdalen: Myth and Metaphor* (New York: Harcourt Brace, 1994); and Sandra Rushing, *The Magdalene Legacy* (Westport, Conn.: Greenwood Pub., 1995).

29. Lk 7:36–50.

30. Jn 8:1–11 and 12:1–8.

31. Mk 14:3–9.

32. Ruether, *Sexism and God-Talk,* 10–11 (see Intro., n. 2).

33. Anselm of Canterbury, "Prayer to St. Mary Magdalene," in *The Prayers and Meditations of St. Anselm,* ed. and trans. Benedicta Ward (London: Penguin Books, 1973), 201.

34. Feast day November 22, cited by Kathleen Norris, "The Virgin Martyrs: Between *Point Vierge* and the *Usual Spring,*" in her *The Cloister Walk* (New York: Riverhead Books, 1996), 186–87. Key studies of the import of virginity include Rosemary R. Ruether, "Misogynism and Feminism in the Fathers of the Church," in *Religion and Sexism,* 150–83 (see ch. 2, n. 15); Jo Ann McNamara, *A New Song: Celibate Women in the First Three Christian Centuries* (New York: Haworth Press, 1983); Elizabeth Clark, *Ascetic Piety and Women's Faith* (Lewiston, N.Y.: Edwin Mellon Press, 1986); and Brown, *Body and Society* (see ch. 4, n. 13).

35. Maureen Tilley, "The Passion of Perpetua and Felicity," in Schüssler Fiorenza, *Searching the Scriptures,* 2:829–58.

36. Valerie Saiving, "The Human Situation: A Feminine View," in *Womanspirit Rising: A Feminist Reader in Religion,* ed. Carol Christ and Judith Plaskow (New York: Harper & Row, 1979), 25–42. Saiving criticizes the way exhortations to humility and self-sacrifice are traditionally directed toward women. Such teaching may be legitimate and necessary for men whose social status and prestige open them to temptations of arrogance and *hubris.* But since women are socialized from birth to be pleasing to others, to be needful of approval, and to give of themselves to others, they are much more likely to be tempted to diffuseness of self and lack of self-assertion than to pride. If so, encouragement to self-sacrifice actually works counter to a mature spiritual personality and leads instead to dependency and pious masochism.

37. Patrick, "Narrative and the Social Dynamics of Virtue," 77–78 (see ch. 2, n. 8); see contrasting readings in K. Norris, "Maria Goretti: Cipher or Saint?" in *The Cloister Walk,* 223–36; and Eileen Stenzel, "Maria Goretti: Rape and the Politics of Sainthood," in *The Power of Naming,* ed. Schüssler Fiorenza, 224–31 (see ch. 2, n. 5).

38. Norris, *The Cloister Walk,* 189.

39. Tilley, "The Passion of Perpetua and Felicity," 836.

40. Norris, *The Cloister Walk,* 193.

41. See Eamon Duffy, "Holy Maydens, Holy Wyfes: The Cult of Women Saints in 15th and 16th Century England," in *Women in the Church,* ed. W. J. Sheils and Diana Wood (Cambridge, Mass.: Blackwell, 1990), 175–96; and Kevin Brownlee, "Martyrdom and the Female Voice: Saint Christine in the *Cité des dames,*" in *Images of Sainthood in Medieval Europe,* ed. Renate Blumenfeld-Kosinski and Timea Szell (Ithaca, N.Y.: Cornell University Press, 1991), 115–35. Similar connections between female self-definition and pain are made by Frederick Klawiter, "The Role of Martyrdom and Persecution in Developing the Priestly Authority of Women in Early Christianity: A Case Study of Montanism," *Church History* 49 (1980): 251–61; and Sara Maitland, "Rose of Lima: Some Thoughts on Purity and Penance," in *Through the Devil's Gateway: Women, Religion, and Taboo* (London: SPCK, 1990), 60–70.

42. *Productions of Mrs. Maria Stewart* (Boston: Friends of Freedom and Virtue, 1935); quoted in Elisabeth Schüssler Fiorenza, *But She Said: Feminist Practices of Biblical Interpretation* (Boston: Beacon, 1992), 157.

43. Karl Rahner, "Dimensions of Martyrdom," *Theological Investigations* 23, trans. Joseph Donceel and Hugh Riley (New York: Crossroad, 1992), 111. Insightful essays about martyrdom in different parts of the world today which, however, do not include feminist analysis, are collected in *Martyrdom Today,* ed. Johann Baptist Metz and Edward Schillebeeckx (New York: Seabury Press, 1983); and in *Revue Catholique Internationale Communio* 12, no. 2 (March–April 1987): 1–125, under the title "Bienheureux persécuté?"

44. Donna Whitson Brett and Edward Brett, *Murdered in Central America: The Stories of Eleven U.S. Missionaries* (Maryknoll, N.Y.: Orbis, 1988), 328. See Judith Noone, *The Same Fate as the Poor* (Maryknoll, N.Y.: Orbis, 1984, rev. 1995); Ana Carrigan, *Salvador Witness: The Life and Calling of Jean Donovan* (New York: Simon and Schuster, 1984); and D. C. Kazel, *Alleluia Woman: Sister Dorothy Kazel OSU* (Cleveland: Chapel Pub., 1987).

45. Norris, *The Cloister Walk,* 193.

46. Tilley, "The Passion of Perpetua and Felicity," 852; see the role of the body in Francine Cardman, "Acts of the Women Martyrs," *Anglican Theological Review* 70 (1988): 144–50.

47. Renny Golden, "Sanctuary and Women," *Journal of Feminist Studies in Religion* 2 (1986): 147.

48. Jane Grovijahn, "Grabbing Life Away from Death: Women and Martyrdom in El Salvador," *Journal of Feminist Studies in Religion* 7 (1991): 28.

49. Ibid.

50. Quoted in ibid., 19.

51. Rich, "Resisting Amnesia," 148 (see ch. 2, n. 6).

52. See Mary Daly, "European Witchburnings: Purifying the Body of Christ," in her *Gyn/Ecology: The Metaethics of Radical Feminism* (Boston: Beacon, 1978), 178–222.

53. See Gerda Lerner, ed., *Black Women in White America: A Documentary History* (New York: Random House, 1972).

54. Mona Higuchi, "Bamboo Echoes," displayed at the Isabella Stuart Gardner Museum in Boston, Fall 1996, accompanied by explanatory broadsheets.

55. George Eliot (Mary Ann Evans), *Middlemarch,* ed. Gordon Haight (Boston: Houghton Mifflin, 1955), 612–13.

56. Rich, "Resisting Amnesia," 155.

57. See the excellent discussion of different methods by Emily Cheney, *She Can Read: Feminist Reading Strategies for Biblical Narrative* (Valley Forge, Pa.: Trinity Press International, 1996), 11–27, who goes on to propose reading strategies of her own.

58. Mt 7:9, reprised by Elisabeth Schüssler Fiorenza, *Bread Not Stone: The Challenge of Feminist Biblical Interpretation* (Boston: Beacon, 1984).

59. See Phyllis Trible, "Bringing Miriam out of the Shadows," *Bible Review* 1 (February 1989): 14–25, 34; and idem, "Eve and Miriam: From the Margins to the Center," in *Feminist Approaches to the Bible,* ed. Hershel Shanks (Washington, D.C.: Biblical Archaeology Society, 1995), 15–23.

Chapter 9: Companions in Memory

1. Johann Baptist Metz, *Faith in History and Society,* trans. David Smith (New York: Seabury, 1980); especially "The Dangerous Memory of the Freedom of Jesus Christ," 88–99; "The Future in the Memory of Suffering," 100–118; and "Categories: Memory, Narrative, Solidarity," 184–237. In what follows I draw from Metz's analysis and amplify it in the light of the communion of saints.

2. Gustavo Gutiérrez, "Where Hunger Is, God Is Not," *The Witness* (April 1977): 6.

3. Daniel Berrigan, *Steadfastness of the Saints: Peace and War in Central and North America* (Maryknoll, N.Y.: Orbis, 1985), 20; see also Mary Hunt, "Dead but Still Missing: Mothers of the Plaza de Mayo Transform Argentina," in *The Spectre of Mass Death,* ed. David Power and Kabasele Lumbala (London: SCM Press and Maryknoll, N.Y.: Orbis, 1993), 89–96.

4. bell hooks, *Yearning: Race, Gender, and Cultural Politics* (Boston: South End Press, 1990), 116.

5. Ibid., 43.

6. Albert Friedlander, *Riders towards the Dawn: From Holocaust to Hope* (New York: Continuum, 1994), 315.

7. Rich, "Resisting Amnesia," 141 (see ch. 2, n. 6).

8. Johann Baptist Metz, "Theology Today: New Crises and New Visions," *Proceedings of the Catholic Theological Society of America* 40 (1985): 11. Metz judges danger to be a basic quality of the experience of Jesus, though for the most part Christian tradition has disregarded this.

9. Plaskow, *Standing Again at Sinai,* 90 (see ch. 3, n. 25).

10. In a field of rich resources, I find these writings most helpful: Stephen Crites, "The Narrative Quality of Experience," *Journal of the American Academy of Religion* 39 (1971): 291–311; Terrence Tilley, *Story Theology* (Wilmington, Del.: Michael Glazier, 1985); and Nicholas Lash, "Ideology, Metaphor and Analogy," in *The Philosophical Frontiers of Christian Theology,* ed. B. Hebblethwaite and S. Sutherland (Cambridge: Cambridge University Press, 1982), 68–94.

11. Martin Buber, *Tales of the Hasidim* (New York: Schocken Books, 1947, 1978), v–vi.

12. As told to Anna Peterson, "Religious Narratives and Political Protest," *Journal of the American Academy of Religion* 64 (1996): 27.

13. Ibid., 33.

14. Walter Benjamin, "Theses on the Philosophy of History," *Illuminations: Essays and Reflections,* ed. Hannah Arendt (New York: Harcourt, Brace, 1968), 258 (thesis VII).

15. Toni Cade Bambara, "Salvation Is the Issue," in *Black Women Writers (1950–1980): A Critical Evaluation,* ed. Mari Evans (New York: Doubleday, 1984), 41.

16. Robert McAfee Brown, *Elie Wiesel: Messenger to All Humanity* (Notre Dame, Ind.: University of Notre Dame Press, 1983), 6–7.

17. René Girard, "History and the Paraclete," *Ecumenical Review* 35 (1983): 6.

18. Ibid., 14.

19. See Sharon Welch, *Communities of Resistance and Solidarity: A Feminist Theology of Liberation* (Maryknoll, N.Y.: Orbis, 1985); Jon Sobrino and Juan Hernández Pico, *Theology of Christian Solidarity* (Maryknoll, N.Y.: Orbis, 1985); Gregory Baum and Robert Ellsberg, eds., *The Logic of Solidarity* (Maryknoll, N.Y.: Orbis, 1989); and Ada María Isasi-Díaz, "Solidarity: Love of Neighbor in the 1980s," in *Lift Every Voice: Constructing Christian Theologies from the Underside,* ed. Susan B. Thistlethwaite and Mary Potter Engel (San Francisco: Harper & Row, 1990), 31–40.

20. Welch, *Communities of Resistance and Solidarity,* 45. See Michael Himes and Kenneth Himes, "The Communion of Saints and an Ethic of Solidarity," in their *Fullness of Faith: The Public Significance of Theology* (New York: Paulist, 1993), 157–83, who demonstrate how the communion of saints is one aspect of belief that directly connects with an ethic of solidarity in the Catholic moral theology tradition.

21. Dorothee Soelle, *The Strength of the Weak: Towards a Christian Feminist Identity,* trans. Robert and Rita Kimber (Philadelphia: Westminster, 1984), 103.

22. Jn 20:18. For the tradition that ensued from the silencing of Mary Magdalene's voice, see Mary Catherine Hilkert, "Women Preaching the Gospel," in her *Naming Grace: Preaching and the Sacramental Imagination* (New York: Continuum, 1997), 144–65.

23. See Emilie Townes, "Black Women: From Slavery to Womanist Liberation," in *In Our Own Voices,* ed. Ruether and Keller, 179–81 (see ch. 2, n. 19).

24. Isasi-Díaz, "Solidarity: Love of Neighbor in the 1980s," 32.

25. M. Shawn Copeland, "Toward a Critical Christian Feminist Theology of Solidarity," in *Women and Theology,* 3 (see ch. 2, n. 5).

26. Lisa Cahill, "Feminist Ethics, Differences, and Common Ground: A Catholic Perspective," in *Feminist Ethics and the Catholic Moral Tradition,* ed. Charles Curran, Margaret Farley, and Richard McCormick (New York: Paulist, 1996), 184.

27. Lorde, *Sister Outsider,* 112 (see ch. 2, n. 34). See Sharon Welch, "An Ethic of Solidarity and Difference" in her *A Feminist Ethic of Risk* (Minneapolis: Fortress, 1990), 123–51; Ellen Armour, "Questioning 'Woman' in Feminist/ Womanist Theology: Irigaray, Ruether, and Daly," in *Transfigurations,* 171–98 (see ch. 2, n. 32); and J. Scott, "Deconstructing Equality-versus-Difference," *Feminist Studies* 14 (Spring 1988): 33–50.

28. By contrast, see the equation of difference with hierarchy defended by Coleman, "Conclusion: After Sainthood?" 209 (see ch. 1, n. 33); he argues: "Without some notion of hierarchy to guarantee the possibility of otherness, there is no interconnected world, only a congeries of unrelated equals." But this flies in the face of hard-won women's wisdom in the practice of courageous challenge from poor and minority women, hard efforts to hear and be converted on the part of white and middle-class women, and the endeavors of both to form interlinking communities of genuine mutuality where difference is respected in equal regard.

29. M. Shawn Copeland, "Difference as a Category in Critical Theologies for the Liberation of Women," in *Feminist Theology in Different Contexts,* 143 (see ch. 2, n. 34).

30. Schüssler Fiorenza, *Bread Not Stone,* 115 (see ch. 8, n. 58).

31. Copeland, "Difference as a Category," 150.

Chapter 10: The Darkness of Death

1. Martin Marty, "Christian Theology and Modes of Experience," *Dialog* 33 (Winter 1994): 54; not for him the quiet of "here lies" or the desire to "rest in peace" but a hope to awaken in fullness of vibrant life beyond imagining. *Vivit* — he lives.

2. First coined as a technical term by the seventeenth-century Lutheran scholar Abraham Calov, "eschatology" means, in Catherine Keller's exuberant rendition, the study of the end, the logos of the last things, talk of the edge of time, the end of the world, the ultimate of everything. Whether prophetic or apocalyptic in form, it refers to expectation of a final good coming from God; Keller, "Eschatology," in *Dictionary of Feminist Theologies,* 86–87 (see ch. 2, n. 30).

3. Gerard Sloyan, "We'll Not Be There 10,000 Years: Christian Eschatology and the Life to Come," unpublished paper delivered to the American Theological Society (March 1996), 15.

4. 1 Cor 2:9.

5. 2 Cor 5:7.

6. Rom 8:24–25.

7. Brian Daley, *The Hope of the Early Church* (New York and Cambridge: Cambridge University Press, 1991), 217.

8. These studies illuminate the present discussion: John Hick, *Death and Eternal Life* (San Francisco: Harper & Row, 1976); Hans Küng, *Eternal Life? Life after Death as a Medical, Philosophical, and Theological Problem*, trans. Edward Quinn (Garden City, N.Y.: Doubleday, 1985); Brian Hebblethwaite, *The Christian Hope* (Grand Rapids, Mich.: Eerdmans, 1988); Zachary Hayes, *Visions of a Future: A Study of Christian Eschatology* (Wilmington, Del.: Michael Glazier, 1989); Anthony Kelly, *Touching on the Infinite* (Blackburn, Australia: Collins Dove, 1991); Dermot Lane, *Keeping Hope Alive: Stirrings in Christian Theology* (New York: Paulist, 1996); and the survey by Peter Phan, "Contemporary Contexts and Issues in Eschatology," *Theological Studies* 55 (1994): 507–36.

A synthesis of eschatology meant for classroom use is presented from the Protestant perspective by Carl Braaten, "The Kingdom of God and Life Everlasting," in *Christian Theology: An Introduction to Its Traditions and Tasks,* ed. Peter Hodgson and Robert King (Philadelphia: Fortress, 1982), 274–98; and from the Catholic perspective by Monika Hellwig, "Eschatology," in *Systematic Theology: Roman Catholic Perspectives,* ed. Francis Schüssler Fiorenza and John Galvin (Minneapolis: Fortress, 1991), 2:347–72.

9. For one pivotal expression of this idea see Karl Rahner, *Spirit in the World,* trans. William Dych (New York: Herder & Herder, 1968); and his *Hominisation: The Evolutionary Origin of Man as a Theological Problem* (New York: Herder & Herder, 1965).

10. 1 Cor 15:35–44.

11. A problem dealt with even by Thomas Aquinas, *Summa contra gentiles* 4:81; see the insightful analysis of the medieval idea of bodily continuity in Carolyn Walker Bynum, "Material Continuity, Personal Survival, and the Resurrection of the Body: A Scholastic Discussion in Its Medieval and Modern Contexts," *History of Religions* 30 (199): 51–85.

12. For an excellent description of this development see Ignacio Ellacuría, "Utopia and Prophecy in Latin America," 289–328, and J. B. Libânio, "Hope, Utopia, Resurrection," 716–27, in *Mysterium Liberationis: Fundamental Concepts of Liberation Theology,* ed. Ignacio Ellacuría and Jon Sobrino (Maryknoll, N.Y.: Orbis, 1993).

13. See analysis by Ruether, *Sexism and God-Talk,* especially the chapters on body (ch. 3), nature (ch. 9), and the new earth (ch. 10); (see Intro., n. 2).

14. Catherine Keller, "Talk about the Weather: The Greening of Eschatology," in *Ecofeminism and the Sacred,* ed. Carol J. Adams (New York: Continuum, 1993), 30–49.

15. See Sallie McFague, *The Body of God: An Ecological Theology* (Minneapolis: Augsburg Fortress, 1993), and her *Super, Natural Christians: How We Should Love Nature* (Minneapolis: Augsburg Fortress, 1997).

16. Paul Ricoeur, *The Symbolism of Evil* (Boston: Beacon, 1967), 352, 351; see also his "The Hermeneutics of Symbols and Philosophical Reflection," *International Philosophical Quarterly* 2 (1962): 191–218.

17. Robert Schreiter, "Purgatory: In Quest of an Image," *Chicago Studies* 24, no. 2 (August 1985): 167. For historical development, see Jacques LeGoff, *The Birth of Purgatory*, trans. Arthur Goldhammer (Chicago: University of Chicago Press, 1984); and Robert Eno, "The Fathers and the Cleansing Fire," *Irish Theological Quarterly*, no. 3 (1987): 184–202. See also Karl Rahner, "Purgatory," *Theological Investigations* 19, trans. Edward Quinn (New York: Crossroad, 1983), 181–93; and the survey by Klaus Reinhardt, "Das Verständnis des Fegfeuers in der neueren Theologie," *Theologische Zeitung* 96 (1987): 111–22, who interprets purgatory as a symbol of hope.

18. See the plausibility of this connection demonstrated by Hick, *Death and Eternal Life*, esp. 370–71; John R. Sachs, "Resurrection or Reincarnation? The Christian Doctrine of Purgatory," in *Reincarnation or Resurrection? (Concilium* 1993/5), ed. Hermann Häring and Johann-Baptist Metz (Maryknoll, N.Y.: Orbis, 1993), 81–87; and Karl Rahner, *Foundations of Christian Faith*, trans. William Dych (New York: Seabury, 1978), 441–43.

19. Schreiter, "Purgatory: In Quest of an Image," 178.

20. Walter Rauschenbusch, *A Theology for the Social Gospel* (Nashville: Abingdon Press, 1945), 237–38.

21. Flannery O'Connor, "The Artificial Nigger," in *A Good Man Is Hard to Find* (New York: Harcourt, Brace, Jovanovich, 1955), 128–29.

22. Ladislaus Boros, *Living in Hope* (New York: Herder & Herder, 1970), 84.

23. Rauschenbusch, *A Theology for the Social Gospel*, 232.

24. Zachary Hayes, "Visions of a Future: Symbols of Heaven and Hell," *Chicago Studies* 24, no. 2 (August 1985): 162; Hayes's work in this area has guided much of my thinking. For historical development of this symbol, see Colleen McDannell and Bernhard Lang, *Heaven: A History* (New Haven and London: Yale University Press, 1988).

25. Edward Schillebeeckx, *Church: The Human Story of God*, trans. John Bowden (New York: Crossroad, 1990), 137.

26. Ibid.

27. Gordon Graham, "The Goodness of God and the Conception of Hell," *New Blackfriars* 69 (1988): 486.

28. Hans Urs von Balthasar, *Dare We Hope "That All Men Be Saved"?* (San Francisco: Ignatius Press, 1988), including the separate essay "A Short Discourse on Hell"; see discussion by Kevin Flannery, "How to Think about Hell," *New Blackfriars* 72 (1991): 469–81.

29. David Power, *Unsearchable Riches: The Symbolic Nature of Liturgy* (New York: Pueblo Pub., 1984), 73.

30. Karl Rahner, *On the Theology of Death*, trans. C. H. Henkey (New York: Seabury, 1973), 19.

31. Ibid., 22.

32. See Margaret Farley, "Relationships," in *Dictionary of Feminist Theologies* 238–39 (see ch. 2, n. 30). Amid a vast literature, several insightful works

include: Catherine Keller, *From a Broken Web: Separation, Sexism, and Self* (Boston: Beacon, 1986); Carol Gilligan, *In a Different Voice: Psychological Theory and Women's Development* (Cambridge, Mass.: Harvard University Press, 1982); and Paula Cooey, Sharon Farmer, and Mary Ellen Ross, eds., *Embodied Love: Sensuality and Relationship as Feminist Values* (San Francisco: Harper & Row, 1987).

33. Catherine LaCugna, *God for Us: The Trinity and Christian Life* (San Francisco: HarperCollins, 1991), 292.

34. John Zizioulas, *Being as Communion* (Crestwood, N.Y.: St. Vladimir's Seminary Press, 1985), 49.

35. Wolfhart Pannenberg, "Constructive and Critical Functions of Christian Eschatology," *Harvard Theological Review* 77 (1984): 133 (the Ingersoll Lecture on Immortality delivered at Harvard University). In the 1987 Ingersoll Lecture, John B. Cobb works out a somewhat similar notion from the perspective of process theology: "The Resurrection of the Soul," *Harvard Theological Review* 80 (1987): 213–27.

36. Rosemary R. Ruether, *Gaia and God: An Ecofeminist Theology of Earth Healing* (San Francisco: HarperCollins, 1992), 253; a similar argument against personal immortality as an expression of patriarchal ego is made by Cooey, "The Redemption of the Body," in *After Patriarchy*, 106–30 (see ch. 2, n. 24).

37. Rahner, *Foundations of Christian Faith*, 270.

38. Rahner attributes this image to Feuerbach: "Ideas for a Theology of Death," *Theological Investigations* 13, trans. David Bourke (New York: Seabury, 1975), 174; and "The Life of the Dead," *Theological Investigations* 4:347 (see ch. 1, n. 51).

39. Rahner, *Foundations of Christian Faith*, 272.

40. Rahner, "Ideas for a Theology of Death," 175.

41. Rahner, "Immanent and Transcendent Consummation of the World," *Theological Investigations* 10, trans. David Bourke (New York: Seabury, 1977), 289; see also "The Resurrection of the Body," *Theological Investigations* 2, trans. Karl-H. Kruger (Baltimore: Helicon Press, 1964), 203–16; "The Body in the Order of Salvation," *Theological Investigations* 17 (New York: Crossroad, 1981), 71–89; and "The Theological Problems Entailed in the Idea of the New Earth," *Theological Investigations* 10:260–71.

42. Rahner, *Foundations of Christian Faith*, 272.

43. Bartholomew Collopy, "Theology and the Darkness of Death," *Theological Studies* 39 (1978): 39; see critical discussion of this proposal by Florentino Canlas, "Darkness or Light? Rahner and Collopy on the Theology of Death," *Bijdragen* 45 (1984): 251–75 and 384–416.

44. Collopy, "Theology and the Darkness of Death," 53.

Chapter 11: Companions in Hope

1. 1 Pet 1:21; RSV variant; see Karl Rahner, *Meditations on Hope and Love* (New York: Seabury, 1977).

2. Rudolf Bultmann, *"elpis," Theological Dictionary of the New Testament*, 2:521–30, at 523 (see ch. 2, n. 35); see also Gerhard von Rad, *Old Testament Theology*, vol. 2, trans. D. M. G. Stalker (New York: Harper & Row, 1965).

3. See Rom 4:18.

4. Ex 3:7–8.

5. Ezek 37:1–14; Rev. 21:1–5.

6. Dan 12:2–3; for biblical background, see Rudolf Schnackenburg, *God's Rule and Kingdom* (New York: Herder & Herder, 1968).

7. Wis 3:1–3, 7.

8. 2 Macc 7:9.

9. 2 Macc 7:23.

10. 2 Macc 7:29.

11. 1 Pet 1:3.

12. Karl Rahner, "The Hermeneutics of Eschatological Assertions," *Theological Investigations* 4:337 (see ch. 1, n. 51). See explanation by Peter Phan, *Eternity in Time: A Study of Karl Rahner's Eschatology* (London and Toronto: Associated University Presses, 1988), esp. 64–76.

13. The best working out of these metaphors is McFague, *Models of God* (see ch. 2, n. 39); for panentheism, see Johnson, *She Who Is*, 224–33 (see Intro., n. 4).

14. See Thomas Aquinas, *Summa contra gentiles* 3, trans. Vernon Bourke (Garden City, N.Y.: Doubleday, 1956), chaps. 64–77; and his *Summa theologiae* 1 (New York: Benziger, 1956), qq. 4, 8, and 103–9.

15. Karl Rahner, "The Eternal Significance of the Humanity of Jesus for Our Relationship with God," *Theological Investigations* 3:42 (see ch. 1, n. 12).

16. For further exploration of this position, see Piet Schoonenberg, "God or Man: A False Dilemma," in his *The Christ* (New York: Seabury, 1971), 13–49; and Elizabeth A. Johnson, "Does God Play Dice? Divine Providence and Chance," *Theological Studies* 57 (1996): 3–18.

17. See Arthur Peacock, *Theology for a Scientific Age: Being and Becoming — Natural, Divine, Human* (Minneapolis: Fortress, 1993), 72–80, for the nonreducible character of the human person.

18. Hans Küng, *On Being a Christian*, trans. Edward Quinn (Garden City, N.Y.: Doubleday, 1976), 350. Küng's discussion of the meaning of the resurrection runs through pp. 343–81; I have been grateful for these pages for a long time. In what follows, rather than quote Küng directly because of my concern for inclusive language, I draw phrases from these pages and paraphrase his line of thought. See also Küng, *Eternal Life?* 96–118 (see ch. 10, n. 8).

19. For a synopsis of the theology of the resurrection, see Gerald O'Collins, *Jesus Risen: An Historical, Fundamental, and Systematic Examination of Christ's Resurrection* (New York: Paulist, 1987). For biblical interpretation of the Easter texts, see Francis X. Durrwell, *The Resurrection: A Biblical Study* (New York: Sheed and Ward, 1960); Raymond Brown, "The Problem of the Bodily Resurrection of Jesus," in his *The Virginal Conception and Bodily Resurrection of Jesus* (New York: Paulist, 1973), 69–129; and Pheme Perkins, *Resurrection: New Testament Witness and Contemporary Reflection* (Garden City, N.Y.: Doubleday, 1984).

20. Rom 8:11.

21. Rom 4:17.

22. Küng, *On Being a Christian*, 360.

23. Karl Rahner, "On the Theology of the Incarnation," *Theological Investigations* 4:117.

24. Rahner, "The Eternal Significance of the Humanity of Jesus," 40, emended for inclusive language; and "Immanent and Transcendent Consummation of the World," *Theological Investigations* 10:281 (see ch. 10, n. 41).

25. Georgia Harkness, *Our Christian Hope* (New York: Abingdon Press, 1964), 54. Writing in the same vein, Dietrich Bonhoeffer affirms that this is the church's hope which it guards like a treasure: *The Communion of Saints*, trans. R. Gregor Smith (New York: Harper & Row, 1963), 199–202.

26. Rahner, "The Eternal Significance of the Humanity of Jesus," 36; see also J. Gerald Janzen, "Modes of Presence and the Communion of Saints," in *Religious Experience and Process Theology*, ed. Harry James Cargas and Bernard Lee (New York: Paulist, 1976), 147–72.

27. Karl Rahner, "The Life of the Dead," *Theological Investigations* 4:353–54; see also his "Hidden Victory," *Theological Investigations* 7 (New York: Seabury, 1977), 151–58; and "Experiencing Easter," *Theological Investigations* 7:159–68.

28. Mic 6:8.

29. See Edward Farley's analysis of hope as a word of power in need of new retrieval in *Deep Symbols*, 95–112 (see ch. 1, n. 38); and Karl Rahner, "On the Theology of Hope," *Theological Investigations* 10:242–59, and "Faith as Courage," *Theological Investigations* 18, trans. Edward Quinn (New York: Crossroad, 1983), 211–25.

30. Quoted in Jon Sobrino, *Jesus in Latin America* (Maryknoll, N.Y.: Orbis, 1987), 96–97; I am indebted to Melanie May for this interpretation. For the way hope functions creatively as a counterweight to evil in the lives of the poor, see Jon Sobrino, "Evil and Hope: A Reflection from the Victims," trans. Orlando Espín, *Catholic Theological Society of America Proceedings* 50 (1995): 71–84, with response by María Pilar Aquino, 85–92.

31. McFague, *The Body of God*, 202 (see ch. 10, n. 15).

32. Brian Johnstone, "Eschatology and Social Ethics," *Bijdragen* 37 (1976): 47–85, traces the ecumenical reception of this idea; see also Vincent Genovesi, *Expectant Creativity: The Action of Hope in Christian Ethics* (Washington, D.C.: University Press of America, 1982).

33. Ps 142:5.

Chapter 12: Communion of Saints: Friends of God and Prophets

1. Prov 8:35.

2. See Rom 5:20 and Rom 8:1.

3. The ecumenical implications of this idea are probed by Miguel Garijo-Guembe, *Communion of the Saints: Foundation, Nature, and Structure of the*

Church, trans. Patrick Madigan (Collegeville, Minn.: Glazier/Liturgical, 1994). See also T. Howland Sanks, *Salt, Leaven and Light: The Community Called Church* (New York: Crossroad, 1992); Mary Hines, "Community for Liberation: Church," in *Freeing Theology: The Essentials of Theology in Feminist Perspective,* ed. Catherine LaCugna (San Francisco: Harper Collins, 1993), 161–84; Walter Kasper, "The Church as Communio," *New Blackfriars* 74 (1993): 232–44; and Michael Lawler and Thomas Shanahan, "The Church Is Graced Communion," *Worship* 67 (1993): 484–501.

4. Acts 1:14.

5. Lk 8:1–3; 23:49, 55–56; and 24:1–10.

6. Acts 1:15.

7. Acts 2:1–4.

8. Acts 2:15–18; see Joel 2:28–32.

9. *Lumen Gentium,* no. 40 (see ch. 1, n. 9).

10. Ibid., no. 41.

11. Ibid., no. 50.

12. Ibid., no. 49.

13. Joan Chittister, *A Passion for Life: Fragments of the Face of God* (Maryknoll, N.Y.: Orbis, 1996), with icons by Robert Lentz, uses this metaphor of "face" to excellent advantage.

14. See Ellen Ross, "Human Persons as Images of the Divine: A Reconsideration," in *The Pleasures of Her Text: Feminist Readings of Biblical and Historical Texts,* ed. Alice Bach (Philadelphia: Trinity Press International, 1990), 97–116.

15. Edward Schillebeeckx, *Christ: The Experience of Jesus as Lord,* trans. John Bowden (New York: Seabury Press, 1980), 641–42.

16. *Lumen Gentium,* no. 50.

17. Kelly Brown Douglas, *The Black Christ* (Maryknoll, N.Y.: Orbis, 1994), 108.

18. For summary statement of these arguments, see Catholic Theological Society of America, "Tradition and the Ordination of Women," *Origins* 27, no. 5 (June 19, 1997): 75–79.

19. Herman Wegman, "Successio Sanctorum," in *Time and Community,* ed. Alexander Neil (Washington, D.C.: Pastoral Press, 1990), 231.

20. Sherry, *Spirits, Saints, Immortality* (see ch. 1, n. 16).

21. Carolyn Walker Bynum, "Women's Stories, Women's Symbols: A Critique of Victor Turner's Theory of Liminality," in *Anthropology and the Study of Religion,* ed. Robert Moore and Frank Reynolds (Chicago: Center for the Study of Religion, 1984), 119.

22. For examples of contemporary analysis, see Katherine Zappone, *The Hope for Wholeness: A Spirituality for Feminists* (Mystic, Conn.: Twenty-Third Pub., 1991); and Nadya Aisenberg, *Ordinary Heroines: Transforming the Male Myth* (New York: Continuum, 1994).

23. Simone Weil, *Waiting for God,* trans. Emma Craufurd (New York: Putnam, 1951), 99.

24. Theresa Sanders, "Seeking a Minor Sun: Saints after the Death of God," *Horizons: Journal of the College Theology Society* 22 (1995): 183–97.

25. Rembert Weakland, "Story of a Saint of the 1990s," *Origins* 19, no. 33 (January 18, 1990): 535.

26. Ibid., 537.

27. George Tavard, "The Veneration of the Saints as an Ecumenical Question," *One in Christ* 26 (1990): 49.

28. Augustine, Sermon 306c.1; in *Sermons* vol. 9:37 (see ch. 2, n.22).

29. Ibid., S. 273.2 (8:17).

30. T. K. Ware, *The Orthodox Church* (Harmondsworth, England: Penguin Books, 1963), 260.

31. See David Power, *The Eucharistic Mystery: Revitalizing the Tradition* (New York: Crossroad, 1992), 304–16.

32. Gal 3:28.

33. Augustine, Sermon 280.6 (8:75).

34. *Lumen Gentium*, no. 50.

35. Cunningham, *The Meaning of Saints*, 65 (see ch. 1, n. 10).

36. Augustine, Sermon 315.8 (9:133).

37. Rahner, "The Church of the Saints" (ch. 1, n. 12); see also his *The Dynamic Element in the Church*, trans. W. O'Hara (New York: Herder & Herder, 1964).

38. Wyschogrod, *Saints and Postmodernism*, 47 (see ch. 1, n. 16).

39. Matzko, "Postmodernism, Saints and Scoundrels," 35, n. 35 (see ch. 1, n. 16); this is one essay whose extended notes are at least as interesting as the text itself, if not more so.

40. The metaphor is cited from Paulinus by Peter Brown, "The Saint as Exemplar in Late Antiquity," in Hawley, *Saints and Virtue*, 6 (see ch. 1, n. 15).

41. William James, *The Varieties of Religious Experience* (New York: Longmans, Green, 1923), 358, cited by John Coleman, "After Sainthood," in Hawley, *Saints and Virtue*, 221.

42. Matzko, "Postmodernism, Saints and Scoundrels," 36, n. 36.

43. See Thomas McKenna, "Saints and Ecology," *New Theology Review* (August 1994): 47–60; and Belden Lane, "Open the Kingdom for a Cottonwood Tree," *Christian Century* (October 29, 1997): 979–83.

44. Jürgen Moltmann, *God in Creation*, trans. Margaret Kohl (San Francisco: Harper & Row, 1985), 11.

45. Col 1:18 and Col 1:15.

46. John Haught, *The Promise of Nature* (New York: Paulist, 1993), 109–10.

47. Ibid., 129; Haught draws insight from Robert Jay Lifton, *The Broken Connection* (New York: Simon and Schuster, 1979), and extends it to ecology.

Chapter 13: To Let the Symbol Sing Again

1. Karl Rahner and Johann Baptist Metz, *The Courage to Pray* (New York: Crossroad, 1981), 86.

2. Anonymous, in *The Oxford Book of Prayer*, ed. George Appleton (Oxford: Oxford University Press, 1985), 168. For all the usefulness of this book

for some purposes, it is heavily weighted with male authors; quite inexplicable is the omission of the only extended prayer in the New Testament credited to a woman, Mary's Magnificat, Lk 1:46–55.

3. Walter Rauschenbusch, "Prayers for Social Awakening," *Selected Writings,* ed. Winthrop Hudson (New York: Paulist, 1984), 223–24.

4. David Power, "Calling Up the Dead," in *The Spectre of Mass Death,* 114 (see ch. 9, n. 3); I am indebted to this brief but brilliant article for the above examples. See also Walter Brueggemann, "Reservoirs of Unreason," *Reformed Liturgy and Music* 17 (1983): 99–104; and Claus Westermann, *Praise and Lament in the Psalms* (Atlanta: John Knox, 1981).

5. John Paul II, "Visit to Mauthausen," *Origins* 18, no. 8 (July 7, 1988): 124.

6. See "Evening Service for the Sabbath," *The Union Prayerbook,* distributed by Congregation Emanu-el of the City of New York to its radio congregation; copyright 1967; pp. 72–78.

7. Power, "Calling Up the Dead," 114.

8. Rahner, "All Saints," *Theological Investigations* 8:29 (see ch. 1, n. 19).

9. Ibid., 24, 26.

10. Ibid., 26.

11. Julian of Norwich, *Showings,* trans. Edmund Colledge and James Walsh (New York: Paulist, 1978), 225 (long text, ch. 27).

12. Barbara Brown Taylor, "A Great Cloud of Witnesses," *Weavings* 3, no. 5 (September/October 1988): 17. For creative ways to celebrate this feast being worked out in some Protestant churches, in addition to Garrett, "I Sing a Song of the Saints of God" (see ch. 6., n. 43), see Alison Geary, "For All the Saints," *Epworth Review* 20, no. 2 (May 1993): 9–12; and Patricia Fort, "For All the Saints," *Reformed Liturgy and Music* 25 (1991): 41.

13. See F. Cabrol, "Litanies," *Dictionnaire d'archéologie chrétienne et de liturgie* (Paris: Librarie Letouzey et Ané, 1930), 9/2:1540–71; Balthasar Fischer, "Litanies," *Dictionnaire de spiritualité* (Paris: Beauchesne, 1976), 9:865–72; Louis Weil, "The History of Christian Litanies," *Liturgy: Journal of the Liturgical Conference 5,* no. 2 (Fall 1985): 33–37; and Michael Whelan, "The Litany of Saints: Its Place in the Grammar of Liturgy," *Worship* 65 (1991): 216–23.

14. "Litany of the Saints," music by John D. Becker, published by OCP Pub., 5536 NE Hassalo, Portland, OR.

15. Quoted in Plácido Erdozaín, *Archbishop Romero, Martyr of Salvador* (Maryknoll, N.Y.: Orbis, 1981), 73–75; see also James Brockman, *The Word Remains: A Life of Oscar Romero* (Maryknoll, N.Y.: Orbis, 1982).

16. Quoted in Brett and Brett, *Murdered in Central America,* 296 (see ch. 8, n. 44).

17. Quoted in Jon Sobrino, *Companions of Jesus: The Jesuit Martyrs of El Salvador* (Maryknoll, N.Y.: Orbis, 1990), 38–39.

18. Quoted in Brett and Brett, *Murdered in Central America,* 252.

19. Litany written by Ann Heidkamp, *Church and Society* 82 (1992): 79–81.

20. Litany written by Joan Chittister and distributed by Benedictine Sisters, Erie, PA 16503.

21. See A. Llewellyn Barstow, *Witchcraze*, dedicated "For those who did not survive" (see ch. 2, n. 17); and Daly, "European Witchburnings: Purifying the Body of Christ" (see ch. 8, n. 52).

22. Robin Morgan, from Chris Carol, "Hollowmas Liturgy," presented in Rosemary R. Ruether, *Women-Church: Theology and Practice* (San Francisco: Harper & Row, 1985), 225–26.

23. Litany written by William Brackney, *American Baptist Quarterly* 2, no. 4 (1983): 290–91.

24. Litany written by Sanford Culter, "Litany of Contemporary Episcopal Saints," *The Witness* 69, no. 12 (1986): 22–23.

25. Chung, "Welcome the Spirit, Hear Her Cries" (see ch. 1, n. 1); full texts of this key conference including this address are found in *Signs of the Spirit: Official Report of the Seventh Assembly of the World Council of Churches,* ed. Michael Kinnamon (Geneva: World Council of Churches Pub., 1991).

26. Compiled and edited by Margot King (Toronto: Peregrina Pub., 1990–).

27. Text and photo of sculpture in *Church* 9, no. 2 (Summer 1993): 44.

28. Jerome, *Liber contra Vigilantium* 7, PL 23:345–46; quoted in Molinari, *Saints: Their Place in the Church,* 230, n. 165 (see ch. 1, n. 12).

29. Wis 7:27.

Index